An Introduction to Word Grammar

Word Grammar is a theory of language structure based on the assumption that language, and indeed the whole of knowledge, is a network, and that virtually all of knowledge is learned. It combines the psychological insights of cognitive linguistics with the rigour of more formal theories. This textbook spans a broad range of topics from prototypes, activation and default inheritance to the details of syntactic, morphological and semantic structure. It introduces elementary ideas from cognitive science and uses them to explain the structure of language including a survey of English grammar.

RICHARD HUDSON is Emeritus Professor of Linguistics at University College London. His recent publications include *Language Networks: the New Word Grammar* (2007).

CAMBRIDGE TEXTBOOKS IN LINGUISTICS

General editors: P. AUSTIN, J. BRESNAN, B. COMRIE, S. CRAIN, W. DRESSLER,
C. EWEN, R. LASS, D. LIGHTFOOT, K. RICE, I. ROBERTS, S. ROMAINE,
N. V. SMITH

AN INTRODUCTION TO WORD GRAMMAR

An Introduction to Word Grammar

RICHARD HUDSON

CAMBRIDGE
UNIVERSITY PRESS

CAMBRIDGE UNIVERSITY PRESS
Cambridge, New York, Melbourne, Madrid, Cape Town, Singapore,
São Paulo, Delhi, Dubai, Tokyo

Cambridge University Press
The Edinburgh Building, Cambridge CB2 8RU, UK

Published in the United States of America by Cambridge University Press, New York

www.cambridge.org
Information on this title: www.cambridge.org/9780521721646

First published 2010

Printed in the United Kingdom at the University Press, Cambridge

A catalogue record for this publication is available from the British Library

Library of Congress Cataloguing in Publication data
Hudson, Richard A.
   An introduction to word grammar / Richard Hudson.
   p.   cm. – (Cambridge textbooks in linguistics)
   Includes bibliographical references and index.
   ISBN 978-0-521-89690-0 (hardback) – ISBN 978-0-521-72164-6 (pbk.)
   1. English language–Grammar.   I. Title.   II. Series.
   PE1112.H823 2010
   428.2–dc22
   2010022104

ISBN 978-0-521-89690-0 Hardback
ISBN 978-0-521-72164-6 Paperback

Additional resources for this publication at www.cambridge.org/hudson

Contents

Figures

Tables

Acknowledgements

I should like to take this opportunity to thank Helen Barton of CUP for inviting me to write the book, and then bullying me into finishing it; her colleague Sarah Green for patiently supporting me through the production process; and Michael Turner for detailed comments on the style; if the book is readable, thank him! But above all, I'm endebted as always to my wife Gay for putting up with the book. As various people have commented, what a funny way to spend a retirement!

Introduction

This book consists of three parts, each of which is an introduction to a separate discipline: cognitive science, linguistics (a branch of cognitive science) and English grammar (a branch of linguistics).

Part I, called 'How the mind works', is a very modest alternative to Steven Pinker's bestseller of the same name (Pinker 1998a), and is a personal selection of rather commonplace psychological ideas about concepts and mental networks and the activation that flows round them, together with a few novelties such as default inheritance and node building. These ideas are selected so as to provide a foundation for the next part.

In Part II, 'How language works', I make a theoretical point that's exactly the opposite of the one made famous by Pinker, following the mainstream Chomskyan tradition (Pinker 1994). Where Pinker finds a 'language instinct', I find ordinary cognition. Like other 'cognitive linguists', I believe that language is very similar to other kinds of thinking. I also believe that the fine details that we linguists find when looking at language tell us a great deal not only about language, but also about how we think in general. Every single phenomenon that I know about, as a linguist, is just as you'd expect given the way in which (according to Part I) the mind works.

Finally, Part III, 'How English works', gives a brief survey of English grammar. The chapter on syntax summarizes my little 1998 textbook *English Grammar* which supported my first-year undergraduate course on English grammar. The students seemed to enjoy learning to draw dependency arrows and appreciated the idea that this was a skill that they could apply to virtually any English sentence.

I should explain that the book's structure is itself a little like the structure of thought: it's a network. Admittedly, it doesn't look like a network at first sight; if you look at the table of contents you'll see the usual hierarchical structure of parts, chapters and sections. But if you look more carefully, you'll find that most of the chapters and sections correspond across the three parts. For example, Section 2.2 discusses general principles of classification which are then applied in 6.3 to the principles of how we classify words, which in turn lead into the exposition of English word-classes in 10.1.

The structure based on parts and the one indicated by the cross-links between parts correspond to the two structures of the intellectual picture that I want to present. The hierarchical structure follows the academic divisions: Part I is the broad discipline of cognitive science, which includes linguistics (Part II), which includes English grammar (Part III). Each of these disciplines has its own logical structure, so the chapters and sections try to follow this logic. But the cross-links are the book's main point because they show how various general ideas from cognitive science apply to language and explain its characteristics. It's not just that there are some parts of language that are similar to other parts of thinking. What I'm claiming is that the whole of language can be explained in this way, so I have to justify the claim in detail with a link from every section in Part II to some section in Part I.

Fortunately, the corresponding sections in the three parts follow exactly the same order because they follow the same logic, which means that you can read the book either linearly or laterally. A linear reading takes you through a course in cognitive science, then through a course in linguistics and finally through a course in English grammar, each following its own internal logic. A lateral reading takes you from a section in Part I into its corresponding section in Part II and on into a section in Part III – or, if you prefer, in the opposite direction.

How you cope with this choice is, of course, up to you. One obvious solution is to combine the linear and lateral approaches. If you follow this strategy, you'll start at the beginning of Part I, read the first section, then read the corresponding section in Part II, then the one (if there is one) in Part III, then back to the next section in Part I; and so on. This is how I hope more advanced students will read it, and to encourage them I've added a note at the end of most sections in Parts I and II recommending that they should stray into a section of the next part, where (to increase the temptation) they'll also find a summary of this section. This is what I call the '**advanced route**'. But I accept that some readers will prefer to follow a purely linear route which takes them straight through the book, and don't need sign-posts.

If you're a teacher, you may like to know how I would use this book as a textbook for my undergraduate teaching. I would spread it across two years, with Part III for first-year students and Parts I and II for the second year. First-year undergraduates can certainly cope with the grammatical analyses of Part III, especially if they make use of the material on the website; indeed, these analyses aren't much harder than those that are standardly taught in many countries to primary school children. The practical experience of exploring the 'real language' of texts is an excellent foundation for the more theoretical exploration in the first and second parts, and is probably especially important for students who have come through the more or less grammar-free schools of most English-speaking countries (Hudson and Walmsley 2005). I've mapped out a '**novice route**' through the book which basically takes them through Part III, but with little excursions into the corresponding sections of Part II. The 'advanced route' should suit second-year students, who can obviously use their discretion about revisiting Part III.

If you're a student, then I should explain my policy on bibliographical references. I assume that you're a typical modern student with easy access to the internet and more IT skills than time. I also assume that you'd like to be able to follow up some of the research that I quote, but without having to cope with the dense technicalities of research literature. With these two thoughts in mind, I decided to make as much use as I could of two wonderful resources: Wikipedia (en.wikipedia.org) and the second edition of the Elsevier *Encyclopedia of Language and Linguistics* (Brown 2006) which your university may well make available to you online.

Wikipedia is especially good for Part I as it gives easy access to the rather elementary research ideas that I discuss, but please remember to take it with a pinch of salt. As far as I can tell, the articles I recommend are, by and large, sensible and scholarly, but some of the claims are inevitably controversial, and occasional silliness is hard to avoid in a work that anyone can edit. If in doubt about something you find in Wikipedia, try searching in Google, and especially in Google Scholar and Google Books. For Part II, of course, the *Encyclopedia* is the main point of reference. The articles in both sources are written by experts with whom I can't compete; my main contribution is simply to have put their ideas together in an unusual combination.

More material is available on the book's **website** (www.phon.ucl.ac.uk/home/dick/izwg/index.htm) for those who want it, and especially for those who want to hone the skills that Part III tries to develop; it includes an encyclopaedia of English grammar and Word Grammar, but much more besides.

And of course, for those who want to know more about Word Grammar, there are plenty of publications, not least my most recent (2007) monograph, *Language Networks: the New Word Grammar*. There's no better test for ideas than writing a book about them, whether it's a monograph or a textbook, and this textbook is no exception. Consequently I have to report a number of points where I've changed my mind even since writing *Language Networks*: choice sets (3.3), best landmarks (3.4.3), the notation for coordination and dependencies (7.5) and the mechanism for resolving word-order conflicts (7.6). This is as you'd expect. After all, Word Grammar is a network of ideas in my mind, and as I explain in Part I, any cognitive network is forever changing as it tries to adjust to reality.

Where next?

Advanced: Part I, Chapter 1: Introduction to cognitive science
Novice: Part III, Chapter 9: Introduction to English linguistics

PART I

How the mind works

1   Introduction to cognitive science

Although this book is about language, the first part is not about language as such at all, but about general **COGNITION** – i.e. 'knowledge'. Its aim is to provide a general background to the discussion of language in the second part.

Cognition includes everything you might think of as knowledge – knowledge of people, things, events – and may be as general as so-called 'general knowledge' or as specific as what you know about the room you're sitting in at the moment. If we want to understand cognition, we must answer questions such as the following:

- How is it organized in our minds?
- How do we learn it?
- How do we use it in understanding our experiences, in solving problems and in planning actions?
- How is it related to things that we wouldn't call 'knowledge', such as feelings, actions and perceptions?

The main point of this book is to show how answers to these questions throw light on language; or to put it more negatively, how unlikely we are to understand language if we ignore what's already known about cognition.

Cognition is very complex and diverse, so it's hardly surprising that a range of methods have been used for studying it. The term **COGNITIVE SCIENCE** is often used as a cover term for the various different disciplines that explore cognition, including psychology, neuroscience, artificial intelligence, philosophy and (of course) linguistics. (Wikipedia: 'Cognitive science'.) Nor is it surprising that there's a great deal of controversy about findings and theories, so I can't claim that the theory which I present here is the agreed view of every cognitive scientist. Nor, indeed, can I claim to be an expert on cognitive science (in contrast with linguistics, where I do claim some expertise). What I can claim, though, is that the ideas I present in this part are compatible with elementary cognitive science. Most of the things in these chapters can be found in introductory textbooks, though no other textbook presents this particular combination of ideas and theories.

The main differences between the various disciplines that study cognition lie in their research methods, so it will be helpful to outline here the main methods that underpin the research findings, and especially the methods that are used in the research that I present below. **Psychology** uses many methods, but the most relevant for us are experiments which measure the time ('response time') taken by people ('subjects') to perform very specific tasks when sitting in front of a computer in a psychological laboratory. **Neuroscience** uses brain scans which reveal the structure of the brain and which parts of the brain are particularly active at any given moment. **Artificial intelligence** uses computer programs that try to simulate human behaviour. **Philosophy** uses logical argument about how knowledge and thought must 'work'. And **linguistics** uses a variety of methods, including the famous 'grammaticality judgement' and other kinds of self-report made by a native speaker. (Wikipedia: 'Psychology', 'Neuroscience', 'Artificial intelligence' and 'Linguistics'.)

As you can see, these disciplines collectively offer an impressive range of methods for studying human cognition, and the ideal situation will be one in which they all support each other – for instance, where the results of laboratory experiments converge with those of observed behaviour and of brain scans. At present this ideal still lies in the future, but the major debates and disputes lie within the disciplines rather than between them. It would be strange indeed if, say, psychologists all accepted a view of the mind which all neuroscientists rejected. Instead, there is enough diversity within each discipline to allow a synthesis, such as the one that I offer here, which combines at least the greater part of the research findings of all of them.

This is the justification for the first part of my book, in which I try to present a unified view of those areas of cognition that are most directly relevant to language. Having laid this foundation, I shall then be able to show how we apply this general-purpose cognition to language, and I hope to persuade you by the end of the book that language, in spite of its apparent peculiarities, is actually just an ordinary example of human knowledge applied to the particular task of communicating.

There are two reasons for celebrating this result. The first is that it gives us the best possible explanation for the known characteristics of language: they're exactly what we would expect given the kinds of mind we have.

The second reason for celebration is that linguistics acquires a very special role in cognitive science. Language has a far clearer and more intricate structure than any other part of cognition, and only linguistics can explore this structure in detail. Consequently, the window into the human mind that language provides is unusually clear and throws light on areas of thought that other disciplines can't reach. I hope that by the end of the book you'll feel that you have a better understanding not only of how you use language, but also of how you think.

Where next?

Advanced: Part I, Chapter 2: Categorization

2 Categorization

2.1 Concepts, categories and exemplars

One of the most important areas of work in psychology is the study of categorization, which explains how we **CATEGORIZE** or classify items of everyday experience. (Wikipedia: 'Categorization'.) The examples discussed are very familiar and mundane – things like birds, furniture and birthday parties – and the question is how we all manage to find our way through this familiar world so efficiently. How do we know what things are, and what good is this information? The answers are fairly obvious, and make good sense in terms of everyday experience.

2.1.1 Concepts and properties

The main point is that we have a vast stock of **CONCEPTS**, each of which has a set of things we know about it called **PROPERTIES**. (Wikipedia: 'Concept'.) For example, we have the concept 'bird', with the following typical properties:

- It flies.
- It has wings.
- It has feathers.
- It lays eggs.
- It has two legs.
- It has a beak.

If you explore your knowledge of birds, no doubt you can extend this list of properties.

These properties define the general concept 'bird' and distinguish it from other concepts – 'fish', 'aeroplane' and so on. They all emerge in answer to the question: 'what is a bird?' You can explore the properties of any other concept in your mind by asking yourself what you know about it. What is furniture like? What is a birthday party like? In each case, what you're looking for is a list of things that you know – or at least think – about a typical example of the concept in question, including the things that distinguish it from other concepts.

A concept is simply an idea, so it's very different from whatever it represents in the real world (the thing it's a concept 'of'); thus the concept of a bird does not itself fly or have wings, though a bird does and the concept's properties are designed to fit those of the bird. Similarly, birthday parties and accidents have a time and a place, but the concept of a birthday party or an accident doesn't.

A concept, on the other hand, may be real or imaginary, according to whether or not it matches something in the world, whereas the thing it represents either doesn't exist (as in the case of the concepts 'unicorn', 'Father Christmas' and Peter Pan's flight to Neverland) or does exist. A concept exists, but only as an element of someone's mind; in technical terminology it's part of **CONCEPTUAL STRUCTURE**, a term which means much the same as our everyday word *knowledge* but with the extra idea that this knowledge has a structure.

The main point is that the concept is different from the bit of the world that it represents. On the other hand, the only reason for having concepts is to guide us through the world, so the better the fit with the world, the better they guide us.

2.1.2   Inheritance

How does a concept guide us? Imagine life without any general concepts. The problem you face is total novelty – everything you see and hear is new, so you never benefit from experience. When you put something in your mouth, you have no idea what taste or texture to expect – or even whether it's food. You have no concept for 'potato' or 'apple', or even for 'food'. When you want to open a door, you won't know how to do it because you have no concept for 'opening a door', or even for 'door'.

Now return to reality, complete with the millions of concepts that you've learned during your life so far. When you see a potato, you can predict its taste, its texture and the effect it will have on your hunger. How do you know that it's a potato? By looking at it. But how do you know that it will satisfy your hunger? You can't see this or even taste it, and yet you know it for sure. In lay terms, you 'guess' it: you know that the typical potato stops hunger, you guess (from its appearance) that this thing is a potato, so you can also guess that this thing will stop hunger.

This everyday guessing is something cognitive scientists know quite a bit about, and it's generally considered to involve a process called **INHERITANCE** that will be one of the main themes of later sections (starting with 2.3).

The examples concerning doors and potatoes show how concepts guide us through life. To summarize, when we meet a bit of experience (whether a thing, an event or a person), we take two steps:

•   On the basis of what we know already, including its perceived properties – e.g. what it looks or sounds like – we classify it as an example of some concept that we know already.

•   Then we infer more information about it by inheriting further properties from that concept.

In other words, it's concepts that allow us to build on past experience by linking perceived properties to those that we can't perceive.

As we shall see below, the system isn't perfect, but on the whole it works well; and most importantly of all, it works fast. The two steps don't need reflection, but happen almost instantly. For instance, if you're driving on a fast road, you recognize other cars and react to them in a split second. The price you pay for this fast thinking is the possibility of error.

Concepts don't have to represent simple concrete objects, but can represent events as well. Take 'birthday party', in the typical sense of a child's birthday party complete with balloons on the front door, presents, party clothes, games, cake and so on. We all know how the party is organized into sub-events starting with the guests' arrival and ending with their departure; and both parents and children have detailed ideas of what the guests' and hosts' roles involve. If you don't know these things, or if your ideas conflict with those of the birthday girl or boy, then disaster threatens.

The concepts that we've considered so far have been concepts for general notions such as potatoes, birds or birthday parties. As you've probably noticed, all these concepts happen to be the meanings that we would expect to find in a dictionary, so they'll be important for the analysis of meaning (8.7); but word meanings are just the tip of a gigantic iceberg of concepts. The meanings that we give to single words are the concepts that are so general, useful and widely held that society at large gives them a label; but most concepts are far too specific and ephemeral for this – concepts such as 'an undercooked potato' or 'the dust on top of my computer'. Concepts like this don't appear in a dictionary, but they can always be put into words.

2.1.3   Categories and exemplars

Even more specific and ephemeral are what psychologists call **EXEMPLARS** – individual examples of experience – in contrast with the more or less general **CATEGORIES** which we use in categorizing the exemplars. This distinction is so important that some psychologists divide memory into two separate areas which they call (not very helpfully) 'semantic memory' and 'episodic memory', with semantic memory for categories ('semantic' because the categories are meaningful) and episodic memory for remembered exemplars ('episodic' because these exemplars occur in 'episodes' of experience). (Wikipedia: 'Semantic memory' and 'Episodic memory'.)

However, this fundamental distinction is controversial and other psychologists believe that a single memory system includes both kinds of information (Barsalou 1992: 129). This is my view too, and Section 4.3 will suggest that exemplars can turn into categories without in any sense having to move from one system to another. The difference between the two kinds of memory is simply a matter of degree – how specific they are, how much detail about times, places and so on they include, and how long we keep them in our minds.

In these terms, then, the aim of categorization is to put exemplars into categories. The next two sections explain the logical structures that this process creates and how these structures help us to understand our experiences.

Another popular distinction separates 'procedural knowledge', knowing how to do something, from 'declarative knowledge', knowing that something is true. (Wikipedia: 'Procedural memory' and 'Declarative memory'.) Procedural knowledge includes skills such as riding a bike or driving a car which we can't report in words, whereas knowing the properties of birds is an example of declarative knowledge which we can put into words; and crucially for this book, language is often classified as procedural knowledge.

The main reason for making this distinction is that procedural knowledge tends to be so automatic that we can't put it into words, but this is merely a tendency; for example, a driving instructor can put the skills of driving into words, and they are anything but automatic for a learner. Moreover, if we can have declarative knowledge about events such as birthday parties, it's hard to see why we can't use declarative knowledge about driving a car while driving.

A reasonable conclusion seems to be that it's better not to separate procedural and declarative knowledge, especially if we distinguish concepts for procedures from the 'motor skills' (as we shall call them) that are discussed in Section 3.1. Rather obviously, rejecting the distinction between declarative and procedural knowledge undermines the claim that language is procedural. This is a triumph for common sense because we obviously can talk about language – as witness Parts II and III of this book.

Where next?

Advanced: Part II, Chapter 6.1: Types and tokens

2.2   Taxonomies and the isA relation

Another matter of common sense is that our concepts are organized, rather than just a disorganized heap. If you think of 'bird', it's obvious that it must be related to 'feather', 'wing', 'fly' and so on. We explore these relations in Section 3.5, but first we start with the most familiar kind of organization, which is called a **TAXONOMY**.

A simple example of a taxonomy includes 'creature', 'bird' and 'robin', in that order, with 'creature' at the top of the hierarchy and 'robin' at the bottom. As we all know, a bird is a creature – at least that was the assumption behind the dictionary definition quoted above in which a bird was a creature with feathers and wings – and a robin is a bird. But of course a creature is not a bird, nor is a bird a robin, so the expression *is a* defines an unequal relation.

This relation is the basis for any taxonomy, and is so important that cognitive scientists have invented the term **ISA** as the name for the relation, so the concept 'robin' isA 'bird', which isA 'creature'. (Wikipedia: 'Is-a'.)

What distinguishes a taxonomy from a mere list of members is that it allows classification at more than one level. For example, creatures can be classified as birds, animals and fish, but birds can then be subclassified as robins, sparrows and so on. (No doubt a more realistic taxonomy would distinguish higher-level bird classes such as water-birds and land-birds.) A useful bit of terminology allows us to say that 'bird' is a **SUBCLASS** of 'creature', but a **SUPERCLASS** of 'robin'.

2.2.1   The importance of taxonomies

Taxonomies are the most elementary kind of organization because they involve just this one relation. They're also the most useful organization for reasons that we shall explore in the next section. This is why we meet them in so many areas of life; for example:

- Goods are displayed in a supermarket in a taxonomy organized by function (e.g. food contrasting with drink and domestic products and subdivided into subclasses such as breakfast cereals, which then sub-divide to distinguish cornflakes from porridge).
- A restaurant menu is a taxonomy organized according to course and food type.
- The files on your computer are organized in a taxonomy of folders organized by file type or topic.
- A library or a bookshop arranges its books in a taxonomy based on topic, then author.
- A thesaurus is a taxonomy of words organized by meaning.
- A guide to wild flowers is a taxonomy of plants organized in a botanical hierarchy.

And no doubt there's even some kind of taxonomy behind the way you arrange things in your bedroom.

Once you're aware of taxonomies, you find them everywhere; but they're only 'natural' in human society. The world doesn't organize itself in taxonomies; rather, taxonomies are what we use to organize our knowledge of the world. We find them helpful because we think in taxonomies. (Wikipedia: 'Taxonomy'.)

2.2.2   A notation for taxonomies

However simple the basic isA relation may be, the taxonomies that we build in conceptual structure are mostly so rich and complicated that we need an efficient notation for displaying them. Ordinary language is too cumbersome. For example, here's a prose description of a rather simple menu, with our new term *isA* as a rather exceptional verb:

- Pea soup isA soup.
- Chicken soup isA soup.
- Soup isA starter.
- Baked cod and parsley sauce isA fish dish.

- Grilled plaice isA fish dish.
- Liver and bacon isA meat dish.
- Sausage and mash isA meat dish.
- Fish dish isA main course.
- Meat dish isA main course.
- Starter isA dish.
- Main course isA dish.

Worse still, here's a top-down version in continuous prose:

> A dish is either a starter, which may be soup, which may be either pea soup or chicken soup; or a main course, which may be either a fish dish, which may be baked cod and parsley sauce or grilled plaice, or a meat dish, which may be liver and bacon or sausage and mash.

A bottom-up approach isn't much more readable:

> Pea soup and chicken soup are soup, which is a starter; and baked cod and parsley sauce and grilled plaice are fish dishes; and liver and bacon and sausage and mash are meat dishes; and fish dishes and meat dishes are main courses; and starters and main courses are dishes.

It's hardly surprising that actual menus don't use ordinary prose, but instead invent their own special way of showing the taxonomy visually. The same is true of all the other taxonomies mentioned above; in each case, the organization that produced the taxonomy has found what it considers a user-friendly way of guiding users through the structure.

The taxonomies that we find in ordinary knowledge are at least as complicated as any of these, and when we come to language they are even more complex, so we urgently need a visual notation for taxonomies. The obvious system is one which uses the vertical dimension which is conventionally associated with the hierarchy. If we then connect the various categories to one another by means of straight lines, we get a diagram like Figure 2.1.

2.2.3   A notation for isA

This notation works well for simple cases, but taxonomies aren't always simple. One problem is that we shall eventually need to distinguish isA from other kinds of relation for which we shall also want to use lines; but another is that this system ties the taxonomy too rigidly to the vertical dimension, which we sometimes want to use for other purposes.

The solution to both of these problems is to make the isA line itself show both that it means 'isA' (rather than some other kind of relation) and also in which direction it goes – that is, which of the connected items isA the other, which is the subclass and which the superclass.

In Word Grammar notation, a small triangle at one end of an isA line rests on the superclass. The idea behind the triangle is that its large side, the base, rests

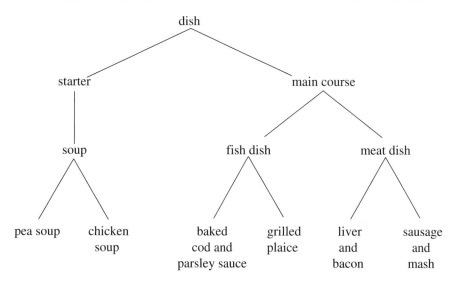

Figure 2.1 *A menu taxonomy in traditional notation*

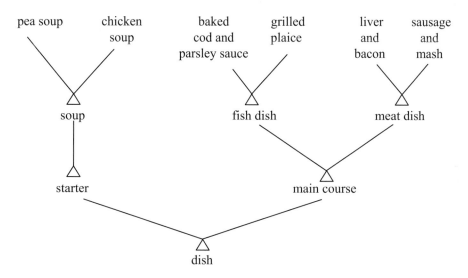

Figure 2.2 *A menu taxonomy in Word Grammar notation*

on the larger class while its apex, which is a mere point, points towards the sub-classes. Figure 2.2 shows how the menu taxonomy looks in this notation, and for good measure it demonstrates the notation's flexibility by turning the taxonomy upside down. In spite of this, the figure conveys exactly the same information as Figure 2.1.

This menu is just an example of how we use taxonomies to classify things. The main point is that classification requires a system of categories, and, in virtually any area of life that you can think of, the system that we use is a taxonomy – a complicated set of concepts nested inside other, more general, concepts, which are in turn nested inside others. In a taxonomy, when you classify something you don't put it into just one pigeon-hole, but into a whole series of pigeon-holes going right up to the top of the taxonomy. For instance, pea soup isn't just pea soup, it's also soup and a starter and a dish.

Where next?

Advanced: Part II, Chapter 6.3: Word-classes

2.3   Generalizations and inheritance

Why should taxonomies play such an important part in our mental life? How do we benefit from organizing our concepts in this way?

The simple answer is that taxonomies allow us to generalize. Taking the example of 'bird', all its properties generalize to all the concepts below it in the taxonomy: if we know that birds have wings and feathers, we can apply this knowledge to robins, sparrows and so on.

This may not strike you as much of a benefit since we already know that robins and sparrows have wings and feathers; and indeed it may well be that we knew these things about robins and sparrows before we created the generalization about birds. (This is a question for the theory of learning which we discuss in Section 4.4.) But generalization allows us to go beyond what we already know in two ways: in dealing with less familiar cases, and in dealing with unobservables.

Suppose you hear about an exotic bird that you've never seen; even if you know nothing else about it, by generalizing from 'bird' you can guess that it has wings and feathers. For the second case, suppose you can see that something is a bird, because it has wings and feathers, but that it's standing on a rock; once again, generalizing from 'bird' allows you to predict that it will fly even though this isn't something it's doing at the moment.

Generalizing from the known to the unknown is crucial throughout life, as we saw in Section 2.1. Knowing that something is a potato opens up a body of knowledge about its flavour, texture, uses, source, cost and all sorts of other things that go well beyond anything we can know directly; and similarly for birds, flying, birthday parties and all the other general concepts that we've discussed already.

2.3.1   How inheritance works (1)

As noted in Section 2.2, the technical name for the mental process which extends our knowledge in this way is **INHERITANCE**, a term from computer science (rather than psychology) based on a metaphor in which concepts 'inherit' the properties of the concepts above them in the taxonomy, rather like

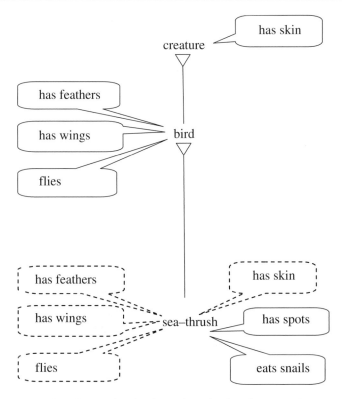

Figure 2.3 *The sea-thrush inherits from 'bird' and 'creature'*

the ordinary legal inheritance in which a person inherits property from their parents. (Wikipedia: 'Inheritance (computer science)'.) Inheritance is what this section is all about, but it's such an important idea that we shall keep on returning to it as we build the theoretical framework needed for a complete account. If you want to see how the story ends, you'll find it summarized in Section 4.5.

Another similarity between logical and legal inheritance is that properties pass down across generations in the taxonomy in the same way that family heirlooms would in an ideal world where nothing got lost. To take the bird example again, if a bird isA creature (which also includes animals and fish), then any properties of creatures pass down to anything which isA bird, in addition to whatever properties 'bird' itself contributes. One thing we know about creatures is that they typically have skin (with jellyfish and snails as potential exceptions), so this property is available for inheritance by any creature, however far down the taxonomy it may be.

Figure 2.3 shows how inheritance might apply to a mythical 'sea-thrush' if it simply copied properties down the hierarchy. The figure shows properties as little boxes of prose (dotted when inherited), but this is just a temporary measure which I replace in Section 3.2. I should also warn you that I'm about to revise this figure (giving Figure 2.5) after a few paragraphs more on the logic of inheritance.

2.3.2   How the mind stores generalizable information

The case shown in the figure concerns a hypothetical bird, the sea-thrush, which inherits the properties shown in dotted boxes and combines them with its unique known properties (having spots and eating snails). The point of the example, of course, is that since sea-thrushes don't exist, you know nothing at all about them and can't draw any information about them from your memory. Accordingly, if you agree that, being a bird, a sea-thrush must fly and have feathers, wings and skin, then you must have applied inheritance to work these facts out for yourself.

How do we know that our minds work like this, storing information at different levels in the taxonomy for eventual use when needed? After all, it's easy to imagine alternative arrangements such as one in which all information is stored repeatedly at every level; in this storage-only scenario, the property of having skin would be stored redundantly for birds, fish and animals as well as at the higher level for creatures, even though it could be inherited.

But although this arrangement is logically possible, it can't be how we actually store information. For one thing, you've just demonstrated your ability to understand new examples, which wouldn't be possible in total storage. Another kind of evidence comes from psychological experiments which show that inheritance takes a measurable amount of time. In a classic experiment, the subjects had to answer questions which might require them to find properties by inheritance, and the crucial variable was how long they took to give the answer (the response time). Each question was about the truth or falsity of a sentence such as 'A canary can sing', 'A canary can fly' or 'A canary has skin'; and it turned out that the response time increased as the property was located further up the taxonomy. For example, singing took less time to confirm than flying, and flying took less time than having skin (Reisberg 2007: 261).

This experiment showed very clearly that some information is inherited, which is rather comforting because the taxonomic organization seems so self-evidently right. On the other hand, the same kind of experiment has also shown that some information is in fact attached to lower concepts as well; such information is technically **REDUNDANT** because it could be predicted. For example, when the question about feathers referred to peacocks, the response time was shorter than for sparrows, suggesting that we store information about feathers with the 'peacock' concept rather than inheriting it via 'bird'.

This finding, of course, is hardly surprising given the prominence of feathers in peacocks, so once again the experimental evidence confirms what common sense probably tells us: sometimes information that could be inherited is already available because it's so important for the concept in question. The main point, however, is that taxonomic organization of concepts allows some information to be stored at higher levels and only inherited by lower-level concepts when needed.

2.3.3   How inheritance works (2)

You may be wondering how redundancy can be avoided in a system where information can be inherited freely. After all, if it takes some extra time and effort to work out whether sparrows have skin, wouldn't it be efficient to store the result for future use? But if we did this for every bit of information that we inherited – involving many thousands or even millions of calculations every day – the result would be a great deal more redundant storage than the experiments suggest. For example, the fact that canaries have feathers would be stored, like the fact that they sing, and yet the experiments show that it takes longer to decide that they have feathers than it does to decide that they sing.

The conclusion must be that we don't in fact remember inherited properties. Even though we can work out that a canary has skin, once we've done so we don't store this as a fact about canaries. This is somewhat surprising, so we need a theory of inheritance to explain it.

The following answer is, as far as I know, unique to Word Grammar, and involves the difference between temporary exemplars in moment-by-moment experience and permanent categories in the mind (2.1). This contrast is important for inheritance because it's exemplars, rather than stored categories, that most urgently need inheritance. Remember that inheritance allows us to go beyond what we already know by adding unknown or unobservable properties – the flavour, texture and food value of a potato, the behaviour expected at a birthday party, and so on.

In each case, what we apply inheritance to is an exemplar, and it's the exemplar that inherits the extra properties. A natural conclusion to draw from this observation is that inheritance **only** applies to exemplars.

If this is right, then inheritance must work as shown in Figure 2.4 (page 20).

The figure assumes a two-person team: a **SEARCHER** who looks for inheritable properties, starting at C and climbing higher and higher up the taxonomy; and a **COPIER** who makes a copy of each property that the searcher finds, and applies it directly to the exemplar. (We shall see in Section 2.5 that the copier is actually quite fussy about the properties it copies, and refuses to copy any that conflict with existing properties.)

If this really is how inheritance works, we need to revise the sea-thrush example. Instead of allowing the category 'sea-thrush' itself to inherit bird properties, we have to create an exemplar node 'E', and apply inheritance to this. The result is shown in Figure 2.5 (on page 21).

But how does this theory of inheritance square with the experiments, where the questions seemed to be about general categories such as 'a canary' rather than exemplars such as a particular canary? The main point of the experiments was to show that the searcher takes a measurable amount of time to climb up the hierarchy, rather than to distinguish exemplars from categories; but they do appear to show that categories can inherit.

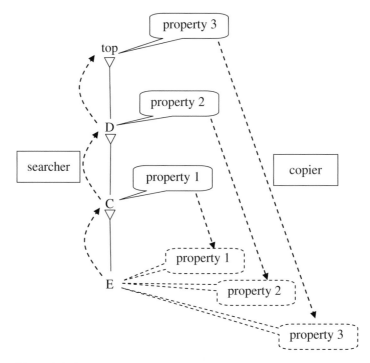

Figure 2.4 *The searcher climbs step by step but the copier sends copies directly*

One possible answer is that this appearance is an illusion, because people actually answer questions about general categories by imagining hypothetical exemplars. When asked whether a canary has skin, you would imagine a canary – an exemplar – and check whether it has skin. This seems quite possible, but of course it would be reassuring to have independent evidence to support it.

2.3.4   Inheritance and logic

And finally, how does this theory relate to traditional logic which goes back to the Ancient Greeks, and which also offers a theory of generalization? (Wikipedia: 'Logic'.) The Greek philosophers developed a theory of what they called 'hypothetical syllogisms', which are very similar to the inheritance process described here. (Wikipedia: 'Syllogism'.) The classic (in every sense) example of a syllogism is this:

- Major premise: All humans are mortal.
- Minor premise: Socrates is a human.
- Conclusion: Socrates is mortal.

In our terms, the major premise is a property of some general category (here, 'human' has the property 'is mortal'); the minor premise is an isA link to this category, and the conclusion is the inherited property. The modern 'predicate

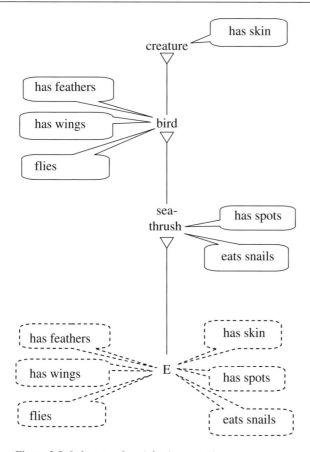

Figure 2.5 *Only exemplars inherit properties*

calculus' is based firmly on this logic (Wikipedia: 'Predicate logic' and 'First-order logic') and provides an unambiguous mathematical notation for it.

Our isA diagrams provide a similarly precise definition of the minor premise, and the property bubbles do the same for the major premise. However, Section 2.5 will explain an important difference between Word Grammar inheritance and classical syllogisms.

Meanwhile it's worth pointing out one immediate advantage of the Word Grammar system. Suppose we only know that Socrates is a Greek, and the fact that he's human is merely implied by the extra fact that Greeks are humans. In the classical system, we can't deduce that he's mortal without first deducing that if he's a Greek, he must be a human; but in the Word Grammar system the inheritance system automatically reaches right up to the top of the taxonomy.

Where next?

Advanced: Part II, Chapter 6.4: Grammaticality

2.4   Multiple inheritance and choices

I said earlier that taxonomies are structures that we invent as a way of imposing order on our experience. They allow us to remember similarities among categories, and in Section 4.4 I shall offer a theory of how we learn taxonomies. The picture of taxonomies that I've presented so far may have left the impression that they organize the world in a neat and orderly way, and it would certainly be pleasant to think that this was true. For example, I would enjoy thinking that all the objects on my desk were arranged neatly into piles according to a clear taxonomy.

2.4.1   Multiple inheritance

If only! The trouble is that the world is a complex place and similarities between objects are messy. For example, one pen is lying on my desk along with all the other things that I've used during the last day or so, but another pen is in a little plastic container along with other tools; similarly, there are various letters on the desk, but some are in a little heap of letters while others have been reclassified as scrap paper; and so on. Maybe you have a cluttered and complicated desk too. Our main problem is not idleness or lack of time, but the complexity of the world we have to deal with. However hard we might try, there's no perfect or 'natural' way to classify everything on a desk so that it has just one proper place.

The same is true of the rest of the world. Things tend to belong to many different taxonomies, each of which reflects some of its properties but not all of them. A pet canary, for example, is a bird, but it's also a pet, a possession and a potential present to someone. In some households, pets are treated as members of the family rather than as animals; they're allowed indoors, named, toilet-trained, pampered, cared for when sick and mourned when dead. If we think of a human family as a collection of humans, the status of a pet makes it (or him or her) almost human. The same complexity is true of virtually everything you can think of: some properties align it with one set of things, and others with another.

This complexity doesn't undermine the principles outlined so far. We still have a taxonomic organization of concepts, and we still have inheritance down the taxonomic hierarchy; but the organization allows any concept, whether exemplar or category, to belong to more than one taxonomy. This requires a slightly more complicated theory of inheritance called **MULTIPLE INHERITANCE**, but this is simply a minor extension of the theory sketched above in which properties may be inherited from more than one superclass. (Wikipedia: 'Multiple inheritance'.)

Figure 2.6 shows the case of the concept 'pet canary', where an exemplar inherits different properties from 'pet' and from 'canary' – a status from one, and a colour from the other.

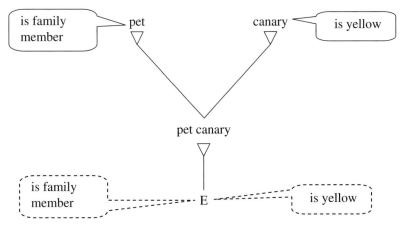

Figure 2.6 *Multiple inheritance*

2.4.2   **Resolving conflicts in multiple inheritance**

The challenge for theories of multiple inheritance is how to reconcile conflicts. Being yellow doesn't in itself conflict with being a family member, but conflicts can and do arise.

Take canaries again. Non-human creatures are part of nature and most western households keep nature strictly outside the house. If a bird comes in through the window, pandemonium reigns until the bird leaves. But family members are allowed inside – in fact, the house is built for them. Where, then, does this leave pets such as pet canaries? As family members they're allowed in, but as non-human creatures they're excluded. We resolve the conflict in favour of allowing them in, using a logical mechanism which we consider in the next section; but in some cases there's no recognized resolution.

The famous case in the literature (Touretzky 1986) is called the 'Nixon diamond' because it involves the American president Richard Nixon and when displayed as a diagram (Figure 2.7 on page 24), the conflict has the form of a diamond. (Wikipedia: 'Nixon diamond'.) The problem for Nixon was that he was both a Republican and a Quaker, and Republicans and Quakers happen to have conflicting views about warfare (Republicans accept it as a means for solving some problems whereas Quakers reject it under all circumstances). Seen as pure logic, the situation should have left him intellectually paralysed and unable to make any decisions, but in fact he resolved the conflict by opting for Republican values – using just the same strategy, in fact, that pet owners use in solving their problem. Figure 2.7 could show his choice as a copy of the 'accepts war' property attached to the 'Nixon' node.

2.4.3   **Choice sets**

Another way to reconcile potential conflicts of this kind is simply to prevent them from arising in the first place, and we do indeed seem to use

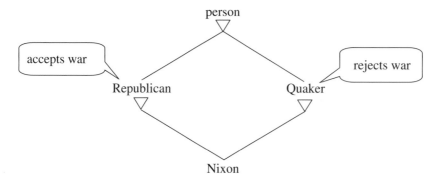

Figure 2.7 *The Nixon diamond*

this strategy in some situations. For example, we assume that Republicans can't also be Democrats; that supporters of one football team can't also support other teams; that men can't also be women; that blue can't also be red or green or yellow; that the number 1 can't also be 2; and so on.

In other words, in each case we have a choice among a group of mutually exclusive alternatives which we can call simply a choice or, more technically, a **CHOICE SET**. One mental benefit of organizing categories in choice sets is to avoid the inheritance of conflicting properties in multiple inheritance, but there are other advantages too.

For one thing, choices save a lot of mental work because once we've identified one of the alternatives, we can ignore all the others; as soon as we know that someone is a man, we can simply assume that they aren't a woman.

But above all, choices are a very efficient way to organize knowledge because they generate questions. Think of the personal questions that any official form asks you: name, sex, date of birth or age, address, occupation, nationality and so on. Each of these is a choice which allows a particular range of mutually exclusive alternatives.

These benefits make choices an important part of our mental make-up, and we shall need to introduce a mechanism for handling them (3.3). On the other hand, it would be wrong to assume that all our categories are neatly lined up in choices. Being a hiker doesn't prevent us from also being a cyclist or a motorist or a pianist or a bird-lover, so these categories are probably not involved in any choices.

Where next?

Advanced: Part II, Chapter 6.5: Lexemes and inflections

2.5   Default inheritance and prototype effects

The messiness of real life is a serious challenge for any theory of categorization. The problem isn't simply the existence of multiple systems of classification, but that the properties we use in classifying don't always line up as we expect them to – in other words, we have to cope with exceptions.

2.5.1   Exceptions and classical definitions

For example, we know that cats have a number of properties such as miaowing, having fur, belonging to human owners and having four legs. But what if some poor cat loses a leg in an accident? Does it cease to be a cat because four-leggedness is a defining characteristic? Clearly not – it simply becomes an exceptional cat.

This exceptionality emerges very clearly in the words we use. For expected, normal properties we use *and* or *so*, but for exceptions we use *but*:

(1)   It's a cat and/so it has four legs.
(2)   It's a cat, but it only has three legs.

Fortunately, cases like this cause us very few problems in day-to-day living because our minds are well adapted to the mess of the world; but they raise serious problems for the classical theory of categories discussed in Section 2.3. According to the classical theory, every category has a definition which consists of a set of 'necessary and sufficient conditions', and which excludes all the other incidental facts that we may know about the category. At least in principle, these two kinds of information should be recorded in two different kinds of reference work: definitions in dictionaries and incidental facts in encyclopaedias.

For example, the category 'even number' can be neatly defined as 'a number that can be divided (without remainder) by 2'. The conditions for being an even number are:

• being a number;
• being divisible without residue by 2.

These conditions are both necessary (something that fails either of them can't be an even number) and sufficient (something that passes them both must be an even number). Taken together they provide a classical definition which you would expect to find in any English dictionary. On the other hand, you wouldn't expect an encyclopaedia entry for even numbers because there's so little to say about them – what incidental facts would you include?

For all its antiquity and neatness, the classical theory doesn't work for the vast majority of our mental categories. What are the necessary and sufficient conditions for being a cat?

If such conditions existed, dictionary-writers ought to be able to find them and ought to agree, but they don't. Here are the entries for 'cat' in two excellent modern dictionaries (Anon. 2003, Anon. 1987):

(3)   A small animal with four legs that people often keep as a pet. Cats sometimes kill small animals and birds.

(4)   A cat is a small, furry animal with a tail, whiskers and sharp claws.
         Cats are often kept as pets.

The only things that these two definitions agree on is that cats are animals, that they are small, and that they are often kept as pets – none of which would, of course, distinguish them from rabbits, guinea pigs or dogs. Moreover, the first definition mentions four legs, but as we have seen, three-legged cats are still cats, so four legs can't be a necessary condition.

The fact is that it's much easier to find exceptions to the classical theory than it is to find examples such as 'even number' that support it, and which all turn out to come from areas of life where clear definitions are important, such as mathematics, science and law. The reason for this result is also easy to see: we don't discover categories in nature, but invent them. Categories are an intellectual device for making sense of experience, so nature doesn't need them; they're needed only by organisms that have minds, such as us.

2.5.2   Categories and prototypes

Before looking at a better theory of categorization, let's consider a little more carefully what categories are. As we've already seen, categories are general concepts from which individual exemplars can inherit otherwise unknowable properties. Consequently, categories must be suitable for this inheritance operation. But all sorts of concepts are imaginable, and it's easy to imagine concepts that would be of no use to us at all – for example, the concept of a thing which has 57 corners and yellow spots. We can certainly imagine this concept and psychologists sometimes do experiments on 'concept formation' to see how easily people can learn arbitrary concepts. (Wikipedia: 'Concept learning'.) Moreover, we can put it into words (as I did in the last sentence); but there's no point in storing it away for future use.

So what kinds of permanent concepts do we find useful? The answer seems to be that our concepts bring together properties that tend to occur together as properties of the same thing. The concept 'bird' brings together beaks, egg-laying, flying, feathers and wings; and 'cat' does the same for fur, purring, four legs, a tail, whiskers and a taste for milk and basking in the sun. As we've seen, the benefit of remembering a bundle of co-occurring properties such as this is that the whole bundle follows from a small subset. You see something using wings to fly and assume it has a beak and lays eggs. In this view of categories, they have no 'definition' – they don't need one. All they need is a sufficiently stable bundle of properties to allow useful predictions. It's no surprise, therefore, that there's no agreed definition of 'cat'; instead, we have a widely agreed bundle of properties that cats typically have, all of which have the same logical status.

The crucial word in the last sentence is *typically*. The bundles of properties that we identify belong to a typical example, which is called a **PROTOTYPE** in the theoretical literature. (Wikipedia: 'Prototype theory'.)

Indeed, according to the version of prototype theory that's built into Word Grammar, the prototype **is** the category. 'Cat' is the name not of a collection or set of cats, but of the typical cat itself. Instead of building clear and water-tight boundaries around categories, as in the classical approach, we build a core example – a typical bird, cat, birthday party or whatever. This core example has all the properties that co-occur, so it plays a critical role in the category.

If the aim of the category is to allow unknown properties to be predicted from known ones, then adding a definition with necessary and sufficient criteria would create irrelevant problems. Suppose something had all the properties of a bird except one of the defining ones; if the definition was crucial, we couldn't classify this thing as a bird, and we couldn't inherit any of its unknown properties. In contrast, by focusing on the central case, we treat all properties equally and aren't worried if a few are missing. In short, categorization is much more robust if it uses prototypes than if it concentrates on boundaries and definitions. It's this focus on clear central cases rather than boundaries that provides the flexibility that we need to accommodate all the mess and irregularity of the world.

The prototype approach doesn't just make good practical sense; psychologists have produced a great deal of evidence that this is how we actually think. The evidence demonstrates what are called **PROTOTYPE EFFECTS** – patterns of behaviour in experiments that can most easily be explained by assuming that in constructing a mental category we build typical members rather than well-defined boundaries. This research shows that category members may have different degrees of 'goodness' as examples, and that some cases are so peripheral that it's even debatable whether they are examples at all. 'Chair' is a better example of 'furniture' than 'TV' is, and 'ash-tray' is a borderline case.

These results emerge from relatively simple experiments using questionnaires where subjects are asked to consider a particular category such as 'vegetable' or 'bird' and to rate things according to how 'good' (i.e. typical) an example of this category they are. For example, if you were asked whether a carrot is a good example of a vegetable, you would probably rate it as an excellent example – on a scale from 1 to 5, it would score 5. But what about a potato? After all, if you are offered 'meat and three vegetables', you wouldn't expect the potatoes to count. Maybe this would score 3, with rice and maize trailing behind at 1 or 2. No doubt you would have some trouble with tomatoes (which we use like vegetables but which grow like fruit), though they are better candidates for vegetable-hood than, say, cherries are.

When a large number of people (such as a lecture-room full of psychology students) fill in a questionnaire like this, it turns out that, for all their uncertainties, they tend to agree. But of course this is only true if they share the same culture; people from different cultures have very different views of how things should be classified.

Moreover, even self-conscious questionnaires must be tapping something real because they tend to coincide with more subtle experiments that measure response times like the one reported in Section 2.2. For example, it takes less time to decide that a carrot is a vegetable than to decide that a tomato is. This research has explored a wide range of everyday categories such as 'bird' and 'furniture', and found the same pattern of prototype effects in each case.

Prototype-based categorization is really helpful to us in dealing with everyday life because it matches the complexity of the world in which we live. It allows us to recognize a tendency for two or more properties to co-occur while recognizing that this co-occurrence is merely a tendency, and not totally regular. For example, we can accept penguins as exceptional birds and ash-trays as peripheral furniture. And of course, when we turn to language, we shall find exceptions right through the system – irregular morphology, irregular syntax, irregular semantics.

2.5.3   Default inheritance

Let's assume, therefore, that our mental categories are prototypes, and consider how this basic insight affects the view of categorization that we developed in the previous sections. The main point of prototypes is that they may have exceptional members, but our discussion of inheritance doesn't allow exceptions because, according to Section 2.3, any exemplar automatically inherits all the properties of every concept above it in the isA hierarchy.

To illustrate the problem, Figure 2.8 shows a very small taxonomy of birds with a couple of properties attached. Sparrows are typical birds, so an example of a sparrow (called 'E1' for 'exemplar number 1') inherits both of the expected properties of 'bird'; but penguins are untypical. Exceptionally, they don't fly. But as things stand at the moment, an example of a penguin will inherit both 'flies' and 'doesn't fly'. Something needs to be done.

The solution is to use a special version of inheritance called **DEFAULT INHERITANCE** (also called 'normal inheritance'; see Frankish 2006), which has been developed in artificial intelligence and logic. In ordinary English, the word *default* means something that happens unless something else happens instead; for example, the default settings on your computer are the settings that the manufacturer chooses, but which you can change or **OVERRIDE**.

Default inheritance works in the same way. The properties of the superclass are the defaults, because they're inherited under normal conditions; but exceptionally, they can be overridden. In the case of penguins and flying in Figure 2.8, 'flies' is a default property for birds, but 'doesn't fly' overrides it. In other words, default inheritance provides a mechanism for resolving conflicts such as the one in Figure 2.8 in favour of the 'lower' of the competing properties, the one inherited from the furthest down the taxonomy.

2.5.4   How inheritance works (3)

A great deal of research in artificial intelligence and logic has been devoted to the mechanics of default inheritance because, although the basic idea is so simple, it can be hard to express in an efficient computer program. The main

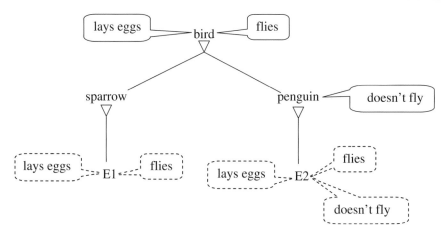

Figure 2.8 *An exception creates an inheritance conflict*

problem is that any property which is inherited at one point in the process may be overridden at a later point. This means that every conclusion is provisional and needs to be checked by searching for possible overriders. In the technical literature this kind of logic is called **NON-MONOTONIC**, in contrast with **MONOTONIC** logics where later inferences never change earlier ones (Bouma 2006).

If we knew in advance which properties might be overridden this wouldn't be too much of a problem, but in fact every property is vulnerable and every single inherited property triggers a search for possible overriders. In a computer system this can be fatal, as it can bring even the fastest computer to a grinding halt; but we know that the human brain, which works much more slowly than any modern computer, in fact takes exceptions in its stride. The conclusion must be that, in the human mind, default inheritance actually works in a monotonic way. But how can this be if every generalization is at risk of being overridden?

Word Grammar offers a theoretical solution to this apparent contradiction. The solution lies in the principle (suggested in Section 2.3) that inheritance should only apply to exemplars, which always stand at the very bottom of the taxonomies to which they belong. Consequently, this is where the 'searcher' always starts; it never starts half-way up the taxonomy. As the searcher works up a taxonomy from the bottom, it inevitably finds the overriding exception, and has it copied by the 'copier', before it finds the default. Consequently, the copier can safely copy every property that it receives from the searcher unless it has **already** inherited a property of the same kind.

Putting it another way, if you think of every property as an answer to a question (e.g. 'Does it fly?'), the searcher stops looking for answers to questions that it has already answered. For example, in Figure 2.8, the searcher starts at E2 and inherits 'doesn't fly' from 'penguin', so by the time it reaches 'bird' on its way to the top of the taxonomy, it can't inherit 'flies' because it already knows that E2 doesn't fly. The result is that it simply ignores this alternative answer.

This simple principle of always starting at the very bottom of the taxonomy guarantees that the first answer found will always be the right one; which is another way of saying that this kind of default inheritance is monotonic. But although we've solved one logical problem, we're left with another: how to decide which properties are 'of the same type' or 'answer the same question' so that one overrides the other. This is a question that we return to in Section 3.5.

Where next?

Advanced: Part II, Chapter 6.6: Definitions and efficiency

2.6   Social categories and stereotypes

Some concepts are richer than others, in the sense that they have more properties; for instance, your concept of a domestic cat is probably richer than the one you have of a puma. Some of our richest concepts are probably those that we build for people, which we can call 'social concepts'. (Wikipedia: 'Social cognition'.)

Because they're so rich and so important, our social concepts provide an essential backdrop to language. For one thing, the complex patterns of knowledge that we find in language aren't so very different in complexity from those that we find among social concepts. For another, one of the main jobs for which we use language is to signal social concepts; we shall explore these 'sociolinguistic' patterns a little more carefully in Section 8.8.

A third reason why social concepts are important for language is that in both language and society, we're participants, and not simply outside observers. What we learn about birds and cats doesn't directly affect the birds and cats, but learning about a society and a language turns us into members of the society and speakers of the language. This produces an important feed-back mechanism which reinforces some behaviour patterns: we reproduce in our own behaviour the behaviour that we observe around us, and since others are observing our behaviour, this encourages them to do the same. Individual creativity does exist and is important, but what is most striking about both social behaviour and language is our sheep-like conformity (Hudson 1996: 10–14).

2.6.1   The richness of social categories

Just as in other areas of cognition, social categories may be more or less general, ranging from individual people to general social categories. For each of us, of course, the most important individual in our mental world is ourselves. We must each have a concept node which we can call 'me'; but of course my 'me' is different from your 'me'. One of the properties of mine is being called 'Richard', but you may have a different name; and so on through all the other

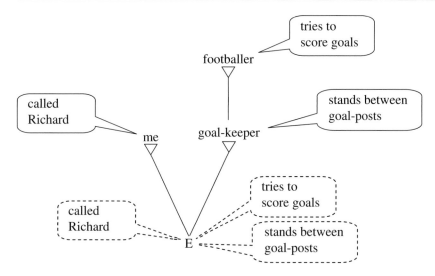

Figure 2.9 'Me' as goal-keeper

personal properties you can think of – age, sex, size, skin colour, hair colour and so on.

It is this vast range of properties that justifies my claim that our social concepts are especially rich. This preoccupation with other humans is exactly as we would expect given the obvious tendency for any animal (including humans) to pay most attention to con-specifics – members of the same species. (Wikipedia: 'Intra-species recognition'.) Moreover, each of us knows thousands of other individuals, each represented in our minds by a different concept node with a more or less rich set of properties.

Apart from what we know about individuals, we also have a vast range of more general category concepts for different kinds of people – men, footballers, goal-keepers, drivers, Brits, Londoners, professionals, fathers and so on and on. Each of these categories has a range of properties which members can inherit; for example, men have deep voices, footballers try to score goals, goal-keepers stand between the goal-posts, and so on. Each individual in your mind can inherit all sorts of properties in addition to the ones that you've stored specifically for them.

To take a very simple example, in the unlikely event that I was to play football and acted as goal-keeper, I would be able to inherit a few properties telling me what I was supposed to do. This hypothetical situation is displayed in Figure 2.9, where as usual the dotted property boxes are inherited.

2.6.2   Inheritance and stereotypes

Social concepts inherit properties in just the same way as other concepts. First, it's only exemplars that inherit at all (2.5), which is why Figure 2.9 includes E', standing for the exemplar that inherits, as well as 'me'. E isA me on that particular occasion when I was playing football; this may strike you as an odd way of thinking about me, but it must actually be how we all think not only about ourselves but also about other people. We have a more or less permanently stored memory of the person concerned, but we also have an exemplar concept for each occasion. This is why we can talk about someone 'not being their usual self' when they are not as we remember them, and also how we cope with me being a goal-keeper on one occasion but not on another.

The second principle that social inheritance shares with inheritance in other areas of thought is that social properties often require multiple inheritance (2.4). E in Figure 2.9 is typical in inheriting both from the permanent 'me' and from 'goal-keeper'. If you know that I am a male Londoner, then you inherit one set of properties from 'male' and a different set from 'Londoner', and similarly for all the other social categories that I belong to (retired, father, grandfather, husband, white, driver, cyclist and so on). With luck, these different superclasses are based on completely different properties. Consequently they can combine freely without conflict, but luck doesn't always hold and conflicts are possible, as in the famous case of the Nixon diamond (2.4). Such conflicts are especially likely to arise in relation to the social categories that sociologists call 'roles' which each define a set of behaviours, rights and duties. (Wikipedia: 'Role'.) Any working parent knows how the 'parent' and 'employee' (or 'colleague') roles pull in opposite directions.

The third shared principle is default inheritance, based on the idea that our social categories may have exceptional members who lack some of the expected properties. The general principle applies to humans in just the same way as we saw with birds and vegetables, but with humans its negative consequences matter a great deal more because this is the territory of socially transmitted **STEREOTYPES** and prejudice. (Wikipedia: 'Stereotype'.) For instance, if we associate football fans with hooliganism, there is a real danger of being seriously unfair to all those football fans who behave well. The trouble with default inheritance is that once an association is established in our minds, it's hard to learn from experience that it's wrong, and especially so if the association is accepted by other people and helps us to bond with them. If we think that football fans typically misbehave, then seeing fans who are behaving well need not affect our belief – we can shrug our shoulders and talk about exceptions. The same is true for all the other prejudices that you can think of that are based on race, sex, sexuality, age, nationality, religion and so on. Unfortunately, these prejudices are the price we pay for the flexibility that we gain from default inheritance. The better we understand how our minds work, the easier it should be to overcome or weaken our prejudices.

2.6.3   I-language and I-society

Social categories are highly relevant for understanding language because we use them to build a complex mental map of the society in which we live and in which, crucially, we learn language and use it. Noam Chomsky has invented the term **I-LANGUAGE** (with 'I' for 'internal' or 'individual') for the mental map that learners build for language (Wikipedia: 'I-language'), in contrast with the external reality of language which he calls 'E-LANGUAGE'. It's helpful to have a similar name for the individual mental map of society that each of us constructs: **I-SOCIETY**, in contrast with 'E-SOCIETY', all the individual people and institutions who are actually out there (Hudson 2007b). One of the unique features of Word Grammar is the attempt to explore the relations between these two mental maps, I-language and I-society (8.8).

Chapter summary:

- We think in **concepts** (e.g. 'bird'), which each have a bundle of **properties** ('flies', 'lays eggs'); in contrast with the classical tradition, these properties all have the same status, without any distinction between 'defining' properties and the rest.
- Concepts may be more or less general, ranging from very general **categories** (e.g. 'creature' or even 'thing') to the most specific categories (e.g. 'me'), with individual **exemplars** as the most specific of all. They are arranged in a **taxonomy** in which each concept 'isA' at least one more general one; so 'me' isA 'man' and 'man' isA 'human'.
- Exemplars **inherit** properties from the concepts above them in the taxonomy, so we can guess properties that we couldn't otherwise know (e.g. 'flies' for a bird that is standing still).
- **Multiple inheritance** allows exemplars to inherit from multiple sources at the same level (e.g. from 'pet' as well as from 'bird').
- **Default inheritance** allows exemplars to have or inherit exceptional properties that **override** the default properties that they would otherwise inherit (e.g. penguins don't fly), in contrast with classical logic which doesn't allow exceptions.
- The possibility of exceptions means that the properties of a concept describe the typical example, or **prototype**, more accurately than its less typical examples; e.g. sparrows are more typical birds than penguins are.
- The same logic applies to all kinds of categories, including social categories, where widely shared prototypes are called '**stereotypes**' and may carry negative prejudice as well as positive properties.
- The categories and properties in our minds provide a mental map of the social world, **I-society**.

Where next?

Advanced: Part II, Chapter 6.8: Social properties of words

3   Network structure

3.1   Concepts, percepts, feelings and actions

In Chapter 2 properties were presented as little fragments of ordinary English prose such as 'flies' or 'has wings', but this was just a temporary measure. Obviously we don't actually have little bits of prose in our minds; if we did, how would we understand them without getting into the infinite regress of using other little bits of prose, and so on and on? The question is, then, what is a property? If it's not a bit of English prose, what is it?

One possible answer is that our minds contain two different kinds of things: concepts and properties. In this theory, there would have to be cross-links between the concepts and the properties, but they would have fundamentally different characteristics; for example, concepts and properties might be organized differently.

This is actually very similar to the way in which a dictionary works. A dictionary consists of thousands of little paragraphs each of which is dedicated to one word, called its 'head-word', and head-words are organized alphabetically. These would be the dictionary's 'concepts', while its 'properties' consist of the material in the paragraphs – the pronunciation, the part of speech, the semantic definition and so on. In this arrangement, the list of concepts is completely separate from the properties, to the extent that in a bilingual dictionary the two are in different languages.

Dictionaries work (more or less), so this approach must be suitable for them; but as a theory of how our minds work it faces a very serious question: what do properties consist of? We have just rejected out of hand the possibility that they might consist of English words such as 'flies' and 'has wings', but there are other possibilities.

The idea that concepts and properties are different kinds of things is almost certainly right for some properties, namely properties that involve percepts, emotions or motor skills, which we'll now consider in turn.

3.1.1   Percepts

PERCEPTS are units of perception – mental representations for images, sounds, smells and so on. (Wikipedia: 'Percept'.) For example, your concept 'cat' almost certainly includes something like a picture of a typical cat.

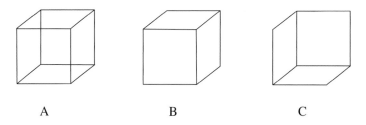

Figure 3.1 *The Necker cube (A) with its two interpretations (B, C)*

This is what you use in order to recognize a cat, and is derived (like all the other cat properties) from your experience of individual cats.

However, it's much more abstract than a photograph. For one thing, it's selected for typicality to the exclusion of exceptional cats such as those with three legs, and chooses a typical viewpoint such as the view from in front or one side, rather than from the rear or from underneath. (You may of course have a number of alternative images of a cat showing different poses – standing, sitting, lying, sleeping and so on.) Moreover, your percept of a cat is interpreted in terms of what you know about cats, so ambiguities are removed.

This process of ambiguity removal is easy to demonstrate with one of the favourite pictures in any psychology textbook, the Necker cube, named after a Swiss scientist who produced the first example in 1832. (Wikipedia: 'Necker cube'.) This is a very simple geometrical structure shown as A in Figure 3.1, which shows how your mind imposes an interpretation on the information fed to it by your eyes.

Look at A, and try to see it merely as a collection of lines. Most people can't do this because their minds immediately interpret the lines as the edges of a cube. The point is that there are two distinct ways to interpret the lines, either as a top-down view of a cube (B) or as a bottom-up view (C). What you can't do (unless you're very unusual) is to see it in both views at the same time; if so, you probably find that the view 'flips' every few seconds. This is because you create a percept of a three-dimensional cube out of the pattern of lines in A, and your percept must be either B or C, and cannot be both B and C or something in between.

Coming back to cats, the point of the Necker cube is that your mental image of a cat must be a percept: a tidied-up interpretation of a typical cat in a typical pose viewed from a typical angle. This is already half-way from a photograph to a concept, but a concept it is not.

A percept is mono-modal and analog, like an analog photograph or audio recording which reproduces just one modality (vision, hearing or whatever); but a concept is multi-modal and digital. Your concept 'cat' brings together properties from different modalities – a typical cat appearance, a typical purring sound and miaowing sound, a typical cat smell, the typical feel of a cat's fur – and these properties are 'digital' in the sense that each property is inheritable as a separate element. Moreover, concepts are organized in taxonomies, but there's nothing like this for percepts.

In short, a concept may have percepts among its properties, but concepts and percepts are fundamentally different kinds of objects in our minds. Percepts are important in language because they probably hold our memories for speech sounds, but they're distinct from the concepts that represent words and so on.

3.1.2   Emotions

Another kind of property involves **EMOTIONS**. (Wikipedia: 'Emotion'.) For example, seeing a kitten probably triggers a very different emotion in you from what you feel if you see a large spider; and the total range of emotions includes liking, hatred, fear, disgust, anxiety, envy, hope, joy and desire.

Emotions are very different from concepts because they're global states affecting the entire mind. Although you can think of a kitten chasing a spider (at least two concepts entertained at the same time), it's very hard to keep two emotions separate if you feel them at the same time. Another difference is that emotions drive us to action – in evolutionary terms, they probably evolved to push us to 'fight or flight' – whereas concepts are simply classifications of experience. We all know an emotion when we feel it, but most of us find them very hard to analyse, so I shan't try.

All that matters for present purposes is that some concepts are associated with emotions. Emotions generally struggle for recognition in linguistic theory, but they are actually rather important, not only because we use language to express them (think of the emotions expressed, in different ways, by *hooray!*, *snug*, *terrorist* and *What on Earth happened?*) but also because our feelings about other people influence the way we talk to them and whether we copy them in our own speech (Hudson 2007c: 246–8).

3.1.3   Motor skills

Alongside percepts and emotions there's a third kind of mental object that functions as a property of concepts without itself being a concept. This is what psychologists call 'motor programs' or **MOTOR SKILLS**. (Wikipedia: 'Motor skill'.) For some people, one of the properties of 'cat' may be the motor skill of stroking (what you typically do to a cat); and if you can ride a bicycle, then 'riding' is linked to whatever motor skills are involved in riding – sitting, balancing, pushing pedals and so on.

Research in neurology has shown that motor skills are controlled by a well-defined part of the brain called the 'motor cortex', with even more precisely defined areas for particular body-parts (hands, tongue and so on). Interestingly, brain scans show that simply reading a verb is enough to trigger activity in the relevant part of the motor cortex; for example, if you read the verb *lick*, the flow of blood increases in the bit of your motor cortex that controls your tongue. (Wikipedia: 'Motor cortex'.) This provides clear evidence for a link between the meaning of this verb (the concept 'lick') and a motor-skill part of your mind.

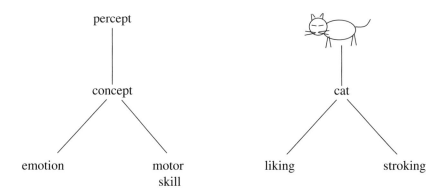

Figure 3.2 *A concept such as 'cat' may be linked to percepts, emotions and motor skills*

Motor skills matter in language because both speaking and writing involve a rich set of motor skills that take years to develop and perfect.

We now have three kinds of mental object that can serve as properties of a concept:

- percepts – abstract and idealized summaries of many occasions when we saw, heard, smelt, tasted or felt the thing concerned;
- emotions – bodily states which lead to action;
- motor skills – the mental patterns that control specific bodily movements.

These possibilities are summarized in Figure 3.2, where I also provide the beginnings of an analysis of my concept 'cat'. Notice that even if you're not impressed by my artwork, my little picture is (I hope) recognizable as a cat; if so, it's possible that your mental image isn't much more sophisticated than this. The words 'liking' and 'stroking' are just place-holders for a proper analysis of an emotion and a motor skill.

Some properties, then, can be defined in terms of mental things that are not themselves concepts. But what about properties such as drinking milk or laying eggs? Percepts, emotions and motor skills aren't relevant here; and the same may well be true of the majority of properties. The next section explains how more abstract properties can be analysed.

Where next?

Advanced: Part II, Chapter 6.9: Levels of analysis

3.2   Relational concepts, arguments and values

Let's assume, therefore, that some properties of some concepts are not themselves concepts, but are percepts, emotions or motor skills. Where does this leave properties such as 'drinks milk' and 'has fur' (for cats) or 'flies' and 'has wings' (for birds)?

3.2.1   Conceptual properties

These properties look very different from the examples considered so far, and not least because 'drinking', 'fur', 'flying' and 'wings' are themselves concepts. We can call them **CONCEPTUAL PROPERTIES**. Thus if purring is a property of cats, equally cats are (in some sense) a property of purring: purring is the sound made by cats. This rather simple idea leads inevitably to the theory that conceptual properties are nothing but links to other concepts.

To see how this works, take the 'bird' example. In this theory, there are concepts for 'flying', 'feather', 'wing' and so on as well as for 'bird', and the properties of 'bird' consist of links to these other concepts. In terms of taxonomies, of course, the other concepts are not at all closely related to 'bird' (for example, 'flying' is a kind of activity, not a kind of creature) and these links cut right across the taxonomic hierarchies. But the taxonomic relations still exist and need to be included in an analysis that tries to understand how the whole system works.

3.2.2   Towards a notation for properties

The result is a rather complicated analysis which combines the taxonomic hierarchy with whatever links are needed from concept to concept. This makes a convenient visual notation even more important. The obvious notation for links between two concepts is a line between them, but in order to emphasize the difference between these links and those for the isA relation, Word Grammar uses curved lines as in Figure 3.3.

What this diagram shows is that 'bird' is related in some way to the concepts 'wing', 'feather' and 'flying', and that although bird isA creature, the same is not true for any of these other concepts. Psychologists call these links 'associations' and describe the memory containing them as 'associative memory'. (Wikipedia: 'Semantic memory'.) There's a great deal of evidence that our minds do in fact contain these associative links between concepts, and we shall review some of the evidence in Section 3.5. This idea, then, is well supported so far as it goes.

The trouble is that it doesn't go far enough. It's not enough to say that a bird is associated with flying, wings and feathers, because the same would be true of a butterfly riding on a feather or of a severed bird-wing (whose function is flying). What's missing is a classification of the associations which would say that the bird's association with its wing is different from its association with flying.

3.2.3   Relations, arguments and values

We need to replace mere associations with **RELATIONS**. In this terminology, the bird has a 'body-part' relation to its wing, and this relation can be

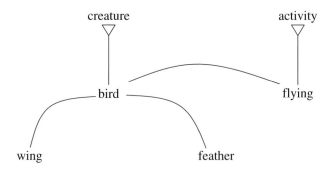

Figure 3.3 *Properties shown as links*

defined even more precisely as a 'front-limb' relation (comparable with our relation to our arms); but it has a 'covering' relation to its feathers (compare our hair)
and a 'locomotion' relation to flying. The point is that the theory must allow us to
distinguish these relations. Psychologists aren't generally interested in these distinctions, but linguists and artificial intelligence researchers are. Consequently
it's these disciplines that provide the ideas that we need.

The first step is to develop a suitable labelling system to distinguish one relation from another, and to distinguish these labels from the basic concept labels;
in Word Grammar, relation labels, unlike entity labels, are written in a 'bubble'.
This allows us to distinguish the 'front-limb' relation from the 'locomotion' relation, but it doesn't tell us which thing related by 'front-limb' is the limb and
which is the owner. In technical terms, we need to distinguish the **ARGUMENT**
from the **VALUE**.

The term *argument* as used here has nothing to do with arguing, but is used in
the mathematical sense where a mathematical operation such as doubling can be
applied to an argument to produce a value. For example, in the equation '$3 \times 2 =
6$', the operation is doubling, its argument is 3 and its value is 6; in other words,
if you take 3 (the argument) and double it (the operation) you get 6 (the value).
Other kinds of relation such as 'front-limb' have a similar structure; for example,
if you take a bird (argument) and look for its front limb (relation), you find a
wing (value). In this way of thinking, a relation is like a journey which starts at
the argument and ends at the value, which is why Word Grammar notation has an
arrow-head pointing towards the value.

Adding these extra bits of information to Figure 3.3 gives Figure 3.4 (page 40).

We now have the beginnings of a proper definition of 'bird' in terms of other
concepts, but of course the analysis also helps to define these other concepts; for
example, one of the things we know about a wing is that it's the front limb of
a typical bird. You can probably imagine how this little network could grow by
adding more properties to each of these concepts, each new property bringing in
further concepts; and how the network might eventually, after a massive amount
of effort (comparable perhaps with mapping the genome), include everything
that some person knows, though it could obviously never include everything that
everybody knows.

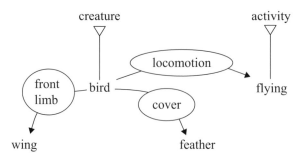

Figure 3.4 *Properties shown as labelled links*

3.2.4   Primitive relations, relational concepts and the relation taxonomy

The big question for researchers in this area is where these relations come from. One view is that they come from a general theory which lists them and defines them once and for all. This approach is particularly popular among linguists, who like to imagine a small set of universal relations with names such as 'agent', 'experiencer' and 'instrument' (8.7.4). (Wikipedia: 'Thematic relation'.) But a moment's thought raises serious questions for this approach. How do very specific relations such as 'front-limb' and 'back-limb' fit into a small set of very general categories? If we don't already have specific relations such as these in our relational tool-kit, why can't we learn them from our experience? Why should we expect the number of relations to be so much smaller than the number of ordinary concepts like 'bird', which is clearly open-ended and very large?

My view is that relations form an equally open-ended collection of concepts to which we can add at any time: a **RELATION TAXONOMY**; the same assumption has been used in a number of successful knowledge-representation systems in artificial intelligence, notably one called Conceptual Graphs. (Wikipedia: 'Conceptual graph'.)

If this is right, then there must be two different kinds of concept. First there are the basic concepts such as 'bird', 'creature', 'wing' and 'flying', which may stand for people, things, activities, times, places and so on and on. For lack of a better term, these are often called **ENTITY CONCEPTS**, or just **ENTITIES**. Entities are the basic building blocks of thought, but what makes each entity distinctive is the way it's linked to other entities by concepts of the other kind such as 'front-limb', 'cover' and 'locomotion', which we can call **RELATIONAL CONCEPTS**.

Although we can shorten this to plain 'relation', it's important to remember that there are also **PRIMITIVE RELATIONS** which are not represented in Word Grammar by relational concepts. We've already met the most important of these, which is the 'isA' relation, and I'm about to introduce three more. Using this terminology, then, we can classify the elements in Figure 3.4 as six entity

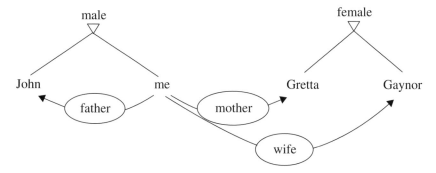

Figure 3.5 *Social relations shown as labelled links*

concepts (creature, bird, wing, feather, flying and activity), three relational concepts (front-limb, locomotion and cover) and two examples of the primitive isA relation.

Relational concepts are very familiar in our social life. Each of us has a mental network which contains all the people we know and what we know about their relations to each other and to us. In this network, the people are the entities and their social relations are the relational concepts. For example, Figure 3.5 shows a tiny fragment of my family network including my father, my mother and my wife, and also classifying us all as male or female.

All these relations are part of what I know about myself and about these people, so they're properties just like the properties of birds listed above. Of course, my relation to my wife is quite different from a bird's relation to its wing, but that's exactly why it's important to distinguish different relational concepts by labelling them.

3.2.5   A notation for relations

Relational concepts need labels to show not only when they are different but also when they are the same. For example, my relation to my mother (Gretta) has enough in common with her relation to her mother (Mary) for us to give them the same label: 'mother'. We might extend Figure 3.5 by adding another arrow labelled 'mother' from Gretta to Mary.

But in the case of entities, we don't use labels to show similarities; for instance, we don't classify a bird as a robin simply by labelling it 'robin'. Instead, we add an isA link from the bird to the category 'robin'. At least in principle, Word Grammar applies the same logic to relational concepts, using isA links rather than shared labels to show that two relations are examples of the same general category. Instead of duplicating the label 'mother' we add isA links from the relations concerned to the general relational category 'mother'.

This purist notation is shown in Figure 3.6, but you can see how impractical it is. It immediately doubles the number of lines in any diagram, so you won't see it again (except when it's essential). For the sake of user-friendliness, we'll settle

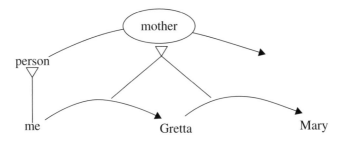

Figure 3.6 *Relations shown as a taxonomy*

for an impure notation in which similarities are shown by isA for entities but by duplicated labels for relationals.

Another impure part of the notation for relational concepts is literally hidden by the labels. As explained earlier, a relational concept applies to an argument and a value, two entities with different statuses; in Figure 3.5, the 'mother' relation between Gretta and me has me as its argument and Gretta as its value. (If you start with me, the mother relation takes you to Gretta – not the other way round.) In other words, Gretta and I have different relations to this (relational) concept, and the notation actually decomposes the relation between Gretta and me into three parts: a relational concept with an argument relation to me and a value relation to Gretta.

But what about 'argument' and 'value' themselves? Should we decompose these relations in the same way, each producing another pair of relations which have to be decomposed, and so on? This outcome would undermine the whole analysis because we certainly don't have room in our minds for an infinite number of relations, but fortunately it can be avoided by declaring 'argument' and 'value' to be primitive relations like 'isA'.

This move gives the following types of relation, each with its own notation:

- primitive relations:
  - 'isA', shown by a straight line with a triangle resting on the superclass
  - 'argument', shown by a curved line without an arrow-head
  - 'value', shown by a curved line with an arrow-head pointing towards the value
- relational concepts, shown by a label inside an ellipse.

In case you're wondering how many other primitive relations I'm going to offer you, the answer is just three, called 'or' and 'identity', plus 'quantity' which I'm about to explain.

As you can see in the last three figures, the notation actually cheats by using an ellipse box to cut what is actually a single curved arrow into two parts, one for the argument and the other for the value. For example, Figure 3.5 shows a 'mother' arrow from me to Gretta. Purists can read this as an example of the 'mother' relational concept with separate relations to its argument and its

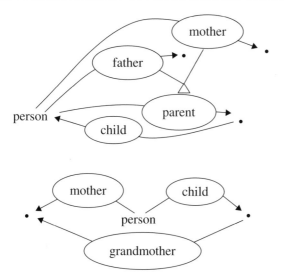

Figure 3.7 *New relations are defined in terms of existing ones*

value; but those who don't care can read it as a 'mother' relation from me to Gretta.

3.2.6   Quantity

This is as good a point as any to mention a primitive relation that's part of the official Word Grammar list (Hudson 2007c: 19–20) but which I'll hardly mention again in this textbook: **QUANTITY**. For example, the 'quantity' of legs that a typical cat has is four, so when we're dealing with a cat exemplar, we expect four legs. On the other hand, a collar is optional, which means that its quantity is either zero or one. Consequently we're not surprised either if it does have a collar or if it doesn't. This mechanism is useful in many areas of cognition, but we can ignore it until we reach valency (7.2).

3.2.7   Defining new relations, relational triangles and recursion

If relational concepts do in fact constitute an open-ended collection, it's easy to see that new relations can easily be defined on the basis of existing ones. On the one hand, we can create specialized concepts such as 'step-mother' as a special kind of mother, or 'parent' as a merger of mother and father; and on the other, we can create new relations on the basis of a chain of relations.

An easy example of both these processes would be 'grandmother', defined as the mother of a parent. Figure 3.7 shows how 'mother' and 'father' provide the basis for both 'parent' and 'child', and how 'grandmother' can then be built on these relations. (The dots in the diagram are a convenient way of indicating a node without bothering to give a name; as I'll explain in Section 3.5, all nodes are really just unlabelled dots, and labels are just a convenience for human readers. You can think of a dot as meaning 'some node or other'.)

The definition of 'grandmother' in terms of two other relations is a typical example of an important network structure, the relational **TRIANGLE**. This pattern plays an important role in syntactic theory (7.2).

Another characteristic of networks which is important in syntax (7.1) is the possibility of using these new relations to define even more general ones such as 'descendant' and 'ancestor' using a pattern called **RECURSION**.

Here's a recursive definition of 'ancestor': a person's ancestor is either their parent, or an ancestor of their parent. This definition is recursive because it includes the term that it's defining, which means that it can apply repeatedly through a long chain of relations. For example, since my father is my ancestor and for the same reason his father is his ancestor, the recursive definition means that his father is also my ancestor and so on and on right up through my family tree back to Adam and Eve.

This possibility of creating new relational concepts on the basis of existing ones allows a very rich vocabulary of relational concepts to grow on top of each other, rather like coral polyps.

The main point of this section has been to introduce the idea that an entity concept's properties include some properties which link it to another such concept via a relation which is itself a concept. According to this theory, therefore, conceptual structure consists of two kinds of concept – entities and relations – with a separate taxonomy for each kind. But that's not all, because the relations link pairs of entity concepts to one another.

This degree of complexity and detail is typical of models in artificial intelligence and linguistics, though less typical of psychological models. On the other hand, the Word Grammar model isn't actually that complex compared with a lot of complex systems that you're probably quite familiar with already, such as the internet or even the remote control for your TV; and of course, the whole point of this theory is that your mind already has precisely this degree of complexity. The main challenge for you may not be so much the complexity as the unfamiliarity of thinking about your mind in this way. Section 3.4 will try to help you by applying the general ideas to three very familiar and quite concrete areas of thought.

Where next?

Advanced: Part II, Chapter 7.1: Dependencies and phrases

3.3   Choices, features and cross-classification

Section 2.4 introduced the idea that some categories are grouped together as choices: man or woman, Republican or Democrat, 1 or 2 or 3 or…

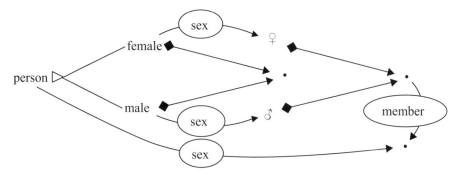

Figure 3.8 *Sex as a choice between 'male' and 'female'*

and so on. We can now consider how to build these choices into a network, with the help of a new primitive relation called 'or'.

Think of sex (aka 'gender', a term that I prefer to keep for grammar), one of the most important choices that we make when classifying people. Sex contrasts 'male' and 'female' and we assume that everyone must have either male or female sex, and nobody can have both. The question is how to include this information in network structure.

3.3.1   Features

The first step is to recognize that the sex called 'male' is different from the type of person we call 'male'. A male person has the sex 'male', which isn't a person but a property of a person. Similarly, an old person has the property 'old age'; but old age isn't itself a person.

What then is the sex 'male' or the age 'old'? It's a concept, but a very abstract one compared with, say, 'person'. It probably doesn't have any properties of its own, and its main job in our minds is to help us to organize our ideas into contrasting sets of alternatives. Even more abstract is the relation 'sex' or 'age', which links a person to one of these concepts. To anticipate the discussion of such things in language (7.3), we can call sex and age a **FEATURE**. A feature is a kind of relational concept whose value is one of these abstract concepts, shown in Figure 3.8 as the male and female symbols. The diamond arrows are explained below.

3.3.2   A notation for choice sets

The second step in understanding features such as sex and age is to look at the way in which the alternatives are organized so that we know, for example, that 'male' is a possible value for 'sex', but not for 'age'. In each case, the alternatives are defined either by a list of members (e.g. 'male', 'female') or by a description of the typical member ('a measure of time'); in more technical terms, they're defined by a **SET**, a notion that you may have met in mathematics. (Wikipedia: 'Set'.)

In Section 2.4.3 I called this a **CHOICE SET**, a set from which only one member may be chosen (or, if you prefer, a collection of 'opposites'). Each choice set is itself a concept, with its own network node which we can represent in a diagram simply as a dot, such as the dot in the top right-hand corner of Figure 3.8. Its members are the competing alternatives such as 'male' and 'female', so if we know that 'male' belongs to such a set, we can find out by consulting the set node that the only alternative is 'female'.

The relation between 'male' or 'female' and its choice set is different from any other relation we've considered so far, and seems to be another in our small set of primitive relations. The obvious short name for this link is **OR**. If two or more concepts have 'or' links to the same node, then they must be competing alternatives.

In terms of notation, the 'or' relation is shown as an arrow with a diamond at its base. (If you want a mnemonic, think of the diamonds that are sometimes used in flow charts to show decision points because they have a number of alternative attachment points.) You can see this notation in Figure 3.8.

3.3.3   The benefits of features, and their limitations

Like any other relational concept, a feature can be used even when we don't know its value – when, for example, we want to know the value, as when we ask *What's the sex of your baby?* This is the unspecified use of 'sex' shown at the bottom of Figure 3.8 by the arrow linking 'person' to an unspecified member of the choice set, which must of course be either 'male' or 'female'.

Features are important in generalizing about similarities or differences. For example, if we can talk about the feature 'colour', then we can say that my shoes both have the same colour; and then we can generalize to all shoes, saying that one's shoes should always have the same colour. It would be easy to say that they're both brown, or both black, but to make the generalization we have to be able to separate the colour from the shoe and treat it as something that the shoe 'has' (comparable with its sole and heel).

This is what we do whenever we match two things 'with respect to' (or 'in terms of') some abstract feature such as size, colour or whatever – a very commonplace and basic mental operation, but one which requires some high-level mental apparatus. Continuing with shoes, they're also supposed to match for size, so 'size' is another feature; but they must be opposite for whatever we call the left/right contrast – 'leftness'? 'rightness'? This is certainly a feature because we use it for comparisons, but it's one that has no name.

It's very tempting at this point to think that features are so useful that we can use them instead of taxonomies. (Unfortunately, this is a temptation that many linguists haven't been able to resist – Wikipedia: 'Feature (linguistics)'.) For example, if 'person' has the feature 'sex', contrasting values called 'male' and 'female', we might be tempted to dispense with the categories with the same names, 'male' and 'female'. But this would be a mistake, because most subclasses aren't neatly

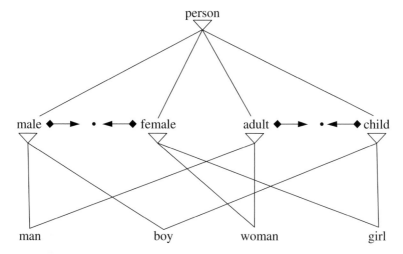

Figure 3.9 *Man, boy, woman and girl defined*

organized in terms of features. What's the 'opposite' of 'shoe', or 'dog'? It's far too easy to think of other examples like these where feature structures just don't seem to be relevant.

Ordinary classification is very much simpler than features and it's important to keep the two ideas separate. However, one of the attractions of features is that they provide very clear evidence for one of the general characteristics of ordinary classification: **CROSS-CLASSIFICATION**.

Take the categories 'male', 'female', 'adult' and 'child', which provide a very basic cross-classification of people in which sex cuts across age to define four categories: 'male adult', 'female adult', 'male child' and 'female child' – in other words, 'man', 'woman', 'boy' and 'girl'. The choices are shown, using the notation introduced above, in Figure 3.9, together with the four categories that the choices allow. The main point is that the analysis does not allow combinations like 'man–woman' or 'man–boy'.

Where next?

Advanced: Part II, Chapter 7.3: Morpho-syntactic features, agreement and unrealized words

3.4   Examples of relational taxonomies

3.4.1   Kinship

Kinship deals with relations between members of a family – a central part of the I-society discussed in Section 2.6. We've already considered a very small set of kinship concepts including the relation between my mother and me (Figure 3.5 and Figure 3.6), but we can now develop these ideas a little.

Take the Simpsons, for example. (In case you don't know who they are, you'll find them well documented in Wikipedia.) The family has five members (plus a cat and a dog which, interestingly, Wikipedia lists as family members, but which I shall ignore for present purposes):

- Homer, the father;
- Marge, the mother;
- Bart, the ten-year old son;
- Lisa, the eight-year old daughter;
- Maggie, the baby.

There are more distant relatives, but this little nuclear family will give us plenty to talk about. Our analysis, therefore, recognizes five Simpson entities: Homer, Marge, Bart, Lisa and Maggie, who could easily be classified for sex and maturity in the taxonomy of Figure 3.9.

What we're concerned with here is not how to classify them as individuals, but rather how to classify their relationships to one another. We need relations such as 'father', 'mother' and 'parent', but we also need to be able to talk about how they fit together – about the relations among the relations, a very abstract idea indeed but (I claim) one that's central to all our thinking.

What's needed is a two-level taxonomy of relations in which sex is ignored at the higher level but recognized at the lower; so, for example, 'parent' divides into 'mother' and 'father' and 'child' into 'daughter' and 'son'. For the other higher-level relations, we have to use somewhat more rarified terms: 'spouse' and 'sibling', but although the term *sibling* isn't part of ordinary English for most of us, there can be little doubt that everyone recognizes the concept. We happen not to have an ordinary name for it, but German does: *Geschwister*, which is a perfectly ordinary word with much the same stylistic feel as our *parent*. The taxonomy is shown in Figure 3.10.

And now for the complicated part: combining these two taxonomies. If there are five entities and everyone is related to everyone else, then there are $5 \times 5 = 25$ related pairs; but to make it even more complicated, every pair involves two different relations depending on who you take as the 'argument' (in the sense defined in Section 3.2 above). For example, think of Homer and Marge: he's her husband, but she's also his wife. This gives no fewer than 50 relations to be defined just in this tiny nuclear family.

The point is not, however, that family relations are too complicated to understand. On the contrary, in everyday life we have no difficulty at all in coping with them. The point is that even our most ordinary cognitive abilities are impressive. Any theory of cognition must recognize these abilities (and especially so if it's laying the grounds for a theory of the most complex cognitive ability of all, language).

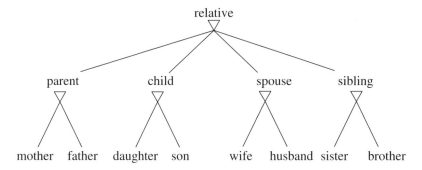

Figure 3.10 *A taxonomy of family relations*

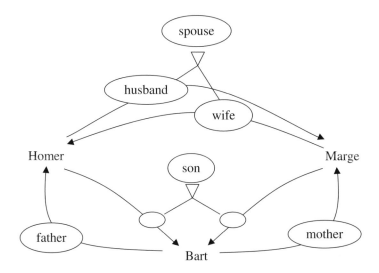

Figure 3.11 *How three of the Simpsons are related*

In practical terms, of course, it's hard to diagram 50 relations. I'll just diagram a few of them and leave the rest to your imagination. Figure 3.11 shows just three of the Simpsons: Homer, Marge and Bart. The main point of this diagram is to show how their relations can be classified via the relation taxonomy in Figure 3.10. As I explained in connection with Figure 3.6 in Section 3.2 above, all the relations should strictly speaking be shown in the same way as 'son', with an isA link to the general category; but this would have made the diagram even more complicated, so I cheated by adding labels directly to the relation arcs.

As I explained earlier, this rather complicated diagram merely lays out for inspection a tiny fragment of what you and I know already and understand without any difficulty at all. Indeed, any two-year-old can recognize basic family relations and their implications in terms of who sleeps with who, who cuddles who (and how), who looks after who and so on. We return to these ideas in Section 8.7.5, where they illustrate the link between language and culture.

Summary of this subsection:

- We have a rich repertoire of relational concepts for distinguishing **kinship relations** which involves a taxonomy and pairs of **reciprocal** relations (such as child–parent).
- We apply these relations in a rich cognitive network for the members of our family whose complexity is comparable with the network we need for language.

Where next?

Advanced: Next subsection

3.4.2   Interpersonal relations

I-society provides our next example as well. I make no apology for this, because social relations provide an important foundation for the even more complicated relations found in language; but in any case, a lot of linguistic choices are sensitive to the social relations between the speaker and hearer. For example, I have a number of names that people choose according to how they see their relation to me: I'm Dick to my wife and friends, Dad to my daughters and either Professor Hudson or just Prof to my dentist. Such linguistic choices involve what sociologists call **INTERPERSONAL RELATIONS**, the relations between two people who interact in some way. (Wikipedia: 'Interpersonal relationship'.)

A particularly important analysis of interpersonal relations was proposed by the psychologist Roger Brown. It recognizes two contrasts: **POWER** and **SOLIDARITY**. According to this analysis, your relation to someone else has a 'vertical' dimension of power in which you're superior, equal or subordinate to the other person, and a 'horizontal' dimension of solidarity, ranging from distant strangers to close intimates. (Wikipedia: 'Power (communication)' and 'Social solidarity'.)

In principle, these two dimensions cross-classify one another, giving six logically possible combinations of superior, equal and subordinate with intimate and stranger. Among intimates, your child (or cat) is a subordinate, your friend is an equal and your mother is a superior; and among strangers, a child is a subordinate, another student is an equal and your boss or professor is a superior.

But the six combinations don't all have the same status when we think of their consequences for behaviour. At least in modern western society, we tend to treat equals and inferiors in much the same way, in contrast with the respectful behaviour we reserve for superiors; and we have many ways of expressing intimacy but very few for showing distance other than the absence of intimate behaviour (Hudson 2007c: 238).

This polarization emerges very clearly in language, where we often find just two options, one for intimate non-superiors and the other for superior non-

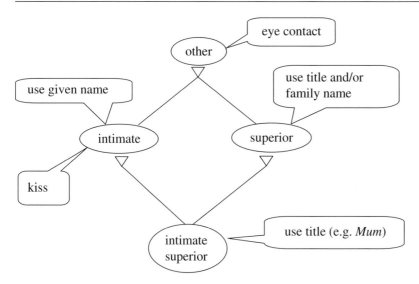

Figure 3.12 *Four interactive relations and their default behaviours*

intimates; for example, French speakers use *tu* when speaking to the first and *vous* to the second, and English speakers use given names to the first (e.g. *Dick*) but titles and family names (e.g. *Professor Hudson* or *Sir*) to the second. These two combinations are the ones where behaviour patterns cluster most clearly, in contrast with other combinations where we may be quite uncertain how to behave. For instance, what do you call your teacher who you've known for years?

It seems, then, that interpersonal relations are organized round just four relational concepts. Simply interacting with someone establishes a basic interpersonal relation which we may call **OTHER**, and which is linked to certain behaviour patterns such as eye contact which show that we are ready to communicate with them. (Wikipedia: 'Social interaction'.)

In addition, there are two special kinds of 'other': **INTIMATE** and **SUPERIOR**, each of which carries various implications for behaviour. These two can combine in the prototypical **INTIMATE SUPERIOR**, one's parents and other senior family members, a relationship with its own special linguistic signal: terms such as *Mum* or *Auntie*, which are used instead of the usual first names demanded for intimates. This analysis is shown in Figure 3.12, which for simplicity shows the relevant behaviours as properties.

This analysis of interpersonal relations shows the benefit of organizing relations in a taxonomy. The analysis only recognizes two kinds of relations, in contrast with the six kinds defined by three degrees of power and two of solidarity, and thereby explains why some power–solidarity combinations are more clearly defined than others.

Moreover, by organizing the categories in this way we allow multiple default inheritance to apply. This allows just the right generalizations, with 'eye contact' applying to all relations, whereas 'use given name' applies by default to typical intimates, but not to intimate superiors. This is why Bart Simpson calls his mother *Mom* rather than the default *Marge*, although he applies other default intimate behaviours such as kissing.

Summary of this subsection:

- **Interpersonal relations** are the relations between people who happen to be interacting at a given time.
- These relations can be analysed in terms of two independent dimensions: **power** (superior, equal or inferior) and **solidarity** (intimate or distant).
- Although the dimensions are independent, they interact in defining behaviour in terms of just two 'clear cases': '**intimate**' and '**superior**'.

Where next?

Advanced: Next subsection

3.4.3   Space and time

For a very different kind of relationship, we turn to relations of space and time, for which we typically use prepositions such as *in*, *behind*, *before* and *during* as in (1) to (4).

(1)   The ball is in the box.
(2)   The ball is behind the box.
(3)   It rained before the party.
(4)   It rained during the party.

In each of these examples, the position of one thing (in space or in time) is defined in relation to another; for example, the ball is located relative to the box, and not the other way round. The first two examples would be good answers to: *Where is the ball?*, but not to: *Where is the box?*

Landmarks

Objectively speaking, the box and the ball may be the same size and in other respects equal, but these sentences assume a particular perspective in which their relation is unequal. Psychologists describe the box as the 'background', or simply 'ground', and the ball as the 'figure', and almost every introductory psychology textbook includes the picture in Figure 3.13 to make the point that what you see – in our terms, your percept (3.1) – depends on how you divide the visual input into a figure and a background. In this example, if you take the white part as the background, then you see two faces (i.e. these constitute your figure); but if the black part is your background, then your figure is a vase. And of course you can switch between the two percepts, but you can't have it both ways at the same time. (Wikipedia: 'Figure-ground (perception)'.)

Figure 3.13 *Figure or ground?*

Although the term 'background' seems reasonable when talking about pictures, it's less helpful when we're talking about balls and boxes, where we don't think of the box as in any sense the 'background' to the ball; indeed, the background in a picture isn't an object but just the part of the picture that's left over when we remove the figure.

A much better term is **LANDMARK**, introduced by the linguist Ronald Langacker, who recognizes that it means much the same as the psychologists' 'background' (Langacker 1987: 233). Landmarks are fixed points that we use for navigating, and are always identifiable objects such as church towers or trees. This comparison is exactly right for balls and boxes, or rain and parties, where we use the box or the party as a fixed point from which the ball or rain takes its 'position' in either space or time. (We shall see below that there is probably no need for the term 'figure'.)

The theoretical claim implied by this discussion is that when we think about where a thing is or when an event happens, we have to think in terms of landmarks; and similarly, when we're planning our own behaviour such as deciding where to put things, we plan in terms of landmarks. Consequently, the first step in saying where something is or should be is to find a suitable landmark.

The Best Landmark Principle

To be suitable, a landmark must combine two qualities: 'prominence' and nearness. These qualities combine to define the **BEST LANDMARK PRINCIPLE**: the best landmark is the one that offers the best balance of

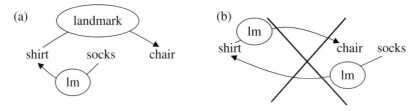

Figure 3.14 *Landmarks tend to be local*

prominence and nearness. Prominence means being easy to find; if you want to tell me where my socks are, there's no point in telling me they're next to my shirt if I don't already know where this is, and in general we choose landmarks that are either already known or easy to find. (Jumping ahead to the ideas of Section 4.2, a good landmark is one that's easy to activate mentally.)

Moreover, an object's landmark should always be easier to find than the object itself, otherwise it's not much help as a clue to the object's whereabouts. Consequently, we typically use larger and more prominent objects as landmarks for smaller and less prominent ones. But size and prominence aren't the only things that count, and in syntax we shall see that a very small word such as *is* can act as a landmark for much more prominent ones on the basis of more abstract structural considerations.

Prominence is balanced against nearness, since a nearby landmark may be more helpful than a more prominent but distant one. Take my lost socks again. If all that counted was prominence, then we might choose the entire house rather than my shirt. But however easy the house may be to find, it's too remote: the area 'in the house' takes much longer to search than the area that's 'by the shirt'.

Our desire to strike the best balance between these two qualities helps to explain a very general fact about landmarks that are linked in a chain so that some landmark A is the landmark for B, which then serves as the landmark for C. What about the relation between C and A?

Suppose you tell me that my shirt is to the left of the chair, while my socks are to the right of my shirt; where do you think my socks are in relation to the chair? In principle, they could be either to the right or the left of the chair, but most of us would assume that they're on the same side of the chair as their landmark, the shirt. In short, we assume the spatial pattern shown in 'map' (a) of Figure 3.14 rather than the one in (b).

Why do we make this assumption? The Best Landmark Principle offers an explanation. If A is the best landmark for B, then in principle it could also have been used for C, but since it wasn't, B must have the advantage of being nearer to C. Putting it more generally, we assume that any object is nearer to its own landmark than it is to the landmark of its landmark.

The Best Landmark Principle doesn't only guide us in interpreting what other people tell us, but it also guides our own behaviour. If we're thinking about where to put socks and shirts, we know it's important to remember where they are and therefore follow the Best Landmark Principle of locating things 'where we can find them', which means in a memorable relation to a memorable landmark. That's why we have furniture such as cupboards that are always in the same place.

Different ways of relating to a landmark

Having found a landmark, of course, we then have to choose a relation to that landmark. Is the ball in the box, or behind it or on it or…? Did it rain before, after or during the party? And so on. This involves another part of the grand taxonomy of relations, the part for relations in space and time. Let's focus on time, because this is the dimension most relevant to language (or at least to spoken language).

The basic temporal relations are, of course, 'before' and 'after', though there are others (until, since, during, at, in, for). If we say that Thursday comes before Friday, we're taking Friday as the landmark for Thursday. We often use the words *before* and *after* to link events, but even then we're really thinking of the times of those events; if we say that it rained before the party, we're taking the party's time as the landmark for the rain's time.

One general question is exactly how these finely classified relations mesh with the basic 'landmark' relation. If the party is the landmark for the rain, how should we add the information that the rain was before the party rather than after it? One possible answer is that we're dealing with two separate relations: the 'landmark' relation which identifies the landmark, and the temporal relation which distinguishes 'before' and 'after'.

But since the temporal relation always involves the landmark, a much easier analysis recognizes 'before' and 'after' as special cases of 'landmark' – 'before landmark' and 'after landmark', as it were. For instance, if the rain was before the party, then the party is not only the rain's landmark, but more precisely it's the rain's 'before landmark'. These isA links are shown in Figure 3.15, alongside an analysis showing that the rain's relation to the party isA 'before', which in turn isA 'landmark'. Notice that 'before' and 'after' are competing alternatives, as you can see from the 'or' relations that link them both to the same choice-set node (3.3).

One reason for this expedition into the vast territory of spatial and temporal relations is simply to show how the theory applies to something other than social relations; but these relations also have a special relevance for linguistics. For one thing, they're needed in the semantic analysis of many words – not only the prepositions discussed above, but also verbs such as *follow* and adjectives like *previous*, and they're even found right in the heart of grammar, in the tenses (where a past-tense verb refers to an event that happened before now).

Above all, we need these relations in the analysis of word order in Section 7.4, where the 'before' and 'after' relations fix the order of words in a sentence. We shall find that these relations are precisely as expected in a sequence of events (words): one word always takes its position from another and stays as close as possible to it. Landmarks and the Best Landmark Principle are exactly what we need.

Where next?

Advanced: Part II, Chapter 7.4: Default word order

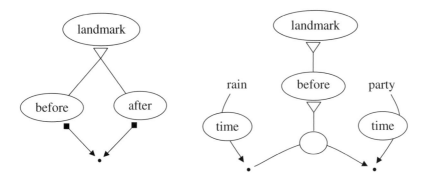

Figure 3.15 *'Before' and 'after' isA 'landmark'*

3.4.4   Chunking, serial ordering and sets

One kind of memory which is particularly important for language is memory for complex events where one thing happens, then another and then another – what psychologists often call 'episodic memory' (2.1).

The episodes that you remember always start off as exemplars, but similar exemplars can turn into general categories (4.3). For instance, you may remember the first time you attended a lecture, but subsequent lectures produced a general memory for what to do before a lecture – finding a seat, sitting down, getting out a notebook, and so on. These general memories for events are sometimes called **SCRIPTS** because they guide our behaviour in much the same way that the script of a play guides actors through it (Wikipedia: 'Scripts (artificial intelligence)'); but of course they also guide our interpretation of other people's behaviour, as when you understand what other students are doing when they come into a lecture theatre, find a seat, sit down and so on.

In order to build an episodic memory you need to be able to recognize two general conceptual elements: **CHUNKS** and **SERIAL ORDERING**. The chunks are the units of behaviour that you recognize, such as 'finding a seat' and 'sitting down', and the ordering is the relation between these chunks: first this, then this, and so on.

The chunks don't define themselves in a mechanical way; instead, we have to find them by looking for things that we can recognize. Although we can't classify chunks until we know what the chunks are, we also can't recognize chunks until we can classify them. The logical problem is obvious, and yet we carry out successful chunking operations every second of our waking lives without even thinking about them. How we do it is one of the greatest mysteries of cognitive science, but the fact is that we do manage to do it. (Wikipedia: 'Chunking (psychology)'.)

Moreover, it's clear that we don't just produce a one-dimensional series of chunks, but a hierarchy of larger chunks containing smaller ones; we recognize 'attending a lecture' as a large chunk, with 'finding a seat' as one of its parts (and maybe something such as 'arriving and settling in' as an intermediate-sized chunk). Each smaller chunk belongs to one larger one, so we need to recognize the relation **PART** between smaller and larger units – scripts within scripts.

Once this miracle of analysis has been achieved, it's quite easy to imagine how we can remember the order of events within a particular script. All we need for this is one simple relationship: **NEXT**, the relationship between one event and the next in the series. (Wikipedia: 'Sequence learning'.) If you're following a route from home to work, then at each turn you know what to do next even if you couldn't easily describe the entire route to someone else. Much the same is true for a tune: if you hear part of a familiar tune, it's easy to supply the next bar or line, though it might be hard to go directly to the end of the tune.

But sequential order isn't necessarily easy to remember; one of the standard tests that psychologists inflict on their subjects is to memorize a sequence of numbers, and it turns out that it's much easier to recall which numbers were in the list than it is to recall the order in which they occurred (Wikipedia: 'Short-term memory'), and the same is of course even more true as the items recede into the past. This is as expected if the 'next' relation is one of the properties of the entities concerned, and is as easily forgotten as their other properties.

When we remember a sequence of similar events such as footsteps or ringing bells we may collapse them into a single **SET**, a collection of items that in some sense behave as a single unit (3.3). Similarly, if we see three people sitting together, we're inevitably conceptualizing them as a set, because it's only sets that have a size (three) and members (people). Although the set consists of its members, the set is more than the sum of its parts because it has properties that the parts don't have: a **SET SIZE** (three) and a **MEMBER DEFINITION** (people). Having recognized these three people as forming a set, we can then remember them as a set rather than as individuals.

A set is therefore one particular way of 'chunking' experience, where we treat a collection of individual objects or events as a single unit which allows us to ignore the differences between them and concentrate on their similarities.

Where next?

Advanced: Part II, Chapter 7.5: Coordination

3.5   The network notion, properties and default inheritance

The title of this section is from a standard psychology textbook. Daniel Reisberg starts his chapter on memory like this:

> **The network notion.**
> Much of this chapter will be devoted to exploring a single idea: that memory connections…**are** our memories. (Reisberg 2007: 252)

In our terms, Reisberg is making a claim about properties. After all, these are information in human memory. For him, it's the relations among entities that give entities whatever properties they have.

3.5.1   The network notion

Of course, it's tempting to think of relations as links between little boxes that are filled with information that's independent of any of the box's relationships. In this view, the 'cat' concept-box holds the cat-essence 'content': it 'has four legs', 'has fur' and so on. The relations only remind us of how 'cat' can link to other concepts.

The box metaphor is appealing – but (according to Reisberg) it's wrong. In reality, there's no box. All the (apparently) internal properties are really external relations. Every property you might put inside is already available outside. For example, that cats purr is a relation of 'cat' to the concept 'purring' – you needn't duplicate 'purring' inside the box.

As Reisberg says, the connections **are** our memories. It's the links from the 'cat' node to other nodes that define our mind's-eye view of 'cat'. But in that case, what is the 'cat' concept?

Certainly not a little object in our minds with the word 'cat' written on it, because that would require a machine in our minds for reading node-labels, and then another machine for reading its internal labels and so on for ever. I put labels on the nodes in my diagrams simply because you and I couldn't understand them without labels; but they're just labels to help me to communicate with you, like the labels that a biology textbook might apply to the parts of the human skeleton. Your concept 'cat' is no more labelled 'cat' in your mind than your shin-bone is stamped with the label 'fibula'. But if your 'cat' concept is neither a box of properties, nor a labelled node, what is it?

The only possible answer is that it's nothing but a node in your mental network. In that view, the only thing that distinguishes it from the nodes for 'dog' or 'purring' is its links to other nodes. It's the only node in the system which is related to 'mammal', 'pet', 'purring', 'fur' and 'stroking'.

But (you may object), how can we avoid infinite regress? If the same is true of every other node (as it must be), and if we can only work out which node is the one for 'cat' by first finding (say) the 'mammal' node, how do we find the 'mammal' node except via nodes such as 'cat'?

This may look like a knock-down argument, but it's not. After all, 'mammal' is defined by relations to a lot of other nodes, each of which is in turn defined in the same way, and so on till we reach the non-concepts discussed in Section 3.1: percepts, emotions and motor skills.

In other words, the only reason why we need labels in our diagrams is because the diagrams are so small. Ultimately, every concept has a unique set of relations, either direct or indirect, to every other concept as well as to a range of non-concepts; if our diagrams encompassed our entire knowledge, we would indeed find that every node was uniquely defined just by its relations to other nodes. We could even rub out all the labels without losing any information at all (Lamb 1998: 59). Of course this is just a fantasy, so we'll continue to use labels throughout this book; but the point is that the 'content' of a concept lies entirely in its relations to other concepts rather than in its label.

This discussion leads to a very important conclusion about how knowledge is organized: it's a **NETWORK** – not a network of things which have their own structure, but simply a network of indivisible nodes, and nothing else. This is the **NETWORK NOTION** that Reisberg refers to above, and which is widely accepted in psychology and other branches of cognitive science; a popular name for the idea is **CONNECTIONISM**. (Wikipedia: 'Connectionism'.)

There are disagreements about details, of course, but it would be almost impossible to deny network connections in the face of the overwhelming evidence that we shall explore in Sections 4.1 and 4.2. In a nutshell, the evidence shows that mental activation circulates from node to node in a way that can only be explained if nodes are connected in a network. In this chapter, our focus is on the network's structure rather than its activity, and we shall take the evidence for granted.

3.5.2   Simple and complex properties and the Recycling Principle

Connectionism is widely accepted and applied in cognitive psychology, but it's much less often combined with the logic of **default inheritance** (2.5). What Word Grammar has to explain is how a property defined by a network link can be inherited; and part of this explanation has to be a precise account of exceptions and how they override defaults.

There seem to be two kinds of inheritable properties: simple properties and complex properties. **SIMPLE PROPERTIES** consist of just one link, such as the one between 'cat' and 'miaowing'. Any cat inherits this link to miaowing, though we'll have to wait till Section 4.5 for a proper discussion of the precise details. And if cats are the only things that miaow, the same link can also be inherited by any example of miaowing. With the exception of isA links, every link can be inherited in this way.

For the sake of variety, let's change examples from birds to cars. One of the properties of a typical car is that its fuel is petrol. This is shown in the left half of Figure 3.16, and a dotted copy is shown inherited by a car exemplar labelled 'E'. As you can see, inheriting a simple property is really simple: the inheriting exemplar receives a copy of the inherited link, complete with isA links to the original concepts.

In contrast, **COMPLEX PROPERTIES** consist of a number of converging links; for example, if a car's motor is in front, this is a convergence of two different relations: the one between a car and its motor, and the one between the motor and its landmark (as defined in Section 3.4.3), the car. This property is shown on

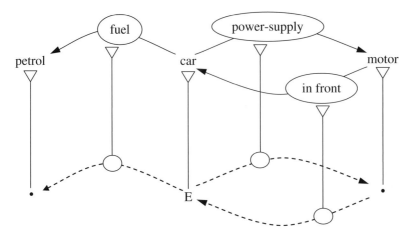

Figure 3.16 *Typical cars are fuelled by petrol and have their motor in front*

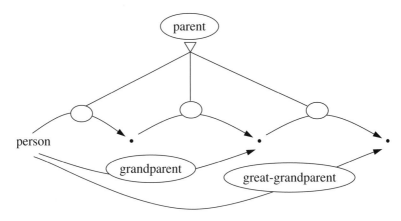

Figure 3.17 *Grandparents are parents' parents and great-grandparents are grandparents' parents*

the right-hand side of Figure 3.16, and can be translated into prose as follows: a car's power supply is a motor that's in the front of the car.

Here too, the exemplar inherits a copy of each relation in a very straightforward way, though this time there's the added twist that the two inherited relations have to converge on the same node. Complex properties are very common in general cognition; for example we find them whenever two relations are converses of each other, as in 'parent' and 'child' or 'husband' and 'wife'.

Sometimes they're a little more complex, as in the case of 'grandparent', which by definition is the parent of a parent – i.e. a complex property involving three links in a little triangle (3.2). This triangular property is shown in the left half of Figure 3.17, and translates into prose like this: a person's grandparent is someone who is also a parent of the person's parent.

Fortunately, the complexity probably goes no further than these triangular properties, because apparently complex relations can generally be broken down into a series of less complex relations. For example, although we could define a great-grandparent as the parent of a parent of a parent, it would be much simpler to say that a great-grandparent is the parent of a grandparent, building on the pre-existing relation 'grandparent'.

Building on existing knowledge is obviously an efficient way to learn, and we might even be tempted to draw optimistic conclusions about resource management. If it's natural for us to make such efficient use of existing resources in our minds, maybe we can rise to the challenge of looking after the physical resources of the world. In this optimistic frame of mind I call it the **RECYCLING PRINCIPLE**: the principle of building wherever possible on existing concepts (Hudson 2007c: 233–6).

3.5.3   How inheritance works (4)

Now that we've separated simple and complex properties, we're ready to return to the main agenda. How does inheritance work?

Inheritance itself is easy. Every link (except isA) is inheritable, either on its own (as a simple property) or in combination with other conceptual links (as a complex property). Moreover, when an exemplar inherits a property, it simply receives a copy of the original, together with isA links to record that it's a copy.

But what about exceptions? Given the network notion, how do we know when two properties are in competition with each other, and how do we know which one wins? This is where the simple/complex contrast becomes really important.

Competition between simple properties can be defined straightforwardly in terms of isA links. Returning to the car example, there are exceptional cars that run on diesel instead of petrol, so 'diesel' is an exception that overrides 'petrol'.

But how do we know that these two properties are in direct competition, so that we can't have both as properties of the same car? Because they're different values for the same relation, 'fuel'; or more technically, because the link to 'diesel' (labelled 'B' in Figure 3.18 on page 62) isA the 'fuel' link to 'petrol'.

And how do we know which of them wins this competition? Because the winner is always the **first** property to be inherited, and exemplar E is bound to inherit the link to 'diesel' before it even considers 'petrol'.

This outcome is simply inevitable given the assumptions made so far:

*   that only exemplars inherit (2.5);
*   that exemplars are attached by 'isA' to the bottom of the isA taxonomy (2.3);
*   that inheritance works its way up the taxonomy's isA links starting with whatever concept the exemplar isA (2.3 again).

Thus at the point where the inheritance mechanism tries to inherit 'petrol' as the value for 'fuel', exemplar E already has link A; this gives a value for this relation, and so the potential link labelled 'C' can't be inherited.

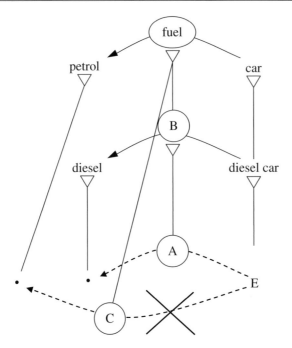

Figure 3.18 *Petrol is the default car fuel, and diesel is an exception*

Complex properties need a slightly different set of principles because it's the relations themselves, rather than their values, that are in competition. For example, although typical cars have the motor in front, some exceptional cars (such as VW Beetles) have it in the rear, and in this case it's the landmark relation 'in front' that competes with 'in the rear'.

The facts are laid out in Figure 3.19, which also shows how we know that the motor can't be both in front and in the rear: because 'in front' and 'in the rear' form a choice set (3.3). Once again, the winner in the competition is the first one inherited. Consequently, the inheritance mechanism must prevent any exemplar from inheriting a link to another node if the exemplar already has a conflicting relation to the same node.

In short, the inheritance mechanism enriches each exemplar by climbing up its isA taxonomy, taking a copy of every conceptual link that it finds except for those that conflict with the links that it has already copied.

Described in this way, it sounds slow and tedious; but in our minds it all happens almost instantaneously – almost, but not quite, because (as we saw in Section 2.2) the time it takes can be measured, albeit in microseconds. That's not quite the end of the inheritance story, which will receive an important refinement that makes it selective (4.5), but it's a considerable improvement on the earlier story.

Where next?

Advanced: Part II, Chapter 7.6: Special word orders

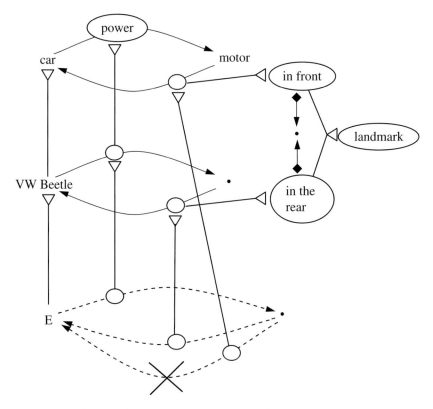

Figure 3.19 *A car's motor is in front by default, and only exceptionally in the rear*

3.6   Do networks need modularity?

One of the big debates in cognitive science concerns the extent to which our minds are **MODULAR**, in the sense of being made up of separate **MODULES**.

Is a mind more like a car or a family? A family has no natural boundaries or divisions – think of the problems involved in deciding which 'family members' to invite to a wedding, for example – and the only clear units are the individual people.

In contrast, a car is highly modular. For example, the car radio is one module and the starter motor is another. Whatever happens to one has no effect on the other, so if the car won't start, there's no point in checking the radio. They're connected physically in that each has a fixed place in the car frame, and they're both fed by the same power supply, but that's all. In manufacturing, modularity is a great idea, apparently, because all the parts can be designed and manu-factured separately and even by different companies. (Wikipedia: 'Modular design'.)

3.6.1   Why our minds aren't modular

But what about our minds? It's widely accepted that the sensory systems of vision, hearing and so on are modular in the strict sense that their internal workings aren't influenced by anything else that's going on elsewhere in our minds. For example, the ambiguous 'face-vase' in Figure 3.13 (3.4.3) still looks like either a face or a vase even if we know, and remind ourselves, that it's actually ambiguous. This is like your car radio not being affected by any other part of the car. In technical terms, the different modules are 'informationally encapsulated'. (Wikipedia: 'Modularity of mind'.)

The question is whether any other parts of our minds are modular in this sense, or indeed in any other significant sense. Some psychologists believe that many parts are modular in the much weaker sense of performing specialized tasks; for example, Steven Pinker argues that we have modules for handling more cognitive processes such as recognizing faces and even behaving romantically (Pinker 1998a).

But any version of modularity faces the question: how did we get that way? And the only possible answer is that this is how our genes built us. If everybody has the same modular structure in their minds, it must be because their brains are organized to produce this effect, and the only possible explanation for that is genetic. Consequently, the claim that the mind is modular goes hand in hand with **NATIVISM**, the claim that its structure is determined genetically. (Wikipedia: 'Psychological nativism'.)

Modularity and nativism are highly controversial when applied to cognition (as opposed to perception). The controversy is probably most intense in connection with language, because the most prominent linguist of modern times, Noam Chomsky, has argued strongly that language is a module which he calls 'the language faculty'. (Wikipedia: 'Noam Chomsky'; and for a particularly clear and authoritative introduction to Chomsky's ideas, see Smith 1999: 17–28.) This is why the issue is important in any textbook on linguistics, and, however briefly, we must consider the evidence for modularity in language.

The main evidence comes from either brain damage or neurological disorders which affect language differently from other mental functions. For example, a genetic condition called Williams Syndrome involves relatively good language combined with extremely low general intelligence; and a stroke in one of the 'language centres' of the brain (Wernicke's or Broca's area) can affect language without necessarily having severe effects on other parts of our behaviour.

These specific effects are well documented and uncontroversial, but they don't seem to point to a language module as such. Although language may be affected, or spared, more than other areas of cognition, no disorder has ever been found which isolates the whole of language, and nothing else. Worse still, it's not even clear what 'the whole of language' would mean, since even linguists cannot agree exactly where the boundaries of language lie – do they include details of pronunciation, for example, and what about word meanings?

In short, the mind isn't like a car, with modular radios, starter motors and so on that can be clearly separated from one another and that can fail completely and utterly. It seems much more like a family, where people form little clusters and groupings but boundaries are both elusive and in general not important. (Wikipedia: 'Language module'.)

3.6.2   Mind and brain

On the other hand, the language disorders found in aphasia and other cases are a fact, and need an explanation. To make the discussion concrete, I'll take a helpful example from the Wikipedia article on aphasia.

Suppose someone who had suffered a stroke wanted to say 'I will take the dog for a walk because he wants to go out'. If the stroke had damaged the part of the brain called Broca's area, they would select vocabulary items accurately but talk very slowly and omit grammatical markers. A Broca's patient might say just 'Dog walk'.

In contrast, damage to Wernicke's area produces speech which is fluent but hardly makes sense at all because of surplus irrelevant words, as in 'You know that smoodle pinkered and that I want to get him round and take care of him like you want before'.

Why should damage in these particular parts of the brain have these particular effects? This is a challenge for any theory based on the network notion. If knowledge in general, and language in particular, is a network – one gigantic network – how can we explain effects as specific as this?

Part of the answer is that similar information tends to be stored in adjacent parts of the brain; the more similar the information carried by two neurons, the closer they're likely to be in the brain. It's hardly surprising, therefore, that brain damage affects different kinds of information according to which part of the brain is affected.

Neuroscientists can pinpoint the parts of the brain that have the main responsibility for various tasks and types of information, and can even produce brain-maps such as the one in Figure 3.20 (based, with the author's permission, on one in Roelofs 2008) which shows a cross-section of the brain, with the front on the left. This is only meant as a rough sketch so please don't take the details seriously.

What this diagram shows, in broad outline, is that Wernicke's area (on the right) is responsible for integrating the word CAT with its syntactic and morphological properties, while Broca's area (on the left) holds the phonetic details. The meanings are general concepts such as 'cat', which are stored in a different part of the brain again, at the bottom of the diagram. The two triangles show the areas that direct brain activity by controlling attention.

Roughly speaking, then, similar parts of cognition tend to be stored close together in the brain. This tendency is enough to explain why patients are affected so differently by damage to Broca's and Wernicke's areas.

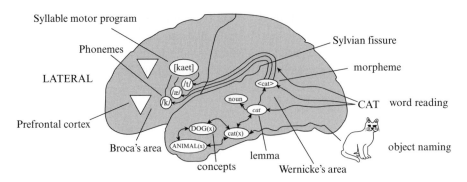

Figure 3.20 *From meaning to sound in the brain*

But this doesn't show that our knowledge is divided into the genetically pre-ordained boxes of modularity; all it shows is that information about one thing tends to be stored near information about similar things. For example, brain damage can prevent an otherwise normal person from naming very specific categories such as objects typically found indoors, or fruits and vegetables (Pinker 1994: 314). Even Pinker, one of the main defenders of modularity, doesn't think we have a module for indoor objects. But if these cases can be explained without modularity, why not all the others too?

3.6.3   The effects of network structure

This tendency for similar bits of information to cluster in the same part of the brain isn't the only relevant characteristic of mental networks. Another is the way that knowledge is organized. As we've seen, every concept is connected to other concepts, and depends on them for its properties. But the number of links varies from concept to concept.

The same is true of computers on the internet, which is a good analogy for the structures in our brain. If my computer crashes, I notice but nobody else does; if a UCL server crashes, several thousand others are affected; but if (Heaven forbid!) the Google or Wikipedia servers were to crash, the whole world would notice.

This is because there are very many more potential links to Google or Wikipedia than there are to my machine; in the technical terminology of graph theory, the internet is 'scale-free', with **HUBS** such as Google that have vastly more connections than most nodes. (Wikipedia: 'Scale-free network'.)

The same applies to conceptual networks: they too have hubs, the general categories that carry rich generalizations that are often inherited, such as the node for 'person' or 'bird' – or, in language, the node for 'word'. If these hubs are damaged, then the whole process of inheritance breaks down because there's nothing to inherit. This kind of damage is bound to have effects that aren't just catastrophic, but also quite specific.

In short, networks have enough structure to explain the effects of brain damage that are claimed to prove modularity. Instead of thinking in terms of 'boxes' of information that can be damaged or spared in their entirety, we need to imagine knowledge as a tightly structured network where concepts may form clusters but where there are no boundaries.

As in human society, clusters shade into one another and distinctions are just a matter of degree; and of course clusters overlap a great deal because of their multifaceted interconnections, with (for example) the concept 'cat' providing a link between the subnetworks for mammals, pets, family members and language (via the word CAT).

3.6.4   Why modularity matters in linguistics

Suppose, then, that we can reject modularity and find satisfactory explanations within the network notion for all the things that are supposed to support modularity. Does it really matter for linguistics? I believe it does, because modularity insulates the study of language from the rest of cognitive science.

If language was a module, there would be no pressure on us to explain it in terms of the general principles that apply to other parts of cognition. For example, word-classes inside a language module could be organized quite differently from general categories such as 'bird', and there would be no point in looking for similarities between the two. It's all too easy, given this approach, for linguistics to develop the kind of highly rarified analysis for which modern linguistics is infamous.

In contrast, if language really is just an ordinary part of general cognition, then we would expect it to follow principles which apply elsewhere and should be deeply suspicious of any analysis which makes language look unique. Maybe, after a great deal of research along these lines, it will turn out that some characteristic of language really is only found in language; but in that case, we shall have learned something really important which didn't simply follow from the assumptions with which we started.

This is the approach that underlies work in **COGNITIVE LINGUISTICS**, a trend in linguistics that dates from the 1980s and that includes Word Grammar. (Wikipedia: 'Cognitive linguistics'.) Cognitive linguists try to explain what we find in language by relating it to more general properties of cognition – a much more satisfying kind of explanation than one which denies that any further explanation is possible. The general aim of Part II is to show how far this approach can already take us, but Section 7.7 considers the special test case of syntax.

Chapter summary:

*   The properties of a concept may include links to at least three different kinds of element which are not themselves concepts:

- **percepts:** visual images, sounds, smells, etc.
- **emotions:** anger, joy, surprise, etc.
- **motor skills:** movements of body parts involved in talking, walking, etc.
- But most properties are **conceptual properties**, which consist of links to other concepts: 'cat', 'purring', 'mother', 'before', etc.
- There are two kinds of concepts:
  - **entity concepts:** 'cat', 'purring', etc.
  - **relational concepts:** 'mother', 'before', etc.
- Relational concepts have an **argument** and a **value**, and can be shown in diagrams by an arrow pointing from the argument to the value, with the relational concept superimposed in an elliptical box. The relations that they define are **conceptual relations**.
- Links between concepts are therefore of two types:
  - **primitive relations: 'isA', 'argument', 'value', 'or', 'quantity'** and **'identity'**
  - **conceptual relations.**
- Relational concepts have their own taxonomy, so a conceptual network is built round an **entity taxonomy** whose entities are linked to each other by relational concepts that belong to a **relation taxonomy**.
- Relation taxonomies are found in every area of knowledge, but are particularly rich in our social knowledge, where very different kinds of relations can be found in **kinship** and in **interpersonal relations**.
- Relation taxonomies are also found in the relations that we distinguish in space and time, where one entity is always located relative to some relatively fixed point, its **landmark**. The precise relation (e.g. 'before' or 'after') is a sub-case of 'landmark'. These temporal relations are important in handling word order in syntax.
- The entities linked to each other by both isA and relational concepts form a **network** in which each node represents a concept that it defines by its links to other concepts (as well as by links to percepts and so on). The **network notion** is the claim that this is all there is to knowledge, so concepts are nothing but atomic nodes in a network. This approach to cognition is called **connectionism**.
- Properties are either **simple properties** (consisting of a single link to another concept) or **complex properties** (consisting of multiple links, either direct or indirect, to another concept). Complexity is minimized by the **Recycling Principle** of building where possible on existing concepts.
- **Default inheritance** enriches exemplars by copying properties across isA links, starting at the bottom of the hierarchy. When two links are in **competition** (defined for simple properties in terms of isA between relations and for complex ones in terms of 'or'), the first one inherited wins.
- The network notion offers an alternative to **modularity** which can explain why neural disorders such as strokes can damage some areas of cognition (including language) more than others. Instead of postulating separate

modules, we look for damage to **hub** nodes which have particularly rich connections to other nodes.

- **Cognitive linguistics** is a recent tradition that denies that language is a module; Word Grammar is part of this tradition. The aim in this approach is to explain characteristics of language as examples of more general cognitive principles.

Where next?

Advanced: Part II, Chapter 7.7: Syntax without modules

4 Network activity

4.1 Activation and long-term memory

One characteristic of knowledge which at first sight seems unrelated to its network structure is that some bits of knowledge are more accessible than others.

Suppose you're a typical Brit and I ask you what the capital of France is. You would probably 'know the answer' – more precisely, recall the answer – immediately; but what about Finland or Serbia? Given time, you could probably find these too, which is why we can't say that you don't know them or that you know them less well.

4.1.1 Accessibility and frequency

The point is that even if your network includes a 'capital' link for each of these countries, this knowledge is easier to find and use in the case of France than in the other two cases. And of course, if I was to ask someone who lived in Finland or Serbia, the relative difficulties would change in favour of their own country.

Why? Because memory is influenced not only qualitatively but also quantitatively by experience. Our theory must explain not only what it means to know that Paris is the capital of France, but also what it means for this fact to be relatively **ACCESSIBLE** or inaccessible.

Psychologists have done a great deal of research on the various things that influence our ability to recall information, and one common theme is that this ability varies in degree according to the nature of our experience of the thing being recalled.

One influence is the emotional impact of this experience; for example, if you were to witness an armed crime, you would probably remember the gun more clearly than other details such as the villain's clothing. (Wikipedia: 'Emotion and memory'.) This is presumably because the gun arouses a much stronger emotion in you than the other details, and more emotional experiences are more likely to be stored and, when stored, are more accessible for recall.

Another influence is the frequency of the experience; this would explain why a Brit might recall the capital of France more easily than the capital of Finland after hearing about Paris more often than Helsinki. This link between frequency and accessibility, called the **FREQUENCY EFFECT** (Harley 1995: 146–8), can be measured experimentally and the results generally produce a pattern that can be expressed as a curve on a graph, known as a 'learning curve' or 'experience curve'. (Wikipedia: 'Experience curve'.)

These curves show in general terms what we all know: that practice makes perfect; but they go further, by showing that later experiences have much less effect than earlier ones. Conversely, psychologists can also produce 'forgetting curves' which show how different kinds of memory gradually become more and more inaccessible with time when we don't access them. In short, 'use it or lose it'. And as we might expect, they show that we lose stronger memories less quickly than weaker ones. (Wikipedia: 'Forgetting curve'.)

The metaphor of **STRENGTH**, with stronger and weaker memories, is a helpful temporary way of thinking about memories as it unifies these various measures. Memories are stronger if they're based on more emotionally charged experiences, and they become stronger with repetition of the experience; and the weaker they are to start with, the more liable they are to weaken with time.

This variable 'strength' is an important quality of our knowledge which we can't ignore; any model of cognition must recognize that some concepts, or connections between concepts, are stronger than others. Moreover, since these strengths reflect experience, they must change through time even if the change is measured in hours or days (in contrast with the very rapid changes that we review in Section 4.2). This constant changing of strengths means that cognition isn't just a static network of connected nodes.

4.1.2   Mind and brain again

But how can we move from a mere metaphor to a better understanding of 'strength'? This requires a brief consideration of the brain.

As we saw in Section 3.6, networks of the **MIND** are carried by networks of the **BRAIN**, but they're not the same things. The brain consists of neurons and neuro-transmitting substances (Wikipedia: 'Brain'), and has the physical structure sketched in Figure 3.20. It's studied by neuroscientists, using methods such as surgery and brain scans.

The mind, in contrast, consists of concept nodes and links, and applies processes such as default inheritance. It has no physical structure, as such, but it has a logical structure defined by the way in which isA links interact with all the other links. It's studied by psychologists and philosophers (Wikipedia: 'Mind') – and, indeed, by anyone who researches any kind of mental activity, including linguists.

But although they're logically quite different, your mind and your brain are obviously linked in some way. The exact nature of this linkage has worried philosophers and theologians for thousands of years as part of the more general question about the relation between minds and bodies (Wikipedia: 'Mind–body duality'), but we don't need to assume any kind of magical or theological connection.

Instead, we need to think of the mind as 'information', which the brain holds in its neurons in much the same way that a computer holds information in its chips and circuits. This view is called the **COMPUTATIONAL THEORY OF MIND**. (Wikipedia: 'Computational theory of mind'.)

Your computer holds information in programs and data files, and you probably understand to some extent how these are related to one another and how they're structured internally even if you have no idea what the various chips and circuits do or how they work. Because of this similarity, it's helpful to think of brains and minds as hardware and software, with the hardware providing the physical resources which hold the information contained in the software.

4.1.3   Activation levels

Our cognitive networks are part of our mind, not part of our brain. For instance, we can be sure that a concept is not held by a single neuron, or even by a single node where many neurons meet.

We simply don't know how neural networks hold mental networks, but the most popular theory is called **PARALLEL DISTRIBUTED PROCESSING**. (Wikipedia: 'Connectionism'.) This is the idea that information is held in a network of neurons whose interconnections have different **ACTIVATION LEVELS** (also called 'weights').

One attraction of this theory is that neuroscientists can measure actual electrical activity and electrical potential in neurons, and can even produce mental activity by applying (very small) electrical charges to the brains of patients who are undergoing brain surgery. (Wikipedia: 'Biological neural network'.) This electrical activity can be observed directly through magneto-encephelography (MEG), and because the activity needs calories which are carried as oxygen in blood, it can also be studied indirectly through functional magnetic resonance imaging (fMRI). (Wikipedia: 'Neuroimaging'.)

We now have a replacement for the metaphor of 'strength'. A strong concept is one which is held (at the level of the brain) by neurons with a high activation level. A useful bit of mental flexibility allows us to simplify this by pretending that concepts themselves have activation; but please bear in mind that it's actually the neurons rather than the concepts that have it.

If emotionally charged concepts are strong, this is because they have a high activation level; if frequently used concepts are strong, this must be because every occasion of use raises the activation level slightly; and so on. The most important conclusion is that a concept in a cognitive network is held by neural structures whose level of activation reflects the previous experiences of the person concerned.

This level changes on two time-scales. In the long term, it varies with frequency, though the effect of frequency is much greater in the first few encounters than in later ones – hence the 'learning curves' discussed in Section 4.1. But in the short term it also varies abruptly in the way I discuss in the next section, before returning after a while to the previous level. To distinguish the levels we can call them the **RESTING ACTIVATION LEVEL** and the **CURRENT ACTIVATION LEVEL**.

Where does this discussion leave our view of the mental network? In a sense, nothing has changed because all the discussion of activation applies to the brain, not the mind. But in another sense everything changes, because this stable mental network is held by a system that's constantly changing. However, it's important to bear in mind that the supposedly stable mental network includes a constantly changing 'fringe' of exemplar nodes, and 'changing our minds' is much more common than we think. Later sections will develop this idea further.

Where next?

Advanced: Part II, Chapter 8.1: Accessibility and frequency

4.2   Activation and working memory

As you no doubt know, psychologists distinguish '**LONG-TERM MEMORY**' from '**SHORT-TERM MEMORY**'. Long-term memory is what we could also call simply 'knowledge', the more or less permanent information that we carry around in our minds, where every concept has some **resting activation level** (4.1). This is contrasted with the much more temporary memory that we use in trying to understand what's going on around us and in deciding what to do about it; this is where we find variations in the **current activation level**.

As you also know, long-term memory has effectively unlimited capacity, and nobody has ever been diagnosed as having run out of long-term memory. In contrast, short-term memory has a very limited capacity, with the famous limit of '7 plus or minus 2' items of information based on the number of unrelated digits most of us can hold in the memory for a few seconds.

Computers once again offer a very convenient analogy: your long-term memory is like a hard disk, which holds vast amounts of information even when it's switched off, while your short-term memory is like the chip for 'RAM' (random access memory), and which has a relatively tiny capacity and loses all useful information when you switch the computer off. (Wikipedia: 'Short-term memory' and 'Long-term memory'.)

4.2.1   Working memory

However, the term 'short-term memory' has generally given way to **WORKING MEMORY** as the name for the constantly changing, limited-capacity system. This change of terminology is driven in part by a new way of imagining the two kinds of memory.

When long-term memory was contrasted with short-term memory, the two were seen as two separate systems of the mind, each supported by a different area of the brain, just like the hard disk and the memory chip on a computer. In this view of memory, information was copied from long-term memory into short-term memory, as a kind of workbench where it could be treated in some way before being cleared by forgetting.

In contrast, the term 'working memory' highlights the activity rather than the limited capacity, and opens the way to a very different view in which there's just one memory. This single memory is both permanent ('long-term') and active ('working'), though different parts of it are active at different times.

This view is by no means universal in psychology, but it does have a considerable amount of support (Wikipedia: 'Working memory') and it's the view that I shall assume here. Indeed, it's the only view compatible with the network notion of memory as one gigantic network.

4.2.2   Spreading activation

What we have to consider in this section is how working memory works. What does activation achieve?

Suppose you have a concept for 'cat'; how do you **RETRIEVE** this concept when you need it? For example, how do you use it for recognizing some observed exemplar as a cat? Your task is to find a concept in your mind that has similar properties to the exemplar, but how do you do it?

You probably have hundreds of thousands of different concepts in your mind – maybe millions – so you certainly can't check through them one at a time until you find the right one. The two keys to the answer are **SPREADING ACTIVATION** and **FIRING**. (Wikipedia: 'Spreading activation'.)

According to this theory, when a concept's current activation level reaches a certain **THRESHOLD**, the concept 'fires' in a little explosion which spreads all its surplus activity among its neighbouring nodes, the nodes to which it's directly connected. This brings its current activity level back to the resting level. I explain below how each firing contributes to the ultimate goal of retrieval.

Let's apply this idea to your cat exemplar. You build a mental node for the exemplar (I'll explain in Section 4.3 how you do this), and make it very active – after all, this is what you're most interested in at the moment. You give it all your mental resources; in fact, you give this node enough activity to make it fire.

Since the node is connected to whatever concepts define its properties – size, shape, purring, fur and so on – the activation spreads to these other concepts. Some of them will receive enough activation to make them fire, and provided sufficient activation reaches them from the exemplar, their activation will converge on a single stored concept that's also connected to these properties, 'cat'. As the only concept that receives activation from all these different sources, it emerges as the winner in the competition for your exemplar and you can decide that you're looking at a cat.

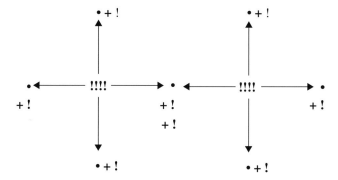

Figure 4.1 *Activation spreads indiscriminately from a node to all its neighbours*

The main point to remember about spreading activation is that the spread of activation is completely random and undirected, with a lot of mess and waste on the way. For instance, when the 'fur' concept fires, its activation doesn't just pass to 'cat', but to every one of the dozens of concepts that you have which connects to 'fur' – 'bear', 'rabbit', 'fur coat' and so on.

Figure 4.1 is an attempt to show this process in general terms, with two very active nodes firing their activation (represented by exclamation marks) equally to all their neighbouring nodes, which thereby each receive the extra activity represented by '+ !'.

What makes this messy process productive is that most concepts which receive activation won't receive enough to make them fire, and that the ones that do fire are the ones where, like the one in the middle of Figure 4.1, activation from several sources **CONVERGES** on a single node.

4.2.3   Priming

We can be sure that activation spreads in this rather clumsy way because we can observe the effects of **PRIMING**. In ordinary English, the verb *prime* means 'prepare for use': we prepare wood for painting, or a machine for operation, by priming it. Similarly, we can prime a concept by raising its activation level.

This is exactly what you do when preparing for an exam – you deliberately prime as many of the relevant concepts as you can by activating them in some way just before the exam. (Wikipedia: 'Study skills'.) But priming of concepts is generally an incidental by-product of experience, and it is incidental, unintended, priming effects that demonstrate the indiscriminate spreading of activation.

We all experience these effects in everyday life; for example, if you watch a scary film, then for a while afterwards you may be more anxious than usual about shadows and unexpected noises, which you associate with the concepts primed by the film. (Wikipedia: 'Social cognition'.) Better still, psychologists have developed experimental methods such as 'naming' or 'lexical decision'

(8.1) which demonstrate priming effects very clearly by showing that priming an item speeds up the retrieval process.

For example, if you were to read the word *nurse* just after you read *doctor*, it would take you slightly less time to retrieve *nurse* than if the preceding word had been an unrelated one such as *lorry*. The time-scales involve tiny fractions of a second, but the findings are extremely robust. (Wikipedia: 'Priming (psychology)'.)

The most important thing that these experiments show is that activating *doctor* has the effect of raising the current activity level of *nurse*, even though you're neither looking for this word nor even interested in it. The only plausible explanation for this finding is that when *doctor* fired, its activation spread, willy nilly, onto all its neighbouring concepts, including the one for 'nurse'.

Spreading activation fits very easily into the view of working memory as the part of long-term memory that happens to be active. Our memory 'works' when we retrieve information, so when a node fires, it joins the 'working' part of memory. The location of working memory varies from moment to moment, as activation energy flows round the brain; and at any given moment, nodes might be firing in numerous different areas of the brain depending on how many different tasks we're dealing with at a time. But wherever nodes fire, their activation spills equally onto all their neighbours.

Moreover, the limited capacity of working memory is easily explained by the limited amount of energy available for activation; the energy that you're devoting at the moment to reading this book is energy that you can't use for other mental tasks, and if you happen to be watching TV while reading, then I fear I'm only getting a fraction of 'your mind' – i.e. of your activation energy.

There's only a finite amount of energy available for activation, so for every winner there's a loser. This limited capacity is important for language, where we shall see that syntax is organized in such a way that we can arrange words in an order that doesn't make too many demands on our hearer's working memory (7.6).

4.2.4   How attention channels activation

The discussion so far has emphasized the indiscriminate way in which activation spreads, and raises the obvious question: how do we manage to channel this aimless activity to suit our aims? For example, why don't we walk around muttering random words to ourselves as the things we see activate word nodes? The answer lies in the converging activation pattern that I showed in Figure 4.1, where one node was selected for double activation, but first we need a little more background theory.

Working memory is the meeting point for a number of different mental activities that psychologists tend to study separately, but which all influence activation. First, and most obviously, it relates to long-term memory, the network of knowledge to which activation applies.

But what is it that decides where activation is applied in the first place? One important influence is **ATTENTION**. We can see a red traffic light, but if we don't pay attention to it – i.e. if we don't notice it – it may not affect our behaviour. (Wikipedia: 'Attention'.)

But that in turn depends on our goals, which are a matter of expectations, motivation, interest and so on – all the things which make up a person's 'personality'. Many psychologists assume that our mind brings all these variables together into a system, often called the **EXECUTIVE SYSTEM**, that manages to integrate them into coherent values and decisions. (Wikipedia: 'Executive system'.)

This is probably the hardest area of cognition to understand because it raises the age-old problem of free will: who makes my decisions? A leading psychologist puts it like this: 'If, in short, there is a community of computers living in my head, there had also better be somebody who is in charge; and, by God, it had better be me' (Fodor 1998: 209). Fortunately, we can leave the ultimate problems for others to solve. Whatever the solution, the fact is that our minds do control activation, at least when we are awake; and dreams are presumably an example of what our minds do when nobody is 'in charge'.

We can now return to the question of how this random spreading activation can serve the very specific purposes of retrieval for which we use cognition. In exploring the retrieval mechanism, we need to explain not only how we do it but also why; in short, we have to treat retrieval as a goal-oriented activity rather than simply as a reaction to a stimulus.

Imagine two contrasting circumstances under which you see a fairly unfamiliar face in a crowd. In one case you are simply part of the crowd; but in the other, you are looking for the person concerned, having (say) arranged to meet them. From a cognitive point of view, these are very different situations, with very different combinations of attention, goals and expectations, and different outcomes.

In the first, you probably won't recognize the face simply because you won't look at it at all, or not in sufficient detail. But in the second, success is much more likely because your brain has already selected the remembered face, and all you have to do is to find a matching face in the crowd – a much smaller challenge than picking a face out of the thousands of faces in your memory. Better still, you're focusing all your attention on this task, rather than on (say) reading a newspaper or thinking about last night's television.

Generalizing from this example, the more activity is applied, and the more nodes are activated initially, the more successful retrieval will be.

To change examples to something more conceptual, suppose you want to remember your friend Jack's birthday. You already know a great deal about the answer: it's a birthday and it's Jack's. Consequently, the parts of your network dealing with Jack and with birthdays are very active.

In my earlier description of spreading activation, activation radiated out from an exemplar node in a random and unguided way. This description is still true,

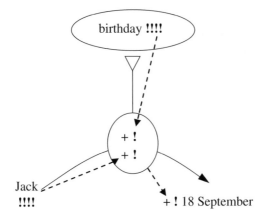

Figure 4.2 *How to retrieve Jack's birthday*

but we now have an explanation for purposeful retrieval, namely that it always involves more than one source of activation.

When activation radiates out from two nodes, it automatically increases on the nodes which they both feed – i.e. on the chain of nodes that links them – and decreases on all the other nodes. In the birthday example, activation goes out from the nodes for 'Jack' and for the relation 'birthday', and (with luck) the two streams of activation converge on a single node. All being well, this is the node you're looking for.

This process can be seen in Figure 4.2, where Jack's birthday is assumed to be 18 September. The very active nodes for 'Jack' and 'birthday' fire their activation to their neighbours, and activation converges on the 'birthday' link specific to Jack. This in turn fires activation to the previously inactive node for '18 September', making it the most active potential answer to the question.

The important thing about this example is the fact that you weren't just interested in Jack; if you had been, his birthday would have been just one of many other properties that would each have received a very small amount of activation. The crucial thing is that your mind also registered your particular interest in birthdays by activating the relational concept 'birthday', which in turn picked out Jack's birthday for special activation.

These complex patterns of activation are important because they provide a way to capture the idea of **INTEREST**: if you're interested in something, you pay attention to it, which in this model translates into high levels of activation. In the same way, they also allow us to define current **GOALS**; for example, if you'd wanted to find Jack's address rather than his birthday, it's the 'address' relation that would have been highly active.

The general idea, then, is that we direct the otherwise random flow of activation by selectively activating a number of different concepts – for example, the 'Jack' node, a current interest in the 'birthday' relation and a query node for Jack's birthday. Although the activation from these three nodes actually spills over onto a host of other neighbours, it rapidly converges on the stored node for

'18 September', the only node that receives activation from more than one other node, and the temporary activation of all the other nodes either vanishes into nothing, or is channelled into this 'winning' node (depending on the details of a model that we can't explore in this book).

4.2.5   The benefits of global activation

This system allows us to use the very crude mechanism of spreading activation to retrieve precisely defined information, and even more importantly, it gives us complete flexibility in the questions we ask ourselves. We can wonder if there's any connection between Jack and 18 September, or whether we know anyone whose birthday is on that day.

We can move from any known to any unknown that we can define in terms of its relations to the known. In terms of the network, we can start with any concept, define our goals in terms of one or more linking relational concepts, and find the target concept.

This flexibility is exactly what we need in dealing with the many experiences and challenges that life presents, but it's particularly important for language, where we have to be able to move either from sound to meaning (listening) or from meaning to sound (speaking) – not to mention the many other ways of using language (8.3).

This model of activation flowing around the network, guided only by general considerations such as attention and interest, is very attractive as a general model of how our minds work, but however intuitive it may be, it's in competition with the modular view considered in Section 3.6, where the mind consists of a collection of modules each of which is dedicated to some specific task.

In the model that I'm describing, there's a single mental network where activation can flow freely from one part to another. One of the many attractions of this view is that it explains the effects of what is usually called **CONTEXT**, meaning everything apart from the current concern.

For example, if you're thinking about Jack's birthday, the context includes other people, other birthdays and even today's date, and the outcome of your search will be the **BEST GLOBAL CANDIDATE**, the node which is most active after activation has converged from everywhere else in the entire network. If the whole network acts as the context for every retrieval process, then anything in the network may affect the outcome, whether or not it's actually relevant.

Sometimes the broader context is relevant; for example, in searching for Jack's birthday you may remember that last year his birthday was on a Sunday. But sometimes it's just a distraction, as it would be if you confused Jack's birthday with his brother Jim's because you've just been thinking about Jim. And of course such mistakes do happen, so the global view is confirmed by our mental frailty. We shall see that the same is true for language, where the global context often interferes with the strictly linguistic processes of speaking and listening (8.3).

Where next?

Advanced: Part II, Chapter 8.2: Retrieving words

4.3   Building and learning exemplar nodes

The idea of activation flowing round the network is standard elementary psychology and neuropsychology, but according to Word Grammar, mental activity goes beyond activation. Our minds also create new nodes and new links.

At this point the theory of the mind parts company radically with the theory of the brain, because nothing comparable is suggested for the brain. No known mechanism could create new brain cells or connect existing ones fast enough to match the proposed creation of nodes in cognition, which must take place within microseconds. This isn't, of course, to deny that the brain plays a part in node-creation; all it means is that the creation of a mental node corresponds to a very different kind of change in the brain such as a complex change in the chemical bonds between neurons.

4.3.1   Building nodes for perceived exemplars

By the end of the chapter I shall have introduced three different reasons for creating new nodes: for various kinds of exemplars, for induced nodes and for inherited nodes. Of these needs, the most obvious is in handling perceived exemplars, the elements of everyday ongoing experience (2.1).

Every time you see a bird, hear a sound or smell a smell, you have to create a mental node to represent it. After all, the whole point of having a mind is so that you can understand exemplars like these with the help of categorization and inheritance. But rather obviously, both classification and inheritance only work if you can hold each exemplar, however briefly, in your mind; and that means creating a node for it.

The node you create when you 'perceive' something is linked to a percept (3.1), but it's not the same thing; for one thing, it can be linked to two percepts each coming from a different organ, as when you both see and hear a bird. The new node is a concept, not a percept.

Take the words that you're reading now: each word consists of letters, and each letter has to be identified and classified. Within the time that it takes to read the word, you must be building not only a node for the word, but also one for each letter. The same may be true for every thing or person that you pay attention to: every pea on your plate, every bend in the road and every pedestrian you avoid when driving.

This claim may sound absurd, but it's hard to see how else your mind might work. How could you recognize the word *This* at the start of the previous sentence without first creating a node and asking: what's this?

It would seem, therefore, that we can create new nodes for elements of ongoing experience – what we can call **EXEMPLAR NODES**. If so, we must do so very fast indeed.

In the case of reading, a normal rate of reading is between 200 and 400 words per minute; even if you're near the bottom of this scale, you can read about three words per second. (Wikipedia: 'Reading speed'.) In this paragraph, the average word has between four and five letters, which means that you're recognizing no fewer than twelve letter exemplars as well as three word exemplars every second. Even if you can ignore some of the more predictable letters, your performance is impressive.

4.3.2   Forgetting exemplar nodes

Now let's push the argument a step further. I'm suggesting that in order to process something that you see or hear, you have to create a node for it. Without this node, you have nothing to classify, and nothing that can inherit properties. But both classification and inheritance require the node to be part of your network, attached by isA to some permanent category node.

It follows that the 'permanent' network has a fringe of very un-permanent exemplar nodes that are changing all the time. The vast majority of them 'disappear', at least for all practical purposes, almost as fast as they appear. Try this question: have you read the word *even* in the last minute? If you don't know, this is because the node that you created at the start of the last sentence in the last paragraph but one is no longer accessible.

How this disappearance came about is hard to tell, especially if we try to explain it in terms of neurons in the brain, and the answer may be different from the mechanism for forgetting items of long-term memory. (Wikipedia: 'Forgetting'.) However, it seems reasonable to assume that nodes remain accessible as long as they have a certain level of activation, so the disappearance of nodes is closely connected with activation levels. Indeed, one view that's popular among neuro-scientists is that the brain holds nodes as activation patterns in a neural network (4.1). If this view is right, a node ceases to be a node when it loses activation.

The link to activation explains why, when we want to, we can prevent these nodes from disappearing by maintaining their activity level. Think what you do when you want to remember a word: you 'rehearse' it (as psychologists put it). By saying it over and over again to yourself, you're at least keeping it active, and with luck, you'll make it so active that it stays accessible for ever. Unfortunately, there's no guarantee that it'll work, because when you eventually stop repeating the word the activation level may simply drop to the level it would have reached without rehearsal.

Another link to activation runs through the notion of 'attention' that we considered in Section 4.2. The whole point of attention is to be selective – we direct activation towards the things we care about and away from irrelevant and unimportant things. The words you're reading now are receiving attention that could have been directed towards other things around you; and while you're reading, those other things are being ignored.

In terms of node-creation, we can assume that attention decides which exemplar nodes are created. If so, although you're creating a vast number of nodes for my words, you're probably creating none at all for these other things. This makes complete sense from a practical point of view if we assume that node-creation takes energy, and that we only have a limited amount of mental energy to cover all the spreading activation and node-creation that we need for thinking.

4.3.3   Remembering exemplars

Let's assume, then, that you create new exemplar nodes for things that you see, hear or otherwise 'perceive'. But perceived exemplars aren't the only things that need concepts in our ongoing experience.

Suppose you plan a meal; each item in the plan is also an exemplar with its own separate mental node. Obviously you don't have a separate node for each pea – just one for 'some peas', but this is still distinct from the generic node for 'pea'.

The same is true for any other planned behaviour. For example, when you unlock a door, you need some kind of plan to guide your actions, and that plan will inevitably include a node for the door, another for the overall action of 'unlocking' and another for the key. These nodes are just like perceived exemplars, with an isA link from each one to some permanent memory node. Consequently, they too belong to the same constantly changing fringe attached to the network and are destined to disappear almost as soon as they're created.

But what happens if an exemplar node does **not** lose its activation? While we're categorizing an exemplar and enriching it, it receives our attention and plenty of activation, but then our attention normally moves on. In a few cases, however, the exemplar is sufficiently special to hold our interest.

Suppose you see a bird which turns out to be a kind of bird that you've never seen before. In that case, you'll have invested a good deal of mental effort in trying to classify it, so it will already have more activation than more straightforward exemplars.

What happens next is pure speculation, but I speculate that it may stay active enough to be still accessible, as an ordinary part of your mental network, next time you see a similar bird. If so, then you can recognize it as 'another one'.

In other words, what started as a temporary exemplar node has turned into something like a permanent category node – you've learned a new kind of bird. Without some mechanism for **LEARNING** such as this, it's hard to imagine how we could ever learn anything from experience.

You may feel that 'learning' is rather a grandiose name for this process, when all you've done is to remember seeing a particular bird on a particular occasion. Nevertheless, the experience has changed your mind permanently, which is at least part of what is meant by 'learning'. In fact, it's hard to see how we could learn generalities without having a collection of specific examples to base them on; at least, that will be the argument of the next section.

However, even a remembered exemplar has some degree of generality, thanks to an important human weakness: selective memory. Remembering an exemplar isn't an all-or-nothing matter, because an exemplar is a complex concept which, like any other concept, has a number of properties – colour, size, time, place and so on. If you remember the exemplar, you're also remembering its properties.

But different properties have different chances of survival into memory. The most likely to survive are those that you're paying a lot of attention to; these are the most active at the time of perception, and they'll stay more active in the coming hours or days. Conversely, properties that receive little attention also receive little activation and don't survive.

This theory explains why you may remember the bird's colour and what it was doing, because these are the kinds of properties that attract our attention. Why? Because they're useful for categorization, so they're interesting.

At the other end of the interest scale are the details of the event, including when and where it happened. When you're classifying birds it really doesn't matter whether it's Monday or Tuesday, and such details receive little or no attention, and correspondingly little activation.

Not surprisingly, then, time and place are much less likely to survive into memory, and you're quite likely to end up with a permanent node for the bird exemplar which has a colour and an activity but no time or place. But that's precisely what distinguishes a general category from a specific exemplar (2.1), and your half-remembered bird is already general enough for a subsequent exemplar to isA it.

We now have the basis for a theory of learning from experience which, once again, applies the Recycling Principle (3.5). In this case, you recycle temporary exemplars as permanent categories. When you experience something, you build a temporary concept for it but if this temporary concept holds your attention it may earn a permanent place in your long-term memory. This is why you may still remember tomorrow something of what you're reading now, and why this may still be in your memory next year – and, of course, why I'm writing this book.

Where next?

Advanced: Part II, Chapter 8.3: Tokens and types in listening and speaking

4.4   Building induced nodes

I mentioned in the previous section that some psychologists believe that our memories contain nothing but exemplars, and in particular no general categories. This is very different from the Word Grammar view in which general categories play a fundamental part. The challenge, therefore, is to explain how we can learn general categories on the basis of experience alone. More precisely, how do we learn the taxonomies that I've been discussing since Section 2.2?

General categories such as 'bird' and 'parent' are somewhat different from the recycled exemplars that we considered in the previous section. Categories are often called **SCHEMAS** in order to emphasize that they are 'schematic' – i.e. mere outlines without any of the specific details that we find in exemplars. (Wikipedia: 'Schema (psychology)'.)

For example, the schema 'dog' must be sufficiently abstract and general to cover all the various shapes, sizes and colours found even among typical default dogs, whereas any exemplar has a specific shape, size and colour. Even if the difference is only a matter of degree, we can't hope to explain the emergence of schemas in terms of the same mechanism as recycled exemplars, not even if these are slightly abstract thanks to selective memory.

How, then, do we learn schemas such as 'bird' from a number of particular exemplars of birds? The question has been much debated in psychology as the problem of **INDUCTION** – how to 'induce' the general from the specific, in contrast with 'deducing' specifics from generalities. (Wikipedia: 'Concept learning' and 'Inductive reasoning'.)

The starting point for the Word Grammar theory is the assumption that we learn enormous numbers of exemplars, as explained in the previous section. But of course one difficulty with this assumption is that even exemplars have properties that involve conceptual schemas, so how does learning start?

How, for instance, can children know that they've just heard an exemplar of a dog barking without already having a 'barking' schema? The answer must be that they start with nothing but the percepts, motor skills and feelings described in Section 3.1. At this stage they link the visual percept of the dog to the auditory percept of the barking, and recognize that this exemplar combined the two.

Having stored a few similar exemplars, they're ready to induce a concept for 'dog barking' as explained below; and once that concept is in place, it can be used for classifying further exemplars. Let's assume, therefore, that even in the earliest stages each exemplar is fitted with property-links to schemas that are also available to other exemplars.

4.4.1   How background activation guides induction

The next theoretical step is to assume that some activation is circulating all the time, even when we're asleep. This assumption is needed even for retrieval, because retrieval sometimes seems to ignore the usual time pressures of working memory, taking hours or even days rather than the usual split second.

For example, suppose I tried unsuccessfully just now to remember the name of a village in Italy that I visited some years ago. That failure may not actually be the end of the search, because my mind may go on hunting even when I think it's given up. In my experience, it's not uncommon for the target to suddenly 'pop up' in memory while I'm asleep, and to be waiting for me when I wake up.

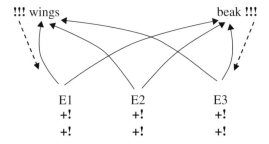

Figure 4.3 *Three bird exemplars have wings and a beak*

The only possible explanation for this phenomenon is that my mind went on searching for the village's name even after I thought I had given up; and since retrieval always involves spreading activation, my brain must have been gradually accumulating activation in the target area. How this happens I don't know, but I assume it must work like ordinary instant retrieval, but with much lower levels of activation.

Suppose, then, that low-level activation is circulating 'off-line' in our brains, maybe during 'down time' when we're not paying attention to anything very much. This activation is available not only for dogged long-term retrieval projects, but also for induction – i.e. spotting generalizations.

Suppose you're a small child who's seen half-a-dozen typical birds but hasn't yet induced the schema 'bird'. All the exemplars you've seen have shared a number of properties such as having wings and a beak. Figure 4.3 shows the state of play in your mind when you have three stored exemplars (E1, E2 and E3) all sharing these two properties. (For simplicity I've omitted various details which I'll restore in Figure 4.4.)

You'll notice that the links define a tightly knit little network with each of the exemplar nodes linked to each of the properties. These shared links mean that all the exemplars are affected equally by activation in any of their properties. If background activation raises 'wings' to its firing point, the activation spills equally onto all three entities, and likewise for 'beak'. But the point is that if **both** properties fire at about the same time, each of the three exemplars receives a double dose.

Moreover, this incoming activation may make some of the exemplar nodes fire, sending activation back to the property nodes and maybe even making them fire again. And so the dense network of links acts as a kind of resonator, magnifying the available activation, in contrast with all the surrounding nodes.

This double dose of activation is the brain's way of saying: 'How interesting – I've spotted a generalization. Things that have a beak also tend to have wings.' But of course, it doesn't actually express the generalization as a permanent part of the network. For this, we need a mechanism to build a new node for a schema. It's hard to be sure what this mechanism might be, but it's tempting to think it may be the same mechanism that we use in building exemplar nodes.

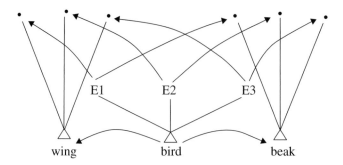

Figure 4.4 *A schema for 'bird' has been induced from a number of exemplars*

Think what your mind has to do when you see a bird singing in a tree. The challenge is that visual and auditory properties come to you via different organs so they reach your brain via different neural pathways. Somehow or other your mind has to work out that the two percepts are properties of the same thing. (Wikipedia: 'Binding problem'.)

Virtually the only clue that shows they belong together is timing: the sights and sounds reach you at the same time. One famous theory for how we integrate these different but co-occurring experiences in our brains is summarized in the saying that 'nodes that fire together, wire together'. (Wikipedia: 'Hebbian theory'.) In this example, your mind 'wires together' the two percepts by creating an exemplar node with both percepts as its properties.

If our brains are capable of creating a new node to wire together the different properties of an exemplar, then they can presumably do the same for stored exemplar nodes that are activated at the same time. Coming back to Figure 4.3, if the three exemplar nodes fire at the same time as 'wings' and 'beak', this mechanism wires them together by creating a new node linked to them all.

In short, this particular mind has discovered the 'bird' schema by induction. And so induction builds our taxonomies while we think we're not doing anything; which is one of the many reasons why 'down time' is so important.

This isn't quite the end of the Word Grammar account of how we create new categories by induction, because the properties have to be suitable for inheritance. We shall see in Section 4.5, that supercategories can't literally share the properties of their sub-cases; for example, the 'mother' link from 'person' can't point at exactly the same node as the one from some particular person, because if it did, any example of that node would inherit the property not only of being the typical mother of the typical person, but also of being the mother of that particular person.

By the same logic, the three bird exemplars can't literally have the same wings and beak; rather, they all have exemplars of the 'wing' and 'beak' schemas. I omitted this complication from Figure 4.3, but we can now see that the typical bird has typical wings and a typical beak, all located at the same level of schematic generality as the bird itself. Consequently, the structure induced from Figure 4.3, with this correction, is the one shown in Figure 4.4. (As before, I've left the relations unlabelled to reduce the clutter in an already overloaded diagram.)

> ### Where next?
> Advanced: Part II, Chapter 8.4: Learning generalizations

4.5   Building inherited nodes

Exemplar nodes aren't the only nodes that we create during day-to-day living and thinking. Thanks to inheritance, we also have expectations which involve further nodes for people and things that we haven't yet experienced.

For example, we expect children to have parents, and when we meet a child we can reasonably introduce a pair of nodes for their assumed mother and father (though as we shall see below, sometimes we don't bother). Similarly, we expect a person to have a name (so a reasonable question is: what's your name?), and we expect events to have causes (so we wonder why, even when we don't know the answer).

4.5.1   Why we need new nodes for inherited properties

These expectations are all properties that exemplars inherit, and in each case the property involves some other predicted entity which we represent to ourselves without knowing anything specific about it.

Figure 4.5 contains two alternative diagrams showing the result of thinking about a child (called here just 'E1', for 'first exemplar') whose mother we don't know but take for granted. For convenience, I've labelled the generic default mother 'M'.

Diagram (b) is simpler than (a), and looks as though it captures the generalization that E1, like any other person, has a mother; but it's wrong. Why? Because it confuses the general and the particular by treating M as the mother not only of the typical person, but also of this one particular person, E1.

This kind of confusion would lead to all sorts of logical problems. For example, according to diagram (b), if you know that Mary is John's mother, then Mary isA concept M. Consequently, by inheritance, she's also E1's mother; but that's certainly the wrong conclusion, so (b) is too simple.

Another reason for rejecting diagram (b) is that only exemplars can inherit (2.3), and since we obviously want E1's predicted mother to be able to inherit properties such as being female, she had better be an exemplar too, in contrast with the non-exemplar M.

Instead of (b), then, we need the slightly more complicated structure in (a). These arguments explain why every inherited property needs an extra node for a predicted but unknown exemplar. These predicted exemplars will play an important part in language structure, and especially in syntax, but it's important

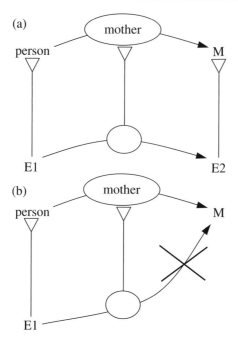

Figure 4.5 *How to inherit a mother*

to recognize them first outside language so that we can then explain language behaviour in terms of more general cognitive principles.

4.5.2   How activation guides inheritance

Let's take stock of the mental activity that I've described so far in this chapter. I've argued that there are two basic types of activity, and that these are divided between the brain and the mind: the brain holds activation while the mind builds nodes. (To activation and node-building I'll soon add a third activity type: binding.)

But I've also argued that these two kinds of activity are closely connected. For one thing, newly constructed exemplar nodes are very active and help to channel the otherwise random spread of activation. And for another, low-level activation is responsible for spotting generalizations, which then trigger the creation of induced nodes.

We can now consider another possible connection between activation and node-building, this time applied to the building of inherited nodes. Take the example of the child E1. The 'mother' property is only one of very many properties that E1 can inherit either from 'person' or from 'child'; I have no idea how many such properties there are, but the number could easily be in the thousands for a rich concept like 'person'.

But most of these properties are irrelevant most of the time. For example, we also know that a person has a blood-group, but this property simply isn't relevant on the vast majority of occasions, so there's no point in inheriting it.

One theoretical possibility is that we actually inherit everything regardless of how useful or interesting it is. A much more plausible idea, though, is that we inherit selectively, concentrating on properties that happen to be **RELEVANT** to our current purposes. In the example of thinking about child E1, we don't bother to inherit the property of having a blood-group unless it happens to be relevant.

But this theory raises a different question: how do we do it? How do we distinguish relevant properties from irrelevant ones? As always, a good candidate for the mechanism we need is spreading activation.

Unfortunately there's very little research on the interaction of spreading activation and default inheritance for the simple reason that these two mental activities have been studied by different research communities: psychology and artificial intelligence. Consequently, what follows is nothing but an untested guess, but an untested guess is better than no idea at all, and this particular guess does have the merit of meshing reasonably well with everyday experience as well as with the tested ideas I've offered so far.

My guess is that exemplars only inherit properties that are active. Sometimes the 'blood-group' property will be active for a child because of the observer's current interests, but most of the time we're not particularly interested in blood-groups and this property is 'switched off' because its activation level is too low to reach the threshold for firing.

Suppose this guess is correct. On the one hand it raises questions that can only be answered by careful research into the details of how inheritance and activation interact. How much activity is needed to trigger inheritance? For example, is inheritance really an all-or-none matter, as I have presented it so far, or might there be some arrangement which allows a property to be inherited to some degree? And on the other hand, the guess suggests explanations for one of the trickiest challenges in the study of cognition: the effect of **CONTEXT** on our thinking.

How we think about a tree, for example, depends on all sorts of considerations which vary from time to time. Are we currently thinking as an artist, a botanist, a timber merchant or a tree-climbing enthusiast? One and the same person could, of course, combine all these interests, but with just one of them dominant at any given moment.

Relative dominance translates into attention and activation levels, providing a link between the context and activation. This in turn explains how the inheritance system can distinguish between active properties, which are relevant, and inactive ones which aren't. The result is that only relevant properties are inherited. (Wikipedia: 'Relevance'.)

In such cases we might say that since the different viewpoints are all capturing a different aspect of truth, they're all 'right'; but even the notion of rightness or truth seems to be able to vary with context. (Wikipedia: 'Contextualism'.) For example, are you an animal? Well, it all depends on what you mean – in other words, it depends on the context. In a biological context, you definitely are an animal – a primate, closely related to chimpanzees, and so on.

But if the context is non-scientific, then you definitely aren't an animal, because animals are what we contrast ourselves with; we talk about 'animal rights' (in relation to humans) and 'cruelty to animals' (inflicted by humans). (Wikipedia: 'Context (language use)'.) Moreover, you inherit a nationality as a non-animal and a species as an animal. And so on.

Our minds are able to contain these contradictory assumptions quite happily because they apply in different contexts; and all this is as we would expect if inheritance follows attention and activation.

This section completes the discussion of inheritance that started in Section 2.3, so it may be helpful to summarize the Word Grammar theory of inheritance. The mechanism seems to work as shown in the textbox.

This mechanism is absolutely fundamental to all our thinking, and explains how we can combine the bold generalizations of defaults with the flexibility provided by exceptions and by sensitivity to context.

This flexibility explains the 'prototype effects' of classification that accommodate the irregularities of the real world (2.5), and also allows us to deal creatively with new kinds of experience. Without our ability to accommodate exceptions and to be influenced by context, we would be locked into a rigid system of categories which would probably be more of a hindrance in living than a help.

How inheritance works (final summary):

- **Only exemplars** inherit, so inheritance only applies when an exemplar E is attached by an isA link to some permanent concept C; for instance, E isA 'child', which isA 'person'.
- Inheritance consists of two closely related activities: **searching** for **source concepts** and **inheritable properties**, and **copying** the latter.
- The **searcher** chooses source concepts **recursively** up the taxonomy, starting with concept C; so having inherited from C, the searcher chooses any concept that C isA, and then any concepts that these concepts isA, and so on up the taxonomy. If the taxonomy branches, the inheritor visits all branches, so inheritance is **multiple**.
- For each source concept, the searcher chooses all its properties that are sufficiently **relevant** to be **active**. For example, E probably inherits the active 'mother' property but probably not 'blood-group' because this is unlikely to be sufficiently active.
- The searcher also ignores properties that **compete** with properties that E already has; so inheritance is only **by default**. Two properties are in competition if their relational concepts are directly linked,
  - either by isA for simple properties (as shown in Figure 3.18 for the competition between diesel and petrol as the value for 'fuel')

- or by 'or' for complex properties (as in Figure 3.19, for 'in front' versus 'in the rear').

- The copier makes a **copy** of each selected property, with new nodes for both the property's other nodes: its relational concept and the latter's argument or value. Each of these new nodes isA the corresponding node in the source property.

Where next?

Advanced: Part II, Chapter 8.5: Using generalizations

4.6   Binding nodes together

The discussion so far has focused on two kinds of activity in a mental network: activation and node-creation. This section discusses a third activity in which two existing nodes are 'bound together' to show that they are, in some sense, 'the same concept'.

When we bind one node to another, the first step is to select the other node, and the second is to establish a special link between the two. Before I discuss the mechanism, I want to show informally that the same pair of steps, using the same basic selection mechanism, seems to be used as a tool in several different operations: classifying, retrieving from memory, predicting and planning. We consider these operations one at a time, starting with **classification**.

4.6.1   Recognizing and remembering

Suppose you look out of the window and see a bird flying past. How do you recognize it as a bird? We've already seen (4.3) that the first step is to create an exemplar node E and attach to it as many observable properties as possible. There must be a brief moment when E is in your mind, but when it has the status of an 'unidentified flying object', all you know about it is that it's a small moving object in the sky which you can see.

Your task, in the next split second, is to find a category into which E will fit, given its known properties, and then to link E to it via an isA link. Once this is in place, inheritance can enrich E, but until you've decided what E is (or rather, isA), you can't do anything with it except wonder.

Now suppose that I'm trying to **remember** where I put something; in my case, it's often my spectacles that I've mislaid, so let's take that as an example. Since I know that I put my spectacles somewhere, I'm trying to recall an incident in which I put my spectacles down. And of course if I can remember this incident, I'm hoping to be able to remember where it happened.

Here too I start with a hypothetical temporary concept that has a handful of properties (involving spectacles and me), and which I'm hoping to identify with a stored concept that has the same properties. But of course, unlike the bird example, I'm not trying to classify a new bit of experience; rather, I'm trying to find a memory of an old bit of experience.

4.6.2   Anticipating and planning

Now let's consider a very different challenge, **anticipation**. Suppose you see a flash of lightning and recognize it as a flash of lightning. One of the things you know about meteorology is that lightning is usually followed by thunder, and you may even know that the time-lag between the two indicates how far away the storm is (four seconds per mile, I was told).

Given this strong linkage between lightning and thunder, you may be sufficiently interested in the future thunder to deliberately listen for it. If so, then on seeing the lightning you think: 'Aha, lightning. That means thunder, so let's listen for it … Aha, there it is.' In these thoughts, the first 'it' is a hypothetical temporary node and the second is the eventual thunder, your target category.

As you can see, the challenge of linking the empty exemplar to the target is much the same as in the two previous examples, but in this case we're in a very different area of psychology: anticipation of a future event rather than classification or recall.

And finally, suppose that you're not anticipating an event, but **planning** it. For instance, your mobile phone rings, and you have to decide what to do. Once again you have a hypothetical temporary node standing for the action you're looking for and that you're hoping to identify with the retrieval target, some stored action. One possible target category is to answer the phone, but no doubt your mind contains other possibilities as stored action types suited to a ringing mobile phone, such as ignoring it or asking someone else to answer it.

Deciding what to do is called **problem solving** (Wikipedia: 'Problem solving'), and as we all know, solving a familiar problem is much easier than solving an unfamiliar one. Unfamiliar problems call for creative thinking, which is hard to explain; for example, what should you do with your mobile phone if it rings when you've got your hands full of delicate glasses?

These examples are enough to show how many different mental processes use the same mental machinery of attaching a temporary empty node to a permanent target category. In each case the aim is to 'fill up' or enrich the empty node by attaching it to some target node which is fuller or richer in the sense that we know more about it – i.e. it has more properties.

4.6.3   Building an empty node

We now turn to the details of the general mechanism that we use in these cases. For the sake of concreteness, I'll apply them to the example in which you see a bird in the sky and recognize it as a bird.

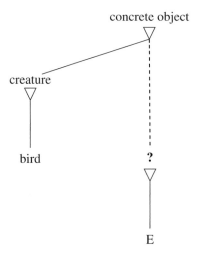

Figure 4.6 *What you know about a bird exemplar*

As I said above, the first thing you do is build a node E for the exemplar. The earlier discussion implied that you know virtually nothing about E except for its observable properties (its size and position). But you actually know more than that.

One very general thing that you know is that you're hoping to classify E. Consequently you can immediately create another node and provide an isA link from E to it. This node stands for the category that you'll eventually select for E. We can call it an **EMPTY NODE**, and represent it in notation as '?', to remind us that it's just a place-holder for the **TARGET CATEGORY** which spreading activation will find. It's shown in the middle of Figure 4.6.

Another equally general thing that you know about E is that it's a concrete object. You can be sure of this for the simple reason that you can see it, and only concrete objects are visible. This immediately reduces the range of possible candidates for '?', so it could be 'bird' but it couldn't be a concept like 'Friday' or 'beauty'.

Showing that '?' is a concrete object isn't as easy as you might think. You may think that all we need is an isA link from '?' to 'concrete object', but this won't in fact do. The reason is that this analysis would rule out 'bird' because there's no isA link from 'bird' to 'concrete object'. Instead, there's a chain of isA links, with at least one concept ('creature') in between.

What we need, therefore, is a variation on the basic 'isA' relation that we haven't needed to recognize so far: **SUPER-ISA**, a relation between a concept and any concept above it in its taxonomy, regardless of the number of intervening isA links. In terms of notation, we can distinguish super-isA from plain isA by using a dotted line instead of the usual solid line, as in Figure 4.6. According to this diagram, then, 'bird' is a candidate because it too super-isA 'concrete object'.

This diagram ignores the observable properties of E, such as its size and the fact that it's in the sky, which will eventually take you to 'bird' as the target; we return to these below. The main point to make is simply that when you wonder what E is, your wondering is already directed to finding a particular kind of concept.

4.6.4   Retrieving the best target

The second step involves retrieval, so you let spreading activation find a suitable stored schema whose properties fit those of E (4.2). When you're searching for some target concept, you activate at least two other concepts that define the target, and leave the rest to spreading activation. In this case, activation is spreading strongly from E and '?', and with luck, the activation from these concepts converges on the target and makes it more active than any other candidates.

One important characteristic of this retrieval mechanism is that it allows a **global** approach (4.2) that takes account of everything we know and selects the best available solution, even if this isn't perfect. The alternative is a simple 'pattern-matching' approach, in which the properties ('patterns', in this terminology) of E are simply compared with those of all the stored categories. (Wikipedia: 'Pattern matching'.)

Simple pattern-matching is what most computer programs apply, and can lead to a great deal of user frustration. For instance, when you log into a secure internet account you may be asked security questions such as your mother's maiden name or the first school you attended; but all the computer can do is to match the patterns (the letters) that you type in against those that it holds in its database, and it objects to the slightest difference between the two.

The reason why we find this approach so frustrating is that our minds don't work like that. Unlike machines, we humans are prepared to tolerate the odd error provided the global fit is 'good enough', and we're not thrown by little things such as mispellings – in fact you may not even have noticed the deliberate one in this sentence. So long as most of the letters in a word are right, and the word fits comfortably both into the surrounding sentence and into the overall context, we overlook deviations.

The same is true of the unidentified flying object, where we look for an interpretation which makes the best fit not only with the object's perceived size, shape and so on but also with its behaviour and the totality of the situation. And similarly for the place where I left my spectacles and the predicted thunder; in each case, the search takes global account of everything we know.

The benefits of a global approach seem rather obvious when we think informally, especially in comparison with more rigid pattern-matching approaches. Consequently, this common-sense notion is sometimes discussed in artificial intelligence, where it's been named the **BEST FIT PRINCIPLE** (Winograd 1976). It's also applied in mathematics, where there are well-developed techniques for finding the best fit between a simple line and a series of data points. (Wikipedia: 'Curve fitting'.)

Unfortunately, it also turns out to be an extremely difficult principle to apply more generally. (Wikipedia: 'Global optimization'.) For example, one famously difficult problem is called the 'travelling salesman problem'. It sounds easy: given a number of cities and the costs of travelling from any city to any other city, what is the least-cost round-trip route that visits each city exactly once and then returns to the starting city? The trouble is that gains on visiting one city may easily be offset by losses on other cities.

4.6.5   How spreading activation helps

One approach, of course, would in theory be to consider all possible routes, cost them all and choose the cheapest; but the number of possible routes rises much faster than the number of cities. However sensible a consideration of all possibilities may be for three or four cities, it's anything but sensible for 100.

This objection becomes even more telling when we impose a time constraint, as we must in cognition. When looking for the best fit, we typically finish the job in microseconds and certainly don't have time to consider even one alternative, let alone thousands of them. In any case, there would be no point in choosing the best fit if, in order to find it, we had to consider and reject all the worse fits as well. In short, what we need, and presumably have, is a mechanism that takes us directly (and fast) to the best fit.

This mechanism is spreading activation. Activation spreads fast and accumulates where different sources converge on a single node. What counts is the overall activation pattern, and not the details. Accordingly, the winning concept is the one that gives the best overall performance even if it fails on one or two properties.

In exploring the effects of this activation, we start once again with your task of classifying E, the flying bird. Let's consider your mind at some point before you spot the bird, i.e. what we can call your 'normal' state of mind.

One of your many concepts is 'bird', with a large number of properties attached; for simplicity, let's assume just two properties, one linking 'bird' via 'location' to 'sky' and the other linking it via 'size' to '5 cm'. This is the state of play shown in Figure 4.7 on page 96, where I've assumed, again for simplicity, that none of the concepts have any activation at all.

Let's now move forward to the point where you've noticed the object E and recorded those of its properties that you can see – properties which, of course, consist of links to stored nodes in the permanent network (for size, shape, location, movement and so on). In our example we can assume that E is also linked to '5 cm' and 'sky', as shown in Figure 4.8 (where I've simplified by omitting the relation labels).

As before, the exclamation marks stand for activation, and the dotted arrows show how it spreads from E to these two concepts, which in turn become

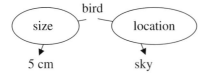

Figure 4.7 *What you know about 'bird'*

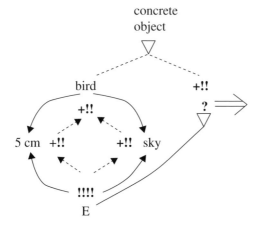

Figure 4.8 *What you know about bird E*

sufficiently active to fire and pass their activation on to 'bird'. Since their activation converges on 'bird', this becomes especially active and you're well on the way to recognizing E as a bird, especially since 'bird' super-isA 'concrete object'.

4.6.6   The 'identity' relation

The double-shafted arrow in Figure 4.8 is needed for the second part of the binding operation. Having selected 'bird' as the global winner, you have to link it to '?' in such a way as to show that '?' and 'bird' are the same. What exactly does this mean in network terms?

One possibility is that the two nodes simply merge into a single node. This would be a clean and simple solution, but it's almost certainly wrong because we can 'undo' the merger mentally. This is what happens whenever we change our minds about classification. If classifying E as a bird meant merging '?' into the 'bird' node, we could never backtrack because we couldn't separate the properties of '?' from those of 'bird'.

What we need, therefore, is a way of equating two nodes while still maintaining their separate identities. One way to do this would be to use an isA link, giving '? isA bird'. This may be the solution, but it doesn't seem right because it introduces a redundant isA link; instead of concluding that 'E isA bird', you're actually concluding that 'E isA ?' and '? isA bird'.

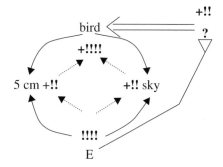

Figure 4.9 *You decide that E isA 'bird'*

The alternative I prefer is to introduce the last primitive relation, called **IDENTITY**. Identity is a link between two nodes which are functionally equivalent, so that their properties are interchangeable. In our bird example, an identity relation between '?' and 'bird' means that they count, in network terms, as the same though the nodes are distinct.

The notation for identity is an extended 'equals' sign '='. However, the concepts that it relates aren't equal because one is, at least relatively speaking, empty and seeks the other to enrich it. This is why the equals sign has an arrowhead at one end pointing from the empty node to the target node. In Figure 4.8, the arrowhead points at nothing because it's still 'searching', but in Figure 4.9 it points at 'bird'. This diagram shows the end (at last!) of your little project of classifying that bird.

What you have to remember is that, although this project has spilt over a couple of pages of this book, it took your mind a very small fraction of a second. Speed is essential, so what you need is a 'quick and dirty' method such as spreading activation rather than a slower and more careful approach which might produce fewer mistakes.

This example illustrates the mechanics of what I call 'binding', the process of finding a suitable stored concept and identifying it with some empty node. In using this term, I'm thinking of two different uses of the term. Linguists and logicians use the term **BINDING** for the pattern in a sentence such as *John hurt himself*, where the person referred to by *himself* is 'bound by' the person referred to by *John*. (Wikipedia: 'Binding (linguistics)'.)

As I mentioned in Section 4.4, psychologists also use the same term for a somewhat similar mental process in perception which 'binds' the elements of different kinds of perception together into single units. For example, vision actually processes shapes and colours separately, and so an early stage of perception recognizes something green and something square, but a 'binding' operation is needed before we recognize a green square.

I shall suggest that the linguists' binding is actually a special case of the much more general process that I'm describing here (8.7.3), but I don't know whether the same can be said for what psychologists call binding. At any rate, it's possible that the two have some similarities in terms of brain mechanics.

4.6.7   How binding helps us to remember, anticipate and solve problems

However, I'm more confident that the binding mechanism used in classification is the same as the one we use in the other mental processes that I described earlier. Let's see how it applies to them.

In remembering where I left my spectacles, I activate an empty node '?' and whatever properties define it – i.e. the properties defining an event in which I put down my spectacles. Activation from these properties hopefully converges on a stored memory of the occasion, defining it as the best global candidate. An identity link between this and '?' records the binding.

In anticipating thunder after lightning, I similarly activate '?' and the properties of thunder, but in this case I have to wait for converging activation from a future exemplar E. If I hear a number of different noises, I choose the one that makes the best global fit.

Finally, in problem solving I create '?' for the solution, with a specification of the desired outcome and plenty of activation. If I'm lucky the activation from the properties in the specification will converge on a stored solution. If not, I have to think 'outside the box', which means creating a new concept.

In short, the claim of Word Grammar is that we apply the same mechanism of binding guided by activation to the past, the present and the future: to retrieving memories, to classifying present experiences and to anticipating and planning future events. Moreover, we shall see how important this same mechanism is in various apparently unrelated areas of language use (8.6).

Word Grammar makes similar claims for activation, inheritance and node-building, all of which play an important part in our use and learning of language as well as in areas of life that have nothing to do with language.

If these claims are true, they matter greatly. They suggest that our minds use a very small number of very general mechanisms for achieving an astonishingly wide range of tasks – a very different view of the human mind, and of human nature, from the idea that our minds consist of a collection of task-specific 'modules' (3.6).

Chapter summary:

- How easy it is to find a concept – its accessibility – depends on its **strength**, which depends on our previous experiences with it.
- The brain network that supports your mind carries electrical **activation** which is moving around the network all the time. Each neuron has a **resting activation level** and a threshold level at which it **fires** and spreads

its surplus energy equally to all its neighbouring neurons. This is called **spreading activation**. One consequence of this automatic spreading is **priming**, in which one concept is temporarily 'primed' (i.e. becomes more accessible) by activation spilling over indiscriminately from a neighbouring concept.

- Although the spread of activation is completely automatic and outside your control, it is you that channels the available resources towards certain nodes through **attention**, controlled by your **executive system**; what you pay attention to depends on your **interests** and needs. Only a limited amount of energy is available, and the part of your network which is currently active is described as your **working memory**.

- Physical activation in your brain translates into more abstract 'activation' in your mind, where it serves a number of different functions:
  - guiding **retrieval** – remembering specific things (e.g. your friend Jack's birthday)
  - guiding **inheritance** so that properties are inherited only if they are **relevant** to the immediate **context** (e.g. Jack's birthday may or may not be relevant, so you won't inherit it every time you see him).
  - guiding **binding** so that the outcome makes the **best fit** between the global properties of the situation and the target
  - guiding **induction** so that new categories reflect true generalizations about two or more co-occurring properties (e.g. birds tend to share the same size, shape and so on).

- **Node creation** has a number of different functions:
  - creating nodes for individual **exemplars** and their properties (e.g. for a bird that you see, or for one that you would like to see)
  - creating nodes for inherited properties (e.g. for the beak that you expect a bird to have)
  - creating nodes for **general categories** (e.g. 'bird'), based on a number of exemplars all sharing the same properties.

- **Binding** ties an **empty exemplar** to a **target category** by a primitive **identity** relation. Identity signals that the nodes are functionally identical, while still allowing them to be treated separately (and, if need be, distinguished). Binding always selects the most active candidate node as the target, thereby guaranteeing the **global best fit**. Binding has different functions:
  - accepting the best categorization for an exemplar (e.g. deciding that what you can see is a bird)
  - accepting the answer to a search of memory (e.g. recognizing that the activated date is your friend Jack's birthday)
  - accepting something which is anticipated (e.g. the thunder expected after a flash of lightning)
  - accepting the best solution to a problem (e.g. how to react when your phone rings).

- We can **remember** individual events by simply keeping their exemplar nodes active, though the memory may lack details such as time and place (e.g. you may remember seeing Jack's brother, but can't remember when or where).

- **Induction** creates new general categories as superclasses for lower-level categories that share the same range of properties (e.g. 'bird' has the properties that tend to be shared by all exemplar birds), and can apply repeatedly to produce a **taxonomy** of increasingly general categories.

Where next?

Advanced: Part II, Chapter 8.6: Binding in word recognition, parsing and pragmatics

PART II

How language works

5   Introduction to linguistics

Linguistics is the study of language structure, which means grammar, pronunciation, vocabulary and meaning. Anyone who thinks about how language is organized is doing linguistics.

By this definition, linguistics is a very old discipline indeed; in fact, it's almost as old as written language itself. (Wikipedia: 'Linguistics'.) The earliest linguists may have been the grammarians who covered clay tablets with verb forms in Babylon in the second millenium BC (Gragg 1994).

More recently, the Ancient Greeks built the foundations on which our modern grammars rest, and during the Middle Ages grammar was one of the three main parts of the school curriculum (part of the 'trivium', or 'three ways', from which the modern word *trivial* is unfortunately derived). More recently still, we (in the UK) still have some 'grammar schools', many of which date back to the fifteenth or sixteenth century.

5.1   Description

Much of the early work on language structure was brilliantly insightful and survives in modern linguistics, though the study of language has always run the danger of attracting its fair share of dogma, ignorance and thoroughly bad science.

For example, one popular activity among the educated is to complain about the 'mistakes' made by the uneducated, such as using 'double negatives' like *I didn't say nothing*. Such 'prescriptive' comments are simply wrong because the forms in question are not mistakes any more than an English sentence is a 'mistake' compared with its French translation. (Wikipedia: 'Linguistic prescription'.)

Prescriptive linguistics claims to find faults in language and tries to fix them, whereas **DESCRIPTIVE LINGUISTICS**, as its name suggests, tries to 'describe' language as it really is. Of course, there's nothing wrong with trying to fix problems, and descriptive linguists have always been driven in part by a desire to solve practical problems.

For the Babylonian linguists, the problem was that scribes didn't know Sumerian (a dead language), so Babylonian linguists produced teaching aids such as lists of words and word-forms. Medieval linguists addressed a similar problem with a different dead language (first Latin, and later Greek). For many modern linguists, the problem is again based on the need for people to learn more 'language', whether in the form of a foreign language or the parts of a first language that are only learned in school (writing and the 'educated' language).

In each case, the problem requires a correct diagnosis before the remedy can be determined, and (as in medicine) a correct diagnosis requires careful description and analysis. The trouble with prescriptive linguistics is simply that it gets the diagnosis wrong.

What's the problem with *I didn't say nothing*? According to prescriptive linguistics, it's simply incorrect under all circumstances. Why? Because it 'really' means 'I said something', whatever its users may intend it to mean.

Descriptive linguistics takes a very different view. It takes the user as the ultimate authority on what it means; if a particular user says it means the opposite of *I said something*, that's what it does mean for that user (even if other users think differently). But there is a problem. The trouble is that different kinds of English apply different rules, and the rules of Standard English are different. And why is this a problem? Because Standard English is the English of education and power, a language that every English speaker should be able to use when needed.

The descriptive and prescriptive approaches aren't just equal alternatives. Prescriptivism is very bad science, and deeply misleading as a diagnosis. The prescriptive mis-diagnosis of double negatives is just one example of the ways in which the study of language can fall short of the highest academic standards.

5.2   Detail

Double negatives illustrate another important characteristic of linguistics. It's always been heavily involved in the **fine detail** of language structure – lists of words and word-forms, very specific syntactic patterns, the details of spelling or punctuation, detailed correspondences between languages, and so on.

But anyone who works on fine detail in any subject also needs a general framework of ideas to hold all the detail together. Over the centuries, linguists have evolved a widely accepted collection of **categories** and **terms** which constitute a METALANGUAGE – a language for describing language.

Linguists have also developed a superb **notation** for language which we all take for granted: **writing** – one of the main pillars of civilization; and it's hardly surprising that written records of linguistic analysis go back almost to the beginning of writing, since the skills of reading and writing have to be transmitted from generation to generation.

Our alphabet has very ancient roots indeed, which go back, through Latin and Greek, to the Phoenicians who lived in the Eastern Mediterranean 3,000 years ago. Interestingly, we still respect the same very odd order of letters as the Phoenicians did (starting with 'aleph', then 'beth', which turned in Greek into *alpha* and *beta*, hence our *alpha-bet*). (Wikipedia: 'Latin alphabet' and 'Phoenician alphabet'.)

As for our metalanguage, much of it dates back 2,000 years, such as *grammar* and *lexicon* (from Greek), and *verb* and *letter* (from Latin). Rather fascinatingly, our terms 'first person' (for *I* or *we*), 'second person' (for *you*) and 'third person' (for the rest) may date back to the Babylonians, who at least sometimes listed verb forms in that order (Gragg 1994); if so, then the age of these terms may be an amazing 4,000 years.

5.3   Data

This ancestry puts linguistics in a rather special position compared with other sciences. In age, it matches mathematics and astronomy, which also have strong roots in ancient Babylonia, but what makes it special is that it's a 'human science', an objective study of human behaviour and knowledge. Like their colleagues in mathematics and astronomy, modern linguists build on the work done by something like 140 generations of earlier scholars (assuming four generations in 100 years, and 4,000 years of linguistics); but unlike other scientists, linguists are analysing and cataloguing their own culture in great detail.

When the Babylonian scribes wrote lists of words on their clay tablets, they were simply writing down what they knew, just like a British school teacher writing the word *cat* for children to copy. The facts were extremely clear and completely unproblematic: either you knew them, or you didn't. Modern linguists still use the same technique in a great deal of their work, though we now have a range of alternative methods which we can turn to when needed for more sophisticated work. And of course we have to use somewhat special techniques if we're trying to analyse someone else's language rather than our own.

5.4   Differences

We can now contrast linguistics with the other branches of cognitive science that I introduced in Chapter 1: psychology, neuroscience, artificial intelligence and philosophy.

In terms of age, philosophy is as ancient as linguistics, but the other branches are much younger. Psychology goes back to 1879, when Wilhelm Wundt founded the first psychology laboratory in Leipzig in Germany, and neuroscience has a similar age thanks to careful observations of brain damage and its effects. Artificial intelligence is even younger, starting a couple of decades after the first computers were built in the 1940s. (Wikipedia: 'History of Western philosophy', 'Psychology', 'Neuroscience' and 'Artificial intelligence'.)

More importantly, all the others except philosophy use much more sophisticated methods than linguistics: experiments, surgical observation, brain-scans and computer programs. This is very different from the 'self-report' that linguists use, when they ask themselves about their language: How do I say this? What does this word mean? Can I say this? Asking someone else about their language isn't very much more sophisticated.

In this sense, linguistics is very much easier than any other branch of cognitive science because we're all full of easily accessible data which, by and large, is uncontroversial. Each of us is a more or less typical example of people who speak 'our language' precisely because we try our hardest to make our language identical, in every detail, to the rest of our community (Hudson 1996: 10–14). We do, of course, have much more sophisticated methods that we can fall back on when this simple approach lets us down (Schütze 2006), but these methods would count as overkill if we wanted to know, for example, what the past tense of the verb *walk* was.

This ready supply of data has the important consequence that linguists can pay a great deal of attention to details of language structure such as the rules for forming past-tense verbs, complete with exceptions and uncertainties. This is something that the research methods of psychologists and neuroscientists don't allow.

For example, although psychologists can demonstrate a priming effect from *doctor* to *nurse* (as explained in Section 4.2), the best explanation they can offer is that the words are 'related in meaning'. Even if they were interested in the details of this relation (which on the whole they aren't), their methods wouldn't help them to push the analysis any further. Nor do such details interest philosophers.

Artificial intelligence, on the other hand, does allow detailed analysis, because its aim is to simulate human behaviour in fine detail. If the aim is to produce, say, a computer program that can answer questions about English sentences, then the computer needs to know a great deal of detail about words including such minutiae as irregular past tenses and precise meanings. But in the area of language, AI generally uses ordinary analyses produced in the usual way by linguists.

For matters of structure, the experts are linguists because our methods are the only ones that produce the kind and amount of detail that is needed.

It would seem, therefore, that linguistics and the other disciplines are truly complementary: where one is weak, another is strong, and if we want a complete picture, we need all the disciplines, with all their strengths. If we want to know how the mind works, we ask a psychologist, a neuroscientist or an AI expert; but if we want to know details of how language is organized, we ask a linguist. This much is uncontroversial.

5.5   Divisions

Unfortunately, the long history of linguistics raises a problem in this connection. When linguistics started, there was no cognitive science and very little guidance about how the mind works. Moreover, it's always been tempting for linguists to think of language as somehow separate from individual minds.

The separation of languages from minds is encouraged by the fact that so much work in linguistics has concentrated on the 'language' of an entire community – Standard English, Classical Latin, Sumerian or whatever. In this view, the language is in some sense 'out there' in the community, in much the same way that, say, the solar system is 'out there' in space. Individual people may or may not know the language (or the solar system), but the language doesn't need speakers or knowers in order to exist. Indeed, a dead language is dead precisely because it doesn't have speakers, but it still exists. Consequently, for most of its history linguistics has simply ignored the speaker except as an incidental source of data. Questions about how people learn, store or use their language have simply not arisen.

This description is no longer true of linguistics taken as a whole, thanks to the rise of psycholinguistics as a sub-discipline. (Wikipedia: 'Psycholinguistics'.) As we shall see in the coming chapters, psycholinguists have learned a great deal since the 1950s about the learning, storing and using of language (Altmann 2006).

Moreover, thanks to Noam Chomsky linguists now have a more or less standard terminology for talking about language in relation to the mind. Our knowledge of language is our **COMPETENCE** or **I-LANGUAGE** (for 'individual' or 'internal' language), in contrast with the things we do with this knowledge, which is our **PERFORMANCE**. (Wikipedia: 'Transformational grammar'.)

Nevertheless, this swing to psychology has had very little impact on theoretical linguistics. Most theories of language structure continue to ignore elementary psychology even when claiming (as Chomsky's theory emphatically does) that language is part of the individual's mind. This is certainly true of the four dominant theories, namely Minimalism, Head-Driven Phrase Structure Grammar, Lexical Functional Grammar and Optimality Theory. (Wikipedia: 'Linguistic minimalism', 'Head-driven phrase structure grammar', 'Lexical functional grammar' and 'Optimality theory'.)

All these theories grew out of a major twentieth-century movement called **STRUCTURALIST LINGUISTICS** (or just 'structural linguistics') whose main point was that a language was a structured collection of units separate from everything outside the collection. (Wikipedia: 'Structural linguistics'.) The positive side of the structuralist approach was its focusing of attention on the complex internal structure of language.

But it also had the negative effect of encouraging linguists to ignore everything outside language, and in particular, to assume that language is organized differently from everything else in our minds. This effect has persisted. For instance, theories of language structure typically make no provision either for activation spreading through network structures or for default inheritance, the two pillars of cognitive psychology that played such a prominent role in the first part of this book.

5.6   Developments

However, like so many generalizations, this one has exceptions. In the 1980s a number of linguists (including me) started to develop theories of language structure which did build on cognitive psychology and artificial intelligence. What evolved was a movement called **COGNITIVE LINGUISTICS** which now includes a significant minority of linguists. (Wikipedia: 'Cognitive linguistics'.)

Cognitive linguistics is a 'movement' rather than a 'theory' because it's united only by a few very general assumptions, including the assumption that language is part of general cognition, and not a distinct module (as I explained in Section 3.6). But within the movement there are a number of distinct and reasonably well-articulated theories:

*   Cognitive grammar;
*   Construction grammar;
*   Word Grammar.

(Wikipedia: 'Cognitive grammar', 'Construction grammar' and 'Word Grammar'.)

Which brings us to **WORD GRAMMAR**, the subject of this book. I have been developing this theory since about 1980 (Hudson 1984, Hudson 1990, Hudson 2007c), and no doubt it will go on developing as we find new ways of bridging the gap between cognitive science and linguistics.

If pushed for a one-sentence summary of Word Grammar, I'd summarize it in the words of another cognitive linguist: 'knowledge of language is knowledge' (Goldberg 1995: 5). The best possible theoretical explanation for the organization of language is to show that it's typical of the organization of knowledge in general. What I hope to have achieved is a marriage of the general insights of cognitive science into how our minds work with the enormous amounts of detail that linguists analyse. This is what I offer in Part II, which is linked, section by section, to the cognitive science of Part I.

Where next?

Advanced: Next chapter

6 Words as concepts

6.1 Types and tokens

Summary of Section 2.1:

- Knowledge, or **conceptual structure**, consists of **concepts** (e.g. 'bird') and their **properties** (e.g. 'it flies').
- **Exemplars** are specific concepts which are tied to particular experiences (e.g. 'that bird over there').
- **Categories** are general concepts. We use them to **categorize** (i.e. to classify) exemplars.
- Once we have categorized an exemplar, it can **inherit** the properties of the category (e.g. 'that bird over there' can inherit 'it flies'). This is how we use past experience to guide us through the present and predict the future.

The question for this section is how the ideas from Section 2.1 apply to language. Which parts of language are concepts, and how does the contrast between exemplars and categories apply in language?

6.1.1 Language as concepts

Linguists often assume that the only point of contact between conceptual structure and language is in meaning, where words act as the names for concepts such as 'dog'. One influential theory of meaning even uses the term 'conceptual structure' for meaning (Jun 2006), implying that nothing else in language is part of conceptual structure. For the historical reasons that I explained in Chapter 5, most theories of language structure recognize even less connection between language and conceptual structure, with language and conceptual structure co-existing in some undefined way.

In contrast, cognitive linguistics insists that conceptual structure includes the whole of language: not only meanings, but also words, word-parts, sentence structures and even sounds. This is the view that I shall now explain and defend.

Think of the word *dog*. How could this be a concept? Remember, we're talking about the thing that is written with three letters and pronounced with two consonants and a vowel, not the thing that barks and has four legs. You're probably willing to accept 'dog' as a concept, but what about the word *dog*? (Notice how useful it is to use the standard notation of linguistics, where *italics* are used for words and 'quotation marks' for their meanings: *dog* means 'dog'.)

It's true that we tend to think of words as the labels for concepts, rather than as themselves being concepts, but there's no good reason for this distinction. Put simply, knowledge consists of concepts, so if the word *dog* is something you know, it must be a concept. Moreover, once we accept it as a concept, we find that it's actually very similar to the concept 'dog'.

One similarity between *dog* and its meaning 'dog' is that both are 'defined' by a number of properties. Whereas 'dog' has properties such as four legs and a bark, the word *dog* has properties such as the following:

*   It's spelt <dog>.
*   It's pronounced (in England) /dɒg/.
*   It's a noun.
*   It means 'dog'.
*   It's an English word.

(Once again, the notation is important: <...> for spelling and /.../ for pronunciation.)

Another similarity between *dog* and 'dog' is that they're both general categories from which exemplars inherit properties that aren't already known. For instance, just as an observed (but non-barking) dog inherits (in our minds) the property of barking, so an observed example of the word *dog* inherits the property of being a noun.

It seems rather obvious, then, that *dog* and 'dog' are both concepts. Equally obviously, they are also very different kinds of concept. But the differences between a word and an animal are probably no greater than those between 'dog' and other concepts such as 'birthday party', '7' or 'tall'.

6.1.2   Declarative and procedural knowledge

Even linguists who don't immediately think of words as concepts would probably not disagree with this conclusion, and would certainly accept the premise that a word has properties such as the ones I listed above. On the other hand, it's important to recognize that some psychologists would disagree.

For them the question is whether knowledge of language is an example of declarative or procedural knowledge (a contrast introduced in Section 2.1), and many psychologists believe it's procedural. Put simply, their view is that a word is an instruction for relating a sound to a meaning:

(1)   If you hear X, then understand Y.
(2)   If you mean Y, then say X.

The instruction in (1) tells us what to do when listening, while the one in (2) guides our speaking. If a word is a procedure, it can't be a concept because concepts belong to declarative knowledge.

In contrast, most linguists prefer a single declarative statement: the meaning of Y is X. The advantages are rather obvious to us. After all, the procedural analysis implies that we could link a sound to one meaning when speaking but to a different one when listening. However, I also suggested in Section 2.1 that the general distinction between declarative and procedural knowledge may not be as important as psychologists think, in which case there's no point in debating the question.

6.1.3   Types and tokens

Assuming, then, that a word is a concept, what about the distinction between categories and exemplars, such as that between the category 'bird' and the exemplar 'that particular bird over there'? In this case, linguists make just the same distinction as psychologists do, but we use different terminology. We call categories **TYPES** and exemplars **TOKENS** (Wetzel 2006). (Wikipedia: 'Type–token distinction'.)

For example, consider the sentence in (3):

(3)   The cat sat on the mat.

In this sentence there are six word-tokens, but only five word-types because the word *the* is repeated. Each 'distinct word' is a different type, so if the words in this sentence were the only English words you knew, you would know precisely five words: *the*, *cat*, *sat*, *on* and *mat*. Each of these would be a general category which could justify any number of exemplars.

The distinction between types and tokens is applied in a well-known measure, the '**TYPE–TOKEN RATIO**'. In example (3), the type–token ratio is five types to six tokens, or 5/6 (i.e. 0.8). This measure is an indication of 'lexical diversity', i.e. the range of vocabulary, in any piece of writing or speech. The lower the ratio, the more repeated types there are, and every token which repeats the type of an earlier token brings the ratio down. At one extreme, a string of ten tokens all of the same type would score close to zero (1/10 = 0.1), while at the other extreme ten tokens which all belong to different types would score one (10/10).

The type–token ratio has many uses, from measuring how children's vocabulary grows with age (Theakston 2006) to identifying the style of an author (Rudman 2006). It's very easy to use, provided you take one basic precaution: when comparing samples of texts, always compare samples of the same length, because the type–token ratio always tends to go down as the sample gets longer and contains more candidates for repetition.

The main point, for present purposes, is that types and tokens are fundamentally different, and the difference matters in any discussion of language.

The rather obvious difference between types and tokens plays an important part in Word Grammar. Most other theories pay very little attention to it, so there isn't even a standard notation for distinguishing a token from the type that it belongs to. When we write *the* in a sentence such as the last one, this is a token of

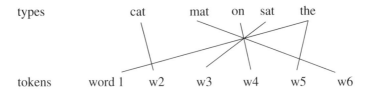

Figure 6.1 *Types and tokens distinguished*

the type *the*; but notice that we use the same notation in both cases. This doesn't matter in most theories because they're only concerned with language systems, and only types, not tokens, belong to the language system.

Cognitive theories are different because they're concerned with cognition, and tokens are part of cognition: we build concepts for them, we categorize them and we let them inherit properties. In ordinary life it's easy to appreciate the difference between exemplars and categories; so when we see a bird, we know that we haven't seen the category 'bird'.

In language the difference between types and tokens is less obvious, and especially so in writing because we write tokens and types in the same way. But this is very confusing because a token's properties are always different from those of its type. An irregular token such as a mis-spelling has properties that conflict with those of its type, but even a regular token has a time, a user, a context and so on which are missing from its type.

6.1.4   A notation for types and tokens

In a cognitive theory such as Word Grammar, then, it's essential to distinguish tokens from their types. How we make this distinction is merely a matter of convenience and convention, so I shall simply follow the convention that has evolved over the years in Word Grammar (Hudson 2007c: 44), and which is illustrated for sentence (3) in Figure 6.1. According to this diagram, the first word-token is an example of the word-type *the*, and so is the fifth word; the second is an example of *cat*; and so on.

In this notation, each token has a label such as 'word 1' which gives two pieces of information: its general type (e.g. 'word', 'morph') and its position in sequence (1, 2 and so on). The positional information reminds us that linguistic units are always ordered one after the other; and the abstractness of the label reminds us that for a split second, we don't know any more than this. It's only after some intellectual work that we can recognize the tokens as examples of the types *the*, *cat* and so on. (We consider this process more carefully in Section 8.3.)

The notation for tokens is enough to distinguish them from types, but later sections will introduce a more sophisticated notation for types as well, which will allow us to use simple italics as an easy notation for tokens. As you can see, I'm gradually moving us away from the notation that we all learned as children.

Ordinary writing is already a very sophisticated notation which shows a great deal of information about pronunciation, lexical identity and grammar; for

instance, when we decide to write *bear* rather than *beer*, we indicate pronunciation; but when contrasted with *bare*, the spelling *bear* shows lexical identity (the
noun or verb *bear* rather than the homophonous adjective *bare*).

As for grammar, writing shows intra-word morphology through spellings (e.g.
bear versus *bare*) and inter-word syntax through punctuation, as in (4) and (5).

(4)   I love her; money affairs don't interest me.
(5)   I love her money; affairs don't interest me.

The trouble with ordinary writing is that it tries to do too many things at once,
and ends up confusing them and not doing anything consistently or thoroughly
enough for our purposes. It confuses pronunciation and lexical identity and only
gives a partial indication of syntax; and above all, it doesn't distinguish types and
tokens. This is why we need a special notation.

Figure 6.1 shows how the tokens and types are related to one another, with
word 1 linked to *the*, word 2 to *cat* and so on. This is the relation that allows
inheritance of properties, which is the main benefit of having general concepts.
In Section 2.1 we saw how this applies to everyday experiences such as seeing a
cat: as soon as we know that it's a cat, we can guess that it enjoys being stroked,
likes cream, purrs and has all the other properties of a typical cat.

Just the same is true of words. As soon as we categorize a word-token, we
can guess its meaning, its typical pronunciation, its word-class, its language and
various other properties which will emerge in later discussion. These inherited
properties combine with the properties that we already know such as its pronunciation (if we're listening) or its meaning (when talking); and the result is a
greatly enriched conceptual structure for the token. As described, this process is
precisely the same as we would apply to anything else in our experience.

The main question for a theory of language, of course, is what exactly the
properties of a word are; and the Word Grammar claim is that the word is so central to language that once we have answered this question, together with the other
sub-questions that it raises, we shall in effect have a complete theory of language
structure. Indeed, the rest of this book can be seen as an attempt to answer this
question, starting with the list of properties in the next section.

Summary of this section:

- Words are concepts and their properties include their meaning, their pronunciation, their word-class and their language.
- Like other concepts, they may be either general categories (e.g. the word
  the) or specific exemplars; but in the terminology of linguistics, exemplars are **tokens** and categories are **types**.
- In Word Grammar notation, tokens have complex labels consisting of a
  general category followed by a number showing the token's position in
  sequence (e.g. word 1 or w1).
- The **type–token ratio** of a text is a useful measure of the diversity of
  vocabulary in the text.

- When a token is categorized by being linked to some type, it can inherit all the properties of this type, thereby greatly enriching its known properties.

Where next?

Advanced: Next section

6.2   Word properties

This section follows directly from the previous one, rather than from a section in Part I, because it builds on the ancient tradition of linguistics rather than on cognitive science.

All the effort that our ancestors devoted to the study of language bore a great deal of fruit in the form of a detailed understanding of the structure of language. As I explained in Chapter 5, linguistics is very strong on detail, and because language itself is probably organized more clearly and consistently than any other part of human culture, it's in language that we have the clearest insight into the details of conceptual structure. Much of this detail is widely agreed, and even traditional. What follows, then, is something approaching a complete list of the properties of words.

Before I start, you may expect a definition of 'word'. There are actually strong theoretical reasons for avoiding definitions, which emerge in Section 2.5, so I'll simply assume that we all know roughly what a word is, but as the discussion progresses this understanding will become deeper and more sophisticated. For the time being, you can assume that a word is the kind of thing that we write between word spaces.

On the other hand, we do need to bear in mind the one step towards sophistication that I've already introduced, which is the distinction between word-types and word-tokens (6.1). Their properties are slightly different and I shall need to distinguish them in the following list.

6.2.1   Properties of a typical word

Here, then, is a list of the kinds of properties that a typical word has:

- a **MEANING**, which is a little cluster of concepts which combine a fixed 'dictionary meaning' with a variable 'contextual meaning'; this idea is expanded in Section 8.7.2.
- a **REALIZATION**, which is again a cluster of concepts that combine a fixed 'dictionary form' with a variable 'word-form' as I explain in Section 6.7. The realization makes the word audible in speech or visible in writing, so it 'realizes' the word in the sense of making it more real. The precise nature of this realization is a matter of debate, but

Section 6.9 explains that in Word Grammar the realization is a 'form' which in turn is realized by sounds or letters.

- a **WORD-CLASS**. As explained in Sections 6.3 and 8.4, word-classes allow generalizations.
- a syntactic **VALENCY**, showing how the word combines with other words; for example, the verbs *try* and *attempt* both combine with *to* followed by another verb (as in *try/attempt to go*), but whereas *to* is optional after *try*, it is obligatory after *attempt* (so we can simply try, but we can't simply attempt).
- a **LANGUAGE**. Every word belongs to some language or other.
- a **FREQUENCY**. Some words occur more frequently than others, but this isn't just an objective fact; native speakers are aware of these differences, and are able to make reasonably accurate 'subjective frequency estimates' about particular words; for example, English speakers know that *smile* is more common than *smirk* (Barsalou 1992: 64–7).
- a **SPEAKER**, an **ADDRESSEE** (the person addressed), a **TIME** and a **PLACE**. These properties belong primarily to word-tokens, and a typical word-token has all four properties – we know who spoke them, to whom, when and where. These properties typically don't generalize, but in some cases they do; for example, *good morning* and *good evening* are used at different times.

6.2.2   Other properties available to some words

In addition to these typical properties, some words also have one or more of the following:

- a **STYLE-LEVEL**. Some words are only used in very formal styles (e.g. *attempt*), while others are only used in very casual styles (e.g. *have a go*).
- a **SPEAKER TYPE**. Some words are only used by some speakers; for example, *bonny* is only used by speakers from Scotland (or nearby), and *gee-gee* only by (or to) small children.
- a **SOCIAL RELATION**. Some words are only used when a particular social relation holds between the speaker and either the addressee (e.g. *Sir*, *thank you*, *hello*) or the person referred to (e.g. *Mrs Brown*).
- an **EMOTION**. Some words are only used when the speaker is experiencing a particular emotion such as joy (*hooray!*), anxiety (*oh dear!*) or anger (*damn!*). These words illustrate the possibility of linking a concept directly to an emotion that we raised in Section 3.1.
- an **ETYMOLOGY**. For some words, some of us know something about their history (e.g. *nice* comes from Latin *nescius*, meaning 'ignorant').
- **LEXICAL RELATIONS**. If one word is 'derived' from another in the various ways explored in Section 6.7, then there is a lexical relation between them (as in *farm – farmer* or *possible – impossible*).

- **COGNATES**. If we know the etymology of a word, we may also know other words with the same origin, either in our own language or in other languages; for example, the etymology of *nice* means that one of its cognates in English is *science*.

- **TRANSLATION EQUIVALENTS**. Some people know how to translate some words of their own language into other languages (e.g. the French for *nice*, in one of its senses, is *gentil*).

Every one of these kinds of information is psychologically real for some speakers, though some of them are optional extras; for example, it's possible to be a first-rate fluent speaker of English without knowing any etymologies. The fact is simply that such facts are among the possible properties of a word.

6.2.3   Word properties in dictionaries and in linguistics

Good dictionaries include many of these properties in their word entries. For example, here are the first few lines of the entry for *nice* in the *Collins Cobuild English Language Dictionary* (Anon. 1987):

> **nice** /naɪs/, **nicer, nicest. Nice** is a very common word, especially in informal spoken English, which is used to express pleasure, approval, or admiration of a very general kind. 1. [ADJ QUALIT = good]...

Notice how this entry includes a pronunciation, lexical relations to *nicer* and *nicest*, frequency, style-level and feelings, as well as the expected word-class (ADJ) and a general description of the meaning (QUALIT = good), before giving details of the various meanings.

In contrast with dictionaries, however, most linguistic theories ignore most of this information and recognize only properties that link a word to other things that are 'inside' language – sounds, meanings, word-classes, syntactic valency (Allan 2006a). This restriction makes no sense at all if the aim is to analyse and understand what we know about words, so Word Grammar spreads the net as wide as possible.

Later sections will discuss most of these properties in more detail. Meanwhile, the most obvious points that arise out of this section are, first, that an astonishing range of different things are known, or at least knowable, about words, and second, that many of these properties involve concepts that are outside the language concerned or even outside language – meanings, etymologies, feelings, social relations and so on.

Summary of this section:

- A typical word has the following mental properties for all speakers: a **meaning**, a **realization**, a **word-class**, a syntactic **valency**, a **language** and a **frequency**.

- A typical word-token also has: a **speaker**, an **addressee**, a **time** and a **place**.
- Other properties that some words may also have include: a **style-level**, a **speaker type**, a **social relation**, an **emotion**, an **etymology**, **lexical relations**, **cognates** and **translation equivalents**.

Where next?

Advanced: Back to Part I, Chapter 2.2: Taxonomies and the isA relation

6.3   Word-classes

Summary of Section 2.2:

- Concepts are organized in **taxonomies**, which link concepts upwards to their **superclasses** and downwards to their **subclasses**.
- The relation between a concept and its superclass is called **isA**.
- In Word Grammar notation, the isA relation is shown as a line ending in a small triangle whose base rests on the superclass.

The taxonomy of words is the most famous part of traditional grammar. Ever since Indian scholars invented word-classes for their language in about the fifth century BC, followed by Greeks in the second century BC, word-classes (also known as 'lexical categories' or 'parts of speech') have formed the basis for the study of grammar (Anward 2006). Not surprisingly, the details vary from language to language, and the analysis has varied (though astonishingly little) over the centuries and according to the analysts' assumptions.

A rather traditional list of word-classes for English is given below:

- noun
- adjective
- pronoun
- preposition
- verb
- adverb
- article
- conjunction.

This list dates back, with minor changes, to the second century BC – an extraordinary example of cultural continuity. The original names for the word-classes were in Greek, but the English names are derived from Latin terminology. Modern linguists would want to make a number of other changes, but for present purposes we can stick to the traditional analysis.

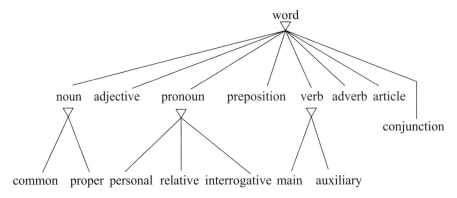

Figure 6.2 *Traditional word-classes as a taxonomy*

Each of these classes is a major class of words, so each one isA word; this is the top of the taxonomy for words shown in Figure 6.2. But the traditional classification goes much further by further subdividing some of these classes. Nouns are divided into common and proper; pronouns are personal, relative or interrogative; verbs are main or auxiliary; and so on. A century ago, a typical grammar book for use in schools would lay out the classes and subclasses in immense detail, and modern scholarly grammars do the same, although the details are different. In short, the word-class system is a true taxonomy.

Where next?

Advanced: Part III, Chapter 10.1: Word-classes
Novice: Part III, Chapter 10.2: Inflections

6.4   Grammaticality

Summary of Section 2.3:

- The main benefit of organizing knowledge in taxonomies is to allow general information to be applied, by **inheritance**, to more specific cases. This is helpful in at least two cases: when dealing with an unfamiliar kind of exemplar, whose properties we don't know; and when we need to know properties that we can't observe or know directly.
- A concept can inherit properties from every concept between it and the top of the taxonomy. This process is psychologically real, and takes a tiny but measurable amount of time.
- Inheritance allows properties to be generalized by being attached to higher concepts, but even generalized properties may also be attached to lower concepts as well, in which case the information is **redundant**.

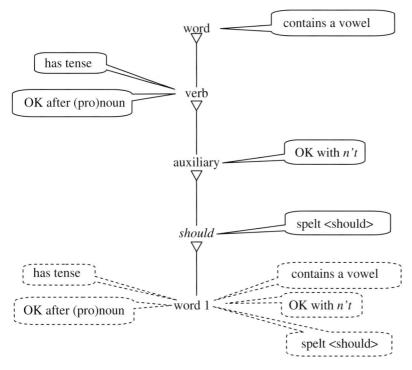

Figure 6.3 *Inheritance in a taxonomy of word-classes*

- But inheritance doesn't clog up the taxonomy with redundant information because it only applies to exemplars.
- Inheritance is a process that can be imagined as being carried out by two workers: a '**searcher**' who climbs up the tree looking for inheritable properties, and a '**copier**' who makes a copy of each property and passes it to the exemplar.

As in any taxonomy, each of the word-classes discussed in Section 6.3 has a number of properties that generalize to all their subclasses. Take 'verb', for example. A typical verb has the following properties, as well as many more:

- It can have a tense, either past or present (e.g. *eats/ate*).
- It can be used with a preceding noun or pronoun (e.g. *John eats*).

These properties, summarized as 'has tense', 'OK after (pro)noun', are displayed in Figure 6.3.

The figure also includes one property each for 'word', 'auxiliary' and *should*: that a typical word contains at least one vowel, that a typical auxiliary verb such as *should* can combine with *n't* to give *shouldn't*, and that *should* is spelt <should>. These properties are merely examples, of course; in each case the actual list of properties would be very much longer. As you can see, this figure is very similar to the one for birds in Figure 2.5 (Section 2.3), including the inherited properties shown as dotted boxes.

6.4.1   Good grammar

What Figure 6.3 shows, then, is that a typical token of *should* will have tense, contain a vowel and so on. In the terminology of grammar, a token that has these properties is **GRAMMATICAL**, and the little network which allows it is a fragment of a **GRAMMAR** of the language. (In this slightly technical sense, the 'grammar' includes the dictionary as well as the grammar in the more conventional sense; we'll see in Section 6.5 that the grammar and dictionary can't be separated, so the terminology isn't actually as inconsistent as it may seem.)

What our grammar does is exactly the same as what a grammar-book for a foreign language does: it tells you what the language allows. To take a simple example, English allows us to add *n't* to an auxiliary verb (converting *should* to *shouldn't*, for example). This is something that English allows, though other languages don't.

Inherited properties are, by definition, 'OK'; and so are properties that don't interfere with inherited properties (such as the speaker, time and place). But if a word-token has properties that conflict with inherited properties, they are not OK, and by implication the word isn't OK either. To take a rather obvious example, *shouldn't* may be a fine English word, but it's a terrible French word; and slightly less obviously, *gotn't* is a bad English word because *got* isn't an auxiliary verb, and only auxiliaries take *n't*.

This contrast between good and bad is called **GRAMMATICALITY**, and a very useful bit of notation is the star that linguists use for showing ungrammaticality; for example, to show that *gotn't* is ungrammatical, I could have written **gotn't*.

It isn't only in language that we separate good and bad in this way. The stored concepts provide precedents for future exemplars, so we can distinguish the expected and typical from the unexpected; for example, a cat with four legs is typical and expected, whereas one with five legs surprises us, and we might even go so far as to say that it's impossible outside fairy stories. In linguistic terminology, a four-legged cat is 'grammatical' whereas a five-legged cat is 'ungrammatical'.

In fact, we can push the similarities between cats and words further. When you see a cat, there are four possibilities:

*   You recognize it as a particular cat, say the neighbour's cat Felix.
*   You recognize it as Felix, but with some unexpected property – say Felix after losing a leg in an accident.
*   You know it's an ordinary cat, but don't recognize it.
*   It has five legs and you know it's impossible – maybe you're dreaming.

The same is true in language, where a native speaker can easily distinguish familiar and unfamiliar tokens, and in both cases typical and untypical tokens. For example, the following facts are obvious to a native speaker of English:

- *kick*: You recognize this as an existing word.
- *kik*: You recognize this as a mis-spelt version of *kick*.
- *keck*: You know this is at least potentially an ordinary English word, but you don't recognize it.
- *krk*: You know this is simply impossible.

No doubt you agree – unless you happen to know some Czech, in which case you'll recognize *krk* as the word for 'throat'.

What these examples show is that we know a lot about English words and word-classes, and thanks to inheritance we can apply this knowledge to word-tokens such as these. A word-token such as *kick* is grammatical and recognizable because it sits comfortably at the bottom of the taxonomy and inherits freely not only from the word-classes, but also from a particular word (6.5); *kik* is partly ungrammatical but recognizable; *keck* is grammatical but unrecognizable because there is no particular word *keck*; but *krk* has such a weird spelling that we can't even classify it as a possible English word, let alone identify it with any particular one.

Summary of this section:

- A full analysis of a language which includes all the words and word-classes of the language is a **grammar** for that language.
- Word-tokens are **grammatical** if their properties are compatible with all the properties that they should inherit from the grammar.

Where next?

Advanced: Back to Part I, Chapter 2.4: Multiple inheritance and choices

6.5   Lexemes and inflections

Summary of Section 2.4:

- Most concepts belong to more than one taxonomy, and inherit from each one by an extended version of inheritance called **multiple inheritance**.
- The properties that a concept inherits from different taxonomies can conflict, so we need to understand how conflicts are avoided and, when not avoided, how they affect our thinking.
- Mutually exclusive concepts are related through a **choice** concept that prevents us from selecting more than one of them.

The ideas in Section 2.4 apply even more clearly in language than they do in cases such as canaries, which both isA 'bird' and 'pet'; so an understanding of this area of grammar extends well beyond language into fundamental parts of our thinking.

The grammatical concepts are simple, so we can illustrate them with an easy example: *books*. How do we classify this word? We know that *book* is a noun; but what about the *s*? As you're no doubt aware, grammarians use the term 'plural' to contrast words like *books* with the 'singular' *book*. This means that *books* shares properties not only with its 'singular' counterpart, *book*, but also with other plural nouns such as *dogs*, *mice*, *sheep* and *people*. Notice that the other plural nouns don't necessarily contain the suffix *-s*, so we can't say that it's this suffix that is in some sense plural; what we're classifying is the entire word.

Consequently, this word isA not only *book*, but also 'plural' – a classic case of multiple inheritance. From *book* it inherits its basic meaning ('book'), most of its realization (*book*) and its word-class; from 'plural' it inherits the plurality of its meaning ('more than one'), the last bit of its realization (*-s*) and a more precise word-class ('plural'). The formal details can wait till Section 7.3, and the main point here is just that a word such as *books* has two independent sets of properties which are inherited from two separate sources.

6.5.1   Lexemes and inflections

Our most urgent need is terminology for distinguishing the sources: **LEXEME** and **INFLECTION**.

- The lexeme is the basic 'dictionary word', *book*, which is what you would expect to find listed in a dictionary; one of the most obvious properties of a lexeme is that it's realized by a **STEM** – the basic part of the word as defined by the dictionary, such as *book*. Lexemes are what we classify in word-classes as nouns, verbs and so on.
- The inflection is a new word which we create by 'inflecting' it (which medieval grammarians thought of metaphorically as a kind of 'bending' of the word). In contrast with lexemes, inflections are realized by a specially altered version of the stem that Word Grammar calls a **VARIANT**; for example, *books* is the 's-variant' of *book*.

Apart from 'variant' (a Word Grammar speciality discussed in Section 6.7), this terminology is standard among linguists, though you may also find 'lexical item' or 'lexical word' for 'lexeme'; 'inflectional category' for 'inflection'; and 'base' or 'theme' for 'stem' (Wikipedia: 'Lexeme' and 'Word stem'; Julien 2006).

To support this distinction, many linguists also have a special notation in which lexemes are written in capital letters throughout: BOOK, DOG, etc. In this notation, then, the lexeme BOOK covers not only *book* but also *books*, and a more accurate name for the word *books* would be 'BOOK, plural' – i.e. a combination

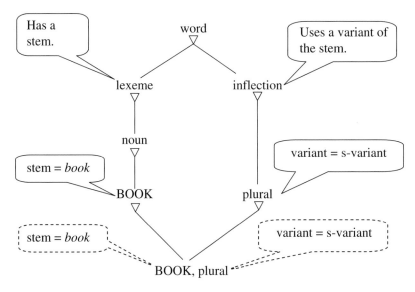

Figure 6.4 *How the lexeme BOOK is related to the inflection 'plural'*

of BOOK and 'plural'. Figure 6.4 shows the relevant part of a word taxonomy which separates lexemes from inflections.

What allows lexemes and inflections to interact smoothly, without creating the kinds of conflict that we saw in the 'Nixon diamond' (2.4), is that lexemes and inflections are two very different kinds of 'word', with different kinds of properties.

Lexemes are what we think of immediately as 'dictionary words', with basic meanings, realizations and so on that we might find in a dictionary.

Inflections, on the other hand, have a rather more complicated status. On the one hand they're independent of lexemes, providing concepts such as 'plural', a kind of information that the grammar cannot find in the ordinary lexeme taxonomy. This information plays an important part in the grammar of some languages, but less important in other languages. (Its role in English is relatively small, as we see in Section 10.2.)

On the other hand, inflections are also closely related to individual lexemes because these are what they're built out of. For example, the inflection *books* is obviously built out of the lexeme BOOK by adding *-s* to the realization and some kind of plurality to the meaning. These changes are general enough to apply to any noun, so we find very regular pairings which are easily displayed in a table such as Table 6.1 on the next page.

6.5.2   Marked and unmarked inflections

You may notice that this table doesn't include a column for 'singular'. This is because the singular properties are the same as those of the lexeme; in fact, the singular **is** the lexeme. The inflection is just a small variation on the lexeme's

Table 6.1 *Some English noun lexemes and their plurals.*

Lexeme	Plural
GIRAFFE	giraffes
EXPLANATION	explanations
CACTUS	cacti
PERSON	people

Table 6.2 *Two Latin nouns by number and case.*

Lexeme	Number	Case				
		Nominative	Accusative	Genitive	Dative	Ablative
AMIC 'friend'	singular	amic-us	amic-um	amic-i	amic-o	amic-o
	plural	amic-i	amic-os	amic-orum	amic-is	amic-is
URB 'city'	singular	urb-s	urb-em	urb-is	urb-i	urb-e
	plural	urb-es	urb-es	urb-ium	urb-ibus	urb-ibus

basic pattern, so the word *book* is simply the lexeme BOOK, without any inflection, in contrast with 'BOOK, plural', the word *books*. In another piece of standard terminology, the plural is **MARKED** (by the ending *-s*) while the singular is
UNMARKED, i.e. the same as the basic form. (Wikipedia: 'Markedness'.)

In this analysis, the singular and plural of a noun are unequal partners in much
the same relation as pairs in the real world such as tea without or with milk, eggs
before or after scrambling, and potatoes before and after peeling. Note that these
pairs don't necessarily involve the addition of something extra; in the case of
peeling, the basic potato is larger than its peeled variant. The same is true with
words, where the basic word may be longer than its variant; an example from
English is *cactus – cacti*, but there are better examples in other languages.

6.5.3   Intersecting inflections

English nouns are very simple compared with the inflectional patterns found in other languages such as Latin. English nouns have just one marked
form and one unmarked one, but Latin nouns have ten marked forms and no
unmarked ones. Two typical Latin lexemes, each illustrating a different pattern,
can be found in Table 6.2.

Each of the inflections in the table is defined by the intersection of two different inflectional patterns:

- number (shown here as singular or plural, but more accurately 'plural' and its absence);
- 'case', a contrast in the noun's form that is related to its grammatical
  function in the sentence (Wikipedia: 'Grammatical case'), described

Table 6.3 *The present-tense inflections of the French verb PORT, 'carry'.*

	Singular	Plural
First person	port-e	port-ons
Second person	port-es	port-ez
Third person	port-e	port-ent

traditionally in terms of inflections such as 'nominative' and 'accusative'. For example, in sentence (1), the nominative case of *amicus* marks it as the grammatical subject of *vidit*, whereas the accusative *urbem* is its object. (There is a full discussion of the relations 'subject' and 'object' in Section 7.1.)

(1)   Amicus urbem vidit
             friend city saw
             'A/the friend saw a/the city.'

What may strike you as extravagant complexity is quite normal in many of the world's languages, and not just in the dead ones (like Latin). Take modern French, for example. You've probably seen verb 'conjugations' (a traditional name for verb inflections, contrasting with 'declensions' for nouns) displayed in lists like Table 6.3.

French verbs have the following inflections which combine with one another:

- two numbers (according to whether the subject is singular or plural);
- three persons (according to whether the subject is 'I', 'you' or something else);
- five tenses or 'moods' (present, past simple, imperfect, future, conditional, present subjunctive, imperfect subjunctive).

These contrasts give $2 \times 3 \times 5 = 30$ inflections per verb, to which we could add three imperatives, two participles and an infinitive, making a total of 36 inflections. (Wikipedia: 'French conjugation'.)

Many languages have even more inflections; to take a rather extreme case, modern spoken Basque (a non-Indo-European language spoken in Spain and France) has an inflectional system for nouns which allows them to keep acquiring extra inflections, so in theory at least a single noun lexeme might have 458,683 distinct inflections! (Wikipedia: 'Inflection'.)

Inflections form groups of inflections which are mutually exclusive, so the grammar needs to rule out combinations such as 'singular and plural' or 'nominative and accusative'. The first of these is easy in English, because 'singular' is really just a name for 'not plural'. Either it isA 'plural' or not, and there's nothing more to be said.

Latin is more complicated because none of the inflections are unmarked. We need to rule out 'singular and plural' or 'nominative and accusative' while allowing combinations such as 'singular and nominative'. This is where the mechanism of choices and choice sets (3.3) comes into its own, with 'singular' and 'plural' in one choice set and the cases in another.

6.5.4   Sublexemes

The main point of this section is the interaction between two separate taxonomies for words, the one for lexemes and the one for inflections. But another point which is almost as important is the flexibility that taxonomies offer for any amount of subclassification.

This is important because it solves a notorious problem of linguistics. How big is a lexeme? Take the word *foot* in the joke sentence (2).

(2)   He grew a foot.

Does this mean that he got a foot taller or that he acquired an extra foot? Clearly it could mean either, but the question linguists struggle with is whether we're dealing here with two different lexemes spelt <foot> or just one (Koskela and Murphy 2006).

In one view we have 'homonymy': two lexemes which happen to share the same realization. In the other, we have 'polysemy': one lexeme which happens to have two meanings. Presented in these terms, it's an important distinction for which we might hope to find clear theoretical guidance. Should we for instance give priority to the radical difference of meaning and opt for two lexemes, or should we be more impressed by the irregular plural (*feet*) that both meanings share, which points to a single lexeme?

For most linguists the choice is a stark one between two completely different lexemes and one; and to make matters worse, there are no reliable principles to base the choice on. Word Grammar offers an alternative: extending the taxonomy downwards to recognize **SUBLEXEMES** within lexemes.

In this approach, there's a single lexeme FOOT which explains the shared irregularity in the plural, but we can also create additional sublexemes to explain the different meanings. For the measure meaning, we can create $FOOT_{measure}$, which isA FOOT. As an example of FOOT it inherits the past tense *feet*, but provides its own meaning.

Better still, we have the option of assigning the concrete body-part meaning either to another sublexeme or to the basic lexeme FOOT itself; and of course the same choice is available to anyone learning English. If the body-part meaning belongs to a sublexeme, FOOT has no meaning; but even if it belongs to FOOT, it's merely the default so the measure meaning can override it (as explained in the next section). Either way, we avoid the agonizing choice between one lexeme and two by recognizing at least two closely linked (sub)lexemes. The flexibility that this facility provides is just what's needed in any realistic analysis, as emerges from the analyses in Part III.

Where next?

Advanced: Part III, Chapter 10.2: Inflections
Novice: Part III, Chapter 10.3: Word-class properties

6.6   Definitions and efficiency

Summary of Section 2.5:

- Our minds are good at handling generalizations that have exceptions because our mental categories are **prototypes** which define typical cases but also accommodate exceptional cases.
- The inheritance logic that allows this flexibility is called **default inheritance**, because properties may be **overridden** by exceptional properties, so they are only inherited 'by default'.
- Unlike other versions of default inheritance, the way the logic is applied in Word Grammar is **monotonic** (i.e. later inferences never overturn earlier ones) because it only applies to exemplars, so the searcher always finds overriding properties before it finds default properties.
- In contrast with the 'classical' logic which has dominated theories of how we categorize and generalize for 2,000 years, categories have no definition (consisting of the conditions that are necessary and sufficient for membership). Instead, each category has a bundle of properties that tend to coincide and that 'define' only the prototype.

The present section considers how these general ideas about categories apply to the word-classes that we reviewed in Section 6.3. What difference does it make if word-classes are built round prototypical members while also allowing exceptional members?

The first difference is that we don't need to worry about definitions. Traditional discussions of word-classes start with definitions such as 'A noun is the name of a person, place or thing'. (For a range of examples, try typing 'define: noun' into Google.) You may have learned something like this in primary school, but it's very easy to undermine any such 'notional' definition, i.e. one based on meaning.

How do you recognize 'things' in such a way that you know that thunder is a thing in (1) but not in (2)?

(1)   I heard the thunder.
(2)   It heard it thunder.

The definition implies that you first recognize thunder as a thing, and on the basis of that classification you classify its name – the word *thunder* – as a noun. But surely that puts things the wrong way round? It's much more likely that you actually recognize the word-class before you classify its meaning.

Even without a deep understanding of grammar you can probably see that *thunder* in (1) is like the noun *dog* in *I heard the dog*, whereas in (2) it's like the verb *bark* in *I heard it bark*. English happens to have two separate lexemes, a noun THUNDER$_{noun}$ and a verb THUNDER$_{verb}$, which share the same realization but have different grammatical properties; for example, the noun can be used immediately after *the* but the verb can't. If there is a difference of meaning between the two lexemes, it's far too subtle to use as the basis for a workable definition.

6.6.1   Definitions or descriptions?

In any case, the theory of categorization in Section 2.5 provides much deeper objections to definitions. We don't learn ordinary concepts such as 'cat' and 'birthday party' via definitions, but via exemplars; and the same is true for the concepts that we construct when building our own mental grammar. Why, then, should we expect to be able to pin down these concepts with home-made definitions?

According to the theory of categorization, the nearest we get to a 'definition' of a category is a list of its properties, so it would be as misguided to look for a 'true' definition of 'noun' as it would be to choose between the two definitions of 'cat' in Section 2.5. To focus on definitions is to miss the main point of categorization.

Categorization isn't mere classification for its own sake, like classifying a handful of pebbles into arbitrary heaps – an activity which is finished once every pebble is in a heap, and achieves nothing except a glow of satisfaction at a job completed. Rather, we use categories as tools for generalizing, as with birds and all the other examples discussed in Section 2.3. You recognize a bird by some combination of visible features such as flying and size, and most definitely not by applying some kind of 'definition'. This recognition then allows you to generalize (by inheritance) from 'bird' to your particular bird exemplar. Without this generalization, the categorization process is pointless.

The same applies to word-classes: generalizations are the only reason for setting up word-classes in the first place. This was true for the ancient grammarians of India and Greece, and it still applies in modern linguistics. Word-classes have to earn their place through the generalizations that they permit, and alternative analyses can be judged by the generalizations they allow. This principle isn't just a matter of scientific elegance, but of psychology. We can be sure that our minds do in fact make the generalizations that grammarians try to build into grammars.

The evidence comes from the information that we inherit from general categories, and can be seen most simply in invented examples where we can be sure that we don't draw information from memory. In Section 2.3, the example was the fictitious sea-thrush, and now we can consider the made-up word *grindle*. If all you know about this word is that it can be used in sentence (3),

(3)   He grindles.

which of the following sentences is possible?

(4)   He grindled all night.
(5)   I like his grindle.

For me, the answer is that I'm sure of (4) but I need more evidence before I can vouch for (5); and I guess the same is true for you. How do we know?

We've never seen *grindle* used, and yet we're confident that if it can be used in (3) then it should also be possible in (4). The only imaginable explanation for this ability is that (3) shows us that it's a verb, and then we inherit from 'verb' the possibility of using it in (4). If this explanation is right, then we have solid evidence for the psychological reality of 'verb' as a concept.

6.6.2   Efficiency

A reasonable test for the reality of a word-class, therefore, is how many generalizations it expresses. Clearly, a class that doesn't capture any generalizations at all has no chance of being psychologically real. For example, suppose I proposed a new word-class which contained all the words that begin with the letter <b>: *big*, *butter*, *bring*, *before* and so on. Why is this such an obviously silly idea?

Because this class has no other properties, so it expresses no generalizations at all. If all we know about a word is that it starts with <b>, we can certainly assign it to this class, but this tells us nothing new about it.

In contrast, if we know enough about a word to recognize it as a verb, this tells us a great deal about it that we don't already know. Consequently, we might describe 'verb' as a very '**EFFICIENT**' class. Following this logic, then, linguists generally assume – rightly, in my view – that the most efficient analysis is the one that's most likely to be psychologically real because it's the one most likely to be learned.

The most important general point is that the taxonomy of word-classes is justified by just one criterion: efficiency. Being part of a respectable 2,000-year-old tradition doesn't in itself justify a class, so the traditional word-classes have to be tested just like any other analysis (10.1). The more generalizations an analysis allows, the better; so the analysis that's most likely to be true is the one that expresses the most generalizations.

This principle is very familiar to any linguist, though others may prefer to talk about elegance or simplicity. But in a cognitive approach it is not merely a matter of taste or personal satisfaction for the analyst. Rather, we can argue that the principle of efficiency follows from our theory of how general categories are learned (which I discuss in Section 4.4).

On the other hand, cognitive assumptions also tell us two other things. One is that everyone is different, because everyone applies a slightly different mental apparatus to a different range of experiences; so some of us may arrive at a word-class taxonomy which is less efficient than it might be. Whether, or how often, this happens we have no idea; but we cannot assume without question that the most efficient taxonomy is the one that every adult speaker of English has in their heads.

Another consequence is that the learning of general categories maximizes generalizations, but does not minimize storage. For instance, one of the inheritable properties of nouns is that their plural has the suffix -s; but that doesn't prevent this same property from being stored for individual nouns as well. Indeed, Section 2.3 argues that there is redundant duplication of information on a massive scale, both inside language and outside. If so, then even a regular plural form such as *dogs* may be stored ready-made even though it can also be inherited.

6.6.3   Membership tests for the novice

Where does this discussion leave a novice grammarian? How do you learn to classify words? In the old-fashioned approach you would first learn each word-class name together with its definition, followed by a few examples; and then you would practise identifying examples in a selection of sentences. But I hope to have persuaded you that this approach rests on theoretical sand and goes nowhere.

A much better approach starts with some examples and helps you to discover some of their shared properties for yourself. This allows you to use your own capacity for creating concepts. The goal is for you to refine this new concept until it simply merges with the word-class concept that already exists in your mind. In this way you 'discover' a class of words for which I, as professional grammarian, offer the name 'noun'. As you then gradually discover more properties that these words share with each other your new class turns into the class of nouns that you already had (but couldn't name) before you started to study grammar.

This is basically how grammarians learn their trade, but there's an important snag for the beginner. The trouble is that most of the properties that an experienced grammarian recognizes are too abstract for a novice to understand. I would like to be able to tell you that a noun may act as the complement of a pronoun; but if you don't understand 'complement' or 'pronoun', that's no help.

The problem isn't tied to grammar; exactly the same is true when you're learning any system of concepts, and indeed when you're learning a language. At any point in development, the only way forward starts from where you are at the moment, and the more you know, the easier it is to learn more.

The greatest challenge is getting that first precarious grip of a concept such as a word-class, but more experienced grammarians can help by providing carefully chosen examples supported by **MEMBERSHIP TESTS**; for example, instead of learning that a noun is the name of a person, place or thing, you might learn that a noun is a word that can come between *the* and the end of a sentence. Nobody would suggest that this is a mental property; in fact, it's almost inconceivable that anyone would create a property like that for a word-class because much better alternatives are available in a full grammar, but for a novice wanting to check whether *thunder* was a noun, it might be helpful.

I shall provide membership tests like this in the chapters on English, but even simple tests pose an intellectual challenge: recognizing lexemes. It's easy to apply the noun test to example (1) above, *I heard the thunder*; but what about (6) and (7)?

(6)   The thunder woke me up.
(7)   I heard some thunder.

The trouble is that (6) has *thunder* after *the* but not at the end of the sentence, whereas (7) has it at the end of the sentence but not after *the*, so neither sentence provides exactly the right context to prove that *thunder* is a noun. The evidence from (1) is only relevant if we can be sure that *thunder* in that sentence is an example of the same lexeme as the ones in (6) and (7), in contrast with examples like (8), where it isn't.

(8)   It may thunder.

The difference between (8) and (7) is anything but obvious to a non-human organism such as a computer, so the noun test doesn't help. But most human novice grammarians cope fine in spite of the demands of this rather sophisticated analysis into lexemes. If you know English, the lexeme classification is obvious because the lexemes are already built into your mind, so even apparently simple-minded tests actually build on a great deal of prior knowledge and understanding.

Where next?

Advanced: Part III, Chapter 10.3: Word-class properties
Novice: Part III, Chapter 10.4: Morphology and lexical relations

6.7   Morphology and lexical relations

- The ideas from Section 6.6 are summarised at the start of section 10.3. The main point for present purposes is the idea that generalizations may have exceptions. This is important in morphology because so many rules of morphology have exceptions.

The ideas from Section 2.5 are a good preparation for discussing morphology because so many rules of morphology have exceptions.

Other parts of language have their fair share of irregularity too, but morphology is the area where irregularity looms largest for language learners. If you've tried to learn a Western European language then you may well remember sweating over 'irregular verbs'. For example, foreign learners of English have to learn that the past tense of TAKE is *took*, not the default *taked* (remember: * means 'ungrammatical'), and so on through about 300 other verbs (including the wildly irregular *was/were* of BE and *went* of GO). English isn't alone in this, of course, though there are languages such as Turkish and Chinese which for different reasons have virtually no such irregularities.

MORPHOLOGY is half of grammar, the half that describes changes within a word such as *walk – walked* or *take – took*. In contrast, **SYNTAX** is about the ways in which words combine with each other. In this way we use the word as a way of dividing the data of grammar into two: patterns inside words belong to morphology, and patterns among words are syntax.

For instance, take the last few words of the previous sentence. The nouns *patterns* and *words* have similar morphology, consisting of the suffix {s} added to the basic form of the word; but their syntax is different, because *patterns* is the subject of *are* (as in *patterns are ...*), whereas words is linked by *among* to *patterns* (as in *patterns among words*). The two kinds of patterning are quite different, and independent of one another; irregular morphology, as in *take-took*, has nothing to do with irregular syntax, and although plenty of languages have free word order, none have free order of elements within a word. {{optional extra words: If words are tools, morphology deals with their shapes while syntax deals with their uses.}}

A proper understanding of how language works needs equal coverage of both halves. In an ideal world, this book would contain as many pages on morphology as it does on syntax. The morphology chapters would provide an opportunity to explore fascinatingly different language systems (Iacobini 2006) and some quite well developed parts of Word Grammar theory (Creider and Hudson 1999, Hudson 2000, Hudson 2007c: 63–116). Unfortunately space is limited and morphology has rather limited appeal for students. What follows, therefore, is an extremely potted version of Word Grammar morphology.

6.7.1   Morphs and forms

Section 6.5 introduced some of the main ideas in the analysis of plural nouns such as *books* (Figure 6.4), including the terms 'realization', 'stem' and 'variant'. In that example, the word BOOK is realized by its stem *book*, and the plural 'BOOK, plural' is realized by the 's-variant' of this stem. The main element missing from this analysis is the basic building block of morphology, the unit that does for morphology what the word does for syntax. This is the **MORPH**. (You may recognize this term as the name for a small character from children's TV who could change shape easily; it comes from the Greek word for 'shape'.)

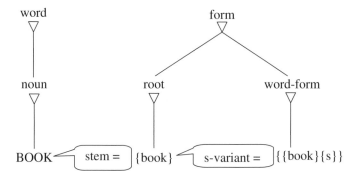

Figure 6.5 *Forms realize words, and word-forms are variants of other forms*

A standard notation for morphs encloses them in curly braces: {…}, so we can recognize two morphs in the word *books*: {book} and {s}. This notation is extended in Word Grammar to more complex morphological structures as well, so when we combine {book} with {s} we get {{book}{s}}. This is called a **WORD-FORM**, and morphs and word-forms together are called **FORMS**.

Forms have their own taxonomy which recognizes very traditional categories such as **ROOT**, **PREFIX** and **SUFFIX**. In this classification, {book} is a root morph and {s} is a suffix – a very different classification from the one found in the word taxonomy.

This double-taxonomy analysis is shown in Figure 6.5, in which the notation starts to cheat in order to prepare for the more sophisticated analyses of Chapter 7 where concepts are linked directly to one another. For instance, BOOK has the property 'stem =', but this is located in the diagram right next to {book} so that you can read it as 'stem = {book}'; in other words, the stem of BOOK is {book}.

6.7.2   Irregularity, partial and complete

What Figure 6.5 shows is just the regular pattern, so the analysis needs to be extended to accommodate irregular examples such as FOOT, with its irregular plural {feet}, and PERSON, with its even more irregular {people}. The system just presented actually provides two points where we can introduce irregularity, one for small irregularities such as {foot} – {feet}, and the other for major ones such as {person} – {people}.

For cases like {foot} – {feet}, where the two forms are recognizably related, we can say that the second is an irregular variant (in this case, an irregular s-variant) of the first. After all, the two morphs both have the same consonants, so {feet} doesn't, as it were, start from scratch.

In contrast, the total irregularity of {people} seems to ignore the stem form altogether; and the difference between {go} and {went} is even more total. In such cases the 'variant' mechanism isn't relevant, so we just say that {people} is the realization of 'PERSON, plural', without trying to relate it to the basic stem {person}.

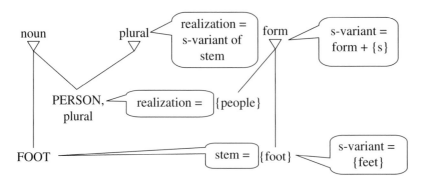

Figure 6.6 *Two kinds of morphological exception*

Figure 6.6 shows how both possibilities are accommodated. In words, the stem of FOOT is {foot}, so by default its plural (i.e. 'FOOT, plural') is realized by the s-variant of {foot}; but the latter's s-variant is in fact the irregular {feet} rather than the default stem + {s}. In contrast, the realization of 'PERSON, plural' is simply {people}, which bears no relation to the stem {person}.

6.7.3   Variants

You may wonder why 'variants' are needed. After all, if {s} marks nouns as plural, why don't we just say that 'plural' is realized by the suffix {s}? Instead of this apparently simple approach, what I am proposing introduces the extra link of 's-variant' between 'plural' and {s}. This link pays for itself in a number of ways.

We've already seen one advantage, in the analysis of irregular forms like {feet}. Without variants, there would be no way to link this form directly to {foot} so as to highlight their shared consonants. All we could say is that {feet} is the irregular realization of 'FOOT, plural', which is exactly the same analysis as for the completely irregular {people}. But if {feet} is a variant of {foot}, the difference isn't much greater than that between a regular pair such as {dog} and {{dog}{s}}.

Another advantage of analysing {feet} as a variant of {foot} is that it separates the morphological pattern from its effects on inflection. This separation is important because the relations between morphology and inflection are often complicated, but in a generalizable way.

Take the form *eaten* – i.e. {{eat}{en}}, which we can call the verb's 'en-variant'. This has (at least) two completely different syntactic uses, as in (1) and (2).

(1)   Someone else has eaten my porridge.
(2)   My porridge was eaten by someone else.

In (1) the inflection is called a 'perfect participle', which is only found after HAVE, but in (2) it's called a 'passive participle', a completely different syntactic

Table 6.4 *Some regular and irregular verb–noun pairs.*

Verb	Noun
speak	speaker
drive	driver
edit	editor
lie	liar
assist	assistant
cook	cook

pattern where (as you can see in (2)) the porridge and the eater have swapped places.

In both cases the verb's morphological form is the same; but this isn't just a peculiarity of the verb EAT. Exactly the same is true for every single English verb, regardless of how regular or irregular it may be. This is an important generalization, but it's impossible to express without variants. With variants, it's easy: any verb's en-variant realizes either its perfect participle or its passive participle.

6.7.4   Lexical morphology

The discussion so far has implied that the only role for variants is in distinguishing inflections from their basic lexemes, but this isn't actually true, and especially not in English, where there are relatively few inflections. A much more important role is to distinguish one lexeme from another one, showing what are called **LEXICAL RELATIONS**.

For example, the {er} of the 'actor noun' WALKER ('someone who walks') distinguishes it from the verb WALK, on which it's based in a rather obvious and regular way. In this case we can recognize 'er-variants', with {{walk}{er}} as the er-variant of {walk}, with exceptions such as those shown in Table 6.4. But, as with en-variants, morphological irregularity is irrelevant to the ways in which these forms are used to realize nouns.

The morphological patterns of variants that are found in lexically related lexemes are very similar to the ones that are used for inflections, and indeed some variants are used for some inflections as well as for some lexical relations; for example, in English the {ing} suffix is used in inflected verbs (e.g. *is walking*) but also in nouns such as *wiring* and *flooring*.

On the other hand, there are also good reasons for distinguishing inflections from lexical relations, not least the fact that inflections such as 'plural' are different from all the other categories, whereas the lexemes linked by lexical relations are just ordinary nouns, verbs and so on (Hudson 2007c: 87–93). The difference can be seen in Figure 6.7, where the noun WALKER is lexically related to (but separate from) the verb WALK, in contrast with *walkers*, which combines it with the inflection 'plural'.

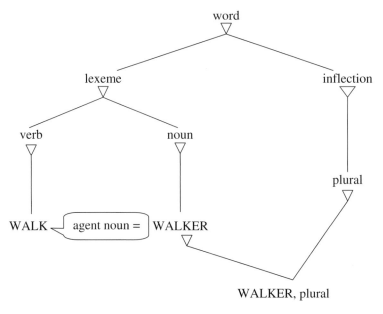

Figure 6.7 *Inflections and lexical relations are different*

In short, a word's morphological structure is highly relevant to its grammatical classification, but the relation is a complex one because the morphology may indicate either an inflection such as 'plural' or a lexical relation such as that between a verb and its agent noun. Moreover, the same morphological structure, such as the presence of {s}, can be used in a number of different inflections (or in different lexical relations). This clear separation of the morphological structure from the more abstract grammatical categories that it signals is why we can be sure that the two are separate.

Where next?

Advanced: Part III, Chapter 10.4: Morphology and lexical relations
Novice: Part III, Chapter 10.5: Social properties

6.8   Social properties of words

Summary of Section 2.6:

- The mental categories that we build for people follow the same principles as those that we build for objects, with the same range of generality from individual exemplars, through individuals, to general social categories.

- Categories for people, whether individual or general, have a particularly rich set of properties which can be inherited in the usual way by multiple inheritance. General social categories are called **stereotypes**.
- The logic of default inheritance allows us to form inaccurate stereotypes which discount counter-evidence as exceptions. These inaccurate properties are **prejudices**.
- Our minds include a 'map' of the society we live in which we can call '**I-society**'.

This section considers the social facts that we all know about words, such as the fact that GEE-GEE is used by or to small children. How do such facts fit into our theory of language?

As I noted in Section 6.2, most linguistic theories make a sharp distinction between a word's 'linguistic' properties, which involve other parts of language, and its 'non-linguistic' properties which don't. For these theories, language is a collection of related linguistic units, and since social categories are certainly not linguistic units, they can't be part of language. Accordingly, the classification of GEE-GEE as a noun is a linguistic property whereas its links to small children are not.

This assumption is quite problematic for working linguists because we all know that social distinctions lie at the heart of language, and the example of GEE-GEE is just the tip of a very large ice-berg. A theory of how language works which has no place at all for social information about the people who use words and the situations in which they use them seems to miss rather an important point about language.

One obvious cognitive fact about the language that we experience is that, at least in ordinary face-to-face communication, we always know who's speaking and who they're speaking to, and we know how these people fit into our I-society. This information about each word-token is easily available to any child when learning language.

When Mummy says (1) to Jimmy, Jimmy knows that she's talking and that she's his mother:

(1)   Jimmy, here's some nice yoghurt.

If all the other people who talk to Jimmy use the same range of words in the same ways, there won't be any special connection between them and Mummy and, as far as Jimmy knows, every human uses these words. But if Mummy speaks one language and Daddy speaks another, Jimmy will soon learn to associate different words with different people (De Houwer 2006). And the same ability allows him to learn any association between a word and an individual or social group.

Later in life we all learn more and more social properties for words as we explore the territory of **SOCIOLINGUISTICS** inhabited by facts such as the following:

*   that BONNY is used by people from Scotland;
*   that ATTEMPT is used by pompous people;
*   that MORPH is used by linguists;
*   that SHIT is used by 'naughty' people;
*   that HARK is used by people in archaic literature.

(Wikipedia: 'Sociolinguistics', Hudson 1996.)

The question for linguistic theory is how such facts relate to our 'I-language', Chomsky's useful name for our mental map of language (2.6). Each of these facts brings together a lexeme, which is definitely part of I-language, with a social category, which is definitely part of I-society. Does this make the fact a part of I-language or of I-society? A reasonable response is to ask why it matters, and an equally reasonable answer is that it doesn't, provided we accept the general idea that I-language and I-society are two rather vaguely defined areas of a single gigantic network (3.5).

Where next?

Advanced: Part III, Chapter 10.5: Social properties
Novice: Part III, Chapter 11: English syntax

6.9   Levels of analysis

Summary of Section 3.1:

*   A concept's properties can be defined, but not by prose statements.
*   Some properties consist of a link to something which is not itself a concept: a **percept** (an abstract representation linked to one perceptual modality – vision, sight, etc.), an **emotion** or a **motor skill**.
*   Most properties cannot be analysed in these ways.

The ideas from Section 3.1 apply most obviously to pronunciation and writing, the least abstract aspects of language.

A speech sound has two main properties: what it sounds like (a percept) and how we make it (a motor skill), though we can of course recognize a sound without knowing how to produce it. Similarly, we recognize a written letter by its shape (a percept), and we use a motor skill to produce it in our own writing. As for emotions, they seem to attach fairly freely to all sorts of linguistic units as illustrated by the list in Section 3.1: *hooray!*, *snug*, *terrorist* and *What on Earth happened?*

6.9.1   The notion of 'levels'

The question, then, is what we can say about all the other properties that make up our I-language. One of the many things that linguists agree on is that they can be separated into a number of different **LEVELS OF ANALYSIS**. At one level we have meanings, at another level units of grammar, and at a third level we have written letters.

Take example (1).

(1)   He drank some coffee.

In terms of meanings, this sentence presents three elements: a person, some coffee and an action that the person applied to the coffee at some time in the past. In terms of grammar, we have four word-tokens with various properties such as being pronouns and verbs; but notice that none of these words is a person or an action, nor does it make sense to ask whether the meanings are pronouns or verbs. And in terms of letters, we have 17 letters, three word spaces and one full stop – but no people, actions, pronouns or verbs.

Each level offers a different kind of analysis for the whole sentence, in terms of a different range of units and patterns. It would be quite impossible to collapse all the levels into one without either creating hopeless confusion or losing a great deal of information.

This is a very familiar cognitive situation and by no means confined to language. For example, if you have books on a shelf then you can 'analyse' them in terms of their size, their colour, their author or their content, and each 'level' of analysis offers a different range of properties and relations; and indeed you could take any one of these levels as the basis for arranging them – in terms of decreasing size, similar colour, similar author or similar content.

Another agreed view of language is that the different levels are arranged in a hierarchy with meaning at one end and written letters or speech sounds at the other. Because we think conventionally of meaning as something lofty and ethereal, linguists always put meaning at the top of the hierarchy and letters and sounds at the bottom, but the direction of the hierarchy is just a conventional metaphor. In these terms, when we speak we start at the top of the hierarchy and have to work down to relatively concrete letters and sounds at the bottom; and when we listen or read we work the other way round, going up the hierarchy from concrete to abstract.

Furthermore, linguists agree that each level provides a guide to the level above it; so letters are clues to words, and words are clues to meanings, but letters or sounds are only indirectly related, through words, to meanings. Because the more concrete elements make the more abstract ones more 'real', this relation between levels is often called **REALIZATION**, a term which I used in Section 6.2 in the list of word properties where I said that words are realized by a word-form.

We might use the same terminology for the relation between a word and its meaning, but it's less clear that it's appropriate here because the meaning doesn't depend on the word for its existence in the same way that a word depends on its concrete realization. For example, the person referred to in (1) would still exist even if he wasn't referred to as 'he'. A much more obvious name for the relation between a word and its meaning is **MEANING**, another term which figured among the properties of words in Section 6.2.

In short, a word exists on one level (syntax), is realized on another (to be discussed below) and has a meaning on a third level.

6.9.2   The level of form

What linguists don't agree about is how many levels there are. Some linguists think that words are simply a link between a meaning and some sounds or letters (Langacker 2006, Lasnik 2006). This is a two-level model with just meaning and sounds (or letters).

Other linguists accept a three-level model, with meanings, words and sounds or letters. This may well strike you as the most obvious analysis since you've been applying the difference between words and letters ever since you learned to write with spaces between words.

But the question is whether sounds (or letters) realize words directly, and many linguists argue that they don't (Aronoff and Volpe 2006). This is also the Word Grammar view (Hudson 2007c: 72–81). In this view, there are no fewer than three levels of analysis for a word such as *squirrels*, in addition to the level where its meaning is analysed:

- as a word, where we classify it as a noun, verb and so on, and describe its syntactic relations to other words; for example, in *Squirrels hibernate* we can recognize a noun acting as the subject of a verb.
- as a form, where we talk about it in terms of morphs, roots, affixes and so on, and where we say how it realizes a word and is itself realized either by a pronunciation or by a spelling; at this level, *squirrels* is a complex word-form {{squirrel}{s}}.
- as a string of letters or sounds, where we talk about consonants, vowels and syllables; at this level, *squirrels* consists of two syllables. These consist in turn of consonants and vowels as follows:
  - in writing: <s, q, r, r, l, s> and <u, i, e>
  - in speech: /s, k, w, r, l, z/ and /ɪ, ə/.

Why do we need an extra level of structure between words and letters or sounds? The main reason is that morphs seem to be mentally real.

6.9.3   Evidence for morphs in the mind

One piece of evidence for this is that ordinary people – not just linguists – look for them in new words. This emerges clearly from **FOLK ETYMOLOGY**, where ordinary people try to make sense of long words (Bauer 2006, Wikipedia: 'Folk etymology').

The classic example is HAMBURGER, which was invented in America but originally named after the city Hamburg (for details of the rather unclear history, see 'Hamburger' in Wikipedia and the online etymological dictionary at www.etymonline.com). At some point in its history, the *burger* part was separated from *ham*, and was then added to *beef* and *cheese* to give BEEFBURGER and CHEESEBURGER. But of course none of these changes make sense unless the people who invented these new words were looking for morphs in the words concerned. Notice that they must have been much more interested in the forms of these morphs than their meanings, because a hamburger never contained ham.

Folk etymology is responsible for a number of other words including BRIDEGROOM and PENTHOUSE, and in each case it's driven by the desire to analyse an incomprehensible long form in terms of shorter existing forms, almost regardless of whether the analysis makes sense in terms of meanings.

The mental reality of forms (between words and sounds) is supported by other kinds of evidence as well. Take speech errors. Someone once tried to say *too thinly sliced*, but instead said: *too slicely thinned* (Stemberger 1985), showing that they had separated {thin} from {ly} and {slice} from {d} before recombining them. Once again, we can be sure that the speaker recognized these units as something more than mere consonants and vowels, because this kind of reorganization never applies to mere sounds. (We look at speech errors in a little more detail in Section 8.2.)

Then there's evidence from the psychological 'priming' experiments mentioned in Section 4.2, where people sit at computers and perform tasks such as deciding whether or not a word that appears on the screen is a real English word by hitting the 'yes' button when they read (say) *nurse* and the 'no' button for *nend*. Although this decision normally takes less than a second, the time taken, measured in milliseconds, reduces when the word concerned has just been 'primed' by a similar word. The delay in recognizing *nurse* is measurably shorter than normal if it follows soon after a related word such as *doctor*.

When applied to morphology, this experimental method shows that forms such as {ness}, {hard} and {er} are mentally real. The evidence consists of priming effects between pairs such as DARKNESS – TOUGHNESS, HARDLY – HARD and even CORNER – CORN (Marslen-Wilson 2006).

The last two cases are particularly interesting because the related words have nothing but their form in common; even though HARDLY is historically related to HARD the two words now have completely unrelated meanings,

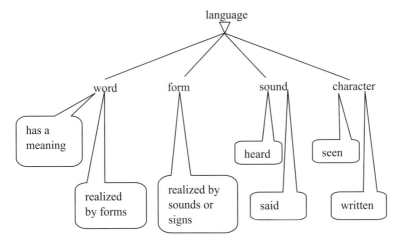

Figure 6.8 *The architecture of language*

and CORNER was never related in meaning to CORN. The only reason for relating them mentally is that {er} is a suffix which in some words has a clear function, so our minds automatically find it even in words where it has no function.

The conclusion is that these word-parts must be in our mental inventory; but crucially they're not just syllables, because priming experiments show that mere syllables don't have the same effect: for instance, SCANDAL doesn't prime SCAN, because *dal* isn't a morph in any other word.

6.9.4   The architecture of language

The evidence from folk etymology and psycholinguistics therefore supports a three-level view of words in which forms are distinct from both words and sounds, and in which each level realizes the level above it as shown in Figure 6.8.

In this diagram, language has four kinds of element: words, forms, sounds and (written) characters. As I pointed out above, sounds and characters both relate to percepts (what sounds sound like and what characters look like) and motor skills to saying sounds and writing characters.

The diagram presents the regular default patterns in which a word is realized by a form, which in turn is realized by sounds or characters. However, default inheritance being what it is, we can expect exceptions. In principle, it's possible that some words are realized directly by sounds or characters; written examples are '&' and 'Z', but spoken examples are harder to find. Nor can we exclude the possibility of forms, or even sounds or letters, having a meaning; indeed, this may well be true for intonation patterns and punctuation marks. Exceptions are to be expected and don't in any way undermine the general pattern.

6.9.5 Why do we divide language into levels?

But why should language be organized in this way? At this point we can only guess, but my guess is that this three-level structuring of words is guaranteed to emerge in any mind that's designed (as ours is) to look for generalizations. However arbitrary may be the relation between pronunciations and the meanings they express (Coleman 2006), some partial similarities are bound to arise even if only by chance. And the larger the vocabulary, the more similarities will be available for spotting. A generalization-hungry mind will always be able to find something to feed on even if it's only as trivial as the fact that MOTHER, FATHER, SISTER, BROTHER and DAUGHTER all end in *-er*.

Moreover, the generalizations aren't simply collectors' trophies, but are used in guiding future behaviour including the creation of new words, so weak generalizations are likely to become stronger through a feed-back loop that makes behaviour patterns more and more general. The outcome, I would guess, is bound to be a system in which the essentially arbitrary relations between meanings and sounds are factored into three levels:

- **SYNTAX**, where words allow generalizations about meanings and especially about how complex meanings are built by combining simpler ones, but no attention is paid to how the words are pronounced.
- **PHONOLOGY** and **GRAPHOLOGY**, where consonants and vowels allow generalizations about pronunciation or writing, but no attention is paid to meaning.
- **MORPHOLOGY**, where forms (morphs and more complex forms) allow generalizations about how words are related to consonants and vowels.

These three levels are recognized in one way or another by virtually every theory of language, but Word Grammar is unusual in giving such a central place to the word. This will be one of the main themes of the next chapter, which explains why syntax is about how words combine with each other rather than, as in other theories, about how sentences are organized.

Summary of this section:

- Language is organized as a hierarchy of different **levels of analysis** in which meaning is conventionally thought of as 'higher' than sounds or written letters.
- The units on one level **realize** the units on the next level up, but meanings are best seen as outside language and related to words by the relation '**meaning**' rather than 'realization'.
- Somewhat controversially, Word Grammar assumes a level of **forms** between **words** and speech **sounds** or written **letters**; this gives a three-

level analysis of words as units organized by **syntax**, by **morphology**, and by **phonology** or **graphology**.

• The level of form allows us to capture generalizations about the relations between syntax and phonology so its existence can be explained in terms of the general cognitive principle of maximizing generalization.

Where next?

Advanced: Back to Part I, Chapter 3.2: Relational concepts, arguments and values

7 Syntax

7.1 Dependencies and phrases

Summary of Section 3.2:

- Properties that can't be defined in terms of percepts, emotions or motor skills are **conceptual properties**, which consist of links from one concept to another.
- The links are not mere 'associations' but **relations** which belong to different types.
- Some links belong to a small number of **primitive** relation types; these include **isA**, argument and value, and quantity.
- Non-primitive relations are themselves concepts, called **relational concepts** (in contrast with the familiar **entity concepts**). A relational concept has an **argument** and a **value**, and belongs to a **taxonomy** of such concepts.
- A concept's **quantity** says how many exemplars are expected.
- Relational concepts, just like entity concepts, can multiply freely according to experience, so (unlike most other theories) Word Grammar does not limit relations to a small vocabulary of supposedly universal relations.
- One way of creating a new relational concept is to define it in terms of existing relations.
- Some such definitions contain a relational **triangle** in which one relation is defined in terms of two others.
- Others allow **recursion** so that they may apply to their own output.

The area of language most obviously relevant to the theory of cognitive relations which I presented in Section 3.2 is syntax, which is all about how words in a sentence are related to one another. Some of the most widely recognized terms in syntax are the names of relations: 'subject', 'object', 'modifier', 'complement', 'dependent', in contrast with the names for entity concepts such as 'noun', 'past' or 'interrogative'.

7.1.1   Syntactic dependencies

Suppose the general theory of cognition does allow an open-ended taxonomy of relational concepts, as Word Grammar claims; how does this affect the theory of syntax? What, for example, does it tell us about a traditional syntactic relation such as **SUBJECT**, the relation between *cows* and *eat* in (1)?

(1)   Cows eat grass.

This relation is a very clear example of a concept which allows generalizations about a large bundle of highly correlated features. The following characteristics all tend strongly to co-occur, so a verb's subject tends to:

- be a noun;
- precede the verb (i.e. in writing, it stands to the left of the verb);
- show agreement with a verb in the present tense (so *eat* is found with a plural subject, and *eats* with a singular one as in *Charlotte eats grass*);
- have its 'subject' form if it's a personal pronoun (so HER has the exceptional form {she} when used as the subject);
- identify the actor if the verb describes an action (so in the action of eating as applied to cows and grass, the syntactic subject has to identify the cows not the grass).

As usual, these characteristics are defaults which can be overridden. For example, passive verbs exchange the default subject for another element (as in *Grass is eaten by cows*). But the main point is that 'subject' is an extremely well motivated concept which allows important generalizations, so it must be mentally real; and of course if it's a concept, then it must be a relational concept.

Now, if syntactic relations are straightforward relational concepts, they must be part of any syntactic structure that we build in our minds for sentences; so in the case of (1), we must recognize a 'subject' relation between *cows* and *eat*, and a different relation (traditionally, **OBJECT**) between *grass* and *eat*. This rather obvious conclusion brings us to one of the most controversial questions in syntactic research, and the one for which Word Grammar is most famous or infamous, according to viewpoint.

The question is: what other relations are there in syntax? For Word Grammar the simple answer is: none. (A slightly more complex answer will emerge in Section 7.5.) This answer is roughly speaking the same as the answer that evolved through 2,000 years of theorizing about grammar in Europe (Wikipedia: 'Grammar: history'); and a significant proportion of linguists working in Europe still take the same view.

This tradition is called **DEPENDENCY GRAMMAR** because syntactic relations always signal an unequal relationship between the words concerned, with one word subordinate to the other. In the terminology of dependency grammar, the subject and object both 'depend on' the verb or are its **DEPENDENTS** (Kruijff 2006).

7.1.2   What is a dependent?

In this view, then, each of the traditional syntactic relations is a **DEPENDENCY** between two unequal words, the dependent and its **PARENT** (the word it depends on). But although individual dependencies such as 'subject' are clearly defined, the more general concept 'dependency' is a little harder to define because it's more abstract. What dependents have in common is that they're subordinate to the parent in a number of senses.

Take a very simple example such as *hungry cows*, where *hungry* depends on *cows*. In what sense is *hungry* subordinate to *cows*? Most obviously, *cows* can occur without *hungry* in places where *hungry* cannot be used on its own, as in (2–4):

(2)   Hungry cows moo.
(3)   Cows moo.
(4)   *Hungry moo.

In this sense, then, *hungry* depends on *cows* for its ability to be used at all. Sometimes the dependent has to occur; for example when the verb is CONSUME, its object is obligatory:

(5)   He consumed his rations.
(6)   *He consumed.

But the general point is that it's the parent that decides whether or not the dependent can be used.

Another aspect of the subordination is in the meaning: the dependent changes the meaning of the parent, not the other way round, so a hungry cow is a kind of cow, not a kind of hunger, and eating grass is a kind of eating rather than a kind of grass. It's important, however, to be clear that this doesn't mean that the dependent is less important, in the sense of carrying less information. On the contrary; for example, if I say someone is a nice person, the crucial word is *nice*, the dependent, not its parent *person*.

Most generally, then, a word's dependents help it to express a more precise meaning than it could on its own, and (incidentally) they may also satisfy some demands of pure syntax. So if you want to talk about cows eating grass, you can't use a single word to express your meaning so you choose one that expresses a more general idea, EAT, and add dependents to narrow its meaning down to eating by cows and of grass. It is in this sense that dependents are subordinate: the parent provides the general meaning which the dependents then narrow down.

Modern dependency theory, then, stands at the end of a long tradition of distinguished work and offers a reasonably well developed and coherent approach to syntactic analysis.

7.1.3   Phrase structure

Unfortunately, however, the most influential theories of syntax take a very different view which develops an idea that was introduced into American

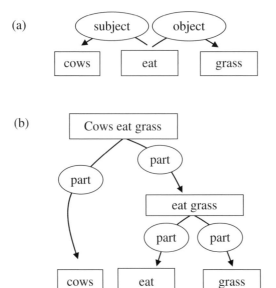

Figure 7.1 *Two syntactic analyses of* Cows eat grass.

linguistics by Leonard Bloomfield in the 1930s (Bloomfield 1933, Percival 1976), ignoring the existing dependency tradition. The idea was that truly 'scientific' linguists needed to build on much simpler concepts than the ones that had evolved in the grammatical tradition, so Bloomfield suggested a procedure for dividing sentences into their **CONSTITUENTS**, or parts, so that the only relation that needed to be invoked was that between a whole and its parts.

Using this kind of part–whole analysis, sentence (1) would be divided first into two parts, *cows* and *eat grass*, and then the latter would be divided into *eat* and *grass*. This more recent tradition is sometimes called 'Constituent structure grammar' (Jacobson 2006), but it's now more often called **PHRASE STRUCTURE GRAMMAR** since Chomsky adopted it as the basis for the 'phrase structure rules' in his early theories. (Wikipedia: 'Phrase structure rule'.)

In contrast with dependency grammar, phrase structure grammar assumes that these part–whole relations are the structure of a sentence. And what's more, there's nothing else, so the traditional dependencies are merely informal descriptions for particular part–whole relations. In this approach, then, *cows* is a part of the whole sentence *Cows eat grass*, so it's the subject, whereas *grass* is part of the 'verb phrase' *eat grass*, which makes it the object. The two approaches are contrasted in Figure 7.1.

7.1.4   Dependencies or phrases?

The popularity of the phrase-structure approach seems strange when compared directly with dependency analysis, which is not only much simpler and more in tune with traditional grammar, but also more plausible as a model of mental structures. After all, if we know that the human mind is capable of enter-taining abstract relations such as 'mother', why should we hesitate to assume the relation 'subject'?

At least part of the reason for this popularity lies in the sociological history of modern linguistics, which developed faster in the USA than in Europe. One consequence of this history is that introductory textbooks rarely even mention dependency analysis, and even less often debate the pros and cons of the two approaches; the honourable exceptions include Matthews 1981 and Atkinson *et al.* 1982. Phrase structure grammarians often talk about dependencies, but only in the same way that they talk about subjects and objects, as a convenient short-hand for talking about the various elements in a sentence's structure. Phrase structure is so basic to their theories that (in my experience of debating these issues) they find it hard even to imagine that another theory might dispense with it.

The crucial questions for distinguishing the two approaches are: what is the subject in a sentence like (7)? And what is it the subject of?

(7)   Hungry cows eat grass.

According to dependency grammar, the subject is the noun *cows*, and it's the subject of the verb *eat*; as for *hungry*, this depends (as a 'modifier') on *cows*. Informally, we can say that *hungry cows* is a phrase, but that's just another way of saying that they're linked by a dependency and there's no question of treating this phrase as a separate element in the sentence structure.

In contrast, phrase structure does recognize *hungry cows* as a separate elem-ent, which can informally be described as 'the subject' because it's part of the larger phrase which we call 'the sentence'. Consequently, even in this informal terminology it's the subject of the sentence, and not of the verb. Each of the extra elements is a phrase, so phrases are a crucial part of the whole analysis; for example, phrase structure grammarians have a classification which parallels that of words, so *hungry cows* is a noun phrase and *eat grass* is a verb phrase. Consequently, the structure is normally shown as a tree whose nodes carry cat-egory labels, as shown in Figure 7.2 on the next page.

This figure contrasts the two analyses even more starkly, and (in my opinion) clearly to the credit of the dependency analysis in (a). Not only is this much sim-pler, but it avoids one of the side effects of the phrase-structure approach which is called 'unary branching' – phrases which have just one part.

The example of unary branching in the diagram is *grass*, which has to be treated not only as a word, but also as a phrase which has just one part. Why? Because *grass* is syntactically similar not only to the noun *cows*, but also to the noun phrase *hungry cows*. Like *cows*, it can be modified by an adjective as in *sweet grass*, but like *hungry cows* it can be used as the subject as in *Grass tastes good*. If this sentence shows that the subject is a noun phrase, then *grass* must be a noun phrase.

Where dependency analysis and phrase structure analysis agree is in recogniz-ing that words are held together by unequal relations. In phrase structure terms,

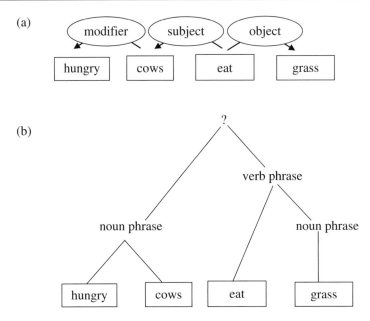

Figure 7.2 *Two syntactic analyses of* Hungry cows eat grass.

every phrase has a **HEAD**, the word to which all its other parts are subordinate and which decides how the whole phrase is classified: if the head is a noun, the phrase is a noun phrase, if it's a verb the phrase is a verb phrase, and so on.

But if *cows*, as the head of *hungry cows*, decides what kind of phrase this is, why do we need the phrase as well as the head word? According to dependency grammar, the phrase node is simply redundant. All we need to say is that *cows*, with *hungry* as its dependent, is the subject (of *eat*).

7.1.5   Evidence for dependencies and dependency distance ▮▮▮▮

The trouble with the phrase structure analysis is not so much that it forces analysts to recognize extra nodes for phrases, but rather that there is no evidence for these extra nodes other than the assumptions of phrase structure which rule out structures more sophisticated than part–whole relations. If our minds can cope with rich relational concepts outside language, why not in syntax too?

In contrast, the dependency approach is supported by a great deal of other evidence showing that the crucial relations in syntax are those between individual words, and not those which involve phrases; in fact, phrase nodes make analysis harder, not easier (Hudson 2007c: 117–30).

For example, it's common for one lexeme to select another – so the verb DEPEND selects the preposition ON (not OF or FROM), OUGHT selects TO (not just a bare infinitive), AT selects WORK (as in *at work*, but not OFFICE in **at office*), in French ALLER ('go') selects the auxiliar ÊTRE ('be') instead of the usual AVOIR ('have'), and so on. In dependency structure these words are all related directly to one another so the selection relations are not only easily stated but mentally plausible; but in phrase structure there's always at least one phrase node between the words, so the selection applies across two or more part–whole links. Why should one concept affect a concept which is so indirectly related to it? In fact, doesn't the selection constitute evidence for the direct link which phrase structure denies?

A very different kind of evidence comes from psycholinguistic measures of memory load, which show that the load increases with the length of a dependency (measured in terms of the number of intervening words). In Word Grammar this measure is called **DEPENDENCY DISTANCE**.

For example, compare the two examples in (8) and (9).

(8)   He looked up the word that he wanted to write but wasn't sure he could spell.

(9)   He looked the girl that he hoped to date but wasn't sure he could name up.

I imagine you agree that (9) is much harder to read, even though the two sentences actually both contain the same number of words in the same syntactic relations.

Why? Because *up* depends on the verb, but whereas in (8) *up* is right next to *looked*, in (9) 13 words separate it from *looked*. This was a problem for you, the reader, because you had to keep *looked* in your memory throughout the time when you were reading those 13 words. For more discussion of memory load, see Section 4.2; we return to the syntactic consequences in Section 7.6.

The main point here is that dependency distance is based directly on dependency structure, but it's very hard to imagine a similar measure defined in terms of phrase structure.

7.1.6   The arguments for dependency structure

To summarize the argument, then, general cognitive theory allows relational concepts, so relational concepts are available, when needed, in every area of life including syntax. This provides a good psychological foundation for the syntactic relations that grammarians have recognized over the centuries, and there's no reason to doubt their mental reality. Nor is there any reason to doubt that what they relate is single words, whose mental reality is clear.

In contrast, phrase structure rests on the dubious psychological assumption that our minds can't cope with anything more complex than a part–whole relation, so it forces the analysis to assume 'whole' nodes (phrases) for which there's no independent evidence, and which complicate the analysis a great deal.

This is not to deny that phrase nodes may, in fact, turn out to be needed in some cases. After all, to deny this would be to commit just the same mistake as I'm pointing to in phrase structure theory – since our minds can process part–whole relations outside language, maybe they also recognize them, alongside dependencies, in syntax. I discuss some part–whole relations in Section 7.5, and there may be others; but recognizing them doesn't detract from the main claim of Word Grammar, which is that dependencies between individual words can support all the common patterns for which other theories assume that phrases are necessary.

7.1.7   Adjuncts and valents in inheritance

Suppose, then, that we recognize dependency relationships between individual words as claimed in dependency grammar, and that the different dependencies form a taxonomy which includes the traditional syntactic relations such as 'subject' and 'object'. Can we say anything general, applying to all languages, about the dependencies that are likely to be needed?

This is a very controversial area of syntactic theory, but there is at least one contrast that's almost bound to be relevant to every language simply because of the way that the logic of inheritance works. This is the contrast between what are called **ADJUNCTS** and other dependents (for which I'll introduce a term below).

Here's a simple example to illustrate the contrast:

(10)   Charlotte moos frequently.

Both *Charlotte* and *frequently* depend on *moos*, and in both cases the dependency can be inherited from the grammar, but inheritance applies differently because *moos* needs *Charlotte*, but merely tolerates *frequently*. To see the difference, consider these two variations on (10).

(11)   *Moos frequently.
(12)   Charlotte moos.

The ungrammatical (11) shows how badly *moos* needs its subject. English present-tense and past-tense verbs have to have an audible subject. In Italian or Spanish, the subject is optional; but not in English. In contrast, (12) is just as grammatical as (10), which shows that *frequently* is merely an optional extra – an adjunct.

The difference between subjects such as *Charlotte* and adjuncts such as *frequently* illustrates a rather obvious characteristic of how relations are inherited. A relation is a property of both the related entities; for instance, if Gretta is my mother, this can be seen as a property either of Gretta (being my mother) or of me (having Gretta as my mother). But in terms of inheritance, the two entities typically play unequal parts. In your mind, I inherit a mother from the universal fact that everyone has a mother; but Gretta doesn't inherit motherhood in this way, because not every woman is a mother.

The same inequality is found in the inheritance of dependencies between words. Although both *Charlotte* and *frequently* depend on *moos*, *Charlotte*'s

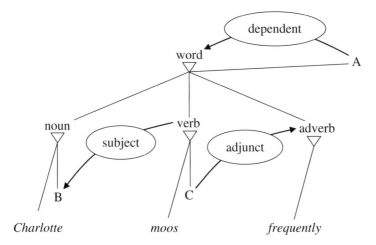

Figure 7.3 *The difference between subjects and adjuncts in a simple example*

dependency is inherited mainly from *moos* but *frequently*'s is inherited mainly from *frequently* itself. The relevant facts are laid out in Figure 7.3.

What this figure shows is that each of the dependencies in (10) is inherited from the two words concerned, but in different proportions:

- *Charlotte* inherits (from 'word') the need for some other word (A) to depend on.
- *moos* inherits (from 'verb') the need for a subject (B), which isA noun and therefore could be *Charlotte*.
- *frequently* inherits (from 'adverb') the need for some verb (C, such as *moos*) to depend on.

In other words, the subject dependency 'comes from' the verb, its parent, whereas the adjunct dependency 'comes from' the adverb, its dependent.

7.1.8   The logical difference between valents and adjuncts ▬▬▬

The example shows the two logical possibilities for inheriting a dependency. Every dependency is inherited by the dependent, at least to the extent that by default every word depends on some other word (A in Figure 7.3). For adjuncts that's enough, though there may be some restriction on the kind of parent that's possible. Notice that C is merely some verb, not the typical verb, so a verb doesn't inherit the adjunct dependency.

The other possibility is illustrated by the subject, which is a property of the typical verb and therefore inherited by every verb. The same is true for objects, such as *grass* in *Cows eat grass*; and more generally for a large range of dependency types that are inherited from the parent as well as from the dependent.

Unfortunately there's no widely accepted general term for dependencies that are inherited from the parent, but dependency theory uses the term **VALENCY** for this property of verbs (Allerton 2006); this area of grammar is the topic of the next section. For example, MOO is said to have a valency of one (including the subject), whereas EAT has a valency of two. The term builds on the theory of 'valency' or 'valence' in chemistry which explains how atoms bond to one another. (Wikipedia: 'Valence (chemistry)'.)

This terminology lies behind the Word Grammar term **VALENT** for any dependent that's inherited from the parent. Since the distinction between valents and adjuncts is merely a matter of logic, it's applicable to every language. Moreover, it plays an important part in the grammars of some languages. In English, for example, valents tend to be closer to their parent than adjuncts, giving contrasts like that between (13) and (14).

(13)   Charlotte eats grass frequently.
(14)   *Charlotte eats frequently grass.

On the other hand, we can't necessarily assume that it's equally important in every language's grammar, nor indeed that it has the same effects even where it is important.

Figure 7.4 summarizes by showing the beginnings of a taxonomy of dependencies for a language such as English. This taxonomy will be expanded in the discussion of the dependencies of English (11.2).

Where next?

Advanced: Part III, Chapter 11.1: Dependencies
Novice: Part III, Chapter 11.2: Valency

7.2   Valency

If we adopt the ideas of section 7.1 (which are summarised in 11.1), syntax is very simple, and remarkably similar to social structure.

Words are gregarious, so each word needs to occur in the company of other words; but simply being next to other words isn't enough. Words, like people, build quite specific 'social' relations with some of the words near to them, and none at all with others; these relations are the dependencies introduced in Section 7.1. Moreover, different words have different social needs, and once again the differences are quite specific and generally clear.

And finally, the needs of different words complement one another neatly so that they can satisfy one another's needs perfectly. For example, IN needs a complement noun, and LONDON needs a parent, so if we combine them to make *in London*, each of the words has its needs satisfied. Syntactic structure is the network of dependencies between words which satisfies their mutual needs; and syntax is the area of grammar which holds all the information about dependency needs.

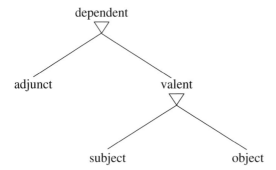

Figure 7.4 *A general taxonomy of dependencies*

The main point about this picture is that syntax consists of nothing but individual words and their relations to other individual words, in just the same way that we may see human society as consisting of nothing but individuals and their relations to one another. Hence, of course, the name of this theory: 'Word Grammar'.

A different analogy lies behind the term **VALENCY** which I introduced in the previous section. In this case, the model for syntax is the chemical 'valency' of atoms which describes their 'social needs' in terms of what other atoms they need to combine with. A word's valency is the set of dependencies that it needs to be involved in and which link it to other words in the same sentence.

Traditionally, these needs are viewed only as a need for dependents (and more precisely, given the terminology of the previous section, for 'valents'), but a word also needs a parent so it would be more logical to include these needs as well. With that extension, then, the study of valency covers almost the whole of syntax, with the exception of coordination and similar structures discussed in Section 7.5.

If we know that every word in a sentence has both the parent that it needs and also the dependents that it needs, and that these dependencies all have the properties that we expect them to have (e.g. in terms of word order), then we can be sure that the sentence's syntax is fine – in technical grammatical terms, that the words are all grammatical (6.4) and the sentence's structure is **WELL-FORMED**.

7.2.1   Parent-valency and sentence roots

But however simple syntax is at the most general level, there is more to be said when we consider the details. Let's start with the need for parents, what we may call **PARENT-VALENCY**.

In principle every word needs a parent, because that's what we expect; so if I say to you simply *Very*, or *Bill*, you look for a parent and, not finding one, look for an explanation. In more formal terms, a word's parent has a default quantity of one, so we're expecting precisely one exemplar – not more, and not less.

Admittedly we can and do say isolated words like this, but only in a context which supplies a parent, such as the question *Are you tired?* or *Who did it?* In the absence of a context like this, we can't use *very* or *Bill* without giving it a parent – *Bill did it* or whatever.

However, the general principle produces a logical problem: if every word needs a parent, how can a sentence ever be grammatically complete? The fact is, of course, that sentences are (by definition) grammatically complete; so every time I put a full stop I'm indicating that no more words are needed to satisfy any word's valency. This is possible because certain words are exceptions to the need for a parent.

In English, the main exceptions are finite verbs (10.2), verbs which either have a tense (past or present) or are imperative; so in (1) and (2), the verbs *believed* and *believe* have no parent, and don't need one.

(1)   They believed me.
(2)   Believe me!

A useful name for such words is **SENTENCE ROOT**, meaning the word on which all the other words ultimately depend. (The terminology invokes the metaphor of a sentence as a plant or tree with words as roots, branches, twigs or leaves, according to the dependency structure.)

Formally, the quantity of potential sentence roots is either zero or one; so we're surprised neither if they have one nor if they don't. In contrast, non-finite verbs do need a parent just like other words; so *believing* can't be used without a parent:

(3)   *Believing me.

In short, we have a generalization (that every word needs a parent), to which there are exceptions – a very familiar cognitive pattern which can easily be accommodated by default inheritance.

Figure 7.5 shows how this little grammar applies to sentence (1), where the sentence root *believed* has no parent (shown by the '0' at the top of the vertical arrow); we'll use the vertical arrow in later diagrams to show the potential dependency of the sentence root. As explained in Section 4.6, the dotted isA lines show the 'super-isA' relation, via a chain of isA links rather than just a single one.

7.2.2   Why finite verbs are special

You may wonder why language is organized like this. Why do words need parents, and why are finite verbs an exception? Why restrict words in this way, and if there are to be exceptions, why not treat, say, prepositions as the exception?

Similar questions arise for all areas of valency: are the facts of valency just arbitrary linguistic facts, rather like the fact that the word for 'table' is feminine

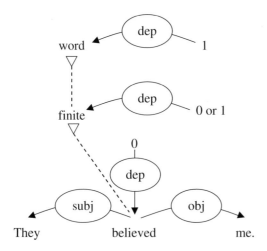

Figure 7.5 *Typical words need a parent, but finite verbs don't*

in French and masculine in German, or are they motivated by the jobs for which we use the words concerned?

Where we can find functional explanations we should of course welcome them, and in many cases this is possible. In the case of syntactic parents, most words need a parent because their meanings don't give the listener enough guidance; for example, *Bill* just guides the listener's mind to the concept 'Bill', but in most contexts that's not enough and leaves the listener asking 'OK, what about him?'

Finite verbs, on the other hand, make a natural exception because their meaning includes what is called an **ILLOCUTIONARY FORCE** which guides the listener; so if I say to you *Bill has died*, you know that this is a new property of Bill that I am inviting you to add to your memory. (Wikipedia: 'Illocutionary act'.) Similarly, the finite verbs in *Has Bill died?* and *Remember me!* each carry the illocutionary force for a question and a command. It seems, therefore, that the facts of parent valency are quite natural consequences of the ways in which we use the words concerned.

Another very general point about valency that arises from this discussion of parents is that valency facts may have any degree of generality, ranging from facts that apply to every word to facts that only apply to a single lexeme or sublexeme. For parents, the main generalization applies to the most general class of all, 'word': a typical word needs a parent. However, this isn't all that valency can say about parents, because a word may be fussy about its parent. Some words only accept parents that belong to certain word-classes; for example, VERY will only depend on an adjective or adverb (as in *very big* or *very soon*, but not **very admire*), whereas REALLY allows parents of any of these classes (*really big, really soon, really admire*), though not a noun (**really surprise* – compare *real surprise*).

7.2.3   Dependent-valency

Turning now to the other kind of valency, **DEPENDENT-VALENCY**, this is the valency that decides what dependents a word needs or allows; which means, of course, that it concerns valents rather than adjuncts.

This valency tends to be more complicated because whereas words typically have just one parent, they often have more than one valent; and partly in order to distinguish these valents from one another, words usually impose more or less rigid restrictions on them in terms of one or more of the properties listed below:

- word-class – e.g. the object of DISCUSS is a noun (as in *discuss linguistics*, but not **discuss that it was raining*);
- quantity – e.g. the object of DISCUSS is obligatory, so its quantity is one, whereas that of, say, SING is optional, with a quantity of either zero or one;
- inflection – e.g. in some languages a verb's valents have different **CASES** (6.5) shown by the noun's inflectional morphology: 'nominative' case for the subject and 'accusative' for the object. The examples in (4) and (5) are from Latin, where case is much more important than word order for distinguishing subjects and objects:

(4)   Homo feminam vidit.
        nominative accusative verb
        man woman saw
        'The man saw the woman.'

(5)   Hominem femina vidit.
        accusative nominative verb
        man woman saw
        'The woman saw the man.'

- word order – e.g. in English the subject typically precedes the verb whereas the object typically follows it;
- lexeme – e.g. SPEND requires one valent to be ON (which in turn, of course, needs a complement noun, as in *spend money on books*);
- meaning – e.g. PUT requires a valent such as *into the box* which defines a place;
- semantic role – e.g. the subject of LIKE refers to the 'like-er', the person who has the feeling, and its object refers to the 'like-ee', the thing that causes the feeling.

7.2.4   Valency as a guide to meaning

The last restriction is the crucial one, because the whole system is designed to guide the hearer to an interpretation in which it's clear how each valent's meaning fits into the meaning of the whole. In principle at least, each valent of a particular word corresponds to just one property of that word's meaning, and the different restrictions on different valents help hearers to distinguish them.

For example, take the subject of the English verb SEE. Suppose I tell you that I saw you; who saw who and how do you know? You know that the 'see-er' was me, and you know this because this is the semantic role of the subject of SEE, and you know that *I* is the subject because of its word order (before the verb) and its form (*I*, rather than *me*).

7.2.5   How to inherit a valent

One complication is that the various restrictions on a single valent may derive from different generalizations applied at different levels in the taxonomy. For example, take the preposition OF, which takes a single **COMPLEMENT** (another grammatical relation; for the name, think how the noun 'completes' the valency) as in *of books*. This complement has to be a noun, and it can't be omitted, so (6) is fine but (7) and (8) are not:

(6)   I was dreaming of books.
(7)   *I was dreaming of she left me.
(8)   *I was dreaming of.

Although these two facts apply to the same tokens, they're inherited from different levels of the taxonomy. The one about being a noun is a general fact about prepositions, whereas the one about not being omitted comes from lower down the taxonomy, maybe even from the lexeme OF itself. The fact is that many prepositions have complements which can be omitted; for example, this is true of IN as in (9) and (10).

(9)   I left the key in the lock.
(10)   I put the key in the lock and left it in.

Similarly, the generalizations about different valents may be inherited from different sources. Take the subject and object in *He liked her*. The verb *liked* isA two general categories: 'past tense' and the lexeme LIKE, each of which contributes one of the valents. As we saw earlier (7.1.7), past-tense verbs have to have a subject (*Liked it*), so the subject comes from the inflection. In contrast, the object comes from the lexeme LIKE, which always needs an object. Consequently, a token of 'LIKE, past' inherits its object from LIKE, and its subject from 'finite verb'.

None of this is problematic or surprising given what we know about multiple inheritance, but it prepares us for a certain amount of complexity in the area of valency.

7.2.6   Syntactic triangles

One particularly important and interesting complication in valency is where valents form themselves into a little three-sided network.

Outside language, we have already seen this kind of pattern in kinship systems where one relation is defined in terms of two simpler relations; for example, my grandmother is someone who is the mother of one of my parents (Figure 3.7 in Section 3.2). It's hardly surprising, therefore, that we find the same pattern in valency.

Consider an auxiliary verb such as HAVE in a sentence like (11).

(11)   He has swum.

We know that *he* is the subject of *has* because the latter needs a subject because of its inflection. We also know that *swum* depends on *has* because we can omit *swum* but not *has* (giving *He has* but not **He swum*). More precisely, *swum* is a valent of *has*.

So far, then, we have recognized two dependencies: *he* is the subject of *has* and *swum* is its valent. But there's also a third dependency which needs to be recognized: *swum* refers to an activity in which there's a swimmer, who (in this sentence) is obviously the person referred to as 'he'.

You may think this is something which can be left to the semantics, but that's not so. Consider (12).

(12)   There was an accident.

In this case, the subject of *was* is *there*; in case you doubt this, just consider the question which we form, in the regular way, by putting the subject after the verb (as in *Has he swum?*). For (12), the question is (13), so *there* must be the subject.

(13)   Was there an accident?

And why do we find *there* in (12)? Because the verb BE allows it as a meaning-less subject that allows the expected subject (*an accident*) to be moved towards the end of the sentence. The crucial point here is that *there* is allowed only because of the valency of BE – a matter of pure syntax, not semantics, because *there* has no meaning of its own. This gives an important test for a subject link: if *there* is used as a meaningless subject, it must be the subject of the verb BE.

Now consider (14).

(14)   There has been an accident.

Once again we have *there* and a form of BE, just as in (12), but in this case *there* must be the subject of *has*. (Once again, if you doubt this, consider the question *Has there been an accident?*) On the other hand, the new test for a subject link shows that the meaningless *there* has to be the subject of a form of BE.

The only possible conclusion is that *there* in (14) is the subject of *been* as well as of *has*. This provides purely syntactic evidence that leads to the same conclusion as the purely semantic evidence from (11), *He has swum*, where I argued that *he* must be the subject of both the verbs, of *swum* as well as *has*, because 'he' is the swimmer.

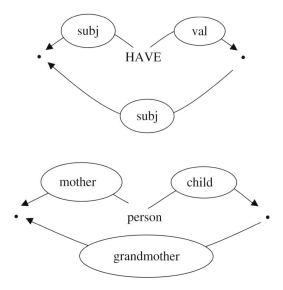

Figure 7.6 *A triangle in syntax and in kinship*

More generally, then, the valency for the auxiliary HAVE is not just a collection of separate dependencies, but a network of interconnected dependencies in which three relations (two subjects and a valent) form a **TRIANGLE** in which one word has two parents. To show how similar this cognitive structure is to the one in kinship that we noted earlier, they are shown together in Figure 7.6. In words, HAVE's subject is also its valent's subject, just as a person's mother is also their child's grandmother.

What's more, the syntactic pattern shows the same possibilities of recursion as the kinship patterns discussed in Section 3.2. My child is my descendant, but so is my child's child, and so on recursively. In just the same way, if I was a verb then my subject would be the subject not only of my valent, but also of my valent's valent and so on and on until we run out of suitable valents.

The cognitive triangle plays an important role in modern syntax. It's the equivalent in Word Grammar of a process called **RAISING** in more mainstream theories (Dubinsky and Davies 2006). Raising is found not only in English auxiliary verbs, but in many other verbs (e.g. TEND), including some (e.g. EXPECT) where the word with two parents is object of one verb and subject of the other, as in *I expect it to rain*. What's more, it's not only found in English but in many other languages too, and not only in verbs but also in other word-classes (notably adjectives such as LIKELY). Section 11.2 includes more about the role of triangles in valency. The same triangle is even found outside valency altogether in the structures created by putting an element in a position other than its default position, as I explain in Section 7.6. Triangles, then, provide a mechanism in Word Grammar for explaining syntactic patterns which most modern theories explain in roughly similar ways.

On the other hand, I have to admit that triangles are also rather controversial in the world of dependency grammar, where most theories make the attractively simple assumption that each word has just one parent. In this world, dependency triangles are impossible because they allow a word to have two parents (as *he* does in my analysis of *He has swum*). Needless to say, these theories have to provide some other mechanism for handling raising which (in my opinion) turns out to be less attractive.

> ### Where next?
>
> Advanced: Part III, Chapter 11.2: Valency
> Novice: Part III, Chapter 11.3: Features, agreement and unrealized lexemes

7.3   Morpho-syntactic features, agreement and unrealized words

> ### Summary of Section 3.3:
>
> - Some concepts are mutually exclusive, so they combine to present a **choice**: for example, a person may be either male or female, but not both.
> - A choice is defined by a **choice set**, a collection whose members exclude one another. The members of a choice set have the relation to it called '**or**', so if two concepts are related by 'or' to the same set, they're mutually exclusive. Conventionally, the notation for 'or' is an arrow with a diamond at its base.
> - A **feature** is an abstract quality such as colour, age or sex which allows comparisons.
> - Two choices may apply to members of the same superclass, in which case they are said to **cross-classify** its members.

7.3.1   Morpho-syntactic features and agreement

Features are very familiar in traditional grammatical descriptions, where they have names such as 'gender', 'number', 'case' and 'tense'.

In learning German, for example, you would learn that any German noun token has a gender (masculine, feminine or neuter), a number (either singular or plural) and a case (nominative, accusative, genitive or dative). A great deal of effort goes into learning how to inflect nouns to show these distinctions; for example, the dative singular of MANN (meaning 'man') is *Manne*, and the dative plural is *Männern*.

A familiar sight in a grammar of such a language is a table in which the options are laid out so as to show how these choices cross-classify the words concerned. Table 6.2 in Section 6.5 shows how the inflections of two typical Latin nouns are cross-classified for case and number, and Table 6.3 does the same for a French verb, showing cross-classification by the subject's person and number. Such tables are traditionally called **PARADIGMS**, after the Greek word for 'model', because they provide typical models of inflectional changes.

Needless to say, the table format is at its most useful when there are just two cross-classifying choices, such as number and case, or number and person. In an ideal world the number of choices should be matched by the number of dimensions in the table, with three intersecting choices (e.g. number, case and gender) displayed in a three-dimensional table, and so on; but more or less effective ways have been found over the ages for making the best of the mere two dimensions of paper.

These distinctions are often called **MORPHO-SYNTAX** because inflections are the meeting point between morphology and syntax. For example, morphology deals with the structural difference between {book} and {{book}{s}}, while syntax recognizes the 'plural' inflection and discusses the syntactic and semantic peculiarities of plural nouns.

Following this terminology, contrasts such as gender, number and case are often called **MORPHO-SYNTACTIC FEATURES**. For example, the feature 'number' has two possible **VALUES**, 'singular' and 'plural'. The obvious question is how this way of classifying nouns in terms of a feature with two values relates to the one I introduced in Section 6.5, where the default 'noun' contrasted with the inflection 'plural' – a very different analysis.

I'll return to this question below but let's start with the evidence for features. Given that we already have a satisfactory way of distinguishing singular and plural nouns, why do we need to recognize the feature 'number' at all?

The answer lies in the earlier discussion of features in other areas of cognition (3.3), where features are used in comparisons. If I generalize that my shoes always have the same colour, I'm using the feature 'colour' in order to pick out just one of my shoes' many properties as the basis for a general comparison. The same is true in language. Morpho-syntactic features are used for comparisons, and it is comparisons that provide the only evidence for their reality.

The comparisons in question are those required by rules of **AGREEMENT**. For instance, the determiners THIS and THAT are said to 'agree' in number with their complement noun, so we have *this book* and *these books* but not **this books* or **these book*.

If we can refer directly to the feature 'number', as the choice between 'singular' and 'plural', then this rule is very easy to express: we just say that the determiner and its complement 'have the same number' – either both are singular, or both are plural. This comparison is just as natural and straightforward as the one you make when you check that your shirt and your tie have matching colour, and so on through myriad 'agreement' rules in everyday life, all of which involve some feature.

But without the option of referring to a feature, agreement is virtually impossible to state in a natural way. It's true that we could still express the rule that a singular determiner is followed by a singular complement noun and a plural determiner by a plural one. But if we're spelling out the details in this way, it would be just as easy to require a plural complement after a singular determiner. An agreement rule such as 'determiners agree in number with their complements' makes much more sense of the facts than does a simple listing of the alternative combinations: 'singular + singular' or 'plural + plural'.

This argument becomes even more persuasive as the facts become more complicated. In languages such as German, determiners also agree with their complement nouns, but agree in terms of number, gender and case (for example, *the man* is translated as *der Mann* in the nominative and *dem Manne* in the dative).

7.3.2   Features and taxonomies

Let's assume, then, that agreement rules provide solid evidence for morpho-syntactic features such as 'number', 'gender' and 'case'. How does this way of classifying words relate to the taxonomies that we've assumed so far?

The first point is that features are only relevant to those word-class distinctions that are mentioned in agreement rules. English probably has just two such rules, both of which mention just one feature: number. The rules are the one for determiners responsible for *this book* and *these books*, and the one for agreement between verbs and their subjects which allows *they are* and *he is* but not **they is* or **he are*.

These two agreement rules both confirm 'number' as a feature of nouns, and maybe of verbs too, but they say nothing about all the other word-classes and inflections. For instance, there would be no point in introducing a feature 'word-class' to contrast nouns, verbs and so on for the simple reason that it would never do any work; and the same would be true even for the contrast between past and present verbs. This is not of course to deny that the word-classes and inflections are needed; what I am denying is that we need to combine them into features.

My conclusion, therefore, is that the taxonomy is basic, and features are quite marginal. In English there may be just one morpho-syntactic feature (number), and if a language had no agreement rules at all, it would also have no features. In contrast, taxonomies exist in every language. This is the reverse of the view found in many of the alternatives to Word Grammar, where features are used instead of a taxonomy.

The Word Grammar view of features, then, is that they are an optional addition to a taxonomy. But precisely how do they combine with the existing taxonomy? How, in English, does the feature 'number' relate to the taxonomic categories 'noun' and 'plural'?

The answer is that features are simply properties of the words classified, along with meanings, realizations and so on.

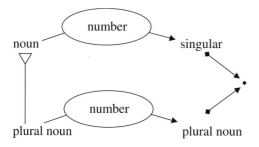

Figure 7.7 *Plural nouns have exceptional plural number*

Take the word *books*, for example. In terms of the taxonomy, this both isA 'common noun' and 'plural'; but its properties include its realization {{book} {s}}, its meaning 'set of books' and its plural number. In contrast, the properties of *book* are {book}, 'book' and singular number.

But notice that although *book* has a number which we can call 'singular', it does not belong to an inflection called 'singular'; it's simply a default noun. In terms of features, 'singular' and 'plural' are equal and competing alternatives; but in terms of the taxonomy, the concepts are not equal. Plural nouns are 'marked' (as explained in Section 6.5), in contrast with the default singulars.

We need to be careful with terminology. If we call the inflection 'plural', we can't use the same term for the value of the number feature, because the value of a feature isn't a word-class, but simply an abstract concept without other properties. In contrast with the 'plural' feature value, therefore, I'll call the inflection 'plural noun'.

Using this terminology, then, nouns have the number 'singular' by default, and the 'plural' of plural nouns is one of their exceptional properties. This analysis is shown in Figure 7.7, where the diamond-based arrows show that 'singular' and 'plural' constitute a choice set.

7.3.3   Unrealized lexemes

Agreement rules play a much more active part in the grammar of some other languages than they do in English, and in those languages they provide important evidence about the nature of syntactic structure. One of the main controversies in syntactic theory where agreement is relevant concerns what traditional grammar called 'understood' elements, words which aren't actually audible or visible but whose presence can be 'felt' in some way.

To take a simple example, consider an imperative such as *Hurry!* What is its subject? One possible answer is that it simply hasn't got one; although we know that the hurrying up is to be done by the person currently being spoken to (the addressee), that information is all in the semantics, so there's no need to duplicate it by pretending that there's a subject in the syntactic structure. In short, it looks like a one-word sentence, and that's precisely what it is. This is analysis (a) in Figure 7.8.

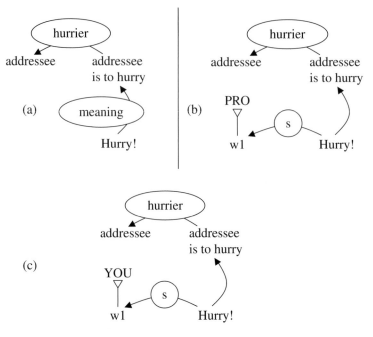

Figure 7.8 *Three alternative analyses of the imperative* Hurry!

Another possibility, though, is that *hurry* has a 'hidden' subject, an extra word which we can neither see nor hear but which nevertheless plays a role in the structure. This view allows two further possibilities: (b) that this hidden word is a special lexeme which is always hidden (an 'unrealizable lexeme'), or (c) that it's an ordinary lexeme which, in this sentence, happens to be hidden – an **UNREALIZED LEXEME**. If it's a special lexeme it is often called 'PRO' (for 'pronoun'), but if it's an ordinary lexeme the obvious candidate is the pronoun YOU.

The three analyses are laid out in Figure 7.8. Which of these analyses is best? The trouble is that in languages such as English there's not much overwhelming evidence for anything more complicated than analysis (a), the analysis that Word Grammar provided until about 2000. More generally, Word Grammar used to claim that syntactic structure should never recognize any words other than the ones we can actually see or hear. Analysis (b) is like the analyses which are popular in the Chomskyan tradition (Wikipedia: 'Empty category'), but for all its popularity, it has very little solid research support compared with either of the other analyses. Analysis (c) is the kind of analysis that does in fact seem to be needed in some languages.

7.3.4   Evidence from polite pronouns

Some evidence for analysis (c) comes from the way in which pronouns reflect social relations (3.4.2). Many European languages have two different pronouns meaning 'you', according to the social relations between the person concerned (the addressee) and the speaker; French is a typical example, with *tu* for addressing an intimate or subordinate such as a small child and *vous* for strangers and superiors. (The same used to be true of English, with *thou* for intimate subordinates and *you* for distant superiors.)

In French, the verb happens to distinguish these pronouns as well, so the present tense of VENIR, 'come', has *tu viens* but *vous venez*. In this case the verb obviously agrees with the subject, but it's the choice of pronoun that drives the choice of verb-form, not the other way round; in short, the pronouns provide the link between the social choice and the choice of verb-forms.

But in the imperative, the pronoun is omitted, just as in English, giving *Viens!* and *Venez!* The choice between the verb-forms follows exactly the same social rules as when the pronoun is used, but there's no pronoun to mediate the choice. In this case, we might consider an explanation for the verb choice which relates the verb forms directly to the social choices, but by far the simplest way to explain the choice of verb forms is to assume that each verb does in fact have either *tu* or *vous* as its subject, although we can't hear or see this pronoun – in other words, to assume an analysis of type (c), with the unrealized lexemes TU and VOUS.

7.3.5   Evidence from case agreement

There are other languages that provide even stronger evidence for unrealized lexemes. For example, take this sentence from Ancient Greek (Hudson 2007c: 177):

(1)   exarkései   soi   túrannon genésthai
       it-will-suffice you(dat) king(acc) to-become
       'it will be enough for you to become king'

The main point of this example is that the suffix {on} shows that the word for 'king', which is the complement of 'to-become', has accusative case. Why? Because 'to-become' has an unrealized accusative subject with which 'king' agrees. Here's the evidence for this claim.

In a simple sentence such as 'Cyrus became king', the words for 'Cyrus' and 'king' would both have nominative case, and in a more complicated one such as 'I believe Cyrus to be king' they would both be accusative because 'Cyrus' is the object of 'believe' as well as being the subject of 'to be'. Examples like these show that the complement of a verb such as 'become' agrees in case (as well as in number and gender) with the verb's subject. A nominative subject demands a nominative complement (Cyrus became king), while an accusative subject demands an accusative complement (I believe Cyrus to be king).

Another relevant fact is that if an infinitive such as 'to become' has an audible subject, then this is accusative, in contrast with the nominative subject required by a present- or past-tense verb. For example, the simple exclamation in (2) has an infinitive 'to suffer' with an accusative 'me' as its subject (Creider and Hudson 2006).

(2)   emè   tatheîn táde
       me(acc)   to-suffer this
       '(To think) that I should suffer this!'

Returning to example (1), then, why should 'king' be accusative? It can't be agreeing in case with 'you', because this word is dative. The only reasonable answer is that 'to become' must in fact have a syntactically relevant but unrealized subject with which 'king' agrees; and that because 'to become' is an infinitive, this subject is accusative. It's hard to imagine a more satisfying explanation.

Moreover, we also know that this unrealized subject must mean 'you', because sentence (1) is about the possibility of you becoming king, rather than about someone or people in general becoming king. This rules out analysis (b) in which the unrealized subject is always the same general-purpose pronoun.

Unrealized lexemes fit easily into the general theory of Word Grammar; after all, a word's realization is just one of its properties along with its meaning, its valency and so on. Thanks to default inheritance, we can recognize that typical words have a realization while allowing some exceptional words not to have one.

On the other hand, recognizing that unrealized lexemes are possible doesn't mean that we can recognize them whenever we feel like it. If linguists can't find clear evidence for an unrealized lexeme, then native speakers probably can't either. Take sentences (3) and (4), for instance.

(3)   I left before him.
(4)   I left before he left.

The mere fact that (3) can mean the same as (4) doesn't necessarily mean that (3) has an unrealized *left*; and in fact the use of *him* rather than *he* in (3) argues against any such assumption.

What we can say is that the agreement patterns found in languages with socially sensitive pronouns or case agreement (Hudson 2007c: 172–81) prove that some lexemes, in some languages, are unrealized. We shall see in 11.3 that English probably has unrealized lexemes as well, but each possible case has to be assessed on its own merits.

Where next?

Advanced: Part III, Chapter 11.3: Features, agreement and unrealized lexemes
Novice: Part III, Chapter 11.4: Default word order

7.4   Default word order

Summary of Section 3.4.3:

- When we think about where something is or when something happened, we think in terms of its relations to some other entity, called its **landmark**.

- For thinking about how something is related to its landmark, we have a range of relational concepts which are expressed by prepositions such as *in* or *after*, dedicated to spatial or temporal relations.
- In selecting a landmark, we apply the **Best Landmark Principle** which prefers landmarks that are near and easy to find ('known'); this principle guides not only our interpretation of the world, but also our own behaviour.
- In the taxonomy of relational concepts, specific relations such as 'after' isA the more general 'landmark' relation.

These general ideas about landmarks in space and time, which are based on how we see the relations between non-linguistic objects or events, provide a good basis for approaching the study of word order in syntax.

After all, if we think of words as spoken events, then we can think of their order in terms of exactly the same temporal relations such as 'before' and 'after' that we recognize in thinking about the relations between other events. Similarly, if we think of words as written objects then we use spatial relations such as 'to the left of'. For simplicity we can concentrate here on speech, avoiding complications such as the various different directions that are available for writing (left–right, right–left, top-bottom).

7.4.1   Parents as landmarks

One of the most important facts about temporal relations is that they generally treat related events as unequal partners, with one acting as the 'landmark' for the other – a coffee after the lecture, the joke during the meeting, the snow after Christmas, and so on. Exactly the same is true of words in a sentence, whose relations to one another involve the very unequal syntactic relation that we call 'dependency' between a dependent and its parent.

A particularly important source of inequality between these words is that the dependent typically treats its parent as its landmark. Consider the example in (1).

(1)   Big books about linguistics are expensive.

The dependency analysis treats *are* as the sentence root, with a parent merely potential, so this is the fixed point from which all the other words take their positions either directly or indirectly. The dependencies in this sentence are shown in Figure 7.9, with the same vertical arrow (for a potential dependency) pointing down at *are* as I used in Figure 7.5. The dependencies carry labels that are explained in Section 11.2 (see Table 11.2).

I'll go through this sentence commenting on each word's position:

- *big* takes its position from its parent, *books*. As a dependent adjective, it stands before its parent noun; in other words, *books* is its landmark, and its landmark relation to *books* is 'before'.

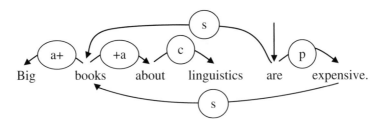

Figure 7.9 *Landmarks shadow dependencies*

- *books* takes its position from *are*. As the latter's subject, its landmark relation to it is also 'before'.
- *about* is 'after' *books* – more technically, *books* is its landmark, with the relation 'after'. *About* has this relation because it is a dependent preposition.
- *linguistics* is 'after' *about* because it's the latter's complement.
- *expensive* is 'after' *are* because it's the latter's 'predicative' (a kind of valent).

Notice how each of these words takes its parent as its landmark, and has its position relative to this landmark fixed by its dependency relation to it.

But you'll also notice that one of the dependencies has no effect on word order. This is the 'subject' link from *books* to *expensive*, which is part of a syntactic triangle (7.2). I'll explain below why this dependency doesn't carry any word-order information, but this diagram introduces a useful convention in which such dependencies are drawn below the words.

This convention for drawing non-landmark dependencies below the words allows us to simplify diagrams considerably by letting 'above-the-word' dependency arrows double as landmark relations. For instance, the arrow pointing from *books* to *big* can now be read either as a dependency (*big* depends on *book*) or as a landmark relation (*book* is the landmark of *big*, with *big* before it).

7.4.2   The continuity of phrases

Now we come to one of the most fundamental questions in syntactic theory: what holds the words in a phrase together? For example, why do the words *big books about linguistics* have to be next to each other, in contrast with other imaginable word orders such as

(2)   *Big books are expensive about linguistics.
(3)   *Big books are about linguistics expensive.

For phrase structure grammarians (7.1), the answer is simple: the words form a phrase, and phrases are by definition continuous strings of words. This notion of continuity means that the words from one phrase can't get mixed up with those from a neighbouring phrase, and it can be translated into the very simple rule

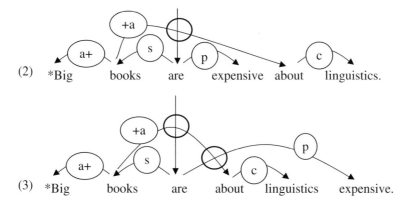

Figure 7.10 *How tangled dependencies show bad word order*

for drawing phrase-structure trees: don't let branches 'tangle'. So long as the branches in a phrase-structure tree don't cross each other, we can be sure that the phrases are continuous.

A very similar answer is possible in dependency grammar, where we can also use tangling as a symptom of a non-continuous phrase; but in this case it's the order-sensitive dependency arrows (i.e. those drawn above the words) that tangle. Figure 7.10 shows the relevant dependencies for examples (2) and (3), where the tangled dependencies are circled. Notice how the tangling in (3) is twice as bad as that in (2), which corresponds to at least my assessment of their structural badness.

But why should tangling be relevant? Because it shows that a phrase has been split by at least one word from outside the phrase; for example, in (2) the phrase *big books about linguistics* is split by *are expensive*, and in (3) by *are*. But why should phrases hang together? As with other syntactic patterns, it's worth looking for an explanation in general cognition.

The words in a phrase stay as close as possible to the phrase's head because of the Best Landmark Principle (3.4.3) which balances prominence against nearness. For instance, given a tree, a house and a church, we would use the church as landmark for the house and would only prefer the house as landmark for the tree if the house was closer than the church to the tree. One of the consequences of this principle is that as we go down a chain of landmarks, we assume that each landmark is nearer to the object located.

Let's see how this applies to words in a sentence, taking the viewpoint first of the hearer and then of the speaker. As hearers, we assume that as we go down a chain of dependencies, each landmark word is nearer to its dependents than any word higher in the chain is. In the case of our example sentence, we assume that *about* is nearer to its landmark *books* than the latter's own landmark, *are*. This is true if the order is ... *books about* ... *are*, but not in *... books are about* ... This means that as hearers we would be misled by the latter.

Now let's switch viewpoint to that of the speaker. Unlike churches, houses and trees, we're in control of the words we say and write, so it's up to us to make sure that the Best Landmark Principle is satisfied. In order to do that, we make sure that words stay as close as possible to their landmarks so as to maximize the benefits of closeness. And so long as we apply that principle, the sentences we produce will have tangle-free dependencies.

7.4.3   Word-order rules

How, then, does a language control its word order?

The least it can do is to say that a typical word is the landmark for all its dependents. Thanks to the Best Landmark Principle, this immediately guarantees that its dependents will all stick as closely to it as possible. Some languages require no more than this, which leaves dependents free to occur on either side of their parent, so long as they keep near to it (Pensalfini 2006). In such 'free-order' languages every dependent merely inherits the property of taking its parent as its landmark. If English had been a free-order language, then both (4) and (5) would have been possible ways of expressing the same meaning.

(4)   This sentence is in English.
(5)   English in is sentence this.

But most languages restrict word order to some extent, and though their restrictions vary widely, there are strong tendencies for dependencies in different kinds of phrases all to follow similar patterns (Siewierska 2006) according to whether they all precede or all follow the phrase's head (7.1).

The most common pattern is **HEAD-FINAL ORDER**, with subjects and objects before verbs, complements before prepositions (which are therefore renamed 'post-positions') and so on. In 'head-final English', (4) would be replaced by (6):

(6)   Sentence this English in is.

A much less common pattern is **HEAD-INITIAL ORDER**, with the reverse order. In 'head-initial English' we would get (7) even in statements, whereas this order is actually only found in questions:

(7)   Is this sentence in English?

Between these two patterns is one which is almost as common as head-final, where a typical word stands between two dependents. This word-order type isn't generally recognized as such, but we can call it **HEAD-MEDIAL ORDER** (a better term than 'consistently mixed' – Hudson 2007c: 161–2). English is a typical example, since every major word-class allows dependents on either side: verbs have their subjects before and their objects (and other valents) after; nouns have adjectival modifiers before and prepositional ones after; and so on.

In each of these word-order types, the general 'landmark' relation is subdivided as described in Section 3.4.3 into 'before' and 'after', and each dependency type inherits one or the other of these relations as a property. Needless to say, the logic of default inheritance also allows exceptions to the default pattern, as with the subjects of certain exceptional English auxiliary verbs (giving *is he* instead of the default *he is*). These three typical patterns are a useful introduction to the wide variety of word orders found in the world's languages, but of course there is actually a great deal more complexity than even this distinction suggests.

7.4.4   Non-landmark dependencies

The discussion so far has assumed that a word can only depend on one parent, but we've already seen (7.2) that this isn't true because some words are involved in a 'syntactic triangle' in which one word depends simultaneously on two others, as in (8).

(8)   He keeps talking.

In this example, *he* must depend as subject not only on *keeps* but also on *talking*, and *talking* depends on *keeps*. In this triangular pattern, which is extremely common in syntax, one word is shared as a dependent by two other words, so it has two parents, not just one; and the question is which of these parents it chooses as its landmark.

The shared parents always have a dependency relation that completes the triangle, with one as the landmark for the other. In (8), *keeps* is the landmark for *talking*, so we say (taking the sentence root as the 'highest' word) that *keeps* is 'higher' than *talking*. And in this example, it's very clear that the landmark for *he* is *keeps*, and not *talking*. This is the analysis shown in Figure 7.11.

The evidence for taking *keeps* rather than *talking* as the landmark of *he* includes all the normal rules for positioning subjects. One such rule requires a verb's subject to stand just before it, so *he* stands just before *keeps* (not *talking*). If the landmark for *he* had been *talking*, the sentence would have been (9) – which is of course impossible.

(9)   *Keeps he talking.

Another rule puts adverbs such as *never* between the verb and its subject. If we add *never* to (8), we get (10) rather than (11).

(10)   He never keeps talking.
(11)   *He keeps never talking.

In contrast there's no reason at all for thinking that *talking* might be the landmark for *he*.

7.4.5   The preference for raising

In this case, then, the verb which *he* selects as its landmark is the higher of the two. This is almost always true, and as already mentioned (7.2.6) the standard name for the pattern is 'raising'. It's easy to imagine the reverse pattern, in which a dependent is 'lowered' to the lower of two parents; but this hardly ever seems to happen. (For an exception in German, see Hudson 2007c: 143–4.) Why not?

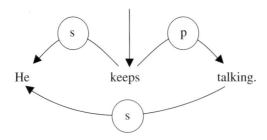

Figure 7.11 *The triangular dependencies of* He keeps talking.

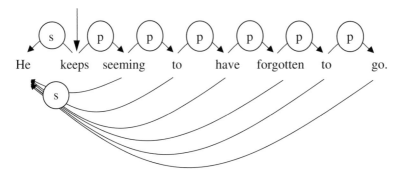

Figure 7.12 *Syntactic triangles can be multiplied freely*

Once again we may be able to explain the syntactic preference for raising in terms of the general cognitive theory of landmarks. The Best Landmark Principle favours landmarks that are better known than the object located, and it's because parents are in some sense 'better known' that they act as landmarks for their dependents. In this sense, therefore, *keeps* must be better known than its dependent *talking*. But if that's so, it must also make a better landmark than *talking* for the shared subject *he*. This explains why languages tend strongly to generalize a raising pattern as the default, though lowering may also be allowed as an exception.

The preference for raising also explains why it's so easy for syntactic triangles to apply recursively. The top triangle is the only one that counts for the position of the shared subject, so further triangles can be added freely without affecting the subject. Figure 7.12 illustrates a rather easily understood English sentence in which there are no fewer than six syntactic triangles with a series of verbs or tokens of *to* which share the same subject. This diagram also shows the benefits of drawing non-landmark dependency arrows below the words.

Where next?

Advanced: Part III, Chapter 11.4: Default word order
Novice: Part III, Chapter 11.5: Coordination

7.5   Coordination

Summary of Section 3.4.4:

- Our memory of complex events, called **episodic memory**, contains both exemplars and general **scripts** which record the typical structure of an event, including the order of events – their **serial ordering**.
- When processing experience we have to first divide it into a hierarchy of classifiable **chunks**, with smaller chunks inside larger ones; consequently, scripts are also organized hierarchically with smaller scripts inside larger ones. Each smaller chunk or script has a **part** relation to the larger script to which it belongs.
- The serial ordering of events within a script is given by the relation **next** between one event and the next.
- One particular kind of chunk is a **set**, a collection of individual **members** which allows us to ignore differences between the members and to treat them conceptually as a single unit. A set's properties are different from those of its members, and include a **set size** and a **member definition**.

One of the main claims of Word Grammar is that the basic chunks that we recognize in language are single words rather than larger phrases, and that the relations between these chunks are dependencies, which are much more abstract and much more meaningful than the 'next' relation that we find (say) between the notes in a tune or the choices made during a journey. Nevertheless, we also recognize the more 'primitive' structuring found in episodic memory, so it wouldn't be surprising if this kind of structure also played some part in language.

7.5.1   Word strings

Take the verb SAY, for example. What kind of thing can we use as the complement of this verb in 'direct speech', i.e. between quotation marks? Here are some examples:

(1)   He said, 'Hello. My name is Dick Hudson. What's yours?'
(2)   He said, 'Hello, testing testing testing. Can you hear me at the back? Testing, testing.'
(3)   He said, 'Bonjour. Je m'appelle Dick Hudson. Comment vous appelez-vous?'

These examples are very different from the 'indirect speech' in examples like (4).

(4)   He said that his name was Dick Hudson.

In this example, the complement of *said* is *that*, whose complement in turn is *was* and so on – a regular structure controlled by ordinary dependency rules. Notice how hard it is to include *Hello!* or *What's yours?* in this structure.

In contrast, direct speech allows anything at all, so long as it consists of words; the words don't have to make a complete sentence (1), they don't have to be grammatically coherent (2), and they don't even have to be in the same language as *He said* (3). In short, when SAY is used with direct speech, its complement is what we can call a **WORD STRING**, a series of words whose internal structure is completely irrelevant except for their sequential order. Given the cognitive apparatus of episodic memory, we can say that a word string is a chunk whose parts are all words, each linked by 'next' to the one after it.

Word strings play an important part in our memory. They include memorized poems, songs and jokes – anything which we remember 'verbatim', including the entire speeches that actors have to memorize. More importantly still, they include clichés, those ready-made chunks of conversation that we all trot out when we can't think of anything original to say such as *trot out a cliché*, or *Lovely weather today*, or *No comment* or *Ah well, you can't be too careful can you?* (Cowie 2006, Wray 2006). A great deal of ordinary language is stored as more or less 'formulaic' word strings; according to one estimate the number of word strings in our memories must be at least as great as the number of individual lexemes (Kuiper 2006).

But even if *you can't be too careful* is stored as a word string, it's almost certainly stored together with its ordinary dependency structure. Similarly, all the word strings used after *said* in (1) to (3) have the same dependency structures within them as they would have had if they had been used on their own. The same is, of course, true of all episodic memory – even if we remember events as a sequence of this, then this, then this, we also remember all the other structure that we impose on them in order to understand who did what when, and why. A word string, then, is a series of words which we remember as a whole, but which may also have a more or less ordinary dependency structure.

7.5.2   Coordination and dependency

Word strings are important for an area of syntax that doesn't fit comfortably into the dependency framework considered so far (or, for that matter, into the phrase-structure framework): **COORDINATION**.

In dependency structures, words have unequal status because one word is subordinate to (i.e. dependent on) another; but in coordination they act as equals. Take the example in (5).

(5)   He saw Arthur, Bill and Charles.

The three proper nouns are coordinated by *and*, which shows that they all have the same relation to the rest of the sentence, so *Arthur* shares the 'object' dependency relation with *Bill* and with *Charles*.

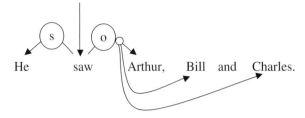

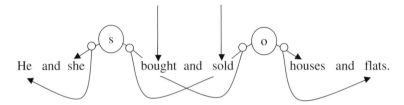

Figure 7.13 *Coordinated words share the same dependency*

Figure 7.14 *Any dependency can be shared by multiple parents or dependents*

More technically, *and* signals that the object of *saw* is a set of words whose members are the words *Arthur*, *Bill* and *Charles* (but not the word *and* itself, which is a mere signal of the set). The set can be shown in dependency notation as a small empty circle, with arrows leading from it to the members as in Figure 7.13.

We have to be careful because the members don't all have the same landmark. In (5), the first name takes its position, in the usual way, from the verb *saw*, just as it would in the simpler sentence *He saw Arthur*; but the same isn't true of the other coordinated names. The most revealing thing to say about them is that they're part of the word string *Arthur, Bill and Charles*, where *Bill* follows *Arthur* and *Charles* follows *Bill* (with *and* providing an added complication which I discuss below). This being so, although the arrow to *Arthur* stands above the words to show that the dependency also carries a landmark relation, the others must not. This is the analysis shown in Figure 7.13.

This **DEPENDENCY-SHARING** pattern is extremely general because virtually any dependency may be shared, and the sharing may affect either end of the dependency – the parent and/or the dependent. Here's a more complicated example:

(6)   He and she bought and sold houses and flats.

In this case there are just two dependencies: one subject and one object; but in each case the dependency is shared by two dependents and two parents. The structure is shown in Figure 7.14.

Notice how the notation leaves the landmark relations free of tangles in spite of the complex dependency relations due to coordination. Just two words have landmarks that derive from their dependency relations: *she* and *houses*; all the rest take their position from one of the coordinated word strings.

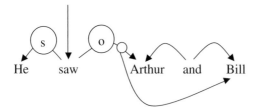

Figure 7.15 *Coordinated items depend on the conjunction*

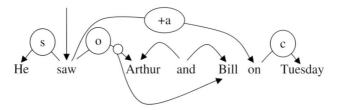

Figure 7.16 *Coordinating conjunctions have dependents but no parent*

7.5.3   Coordinating conjunctions

What about **COORDINATING CONJUNCTIONS** such as *and*, the signal of coordination? Put informally, the rule for *and* is that if two items are coordinated, they are separated by *and*; for simplicity we can ignore the slightly more complex rules for three or more coordinated items.

Somewhat more formally, the internal structure of a coordination seems to involve dependency; for example, in *He saw Arthur and Bill* the coordination is signalled, and indeed made possible, by *and*. This being so, it seems reasonable to say that each of the coordinated items depends on *and*, and also takes it as its landmark. This analysis can be seen in Figure 7.15, where you can see that *Arthur* has two landmarks. It follows *saw* by the usual dependency-based rules, but it also stands before *and*. Since *Bill* follows *and*, the result is precisely the order that we see.

On the other hand, the dependency structure is very unusual in two respects. First, the head word (*and*) has no parent; so even if the words *Arthur* and *Bill* depend on *saw*, there's no reason to believe that *and* does. This means that, like a finite verb, coordinating conjunctions have no parent; but unlike the finite verb, they have no vertical arrow in the notation because no parent is possible even in principle, so other dependencies can freely cross them. You can see this in (7).

(7)   He saw Arthur and Bill on Tuesday.

The dependency from *saw* to *on* crosses the coordinated *Arthur and Bill* just as easily as it would cross either word on its own; in short, the internal structure of the coordination is simply irrelevant to the structure of the rest of the sentence. Figure 7.16 gives the structure of (7).

7.5.4   Non-constituent coordination

The other very unusual characteristic of coordinating conjunctions is that their dependents, the 'coordinated items', aren't words – or at least, not single words. In the examples given so far, the items are all single words, but this need not be so.

The complication isn't just that the coordinated words may have dependents of their own as in (8):

(8)   He saw a man with a wheelbarrow and a boy with a hoe.

This is exactly what we would expect if the coordinated items were single words – each of the coordinated words would have the usual opportunity to have other words depending on it, so the coordinated items would in effect be entire phrases.

What makes things more complicated is that the coordinated items need not be complete phrases. For instance, the rather ordinary example in (9) hides unexpected problems for any theory that ties coordination to complete phrases.

(9)   He visited [London on Tuesday] and [Birmingham on Wednesday].

What's challenging about examples like this is that the coordinated items (enclosed in brackets) each consist of two separate dependents of the shared verb: an object (*London*, *Birmingham*) and a time adjunct (*on Tuesday*, *on Wednesday*). This pattern is often called **NON-CONSTITUENT COORDINATION** (Crysmann 2006; 'constituent' is often used to mean 'phrase'), and is an unresolved problem for most theories.

In Word Grammar, however, we can solve the problem by bringing in the notion 'word string' as defined above: a simple string of words treated as a single chunk. Even if it isn't a phrase, *London on Tuesday* is certainly a word string, and since phrases, as such, play no part in grammar, it doesn't matter whether word strings correspond to phrases or not. In principle, then, we can chop any sentence anywhere we want into two word strings, one of which we can then coordinate with another word string that shares the same relations as the first to the rest of the sentence.

As it happens, the word strings in (9) consist of two dependents of the same verb, but this need not be so; in (10), *London* depends on *to*, while *on Tuesday* depends on *went*, and in (11) even more serious mismatching of the two dependencies leads to some awkwardness but (arguably) not to ungrammaticality.

(10)   He went to [London on Tuesday] and [Birmingham on Wednesday].
(11)   He keeps his collection of paintings by [Rembrandt in the billiards room] and [Goya in the sitting room].

If the coordinated items are word strings, then so are the dependents of a coordinating conjunction; this is unusual, but not quite without precedent because as we've already seen, the verb SAY allows a word string as its complement. Figure 7.17 shows the structure for (10), with square brackets marking the

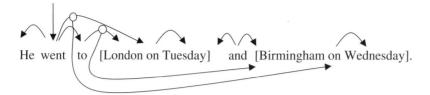

He went to [London on Tuesday] and [Birmingham on Wednesday].

Figure 7.17 *Word strings accommodate non-constituent coordination*

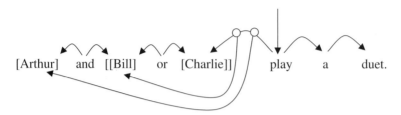

[Arthur] and [[Bill] or [Charlie]] play a duet.

Figure 7.18 *One coordination may contain another*

boundaries of the word strings. In words, the word strings *London on Tuesday* and *Birmingham on Wednesday* depend on *and*, with *London* and *Birmingham* both depending on *to* and the two tokens of *on* both depending on *went*.

7.5.5   Layered coordination

One last point about coordination is that it can be **LAYERED**, exactly as we should expect given that the 'chunks' that we impose on our experience form a hierarchy of chunks within chunks. For example, *Arthur and Bill or Charlie* is ambiguous. It could mean 'either Arthur and Bill on the one hand, or Charlie on the other', or it could mean 'Arthur, and either Bill or Charlie'. Each of these interpretations demands a structure in which one word string is part of a larger one, but of course the interpretation we choose depends on the intended meaning. For instance, (12) demands the second meaning because a duet requires two players.

(12)   Arthur and Bill or Charlie can play a duet.

In this case, the subject of *play* is the set consisting of *Arthur* and another set which contains *Bill* and *Charlie*. The layered structure can be shown using the existing notation as in Figure 7.18.

This discussion of coordination has been directed entirely at examples from English, but many other languages allow similar patterns – though it seems unlikely that they all do because there are other syntactic ways of achieving roughly the same semantic effects; for example, even in English we have alternatives to *and* which have roughly the same semantic effect but involve very different syntactic structures. Two such structures contain either *with* or *as well as*, giving (14) and (15) as rough paraphrases of (13).

(13)   John and Mary visited us.
(14)   John visited us with Mary.
(15)   John as well as Mary visited us.

In contrast with dependency structure, therefore, we can't take it for granted that every language will have coordinate structures in the English sense.

Where next?

Advanced: Part III, Chapter 11.5: Coordination
Novice: Part III, Chapter 11.6: Special word orders

7.6   Special word orders

Summary of Section 3.5:

- The **network notion** (also called **connectionism**) is the idea that knowledge consists of nothing but a **network** of atomic nodes standing for concepts whose properties are defined solely by the node's connections to other nodes.
- The network includes the taxonomies which **enrich** exemplars by linking them to increasingly general concepts, so exemplars inherit properties in the form of a copy of the relevant link (for a simple property) or the cluster of converging links (for a complex property).
- The most complicated link cluster may be a **triangular** property, where one concept is linked to two others which are directly linked to one another. Further potential complexity is avoided by applying the **Recycling Principle** of always building where possible on existing concepts.
- A **simple** default property with relation R is overridden if the exemplar already has a value for the same relation (technically, for a relation which isA R' which isA R).
- A **complex** default property is overridden if the exemplar already has a relation which is in competition with one of the relations in the property (technically, which is in a 'choice' relation to an existing relation).

These general ideas will help us in understanding how special word-order rules override the default rules described in Section 7.4. We shall also move towards an answer to the obvious question which these special rules raise: why do language users need them?

7.6.1   Different default word orders

Word order is one of the areas of grammar which varies most obviously from language to language. As we saw in Section 7.4, head-final, head-initial and head-medial languages impose more or less strict, but different, limits on the position of every dependent; and free-order languages allow dependents complete freedom of position. For example, the sentence *Cows eat grass* could be translated by sentences in which the words occur in any of the following orders:

(1)   Cows grass eat. (Head-final)
(2)   Eat cows grass. (Head-initial)
(3)   Cows eat grass. (Head-medial)

And in free-order languages any of these orders are possible. Moreover, there are even a few languages where the order of subject and object is regularly reversed, with *grass* before *cows*.

It's not just the broad details that vary; the fine details do too. For instance, English and German use word order to distinguish questions from statements (e.g. *They are here* versus *Are they here?*), whereas Italian and Spanish don't. There's a simple reason for this variation: word order is influenced by a great many competing pressures which have to be balanced against each other, and each language offers a different solution to this balancing problem. Each order has its strengths and its weaknesses.

For instance, the head-medial order of English helps us by allowing both the subject and the object to stand right next to the verb, which reduces dependency distances (7.1); but it also prevents us from putting the object or verb first. We can't say **Eat cows grass*, not even when we're talking about eating and this order might be convenient, as in the following imaginary (and grammatically impossible) phrase:

(4)   *Every animal has to eat something, but eat different animals different things – eat blackbirds worms, eat cows grass, . . .

7.6.2   Overriding default word order

Nor do our normal rules allow us to put *grass* first:

(5)   Plants have many uses – flowers decorate our gardens, grass cows eat,
         . . .

But in this case, of course, the required order is in fact permitted: *grass cows eat*. Admittedly, it sounds awkward out of context, but in context you probably wouldn't notice it. Here's a more convincing example, where *the others* is the object of *left* but stands before both this verb and its subject:

(6)   I only brought this book with me – the others I left behind because they were too heavy.

How can this be, if objects are supposed to stand after the verb?

The answer is that we have special rules which override the defaults under special circumstances. Some of these rules treat word order just like other properties that a word may have; for example, although an English verb's subject normally stands before it, the subject of an interrogative auxiliary verb follows it (as in *Have you finished?*). Given the apparatus for inheriting complex properties, such cases are straightforward and can be left to the section on English (11.6).

Other cases, however, are more complicated because they require an extra dependency to override the effect of the existing dependencies. One of the most complex cases is illustrated in example (6), where *the others* is not only the object of *left*, but also its **EXTRACTEE** – an element which is 'extracted' from its normal position.

The same pattern is more familiar in Wh questions (questions introduced by a 'Wh' pronoun such as WHO, WHAT or WHEN); for instance, *who* in (7) is the object of *met*, and would normally follow it as in *He met her*, but because *who* is a Wh pronoun, it stands before the verb.

(7)   I wonder who he met.

Who is clearly the object of *met*, as you can easily see by considering a possible answer: *He met Jane*, where *Jane* replaces *who*; but unlike *Jane*, *who* also has to be extracted from its normal position so that it can stand before the verb it depends on.

Because the Wh pronouns dominate this area of grammar, the word-order rules are often called 'Wh-movement' (Wikipedia: 'Wh-movement'); but it's important to remember that it's not just Wh pronouns that can be displaced in this way.

Returning to the simpler example of *Grass cows eat*, if *grass* is both the object of *eat* and also its extractee, we face a conflict, with 'extractee' demanding a position before the verb and 'object' demanding one after it. Clearly, the extractee wins, but why? As usual, conflicts are resolved by default inheritance, so we need the analysis in Figure 7.19.

In this diagram, the extractee relation (labelled simply 'x') and the object relation point to different nodes, each of which is a word-token which I've labelled simply *Grass* and *Grass1* in the diagram. They have exactly the same properties except that *Grass* inherits a 'before' relation to *eat* from 'extractee', in contrast with the default 'after' relation inherited by *Grass1* from 'object'. The 'before' relation wins because *Grass* isA *Grass1*. That's why I've drawn *Grass1* below the words.

In other words, an extractee link turns what is basically a post-dependent into a pre-dependent.

7.6.3   Forcing a choice between 'before' and 'after'

This analysis raises the technical question about default overriding that I discussed in Section 3.5. How do we know when two relations (such as 'before' and 'after') are alternatives? After all, the word-token *Grass* will inherit

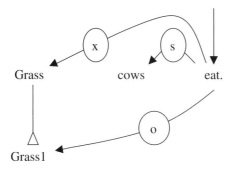

Figure 7.19 *An extracted object*

the object relation from *Grass1*, giving it two different relations to *eat*: extractee and object. So why can't it also have two different landmark relations? Why do properties with 'before' and 'after' conflict, whereas those with 'object' and 'extractee' don't?

The discussion in Section 3.5 distinguished simple properties from complex ones in which two or three relations converge. Word-order properties are complex, in this sense, because they consist of a dependency which converges with a landmark relation. For example, in Figure 7.19 the 'subject' link from *eat* to *cows* converges with a landmark relation (not shown) from *cows* to *eat*. The examples in Section 3.5 concerned the position of car motors, but the principle is exactly the same: the relation between a car and its motor involves two converging relations ('power-supply' and 'in front').

How, then, does the inheritor know when two complex properties conflict? According to Section 3.5, conflicting relations are simply listed as alternatives, using the mechanism of choice sets and the 'or' relation. In this kind of analysis, therefore, 'before' and 'after' are both linked to the same choice set, whereas 'dependent' and 'landmark', or 'subject' and 'before', are not.

To make this more concrete, Figure 7.20 represents the grammar behind the structure in Figure 7.19.

In prose, B is a pre-dependent of A, so B is before A, but since C is a post-dependent of D, C stands after it. The relations 'before' and 'after' conflict because they belong to the same choice set E; so they can't both be inherited as relations between the same pair of nodes. This matters when a word F has both an extractee relation (a kind of pre-dependent) and a post-dependent relation to the same other word, because the conflict can't be resolved. But if we distinguish the values of these relations, as two words G and H, where H isA G, the conflict is resolved in the usual way in favour of H, and H inherits B's 'before' relation rather than C's 'after' relation.

7.6.4   Long-distance dependencies

One complication which adds to the interest of extraction is that it can produce what are called either **LONG-DISTANCE DEPENDENCIES** or

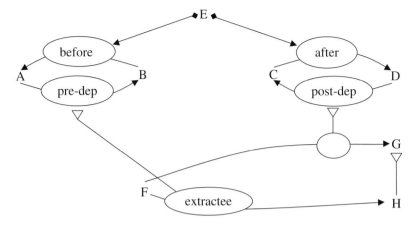

Figure 7.20 *A grammar for simple extraction*

'unbounded dependencies' (Falk 2006). The point is that the extracted item may be a long way from the word from which it is extracted.

This isn't true in *Grass cows eat*, but it is in (8), where *grass* is the object of *eat* in spite of all the intervening words.

(8)   Grass I think I read somewhere that cows eat.

Wh-movement similarly can apply across a great distance when measured in terms of dependencies. Take (9), for example:

(9)   Who do you think they said they invited?

Who is the object of *invited* but it takes its position before the root verb, *do*, which produces a long chain of dependencies between *who* and *invited*.

This long chain is made possible by a recursive rule for extractees which allows the extractee of one word to act as the extractee of that word's complement; this offers the option of applying again to that complement and so on down the dependency chain. In (9) *who* is the extractee of *do*, so it can also act as extractee of the latter's complement *think*, which provides a stepping stone to *said*, and eventually to *invited*.

Each of these extractee links produces the same kind of syntactic triangle that we found in subject-sharing, and as with these other triangles the conflicting demands of the two verbs are resolved by the Raising Principle (7.4) so that the extractee always takes its position from the highest verb – the sentence root *do*.

The structure of (9) is shown in Figure 7.21. The main point of this diagram is to show how an extracted item can take its position from one word while depending on a different word which may be a long way away.

7.6.5   Evidence for hopping

This structure may strike you as unnecessarily complicated. Granted, *who* must have some kind of relation to *do*, as well as one to *invited*, but why link

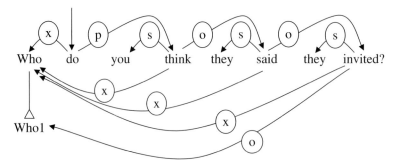

Figure 7.21 *Long-distance dependency*

it to *think* and *said* if these have no effect either on its position or on any other property? Why 'hop' from word to word rather than 'swooping' all the way from *do* to *invited*?

The reason is that each of the 'stepping stones' provides a point where the process may be halted or even blocked. At each point, the speaker has the option of using a verb such as RECOGNIZE which might accept *who* as its object instead of allowing it to hop further:

(10)   Who do you recognize?
(11)   Who do you think they recognized?

Alternatively, the process may be blocked by an inappropriate dependency link, such as an adjunct link from a noun:

(12)   *Who do you recognize the person who invited?

Not all dependencies allow an extractee to hop across them, and in (12) the link from *person* to *who* is one that doesn't. Such dependencies are called **EXTRACTION ISLANDS**, and have generated a great deal of attention in syntactic theory (Falk 2006, Hudson 1990: 354–403). These intermediate dependencies are clearly important in deciding where extraction can apply and where it can't, which is why virtually every syntactic theory adopts a 'hopping' analysis like the one offered here.

Extraction is only one example of a syntactic pattern that overrides the default word order, but other patterns can be analysed in similar ways. Section 11.6 considers some other patterns.

7.6.6   Special word orders and dependency distance

Let's return to the question with which we started this section: why do language users need these special word orders? If it's generally OK in English for the object to follow the verb, why don't we simply accept this as the only possibility? The extra flexibility provided by extraction (and other non-default patterns) must bring some benefits that offset the extra costs that can be measured in terms of extra rules and more complicated structures; but what are these benefits? To simplify discussion I'll focus on extraction.

One of the main benefits of extraction is to reduce dependency distance, the measure that I introduced in Section 7.1. Take example (7) above, which I'm repeating here for convenience:

(13=7)   I wonder who he met.

Extracting *who* has the advantage of putting it next to *wonder*, to which it has a close link because *wonder* needs a Wh-word such as *who*; for example, a mere *that* won't do after *wonder*:

(14)   *I wonder that he met her.

This 'close link' is a dependency, so *who* depends on *wonder*, and the nearer the two words are to one another, the better. Without extraction, *who* would have been separated from *wonder* by *he met*:

(15)   *I wonder he met who.

This dependency between *wonder* and *who* is confirmed by the possibility of stopping after *who*:

(16)   Apparently he met someone last night; I wonder who.

The only possible conclusion is that *who* depends on *wonder*, which leaves *met* to depend on *who* – a nice example of **MUTUAL DEPENDENCY** given that *who* also depends on *met* as its object. (Section 11.6 explores and justifies this analysis in more detail.)

Now given all these assumptions about dependencies, it turns out that (15) is not only unhelpful, but structurally impossible. Figure 7.22 shows the structures for the good (13), with extraction, and the impossible (15), without it.

What's wrong with (15)? First, it's simply not grammatical because *met* comes before *who*, which can't be justified by either of the dependencies between these mutually dependent words. One of these relations must provide the landmark relation that we need. Suppose it's the complement relation (as shown in the top diagram); this won't work because *met* is the complement of *who*, so *met* should come second. Now suppose the landmark relation comes from the object dependency (as in the bottom diagram); this gives the right word order (verb – object), but leaves *met* without a landmark. As you can see, the dependency drawn above the words implies that *met* takes its position from its dependent, contrary to the general principle that landmarks are parents.

The other problem with (15) is its dependency distance. Compared with (13), it has a much longer distance (two separating words) between *who* and *wonder*. In this example, therefore, extraction kills two birds with one stone: it reduces dependency distance, and it avoids a structure which conflicts with basic principles of word order.

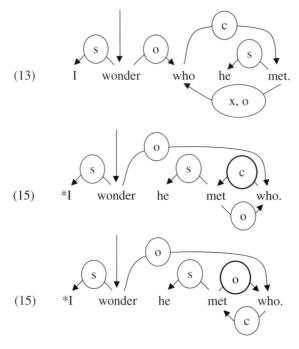

Figure 7.22 *Subordinate questions with and without extraction*

7.6.7   Functional explanations for syntactic facts

What about simpler examples like *Grass cows eat*? How does extraction benefit us as language users? Consider again the more convincing example (6), repeated here:

(17=6)   I only brought this book with me – the others I left behind because they were too heavy.

In this case there's no benefit in terms of dependency; but there is a cognitive benefit in terms of reduced memory load. The relevant words are *this book* and *the others* (meaning, of course, 'the other books'). The latter can only be understood in relation to the former, so they both need to be available in working memory at the same time. The role of working memory is discussed more fully in Section 4.2, but it's quite easy to see that *the others* will be easier to understand (and to produce) if it occurs soon after *this book*.

What these examples have in common is that the structural complexities of extraction are outweighed by clear cognitive benefits; in other words, there's a **FUNCTIONAL EXPLANATION** for the structures found in the grammar (Butler 2006). The function of language is communication, and its structure has evolved to optimize the efficiency of communication. We should be grateful to our linguistic ancestors for developing it into such a user-friendly tool.

Where next?

Advanced: Part III, Chapter 11.6: Special word orders
Novice: You've 'finished'. Congratulations!

7.7   Syntax without modules

Summary of Section 3.6:

- Perceptual systems such as vision and hearing are probably **modules** which are:
  - specialized for particular tasks
  - insulated from information coming in from other parts of the mind
  - fixed genetically.
- Some researchers also argue for **modularity** and **nativism** in cognition on the grounds that brain damage affects different parts of cognition according to which part of the brain is damaged. However, these arguments are weak because:
  - the damage never applies exactly to one supposed module and nothing else
  - a cognitive network, without modules, has enough structure to explain the observed effects in terms of a tendency for related nodes to be stored near to one another in the brain.
- A further argument against modularity and nativism is that cognitive networks have '**hub**' nodes which are extremely richly connected to other nodes and which would therefore have widespread effects if damaged.
- **Cognitive linguistics**, which includes Word Grammar, rejects modularity and nativism in the study of language and tries to analyse language in terms of the same general principles that apply to the rest of cognition.

Those who support modularity and nativism often treat syntax as the 'core' module, the area where language is the most clearly different and autonomous. (Wikipedia: 'Universal Grammar'.) In this section we shall briefly consider these two ideas of difference and autonomy. I shall suggest that syntax is in fact neither different nor completely autonomous.

7.7.1   Is syntax different from the rest of cognition?

How **different** syntax seems to be compared with other areas of cognition depends, of course, on what you think syntax is like, which in turn depends on how you analyse syntactic structures.

There's no doubt that it's possible to analyse syntactic structures in a way that makes them look very different from anything else; and indeed the doctrines of modularity and nativism encourage syntacticians to do just that. If you already believe that syntax is different, there's very little motivation for seeking similarities.

But the crucial question is whether these analyses are the only ones possible. Can syntactic structure be analysed in a way that reveals similarities to other things? Are there parallels outside language to the patterns of word-classes, word order, agreement, valency and so on that we find in syntax?

The whole of this book can be seen as a positive answer to this question. Everything in syntax has parallels outside language: word-classes parallel other taxonomies (2.2, 6.3), word order parallels the way we locate things in space and time (3.4.3, 7.4), agreement parallels the way we match colours and so on (3.3, 7.3), valency parallels the general use of relations as properties (3.2, 3.5, 7.2). Once you start to look for similarities, you find them.

This question matters deeply for syntactic theory. As soon as we discover similarities between syntax and other areas of mental life, we have to explain them. For example, if both syntax and spatial thinking follow the same Best Landmark Principle (3.4.3, 7.4), why should this be so? Is it just a coincidence, or are they both using the same mental tool for locating things?

Moreover, as soon as we find similarities, we face a new challenge: are there any significant differences at all?

There certainly are some differences; most obviously, only syntax is responsible for organizing words so that they can realize meanings and be realized by forms. But that's simply what we mean by syntax; if it didn't have this characteristic, we wouldn't call it syntax.

You could also wonder how similar the word-classes of grammar are to other kinds of classification. Admittedly they have similar abstract properties such as prototypical members and exceptions, but what about the classes themselves? Where else in cognition do you find nouns and verbs?

The modularist answer is that only language has nouns and verbs because these classes are part of our inborn language module; but a cognitivist tries to explain them as a response to the demands of communicating by means of general-purpose thought processes. If you try to use a human mind to talk about human experiences in a human world, then you're almost bound to end up with a class of words for things that happen and another, grammatically different, class for talking about people and objects.

The cognitivist view, then, is that everything in grammar is as expected given the goal of communication and the tools of the ordinary human mind; but of course we can't prove it without very clear theories of the human mind, communication and language. These theories lie in the future, but the search for them is worth a lot of effort.

7.7.2   How autonomous is syntax?

The other question raised by the modularity debate is how **autonomous** syntax is – i.e. how independent is it of other things?

A syntax module would be autonomous in the same sense that a car radio is: its internal workings aren't affected by what happens in other modules, so it does what it has to do regardless of everything else. A syntax module would only apply to truly syntactic objects – words – and would ignore all their characteristics other than those which are truly syntactic – word-classes and dependencies. In contrast, a non-modular syntax would allow some flexibility.

Which view is right? There's certainly some truth in the modular view: syntax does tend to combine words only with words, and to ignore other characteristics. For example, it's true that a string of nonsense can nevertheless be 'grammatical' in the sense that it follows all the rules of syntax; think of Lewis Carroll's poem 'Jabberwocky' (Wikipedia: 'Jabberwocky'):

> Twas brillig, and the slithy toves
> Did gyre and gimble in the wabe:
> All mimsy were the borogoves,
> And the mome raths outgrabe.

But syntax also has some flexibility which allows it to break out of the rigid straightjacket of pure syntax. In particular, it allows words to combine with non-words.

A clear example of **non-words** in valency involves a particular sublexeme of the verb GO, which we can call GO_{action}. This is illustrated in examples like (1), where '[noise]' stands for whatever noise the speaker makes to imitate a train whistle.

(1)   The train went [noise].

For people in my generation, this is the only way that GO_{action} can be used, but this verb has now been generalized to allow speech, as in (2).

(2)   He went 'Wow!'.

But the main point is that the verb's valency specifically requires me, and allows younger speakers, to give it a non-verbal complement – a complement which is not a word.

Admittedly this is a very small detail in the grammar of one language, but it makes an important general point: that grammars can refer to non-words (Hudson 1990: 67–9). But the example is less isolated than you might think. A word can be combined with a noise or shape that it names, as in (3):

(3)   The symbol ¬ is used in logic.

This uses just the same grammatical relation, called 'apposition', that we find in *the word BIG* or *the song 'Oh for the wings of a dove'*. (Wikipedia: 'Apposition'.)

Indeed, in scientific papers formulae are regularly used as the object of a verb such as GET (e.g. *we get X*, where X is a formula), and even a syntactician might write *The correct structure is: X*, where X is a structure diagram. The scholarly apparatus of parentheses, footnotes and hyperlinks adds a further dimension of possibilities for extending language away from the typical patterns of ordinary written or spoken prose.

These possibilities aren't, of course, restricted to writing. The verb GO$_{action}$ can hardly be used except in speech, and it is in speech that we find the detailed interactions between words and gestures that are so important for fluency and effectiveness (McNeill 2006).

The general conclusion is that although syntax is most typically concerned with the relations between words, the same principles that typically combine words can also be used, exceptionally, to combine words with things that are definitely not words. In short, syntax is not autonomous.

Summary of this section:

- Syntax is the area of language where modularity and nativism have been most strongly defended, but even syntax is neither different from other areas of cognition, nor autonomous.
- Syntax isn't **different** because every aspect of syntactic structure has parallels outside language.
- Syntax isn't **autonomous** because non-linguistic objects such as gestures or diagrams can be fully integrated into syntactic structure.

Where next?

Advanced: Back to Part I, Chapter 4: Network activity

8 Using and learning language

8.1 Accessibility and frequency

> **Summary of Section 4.1:**
>
> - Some concepts are more **accessible** than others because of our previous experiences of dealing with them; for example, concepts are more accessible if they're emotionally charged. The most important influence is the **frequency effect**: more frequently used concepts are more accessible. A helpful metaphor for explaining the effect of experience on concepts is **strength**: experience of using a concept strengthens it.
> - 'Strength' in the **mind** corresponds to an **activation level** in the **brain**. According to the **computational theory of mind**, each (mental) concept is held by some pattern of neurons in the brain, where neurons have observable levels of activation. The relation between information in the mind and activation levels in the brain is best explained by **neural networks**.
> - A concept's **resting activation level** reflects previous experiences, whereas its **current activation level** reflects the activity of current thinking.

We all know that some words can be frustratingly inaccessible. We know them, but just can't recall them when we need to.

8.1.1 The frequency effect

These hard to recall words are typically ones that we don't use every day, and are often words that we very rarely use, so frequency clearly plays at least some part in our problems.

This link between accessibility and frequency has been studied intensively in psychological laboratories, so I'll first explain how these experiments work. An experimental subject – typically, a psychology student – sits at a computer terminal on which words are displayed (though they may be presented orally via headphones). As soon as a word is presented, the subject carries out some experimental task, and the computer measures how long this task takes. The time is measured in milliseconds, so whatever differences emerge are likely to be well below the level where subjects themselves are aware of them.

One typical task is called 'naming', in which the subject simply pronounces the word that has appeared on the screen. Another is the 'lexical decision' task, in which the subject decides whether or not the word is an English word, pressing the 'yes' button for (say) *doctor* and the 'no' button for *moctor*. (Wikipedia: 'Lexical decision task', Harley 1995: 143–4.) Other methods exist, but these two are enough to illustrate how such a subjective thing as the accessibility of a word can be studied objectively.

The raw data from the experiment consists of a number (of milliseconds) for each task performed by each subject, which allows the experimenter to ask how long each word takes (per subject, or on average across all subjects), and then to ask whether the length of time correlates with the word's frequency.

This is only possible, of course, if we can also measure word frequencies, but this isn't a problem because there are published lists of words showing how often they have occurred in representative samples of written or spoken English. There are obvious pitfalls in this approach because a word that's common for me may be quite rare for you, but the effects of individual differences among subjects can be reduced by using a large number of subjects and taking their average results.

8.1.2   Accessibility and retrieval

The results that emerge from such experiments show that the more frequent a word is, the less time the experimental task takes.

To see how this relates to accessibility, consider what you would have to do if you were the subject in a lexical-decision experiment. You see on the screen a series of letters such as *doctor*, and you know that you have to press either the green button or the red button according to whether or not you think it's an English word.

However fast you may be, the answer isn't automatic, like a reflex, but requires some thought on your part. You only press the green button if you can **RETRIEVE** the word, which means finding it somewhere in your cognitive network. This is a task that, as an experienced user of English, you happen to do really fast and well, but it still requires mental activity which can be broken down into smaller steps.

In particular, you have to first recognize the individual letters (*d*, then *o*, then *c*, and so on) and their order (*doc*, not *cod*). Each letter is of course a concept in your cognitive network, so you have to use these concepts as stepping stones to take you to the lexeme DOCTOR. We can speculate about how this happens in your mind, but the hard fact that emerges from these experiments is that you find more common words more quickly than rarer ones.

Why should frequency have any effect on retrieval time? Because they both involve **activation**. When you recognize the letters, you're creating a sequence of active nodes; and you 'find' DOCTOR by making it active. The obvious link between these two activation-events is that the activation spreads from the letters to the lexeme in a way that we explore in more detail in Section 4.2. For present purposes the main achievement is an explanation for the effects of frequency on retrieval. How quickly the DOCTOR node responds to the activation reaching it from the letters depends on how active it is already, which in turn depends on how often it has been active before. If it's very frequent, it will already be very active and won't need much extra activity to push it to the level where it counts as 'retrieved'; but if it's rare, much more activity will need to come from the letters to bring it up to whatever level of activity counts as 'enough' for you to press the green button.

8.1.3   Activation levels in a network

But how can a cognitive network as described in Chapter 3 accommodate levels of activation?

One possibility that we might consider (though not for long) is to treat a node's activation as one of its properties, along with all the other properties that are shown by links between concepts; so, for example, one of the properties of 'bird' would be 'preferred locomotion = flying', and another would be 'activation level = 0.56' (or however activation levels may be represented). But that must surely be the wrong way to analyse activation. After all, flying is a property of 'bird', whereas having an activation level of 0.56 is a property of the network node. The activation level is quite different from ordinary properties, and not least in the fact that it doesn't consist of a link to some other concept.

But if activation isn't a property, what is it? The best answer (4.1.2) seems to be that whereas concepts belong to the mind, activation really belongs to the brain and only applies to concepts indirectly through whatever mechanism implements concepts in the neural circuits of the brain. Activation, then, affects the hardware of your brain, and is only indirectly related to the software of your mind.

If we take this distinction seriously, the frequency of a word affects your brain, but not your mind. Take the adjectives GOOD and its opposite, BAD. Somewhat surprisingly, but perhaps encouragingly, GOOD is a lot more common than BAD. (This factlet can be found at www.word frequency. info). How should a cognitive network show that GOOD is more common than BAD?

8.1.4   A notation for activation

Strictly speaking, this difference doesn't belong in this network but in the next network 'down', the neural one; but since we're not dealing in neural networks here, we can invent a convenient shorthand for our cognitive pictures as a reminder of the activation that would be shown properly in a more complete analysis. An exclamation is a very 'active' utterance, so we can use exclamation

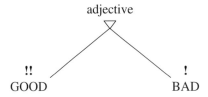

Figure 8.1 *GOOD is more frequent than BAD*

marks to show how much activation there is – one for not much, two for quite a lot and so on. Figure 8.1 includes this rough-and-ready notation. One attraction of this notation is the possibility of showing activation levels changing from moment to moment; this is helpful in later sections.

Every concept has an activation level, though we don't want to clutter diagrams with unnecessary exclamation marks; so even though Figure 8.1 doesn't show an activation level for 'adjective', it must have some degree of activation. What we don't know is how to measure it.

For instance, if a node's activation increases each time it is 'visited' during the processing of some exemplar of experience, the activation on 'adjective' should be equivalent to at least three exclamation marks, because it must have been visited each time that either GOOD or BAD was visited; but this is almost certainly too simple an assumption, because a single exemplar may well affect the activation of different nodes in different ways. Fortunately we don't really need to worry about these mathematical details here, though they will, of course, be crucial for developing the general ideas further.

One particularly important claim about activation that follows from the Word Grammar theory of networks is that it's not just entity concepts that have an activation level. If every concept has activation, it follows that the same must be true of relational concepts. Nearly all the properties of words are carried by relational concepts such as 'meaning', 'realization' and 'dependent'.

Since relations such as these are activated every time we use a word it's fair to assume that they all have very high permanent levels of activation, but even for words there are other relations which are less often activated, such as 'etymology'. A word's etymology is one of its properties (6.2), but even etymology enthusiasts only think about the origins of a handful of words per day, so this would be an example of a rare concept, with relatively low activation.

Summary of this section:

- Psychological experiments such as '**naming**' and '**lexical decision**' show that some words are more **accessible** than others, in the sense that they take longer to **retrieve**.
- The standard explanation for this link between frequency and accessibility is that frequent use increases a concept's **activation**. The result is a

relatively high **resting activation level**, with temporary increases in the **current activation level**.

- A concept's activation level is fundamentally different from its other properties: it belongs to the analysis of the **brain**, not the **mind**, so it has no proper place in cognitive networks (where it can be hinted at by a notation of exclamation marks).
- Activation levels apply to every concept, including superclasses (e.g. 'adjective') and relational concepts (e.g. 'meaning', 'etymology').

Where next?

Advanced: Back to Part I, Chapter 4.2: Activation and working memory

8.2　Retrieving words

Summary of Section 4.2:

- The parts of **long-term memory** that are currently active constitute our **working memory** (which used to be called **short-term memory**), where **current activity levels** are higher than the long-term resting levels.
- When a node's current level reaches a **threshold**, it **fires**, spreading the surplus activation indiscriminately to all its neighbouring nodes. This is called **spreading activation**.
- The main evidence for indiscriminate spreading activation comes from **priming** experiments which show that neighbouring nodes become more active (and therefore more easily retrieved) regardless of how relevant they are to the current task.
- Our **executive system** directs our **attention**, **interests** and **goals**. These choices determine which nodes receive enough ongoing activation to make them fire and activate their neighbours.
- Spreading activation then automatically retrieves the **best global candidate** by **converging** on a single node. In this search, the entire network provides the **context**.

These ideas about activation help to explain how we retrieve words – how we find the words that fit our intended meanings when we're speaking, and how we recognize words when we're listening to others. However, we shall see that speaking and listening aren't the only activities in which we need to find words. Apart from their obvious parallels in the medium of writing – writing and reading – we can search language in various ways that don't fit comfortably into any of these categories.

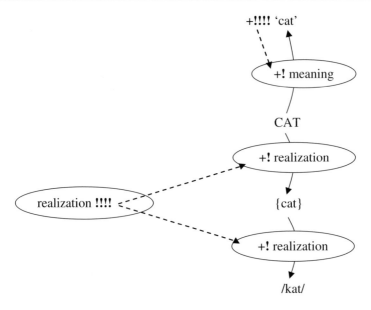

Figure 8.2 *When speaking, thinking of 'cat' evokes /kat/*

8.2.1   Speaking

Consider what happens in your mind when **SPEAKING** (Bock *et al.* 2006).

You have an idea of what you want to say, and the challenge is to find the right words. Clearly this ultimately involves building a series of words into a syntactic structure, but we can leave this more complex process till later (8.3). Meanwhile, we need to understand how you retrieve just one word – say, the word to express the concept 'cat'. Given a network analysis of language, the answer is reasonably simple and obvious.

What do you know at the point where the process starts? Let's not forget the most obvious thing you know, which is that you're talking. This is important, because it defines the target as a string of sounds that you can utter (rather than, say, letters that you could write, or simply a decision about whether a word exists – which is, after all, the target of the lexical-decision task in some psychological experiments). Finding sounds to utter is your general purpose, so all the general language nodes are already highly active, and perhaps especially the 'realization' relations.

In other words, even before you've decided exactly what you want to say, you already have a rich structure of highly active nodes which support the activation from the 'cat' concept and guide it towards the production of a spoken word as shown (in simplified form) in Figure 8.2.

Figure 8.2 shows the state of play in your mind at the point where you start to look for the word for the meaning 'cat'. The most important fact is that activation is spreading out not just from the 'cat' node, but also from the 'realization' one. It's this latter activation that channels the activation from 'cat' in the direction of /kat/ by amplifying the activation on the links between the two. Without this extra activation, an active 'cat' node achieves nothing – you're just thinking about cats.

8.2.2   Speech errors

From the point of view of network theory, speaking is a particularly interesting way of using language because (as I mentioned briefly in Section 6.9) **SPEECH ERRORS** provide clear evidence for the network notion in language (Harley 2006).

Here's a famous example:

(1)   You have tasted the whole worm.

This is an example of a 'Spoonerism' that was reportedly uttered by Dr Spooner, a nineteenth-century Oxford academic, when trying to tell a student that he had wasted the whole term. (Wikipedia: 'Spoonerism'.) What went wrong here was that too many words were active at the same time: the nodes for pronouncing *term* were already active at the point where those for *wasted* were being chosen, and the two realizations changed some of their parts – supported, no doubt, by the fact that TASTE and WORM shared in the over-enthusiastic spread of activation.

Though the details are challenging, it's easy to see how this kind of confusion could happen in a network where activation is switching nodes on and off in a fraction of a second. In this case, the error must have happened because of interference between two words that have both been selected in the normal way by means of activation spreading from meaning to sound. Such examples are very hard to explain without spreading activation.

A different kind of error is found in 'Malapropisms', this time named after a character in an eighteenth-century play:

(2)   I have since laid Sir Anthony's preposition before her.

When Mrs Malaprop says (2), she really means 'proposition', but uses the pronunciation of a similar word instead. (Wikipedia: 'Malapropism'.) The problem here is that activation has correctly selected the lexeme PROPOSITION, but has incorrectly spilled over from the realization of this word onto that of a similarly academic word with a similar pronunciation. Unlike the Spoonerism, the explanation for this mistake lies entirely within the language network, where at least the outlines of an explanation are quite clear.

A particularly important kind of error has been called **ENVIRONMENTAL CONTAMINATION** (Harley 2006). This is what you find when the choice of words is influenced by something in the immediate environment that has nothing to do with the meaning of the current sentence; (3) is an example.

(3)   Get out of the clark!

Apparently, the person who said (3) meant to say *Get out of the car*, but was distracted by a shop sign saying *Clark's*. Examples like this are extremely problematic for any modular theory of speaking in which the processing is all internal to language. In contrast, examples like (3) are exactly what we expect in a language network which is embedded in the total cognitive network. In this model, at the point where the pronunciation of *car* was being planned, the word *clark* was also highly active, and presumably more so than the target *car*.

8.2.3   Explaining speech errors

Although some of these errors are named after eccentric individuals in the past, you don't have to be eccentric to make speech errors. We all make mistakes, and probably more often than we think – according to one estimate, about once or twice per 1,000 words (Pinker 1998b: 40). Speech errors, therefore, confirm the picture that emerges from priming experiments, of a highly active network in which activation spreads in a dangerously random way from each node to all its neighbours (4.2).

The network notion, then, explains why we sometimes say one word while aiming at a different one. The interference comes from a word which is even more active than the target for one of three reasons:

- because it's already planned as part of the same utterance (e.g. *tasted* for *wasted*);
- because it's one of the target word's neighbours in the network (e.g. *preposition* for *proposition*);
- because it's simply prominent in the environment at the moment of speaking (e.g. *clark* for *car*).

In each of these cases, of course, the interference is actually more complicated, just as you would expect in a complex network. In the *tasted–wasted* case, it's no coincidence that when *term* interferes with *wasted* to produce *tasted*, the result involves a form that actually exists: {taste}, which may already have some activation. Similarly for *preposition–proposition*, where you'll notice that *preposition* belongs to the same word-class as the target *proposition*, so the word-class provides a second source of activation. And in the *clark–car* example, both *car* and *Clark's* start with the sound /k/. All these extra links help to raise the activation on the interfering word, much as we would expect given the way in which activation flows round the network.

8.2.4   Listening, writing, reading and other routes
through language

We now turn from speaking to other ways of using language, starting with **LISTENING**. When listening to another speaker we retrieve words by working in the opposite direction. We hear a sequence of sounds, and have to work out which word we've just heard. Hearing /kat/ makes activation spread from this pronunciation and from the 'word' node to converge on CAT, from which the meaning 'cat' and various other properties can be inherited.

There's good experimental evidence for the activation spreading from the phonemes to all the words which contain the same phonological pattern (Mattys 2006): CAT, CATALOGUE, CATEGORY and so on. Priming experiments show that all these lexemes have raised activation levels before rapidly returning to their resting level. Moreover, in the case of long words such as *elephant*, the winner can emerge even before the word has been completely uttered. These experiments show clearly that what we're looking for is a winner, and as soon as a winner emerges, we take it.

Written language offers the same choice of direction for activation, depending on whether we're writing (meanings to letters) or reading (letters to meanings); and in both cases the activation is directed by the activation coming out of the 'word' node. Research has produced a great deal of theory and experimental findings about **WRITING** (Mattys 2006), and even more about **READING** (Rayner and Juhasz 2006, Oakhill and Cain 2006, van Gompel 2006, Balota and Yap 2006), but very little attempt to synthesize an overarching theory of how a single language system might be used for both purposes (or, for that matter, for speaking and listening).

This fragmentation is at least in part due to a fundamental theoretical gap: the lack of a means for channelling activation in the intended direction. As a result, theories of writing or speaking typically assume one series of 'stages' through which processing has to pass and which is different from the series needed for reading or listening. Indeed, some psychologists even suggest that we may have two completely separate mental databases for grammar and vocabulary, one for speaking and the other for listening (Bock *et al.* 2006) – a very hard idea for a linguist to accept, implying as it does that we might pair meanings and sounds quite differently when speaking and when listening.

In contrast, what I'm suggesting is that directionality comes from the activation of at least one other node which defines the target – roughly speaking, the 'meaning' node when reading or listening, and the 'spelling' or 'pronunciation' node when writing or speaking. In this approach the language database is like a single multi-purpose map which we can use for all sorts of routes, depending only on where we choose to start and end our journey.

One of the attractions of this approach is the flexibility with which it credits the human mind. Linguists and psychologists tend to think of words only as tools for communication, and I have no doubt that communication is in fact the main use of language; but many other possible uses exist.

Here are some examples of non-standard but common ways in which one word may evoke (i.e. activate) another in a person's mind, depending on that person's interests:

- For a poet, it evokes words that rhyme or alliterate with it.
- For an etymologist, it evokes its 'etymons' – the words that are derived from the same historical roots.

- For a syntactician, it evokes syntactically similar words, such as those which have a similar valency.
- For a translator, it evokes translation equivalents in other languages.
- For a subject in a psychological priming experiment, it simply evokes the relevant lexeme (4.2).

Even if communication is the most important use of language, all these uses also have to be explained sooner or later by a theory of language, and any theory which can explain these special uses will surely be able to explain the core use of words in communication as well.

Summary of this section:

- We retrieve a word by activating at least two concepts whose activation converges on the target word; so in **speaking** the activation from the meaning and from 'word' converges on the target word, and similarly for **listening**, **writing** and **reading**. Since the direction of retrieval depends on the user's interests and needs rather than on inbuilt procedures, retrieval is not confined to the conventional needs of communication.
- Sometimes the wrong word becomes more active than the target; in speaking, this produces a **speech error**. The interfering activation may come from another word in the same sentence (e.g. **Spoonerisms**), from a closely related word in the network (e.g. **Malapropisms**), or from an irrelevant concept that happens to be active at the moment of speaking (**environmental contamination**). Speech errors are predicted by a network analysis.

Where next?

Advanced: Back to Part I, Chapter 4.3: Building and learning exemplar nodes

8.3   Tokens and types in listening and speaking

Summary of Section 4.3:

- We handle the incidents and objects of ongoing experience by creating **exemplar nodes**, one for each incident and one for each object, and then classifying them (by isA) as examples of general categories. Thanks to these isA links and their other properties, exemplars are temporary parts of the general cognitive network.

- Some exemplars represent objects and events that we **perceive**, but others represent those that we **plan**.
- Exemplars are highly active at first, but their activity level usually drops below the point where we can access them. In a minority of cases, however, it stays high enough for access on future occasions, so the temporary exemplar is '**recycled**', with some (but probably not all) of its properties, as a permanent category. In such cases, **learning** has taken place.

This section explains how these general ideas about exemplars and categories apply to temporary word-tokens and to the permanent lexemes and inflections that we use in classifying them.

8.3.1   Building nodes for word-tokens

When you hear a word-token, and you know that it's a word (rather than, say, a cough), your first job is to build it a node, which, following the Word Grammar convention explained in Section 6.1, we can call 'w1'. Since you know that w1 is a word, you can already add an isA link between w1 and 'word'. However, you also know something about its pronunciation, so w1 already has some properties which in turn involve tokens of various phonological units such as the phonemes /k/, /a/ and /t/ (in that order).

How can we be sure that you build this new node for w1? One kind of evidence comes from our ability to spot mispronunciations and mis-spellings. If you heard someone say *knee* with /k/, you'd undoubtedly notice it and might remember the occasion; but you could only do that if you had already created for that word-token a node that was separate from the one for the lexeme KNEE, because otherwise you can't compare their properties.

In a nutshell, this is what we do when we're listening to another speaker, and something very similar is true when we read. In both cases we create a new node for each word-token, and possibly also for each phoneme or letter. This new token node is very active because it's the focus of our attention, so activation spreads out from it, through its known properties, into the permanent network where the activation is normally channelled to converge with activation spreading from the 'meaning' node. In other words, we're actively 'listening (or reading) for meaning'.

What about speaking and writing? Here too we start by creating a token node, but in this case this node stands for the word that we're planning to say or write. Once again, the token node is highly active, but this time the activity flows in the opposite direction, from meaning to sound. What we know about the word is its meaning – say, 'cat' – but we also know that we're speaking or writing, so we know that we're looking for a realization in terms of sounds or letters.

It's because speakers and hearers start with different purposes that speaking and writing can use the same 'database' – the language network – in spite of taking very different routes through it; and in each case, part of the operation is the creation of a token node for the word being processed.

8.3.2   Learning words

Once the relevant properties of a token have been exploited, we normally forget it; in fact, the pressure for resources is such that word-tokens have typically vanished by the time we've heard or said a dozen or so other tokens (8.6).

But although word-tokens normally vanish from memory within seconds, a few of them last much longer. Just like the unfamiliar bird considered in Section 4.3, an unfamiliar word-token attracts activation in proportion to the intellectual challenge that it poses, and given sufficient activation it may survive till the next token of the same type.

Thus what started as w1, a mere token pronounced (say) /katəgri/, may end as the new lexeme CATEGORY, a general concept to which future tokens can build an isA link. But it's important to remember that in this process the node doesn't change – on the contrary, its changed status comes from the fact that it **hasn't** changed by disappearing.

The preserved node is the meeting point of whatever properties survive from the token, even if this is an incomplete selection based on an inaccurate guess. Suppose, for instance, that John heard w1 during a discussion on Friday about sorting sea-shells, when Mary said: 'What category shall we put this one in?' Since John has never heard the word *category* before, he has to guess its meaning, so he guesses that it means a heap. This is the meaning that survives, along with the pronunciation, till Monday evening when John next hears a token (w2) of the new lexeme; but during that interval he's forgotten when he heard w1 and who was speaking. But on Monday evening the meaning is clearer because the speaker says that stars and planets belong to different categories.

This time John guesses a different meaning nearer to our 'category', but has no problem in reconciling this meaning with the 'heap' one because w2 isA the original w1. By default inheritance, the new meaning blocks the old one. And so we gradually refine the properties of our lexemes through cumulative experience of further tokens, which explains why lexemes can have such a complicated structure of sublexemes (6.5).

The discussion so far has focused on how single word-tokens can turn into lexemes, but the same principles also allow **MULTI-WORD SEQUENCES** to be remembered. For instance, suppose John hears Mary say *I can't put up with the noise*, and suppose he can guess from the context that she means she can't tolerate the noise. The challenge for him is to work out how the words *put up with* can mean 'tolerate', and while he's pondering this all the words receive high doses of activation which keeps them accessible into the future.

Each token can be linked to a familiar lexeme: PUT, UP and WITH, whose grammatical properties suggest a dependency structure in which at least *up*, and possibly *with*, depends on *put*. These dependencies are included among the properties of these tokens, so they enter long-term memory as a network of three word nodes, PUT UP WITH. Any pair of word-tokens connected by a dependency may be stored as a word string (p. 176), providing a vast store of data upon which syntactic generalizations can be based as explained in Section 8.4.

Summary of this section:

- Each token of a word (or of any other linguistic unit such as a phoneme or letter) is given a separate **token node** in the cognitive network, regardless of whether this belongs to a listener/reader or to a speaker/writer. After we've finished with the token, it normally vanishes from memory.
- But some tokens survive, possibly because they're unusually novel and therefore unusually active, and become permanent nodes – lexemes or sublexemes.
- The same survival is possible for **multi-word sequences**, consisting of syntactically linked token nodes.

Where next?

Advanced: Back to Part I, Chapter 4.4: Building induced nodes

8.4   Learning generalizations

Summary of Section 4.4:

- Cognition includes not only exemplars but also general categories (**schemas**). These are **induced** from exemplars as new nodes created wherever a generalization is found.
- Generalizations are found by activation spreading in 'down time' (e.g. during sleep) through the tightly interconnected links formed by shared properties.
- The mechanism for creating induced schema nodes may be the same 'Hebbian' learning that binds the properties of exemplars.

The mechanism for inducing schemas applies to words in much the same way as to other parts of our experience such as birds.

We remember a number of tokens, activation shows us that they share some properties, and we build a new schema which has just these shared properties. We attach the tokens by isA links to the new schema concept, and we have the start of a taxonomy which can grow upwards by generalizations across schemas.

In this theory, the induction processes apply 'off-line', so they apply to the contents of memory rather than to the contents of ongoing experience. The new schema is simply a concept, with just the same cognitive status as the remembered tokens, so if it in turn shares properties with other schemas, induction will result in a more general schema still, and so on till we have the tall taxonomies that we find in language. For example:

- Some tokens of *cat* give the lexeme CAT.
- CAT and some similar lexemes give the word-class 'common noun'.
- 'Common noun', 'proper noun' and 'pronoun' give the word-class 'noun'.
- In the unlikely event that the schema 'word' doesn't already exist, it can be induced from the word-classes.

The more novel tokens we hear, the more generalizations we can induce and the taller and richer our taxonomies can become.

8.4.1   What you can learn depends on what you know already

However, development is actually a great deal more complicated than this. For one thing, properties aren't a fixed set but are growing at the same time as the taxonomies that recognize them. And for another, the properties themselves are based on taxonomies of other kinds that are also growing. These complications are particularly clear in the case of language, where the details of mature language are relatively clear compared with other areas of cognition (Chapter 6).

Adult language seems to involve three separate taxonomies of entities (6.9): words, forms and sounds or letters, and the units in these taxonomies have properties based on various relations (e.g. meaning, realization, variant, language, speaker), including the particularly well developed taxonomy of syntactic dependencies (e.g. pre-dependent, subject).

A child, on the other hand, starts more or less from scratch, with few or none of these complexities in their mind (Lieven 2006). Even an infant comes to know a good deal about the sounds of the adult language, and can certainly remember adult word-tokens in terms of how they sound. These abilities may suggest a schema that we could call 'phonetic word' with very elementary directly observable properties including the sounds and the speaker.

8.4.2   Stages in language learning

A toddler develops this analysis by including more features of the situation – say, associating *no* with stopping current activity – but although this eventually leads to true adult meaning, at this stage it consists of little more than the kind of link between word and situation that adults have for greetings. At the same time, the analysis of sounds develops a stock of phonemes and combination-patterns, so we now have a two-level analysis where 'words' are separate from 'sounds'.

We could call each such item a 'situated phonological word', of which the toddler may have learned several hundred; but notice that as the 'vocabulary' grows, each item of vocabulary also receives a more elaborate set of properties. The ordinary process of induction allows the child to extract generalizations about links between words and situations, but this process works slowly and depends on large numbers of tokens; for instance, it could take dozens of tokens of *more* for the child to notice that adults tend to use it when offering more food.

The real breakthrough is probably the point where the child induces the generalization that words have a 'meaning' – a single concept which the speaker is guaranteed to be thinking about (i.e. which is guaranteed to be active in the speaker's mind) when uttering the word.

At that point, word learning speeds up considerably because the child no longer depends on multiple tokens of a word to work out how to use it. Instead, one token of an unfamiliar word is enough to trigger the question 'What does this mean?', and a guess. Even if the guessed meaning is wrong, it's better than nothing.

Further relations mark the beginnings of syntax as the child learns the relation 'dependent' and particular kinds of dependent, and learns to correlate these with word order. And meanwhile, the child starts to notice the possibility of generalizing about the parts of complex words such as *cats* and *catty*; this is the start of morphology and the separate level of form, separating words from sounds.

In short, what starts as a mere sequence of sounds for the child ends up as a true lexeme with the full paraphernalia of adult linguistic structure, passing through the stages summarized in Figure 8.3.

The route from nothing to full adult cognition is a long one, extending well beyond the first five years which are sometimes claimed to be enough (Nippold 2006), and research has found a great deal of variation from language to language and from person to person. For example, even within my own family one child learned to use the morph {s} in both plurals and possessives soon after combining two words for the first time, whereas another learned the plural {s} well before the possessive, and long after the first two-word combination.

Variation both between individuals and between groups is as expected if we learn language by applying general-purpose mechanisms to the highly variable experiences of different people and different communities.

8.4.3   Learning syntax

What about syntax? As I explained in Section 3.6, this is often presented as something that must be an 'instinct' because it couldn't possibly be learned (Pinker 1994). But in the view of learning that I've just offered, there's nothing remarkable about the learning of syntax.

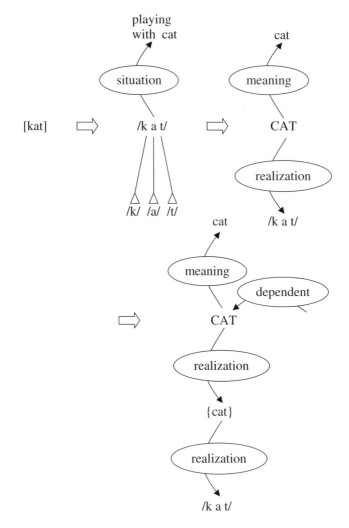

Figure 8.3 *Stages in the learning of the lexeme CAT*

As children, we analyse each word-token in terms of whatever general frame-work of concepts we've managed to build to date, and after some experience and mental development, that framework comes to include syntactic ideas of increasing sophistication, starting with the simple adjacency of the words next to it, and gradually recognizing more abstract dependencies. Once the child recognizes that a word is related to the words on either side, these can be stored as multi-word sequences (8.3), and the induction system can start to find generalizations.

The question, of course, is whether this explanation works for all the very abstract patterns that syntacticians have recognized. Many linguists believe they can (and indeed, I've suggested highly learnable analyses for many of them – see Hudson 1990, Hudson 2007c), but there's clearly a great deal more to be done before we can be sure who's right.

Summary of this section:

- General-purpose induction mechanisms allow our minds to build **linguistic schemas** on memorized tokens or on less general schemas, eventually giving rise to the rich and tall **taxonomies** of language.
- But the **analyses** that a learner gives to new tokens depend on the available schemas, so the properties available for generalization gradually become richer and the child takes several years to develop the complex adult structures for words that include meanings, dependencies and realizations, with forms distinguished from phonemes.
- The same mechanism allows **syntactic** generalizations once the learner recognizes that words have relations to the words before and after them.

Where next?

Advanced: Back to Part I, Chapter 4.5: Building inherited nodes

8.5   Using generalizations

Section 4.5 completed the discussion of the mechanism for inheritance, and ended with a summary which you may want to consult. The present section explains how these general ideas apply to language.

Multiple default inheritance, as described here, is just a formal statement of the logic that grammarians and grammar-users have taken for granted over the centuries. We take it for granted that grammar consists of general facts which apply automatically to individual words, and which may refer to any of the levels of analysis:

- morphology (e.g. plural nouns contain {s});
- syntax (e.g. a verb agrees with its subject);
- phonology (e.g. a short stressed vowel must be followed by a consonant, which allows /kat/ but not */ka/);
- semantics (e.g. a plural noun refers to a set of things).

Inheritance is simply the modern name for the logical process of applying a generalization to a particular case. We also take it for granted that grammatical generalizations can, and frequently do, have exceptions such as 'irregular verbs' (6.7). This is why generalizations only apply 'by default', and the logic is called 'default inheritance'. And finally we take it for granted that the properties of a word may be inherited from more than one source, thanks to two characteristics of linguistic taxonomies.

On the one hand, taxonomies are tall, so that any given word-token stands at the bottom of a long chain of schemas linked by isA. Each of these schemas carries a different range of generalizations; for instance, *cat* inherits its pronunciation and meaning from CAT, its need for a determiner from 'common noun', its ability to act as a verb's subject from 'noun', and its need to be a dependent from 'word'.

On the other hand, the taxonomies of grammar also allow intersecting categories, i.e. two superclasses that share a subclass, as when 'plural' and CAT meet in 'CAT, plural', the grammatical name for *cats*. This is why we need 'multiple inheritance'.

All these logical characteristics of grammar have been known for centuries, but it's only recently that grammarians have been sufficiently interested in the logical niceties to worry about them.

8.5.1   The effects of interest, purpose and attention

It's easy to think of multiple default inheritance as a matter of cold logic, a system for applying generalizations clearly and efficiently, and this view is correct as far as it goes – inheritance does generally give clear answers. But that view would be a mistake because inheritance interacts with the random and messy neural apparatus of spreading activation, as I explained in Section 4.5; we might call this 'warm logic'.

In this psychological (rather than logical) view, we inherit selectively according to what we're interested in (8.2). This explains the obvious differences between the four main modalities of language: speaking, listening, writing and reading.

For instance, when I say *cat* my main concern is its pronunciation whereas my hearer's is its meaning. These are the properties we most want to inherit; in contrast, we really don't care about its spelling, and will never hesitate before pronouncing a word because we don't know how to spell it. According to Word Grammar, these different interests are distinguished by the activation levels in the relational concepts 'meaning', 'pronunciation' and 'spelling'. Once the relevant word has been retrieved 8.2, inheritance applies differently according to whether it's oriented by activation towards the word's meaning, towards its pronunciation or towards its spelling.

But as I point out in 8.2, there are many other ways of applying our knowledge of words, varying in part according to personal priorities and in part with the current activity. For example, how important is spelling? For some people, it really doesn't matter even when they're writing or reading, so I assume that these people have relatively low levels of activation in their 'spelling' node in comparison with, say, professional proof-readers, who tend to be sticklers for correct spelling even when they're not proof-reading.

8.5.2   Special effects of education and the psychological laboratory

Similarly, there's some evidence of variation in the attention individuals pay to syntax, though we need a great deal more research before we can draw firm conclusions. Some research has found that the amount of attention people paid to syntax varied with the amount of education they'd had (Gleitman and Gleitman 1979, Dabrowska 1997).

In one of these studies, less educated people tended to ignore word order in interpreting three-word compounds such as *bird house black*, which they thought might mean 'a black bird who lives in the house'. This interpretation is actually impossible given the syntactic rule that the head noun is always the last one in such a series. Consequently the only way to make these three words refer to a kind of bird would be to put *bird* at the end as in *house black bird*. Given the actual order of the words, the only syntactically correct interpretation makes it refer to some kind of 'black'; and this is in fact the meaning that more educated people found (even when their education was in some completely non-linguistic subject).

At the opposite extreme from the uneducated people in these studies we find linguists, who are famous (or notorious) for paying attention to linguistic minutiae of grammar and pronunciation at the expense of the ordinary meaning. Moreover, no doubt we can all think of occasions when we've sung words whose meaning made little sense or when we've read to a child while preoccupied with some other topic, two activities which don't fit at all comfortably into any of the four standard modalities.

A particularly important example of these special contextual influences is the effect of being the subject of a psycholinguistic experiment. For example, in one series of experiments subjects were asked to say the past-tense forms of English verbs that were flashed onto the screen one after the other (Pinker 1998b: 130). The aim of the experiment was to find whether regular and irregular past tenses took the same length of time to produce, and the results were very clear: regulars such as *walked* were consistently produced faster than irregulars such as *swept*.

The result is a little surprising since irregulars must, by definition, be stored ready-made whereas most regulars are composed as needed; but the facts are robust and demand an explanation. Pinker's explanation assumes a separate process called 'blocking' which applies only to irregulars and 'blocks' the regular form, but this explanation doesn't work if we assume, as in Word Grammar, that exceptions stop the default even from being considered (4.5).

A much easier explanation refers to the peculiarities of this experimental situation, where all the regular examples prime the regular pattern, making it much more active and more accessible than any irregular pattern. Unfortunately, this kind of experimental bias is very hard to avoid, and the fact is that it's very hard to investigate ordinary behaviour experimentally.

The general point is very simple: the network of language provides a map on which we can trace many different kinds of route. Any general theory of language use requires sufficient flexibility to accommodate all uses, so it can't consist of a small number of pre-defined 'mechanisms' for standard activities such as speaking and writing. Word Grammar achieves this degree of flexibility by allowing activity to be directed into different routes according to where our current interest locates activation.

Summary of this section:

- **Multiple default inheritance** is the logic that grammarians have always taken for granted in writing descriptive grammars which allow generalizations, exceptions and cross-classification.
- But the 'cold logic' of inheritance interacts with the 'warm logic' of **spreading activation** to define notions such as '**interest**' and 'purpose'. There's some evidence that different people have different degrees of interest in particular parts of language such as syntax, and that these differences may vary with education.
- The way we use our language also varies according to our current interest. This distinguishes the four main **modalities** of language use: speaking, listening, writing and reading; but it also allows a large number of other uses which can't be accommodated in a theory that includes a separate 'mechanism' for each modality: singing, reading aloud, passing grammaticality judgements and so on.

Where next?

Advanced: Back to Part I, Chapter 4.6: Binding nodes together

8.6   Binding in word-recognition, parsing and pragmatics

Summary of Section 4.6:

- **Binding** involves an **empty node**, which needs to be **enriched**, and a **target node** which is 'the same' and therefore enriches it by adding its properties to those that it already has.
- If the empty node is in a taxonomy headed by some very general conceptual category such as 'concrete object', the target node must be in the same taxonomy; the relation between one node and another which is above it in the same taxonomy is **super-isA**, shown in notation as a dotted version of the usual isA line.
- The relation between the empty node and the target node is **identity**, shown in notation as a double-shafted arrow pointing from the empty node to the target with which it is **identified**.
- According to the **Best Fit Principle**, the target node is the one which has the **best global fit** with the known properties of the empty node, and, thanks to activation spreading from the empty node, it's recognizable as the most active candidate node.

- Binding applies in **classifying** an exemplar, whose node E isA an empty node which is identified (by binding) with some general category; this has properties that make the best global fit with those of E.
- It also applies in other mental activities such as **recalling** an event in the past or **planning** or **anticipating** an event in the future.

This section considers how these conclusions apply to at least three apparently unrelated areas of language: recognizing words, working out how words are related syntactically and finding referents for pronouns.

8.6.1   Recognizing words

Recognizing words is something we do every time we use language, and regardless of how we're using it – for speaking or listening, for writing or reading, or for any of the many other uses considered in Sections 8.3 and 8.5.

In each case, we start with an unidentified token node that already has a few identifying properties – a pronunciation when we're listening, a meaning when we're speaking or writing, and so on – and our first task is to recognize the word as an example of a word-type that we know already. In terms of the activities reviewed in Section 4.6, this is an exercise in **classification**, so we assume that the token node (now called T for 'token' rather than E for 'exemplar') isA an empty node '?' which stands for whatever permanent type node we eventually choose.

Suppose, for example, that you're listening to me, and you've just heard a form T pronounced /kat/. That's all you know about T itself, but you know a great deal more, including the fact that CAT means a kind of pet and is realized by {cat}, which in turn is pronounced /kat/; and you know that we're talking about pets. At that point in time, then, you have a network of concepts in which T, '?' and 'pet' are highly active but {cat} and CAT aren't. This is the state of play shown in (a) of Figure 8.4.

At this point in time, your mind has a small number of highly active 'hot spots' – node T, the node for the syllable /kat/, and the node for 'pet' – each of which is radiating activation to neighbouring nodes. All being well, this activation converges on the node for {cat}, picking this out as the winner in the competition for the best global fit. At this point, the binding mechanism finishes its job by inserting an identity link between '?' and {cat}, so that T is classified as an example of {cat}.

The network can then be filled out by inheritance to show that T is the pronunciation of an example of CAT, meaning an example of a cat, and so on. The main point of the example is to show how spreading activation guides us when we classify linguistic tokens.

This classification process works best when a single winner emerges quickly from the competition for activation. This isn't always the case, and the uncertainties that we sometimes face in deciding precisely what it is that we've heard

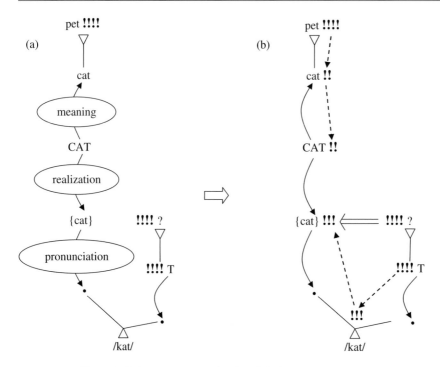

Figure 8.4 *How to recognize {cat} and CAT*

testify to the potential problems, as well as supporting this general model of classification.

8.6.2   The Stroop effect

One of the best known of all psychological experiments provides particularly ingenious evidence in favour of the model. This is called the **STROOP EFFECT** (after the psychologist who invented it in 1935 – MacLeod 2006). In a classic Stroop experiment, a subject sees a word which is written in a particular colour, and the significant measure is the time it takes to name either the word or the colour.

The question is what happens if, say, the word *green* is written in red ink. It turns out that if the task is to 'name' the word – i.e. to read it aloud – its colour has no effect on the speed of reading, but naming the colour of the word takes significantly longer if it contradicts the word (as it does in this case).

A major variation on the classic experiment replaces colours with pictures, which are easier for me to illustrate here. Figure 8.5 summarizes the results of numerous experiments.

Imagine yourself sitting in front of a computer monitor in a psychological laboratory, with instructions to say into a microphone what pictures you see on

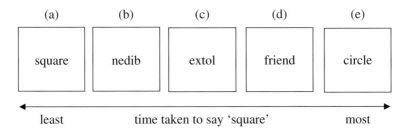

Figure 8.5 *The Stroop effect*

the screen, while ignoring any words you might see. When you see a square, you say 'square', and of course the computer is measuring very precisely how long it takes you to do this.

The snag is, of course, that you can't simply ignore the words; your long training in reading words makes that virtually impossible. Sometimes the word actually helps; that's what happens when the word matches the picture, as in (a). Sometimes it has little or no effect, as in (b), where *nedib* is a 'non-word' – a string of letters that might have been an English word, but isn't. But most words slow you down to a lesser or greater extent, ranging from low-frequency irrelevant words (c) through high-frequency irrelevant words (d) to the contradictory word *circle*, the name of a different shape.

The findings are very robust, but it's only recently, with the arrival of explicit models of language use, that it's been possible to see the outlines of an explanation. In terms of the Word Grammar model, the explanation is reasonably straightforward.

Suppose, again, that you're the experimental subject. You know that you have to say a word, so your problem is simply to choose the right word. Now suppose you've been told to 'name' (i.e. say) the word you see, while ignoring its colour or the picture that accompanies it. The name of the colour or the picture has no effect simply because you have no reason for naming it; so seeing red print or a square doesn't activate the word RED or SQUARE in this experiment any more than it does in ordinary life when you happen to see red things or square things.

But now suppose your job is to name the colour or the picture. In this case you're specifically looking for a word, via a very active 'meaning' link; so when you see red print or a square, you activate the words RED or SQUARE. The trouble is that if you also see the word *blue* or *circle*, you can't help reading it and so your node for this word becomes active as well, and the more active it is, the more competition it offers to the colour or picture name.

Low-frequency words – case (c) – offer weak competition because they're weakly activated; high-frequency words – as in (d) – offer stronger competition; and the hardest competition of all comes from the conflicting name (e). This is because the colour or picture word itself primes all the words that are semantically related; so the more you activate the word SQUARE, the more activation spills over onto the competing word CIRCLE.

In short, the Stroop effect is precisely what we should expect if the Word Grammar model of how we recognize words is right.

8.6.3   Recognizing syntactic relations

We now turn to a very different area of language use, which is usually called **PARSING** (after an old-fashioned school-room activity in which children assigned each word to a 'part of speech', which in Latin is *pars orationis*). This is what we do, when listening or reading, as we try to work out how the word-tokens fit together syntactically.

Given the claims about syntax that I explained in Chapter 7, parsing is almost entirely a matter of matching the needs of the individual words: one word needs a dependent and another word needs to be a dependent, so a dependency link between them satisfies the valency of both (7.2). Binding is relevant because parsing 'binds' the empty node of one word-token's valency to a target node, the other word-token.

For example, consider the analysis of sentence (1) shown in Figure 8.6.

(1)   Short examples sometimes raise problems.

The top diagram shows the empty nodes and targets as separate nodes linked by the identity relation, whereas the lower diagram simply merges the two nodes as in conventional diagrams.

Let's go through this sentence a word at a time – just as in listening, of course, but much, much more slowly. For your sake I'll ignore most of the details.

First you hear *short*, which (after classification) inherits the need for a following noun on which to depend; this word-token is an anticipated exemplar (like the thunder that you anticipate after lightning), so you just name it 'T1' and give it a super-isA link to 'noun'; so you're now actively looking for a noun among the following words.

You don't have to wait long, as the very next word is a noun, *examples*, so you bind T1 to *examples*, as shown in the technically accurate notation of diagram (a), where T1 has a double-shafted identity arrow linking it to *examples*; but this dependency is also shown in the more familiar notation of diagram (b).

Similarly, *examples* inherits the need for a word to depend on, but although *sometimes* is a word, nothing in either its valency or that of *examples* supports a semantic link between them.

In contrast, the next word, *raise*, is an excellent candidate because it's looking for a preceding noun to act as its subject, so a dependency between *examples* and *raise* satisfies both; typically for valents, the dependent and the parent are each bound to the other as you can see in the crossing identity arrows from T2 and T4.

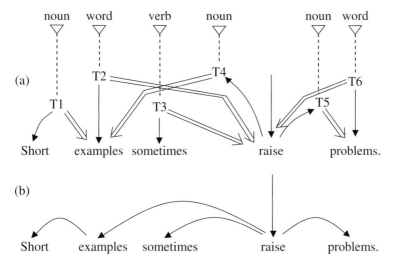

Figure 8.6 *How to parse a simple sentence*

The same pattern of mutual binding can be seen in the other valent of *raise*, its object *problems*. As you can see, once *problems* has been linked to *raise*, all the valency requirements of the individual words are satisfied, so the sentence's syntactic structure is complete.

8.6.4   Ambiguities

One of the advantages of treating parsing as an example of the much more general psychological process of binding is the explanation this provides for the way in which we react to ambiguities. Syntactic ambiguities are extremely common, but we tend not to notice them because we're so good at resolving them.

Take the famous Groucho Marx joke:

(2)   Time flies like an arrow; fruit flies like a banana.

You can see immediately that *flies* is a verb in the first clause but a noun in the second; but how do you do it? And why is the second clause such a shock?

One view of parsing separates a strictly linguistic process, which takes account only of the words concerned, from a 'pragmatic' process which takes account of meanings, context and general knowledge of the world (van Gompel 2006). In contrast, 'constraint-based' theories such as Word Grammar provide a single, very general procedure for dealing with all the uncertainties in one fell swoop, thanks to the Best Fit Principle which favours the analysis that provides the best global fit.

The point of the joke is that the first clause strongly activates a syntactic pattern in which *flies* is a verb and *like* is a preposition, so this syntactic pattern is 'at the front of our minds' when we read the second clause. But equally strong activation comes from what we know about fruit flies and bananas, which pushes us to a completely different syntactic analysis. The pleasure and pain of the joke come, presumably, from the direct competition for the best global fit, with our obvious candidate being overtaken at the last moment.

But although Word Grammar rejects the conventional two-step view of parsing, it does make the same distinction as most other theories between the process of inheriting valency requirements and the process of satisfying them by binding.

This distinction helps to explain why some syntactic structures make heavier demands than others on working memory, and in particular why dependency distance is a good measure of memory load (7.1). The reason is that outstanding valency tokens have to be kept active until they're satisfied by binding, and of course the more such tokens are being kept active, the less activation is available for other nodes. This is why very long subjects are so hard to process, and why therefore, out of consideration for our listeners, we tend to keep subjects short (11.4).

8.6.5   Recognizing antecedents for definite pronouns

So far, then, we've seen two ways in which binding applies to word-tokens: classifying them and finding how they link syntactically to other word-tokens. The third application leads nicely into semantics, the topic of the next section.

The question is how a listener decides who 'he' is in a sentence like (3).

(3)   John says he's ready.

Is it John or someone else, and if someone else, who?

In this case the question is about a personal pronoun, but the problem is much more general, and arises with any **DEFINITE** pronoun, including the word THE which I claim is a special kind of pronoun (10.1). For instance, how do we decide who 'the man' is in (4)?

(4)   The man woke up.

Binding is relevant to both (3) and (4) because the one thing we can be sure of is that the person concerned – 'he' or 'the man' – is someone we already know about. This person (or thing in other examples) is called the pronoun's **ANTECEDENT** (Cornish 2006). More precisely, the antecedent is typically an entity for which we already have a node in our mind, though in some cases (discussed below) we may have to build one by inheritance (Abbott 2006).

Given the promise of an antecedent, our aim is first to find the antecedent, and then to bind the empty node to it. In contrast, *someone* or *a man* would signal to the listener that there's no antecedent, and no point in searching mentally for the person concerned.

Definite pronouns, then, are an invitation to find an antecedent node and to bind the pronoun's empty meaning node to it. For instance, if *he* in (3) refers to John, we give *he* an empty node for its meaning, and then complete this node by binding it to our mental node for John.

Theoreticians generally distinguish two kinds of antecedent according to whether or not they're mentioned by earlier words. If they are, the relation between the two nodes is called 'anaphora', but if it's found in a general non-linguistic context, we have 'exophora' (Huang 2006). In these terms, a link between *he* and John is an example of anaphora if John has just been mentioned, but it's exophora otherwise – if, for example, John has just come into sight but hasn't been discussed.

This distinction is quite unhelpful because it obscures the overriding similarity between the two cases, which is that the speaker knows that the hearer has an accessible node for John. It makes little difference whether this is because John has just been mentioned or because John has just appeared; either way, John is at the top of the hearer's mind, and the speaker knows this.

There are other cases where the antecedent is only available indirectly, via inheritance. Take example (5).

(5)   I've hired a car, but the keys don't work.

Which keys? Obviously the car keys, but this is only obvious if you know that the typical car has keys. To see the point, compare (5) with (6).

(6)   I've hired a car, but the bolts don't work.

Which bolts? In this case there's no obvious link because we don't associate cars with bolts. The fact that (5) is so easy to interpret is a nice confirmation that inheritance works as claimed in this book: if something is a car, then it can inherit the property 'has keys', but not 'has bolts'.

8.6.6   Ellipsis

Definite pronouns aren't the only linguistic devices that trigger binding. We apply very similar processes when dealing with **ELLIPSIS**, as in (7).

(7)   I got my car out of the garage but I locked my keys inside.

Inside what? The preposition INSIDE allows its complement to be suppressed, but if it is, we reconstruct it via just the same procedure as we apply in deciding who 'he' is: we introduce an empty node and try to bind it to a full target one. And just as with pronouns, the target node may be supplied either with or without the help of language.

It seems, then, that definite pronouns and ellipsis both require the mechanism of best-fit retrieval and binding. In both cases, the hearer knows that the current word's meaning is incomplete, and that in order to complete it an antecedent must be found. The hearer also knows what kind of thing the antecedent must be – a person for *he*, some keys for *the keys*, a container such as a car for *inside*. Given this partial specification, the search is for the entity that makes the best global fit, and as usual the winner is the most active relevant node. Once the winner has emerged, all the hearer has to do is to bind it to the incomplete meaning node by the identity link.

If this account of the search for antecedents is right, then it involves precisely the same mental processes as we use in classifying words and in finding their syntactic relations. But most importantly of all, this same process is the one that allows us to recognize a bird in the sky, to anticipate thunder and to solve problems, none of which have anything at all to do with language.

Summary of this section:

- Binding applies when we **classify** a word-token as an example of a particular word-type; the token isA some empty node which super-isA 'word', and our aim is to bind the empty node to the most active word node.
- The **Stroop effect** shows that a competing word may interfere with the finding of a target.
- It also applies in **parsing**, when we link one word-token to another by dependencies; the word's valency identifies a number of dependencies each of which links it to an empty node which super-isA 'word' (or a more specific word-class), so the aim of parsing is to bind each of these empty nodes to the most active earlier word held in working memory.
- The role of activation in parsing explains how we resolve **ambiguities** and also why long dependencies place a heavy load on working memory.
- Thirdly, binding applies when we're finding the **antecedent** of either a **definite pronoun** (e.g. *he* or *the man*) or an example of **ellipsis** (e.g. *inside*), which we represent provisionally as an empty node before binding it to a full target.

Where next?

Advanced: Just read on!

8.7   Meaning

8.7.1   Referential meaning

In the discussion so far I've taken the notion of 'meaning' very much for granted, but it's time to look at it more carefully.

No doubt you agreed when I said (in Section 8.5) that the main uses of language were the ones that linked sounds or written characters to meaning: speaking, listening, reading and writing; but what exactly is meaning? As philosophers have been asking for centuries, what is the meaning of *meaning*? (Hassler 2006, Martin 2006).

Not surprisingly, it all depends on what other assumptions you make, and the assumptions of Word Grammar lead to a very simple theory of meaning: a word's meaning is the concept to which it's related by the link labelled 'meaning'.

That may sound perilously near to being circular, but if you remember the theoretical context, it's actually no worse than saying that the word's realization or subject is the form to which it's linked by 'realization' or 'subject'. As I explained in Section 2.5, there's no point in looking for definitions, because that's not how nature works. Categories don't get their content from a definition, but from the properties that they bring together; so 'cat' has no definition, but neither does 'meaning'. If you want to know what 'meaning' is, you have to look at the network neighbours of this concept.

Social and referential meaning

One problem in thinking about meaning is that a word's meaning isn't simply the information that the word conveys to a listener. If it was, then the meaning of DOG would include the fact that the speaker knows English – an important fact in some contexts, but not what we normally mean by 'meaning'. To be clearer, then, we need to distinguish a word's ordinary meaning from what we shall call its social meaning, which will be discussed in Section 8.8.

A common technical term for ordinary meaning is **REFERENTIAL MEANING**, the meaning that we apply when we use a word to refer to something such as a dog. (The terminology of 'referring' will become clearer in the next subsection.) Having said that, however, I'll keep to simple 'meaning' in the following discussion, with the warning that it's to be taken in the sense of 'referential meaning'.

Meaning as a relation

What, then, can we say about the concept 'meaning'? First, it's a relational concept, and not a special kind of entity. This has to be so because (so far as I know) there's no kind of concept which can't be the meaning of a word.

Even words or word-classes can be meanings – think of the words WORD and NOUN, not to mention the linguist's habit of using words written in italics or capital letters as the names of the words concerned, as when I write that DOG has three letters (whereas 'dog' has four legs). These are examples of **METALANGUAGE**, language about language (Allan 2006b).

In general terms, you can 'put into words' any idea you can think of, and nothing thinkable is un-sayable. Admittedly you may have to use more than one word to say it – for instance, I'm having to use a whole sentence to say the thought that I'm thinking at the moment – but any thought can be a meaning.

The main point is that neither the world nor our minds contain a category of things or concepts that we could call 'meanings', any more than the world of people is divided into 'friends' and others. Instead, 'meaning' is a relation between a word and some concept, just as 'friend' is a relation between one person and another.

The relation 'meaning' takes its place alongside a number of other relations that can apply to words such as 'realization' and 'dependent', each expressing a different kind of property. But unlike 'meaning', the other relations are fussy about the kinds of concept to which they can relate a word: the typical value for 'realization' is a form such as {dog}, whereas for 'dependent' it's another word. You'll notice that forms and words are both part of language (according to Figure 6.8, they both isA 'language'), so these other relations stay inside language, whereas 'meaning' links a word to something which is typically outside language.

In other words, it's meaning that allows us to communicate about the world, unlike the other relations which are part of the 'mechanics' of language. As you can see, we've now got the beginnings of a description of meaning: a relation between a word and a concept which is typically outside language.

We could then go on to talk about how a word's meaning combines (in our minds) with other things. When you combine the word *dog* with the word *owner*, their properties combine in a very regular way which is traditionally described in terms of the 'levels of analysis' discussed in Section 6.9:

- At the level of morphology, the form {dog} combines with {{own}{er}} at least in an ordered string of forms, and possibly even to form a more complex form, {{dog}{{own}{er}}}.
- At the level of syntax, the noun *dog* combines with the noun *owner* via a dependency link.
- At the level of **SEMANTICS**, the meaning 'dog' combines with the meaning 'owner' to form the concept 'dog owner'.

The point is that when you put two words together, one word's meaning combines with the other word's meaning rather than with, say, its realization.

If we add this fact to the earlier summary, we get a respectable description of meaning, as follows. 'Meaning' is a relation between a word and a concept which:

- is typically outside language, though in the case of metalanguage it's part of language;
- combines, on the level of semantics, with the meanings of neighbouring words.

If we think in terms of language use, it's clear that meanings are crucial because they allow us not only to talk about the world, but also to build complex concepts out of simpler ones by merging the meanings of co-occurring words.

Meaning as a link between minds

Before we look at the more technical details of meaning, let's remind ourselves how simple the notion of meaning is in a cognitive theory.

A word's meaning is typically just an ordinary concept such as 'dog' which we would have regardless of language. The qualification 'typically' is particularly important here because there are some concepts which seem to be specialized for language, and which I'll discuss below; but the main point is that language has direct access to the full range of ordinary non-linguistic concepts and can treat any of them as meanings.

Moreover, meaning is just an ordinary property consisting of a relation between two entities, and has exactly the same mental status as any other property. In particular, it receives activation just like any other property, and can be inherited just like any other property. Consequently, if you hear me say the word *dog*, you can be sure of two things: that the concept 'dog' is active in my mind, and that the token of DOG that you've just built inherits the concept 'dog'.

Since this meaning in your mind is also highly active, my saying *dog* has achieved 'one of the wonders of the natural world' (Pinker 1994: 15): a precise coordination of the mental activity in two different minds. In a nutshell, the noises that I make with my mouth tell you very precisely what's going on in one bit of my mind. Better still, of course, if I know that you understand English, then I know that my *dog* will have this effect on you, so I can take it for granted that your 'dog' node is as active as mine is.

This theory isn't just the idea that meaning is based on mental 'associations', because it involves the very specific relation 'meaning' and the equally specific logic of inheritance. (Wikipedia: 'Association of ideas'.)

Suppose, for example, that the last time you heard me say *dog* you were feeling ill. In that case, hearing me say *dog* again might remind you of your illness, but that doesn't mean that illness has something to do with the word's meaning. As I explained in Section 8.4, meaning is a relation that you learned while learning to talk, and which now allows you to select one concept out of all the potentially related or relevant ones, a concept which is consistently associated with the word.

Other kinds of association are covered by other kinds of relation (8.8); but as far as meaning is concerned, the mental structures are reasonably precise. On the other hand, the concepts we invoke as meanings have all the imprecision that we expect in the human mind. For example, precisely where do we draw the line between rain and drizzle? And exactly what do we mean by COSY, LOVE or FUN? Maybe these concepts are vague precisely because we learn them primarily via language, which raises the question of the extent to which language influences our thinking (8.7.5).

Summary of this subsection:

- **(Referential) meaning** is a relation between a word and whatever kind of concept it refers to, not a special kind of entity; in principle, any kind of concept may be the meaning of a word, including the linguistic concepts (words, and so on) that are referred to by **metalanguage**.

Where next?

Advanced: Just read on!

8.7.2   Sense and referent

The first technicality of meaning is a standard distinction between two kinds of meaning. Consider sentence (1).

(1)   A dog barked.

What does *dog* mean here? Is it the general category 'dog', or is it a particular dog that was barking?

Clearly this is a choice that we don't want to make because we'd like to be able to recognize both as a 'meaning', but equally clearly they're very different from each other, so semantic theory uses the term **SENSE** for the general category and **REFERENT** for the particular dog (Sullivan 2006). Similarly, we say that a word 'refers to' its referent, and the relation between them is 'reference'. It's because of its role in referring to referents that we call this kind of meaning 'referential meaning'.

Admittedly, the theoretical tradition in which the contrast between sense and referent developed would actually have applied *referent* to the dog in the real world, rather than to this dog's concept in someone's mind. However, this is the best available terminology since cognitive theory offers no alternatives.

The distinction between sense and referent is fundamental to the Word Grammar theory of semantics, so we need to explore its consequences a little.

Sense/referent and type/token

First, how does it relate to the apparently similar contrast between word-types (lexemes and inflections) and word-tokens? Clearly, the lexeme DOG doesn't have a specific referent, whereas any given token such as the one in (1) does. What DOG has is a sense, so we might be tempted to think that senses belong to lexemes whereas referents belong to word-tokens.

But this would be wrong, because a word-token inherits from a lexeme, so among the other things that it inherits will be the lexeme's sense. That doesn't mean, of course, that it leaves this sense unchanged; on the contrary, as we shall see in Section 8.7.3, the word's dependents have a profound effect on its inherited sense; but the token does have a sense.

Conversely, some lexemes seem to have a referent and virtually no sense; this is the case with names such as FIDO and LONDON, neither of which has a sense comparable with, say, DOG or CITY. And of course the great attraction of a name is precisely that it takes us straight to its referent by inheritance (with obvious reservations about the problems that arise if we know more than one Fido).

In conclusion, then, a typical word-token (other than a name) inherits a sense from its lexeme, but then has its sense enriched by syntax. As for its referent, this

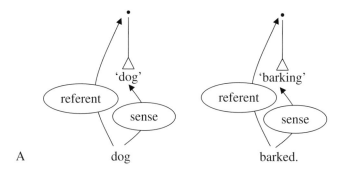

Figure 8.7 *Verbs as well as nouns have a sense and a referent*

is a new exemplar concept, specially created for this word-token. If it's definite, as in *the dog*, then it's intended to be bound to some existing concept (8.6); but an indefinite referent, as in *a dog*, is like a new character appearing on our mental stage.

Referents, senses and word-classes

How is a word's referent related to its sense? The theoretical framework introduced so far provides an easy answer: isA. The reason why we know that a dog is a suitable referent for a token of DOG is because we know that it isA 'dog', the sense of DOG; and more generally, a word's sense is a superclass for the referent.

The same analysis applies well beyond the senses and referents of concrete nouns such as DOG. Take the verb *barked* in (1). BARK has a sense, which is the general category 'barking'. But (1) refers to a particular incident of barking, just as it refers to a particular dog; so *barked* also has a referent as well as a sense. Admittedly the verb's referent is an event rather than a concrete object, but that's because its sense is a kind of event rather than a kind of concrete object. Figure 8.7 shows the start of a semantic analysis of (1), which will be extended below.

Identity-of-reference and identity-of-sense anaphora

The difference between sense and referent is very clear in another area of semantics which I touched on in Section 8.6: anaphora, where a later word takes its meaning from an earlier one.

Semanticists distinguish two kinds of anaphora according to whether they involve the senses or referents of their antecedents (Huang 2006). **IDENTITY-OF-REFERENCE ANAPHORA** is found in definite pronouns (8.6) such as IT, as in (2) and (3).

(2)   A dog barked, and it went on barking all night.
(3)   A dog barked, and it lasted all night.

It refers to the particular dog in (2), and to the event in (3).

In contrast, **IDENTITY-OF-SENSE ANAPHORA** is a link between senses, as illustrated in (4) and (5).

(4)   A dog barked, then another one howled.
(5)   A dog barked, and so did a fox.

In these examples, the anaphoric words are *one* and *so*. *One* obviously doesn't refer to the same individual dog as *a dog*, but it does share the latter's sense, 'dog'; so (4) means the same as *A dog barked, then another dog howled*. ONE doesn't always mean 'dog', but borrows its sense from the earlier word in just the same way that IT borrows its antecedent's referent. The same is true for *so* in (5), which means 'barked' in this case but varies its sense according to which verb is its antecedent.

Another way of showing identity-of-sense anaphora is via ellipsis (8.6), where the word that would otherwise have shown the relevant sense is simply omitted as in (6).

(6)   Her dog barked, and his ~~dog~~ did ~~bark~~ too.

Notice once again how nouns and verbs show the same options for handling senses and referents differently.

Definiteness and ellipsis show how important the sense/referent contrast is in grammar, but it's equally easy to show this in many other areas of grammar.

Referents and senses in inflectional and lexical morphology

Take inflectional morphology, illustrated in (7) by the plural noun and the past-tense verb:

(7)   Some dogs barked.

The inflection of *barked* has no effect at all on the sense, because *barked* refers to something which isA 'barking', just as it would in the present tense. What the inflection changes is the timing of the event referred to. This is the semantic analysis of *barked* shown in Figure 8.8, where 'now' is the time of the word-token itself – i.e. the time of speaking. As you can see, the time of the event referred to takes 'now' as its 'before' landmark.

Much the same is true of the plural inflection of *dogs*, though here the semantic structure is more complex because the plural noun refers to a set rather than to an individual dog. However, the sense is still relevant because it defines the 'typical member' of this set. According to this analysis, then, *dogs* refers to a set whose typical member isA 'dog', the sense of DOG (Hudson 2007c: 224–32).

It's worth pointing out that even the semantics of inflectional morphology, which lies right at the heart of grammar, recycles concepts that are already available in some other part of cognition. The semantics of plurality involves the idea of a 'set' that I introduced in Section 3.4.4, and that of the past tense involves the

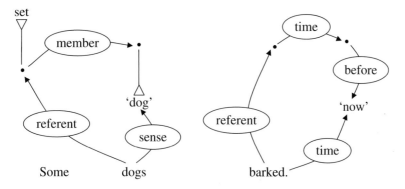

Figure 8.8 *The semantics of plural and past inflections*

'before' relation which is also needed for space and time (3.4.3) and word order (7.4). The concept 'now' also needs some discussion, but I'll come back to this below (8.7.4).

These two examples are typical of the semantic effects of inflectional morphology, which always affects the word's referent rather than its sense. In contrast, the 'lexical morphology' of lexical relations (6.7) always affects senses rather than referents. For instance, changing WALK to WALKER changes the sense (from an event to a person). The distinction between senses and referents could hardly be more important for grammar.

Summary of this subsection:

- Most words have two kinds of referential meaning: a constant **sense** and a **referent** which isA the sense and which varies from token to token. This contrast applies not only to nouns, but also to other word-classes including verbs.
- The sense/referent contrast applies to anaphora, distinguishing **identity-of-sense anaphora** from **identity-of-referent anaphora**.
- It also applies to morphology, where **inflectional morphology** affects referents but **lexical morphology** affects senses.

Where next?

Advanced: Just read on!

8.7.3   Meaning and syntax

The sense/referent distinction is equally important when we consider how meaning is affected by syntax. How is one word's meaning affected by the meanings of the words that accompany it? And how can we integrate the meanings of individual words into a single coherent semantic structure for the entire sentence?

If syntactic structure consists of dependencies between individual words, the first question changes to this: how is a word's meaning affected by the meanings of its dependents? Fortunately, this will also answer the second question because (ignoring coordination) all the words in a sentence are held together by a single word, the root word. This word is affected semantically by its dependents, which are in turn affected by their dependents, and so on down to the furthest dependent, so ultimately the root word's meaning reflects the influence of every other word's meaning.

I'll now explain how a word's dependents affect its meaning, but the important thing to remember in the following discussion is that we're talking about word-tokens, not lexemes. This is important because the token has different properties from the type from which it inherits. For example, in *Fido barked*, the token *barked* has *Fido* as its subject, which isn't true of the lexeme BARK. And similarly, it means 'Fido barked', which again isn't true of BARK.

A word's meaning can be affected by a dependent in one of four ways:

- The default pattern: the dependent's referent combines with the word's sense, as in *Fido barked*.
- Coreference: the dependent's referent merges with the word's referent, as in *the dog*.
- Predicatives: the dependent's sense combines with the word's sense, as in *is a linguist*.
- Idioms: the dependent changes the word's sense in an irregular way that has very little to do with the dependent's meaning.

We'll consider these patterns in turn.

Default: a word's sense is modified by its dependent's referent

Let's make our example sentence even simpler:

(8)   Fido barked.

The word-token *Fido* depends on the word-token *barked*, so *Fido* modifies the meaning that *barked* inherits from the lexeme BARK. Whereas the sense of BARK is simply 'barking', that of *barked* is a particular kind of barking, namely barking done by Fido: 'Fido barking.'

This is a change in the sense, and not in the referent, as you can see from the anaphora in (9).

(9)   Fido barked, which had only once happened before.

What had happened once before? Clearly not this particular incident, but another incident of 'Fido barking'; so the relation between *which* and *barked* is identity-of-sense anaphora, not identity-of-reference anaphora. In short, by supplying *Fido*

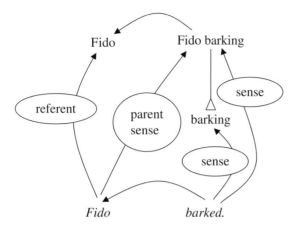

Figure 8.9 *How a dependent's referent most typically affects the sense of its parent*

as its subject, we've changed the sense of *barked* from 'barking' to 'Fido barking'; and the referent isn't just an example of 'barking', but of 'Fido barking'.

A dependent, then, affects a word's sense directly, but its referent only indirectly. Similarly, but perhaps even more clearly, if we changed *some dogs* into *some big dogs*, the dependent *big* changes the sense into 'big dog', but doesn't change the referent set into a big set. Instead, the referent changes into a set of big dogs.

But what about the dependent? Is it the dependent's sense or its referent that affects the modified word's meaning? If we take *Fido* as an example, it must be the referent because names have no sense (except a very general category such as 'dog'). The same is true even when the dependent does have a sense, as in *A dog barked*. What barked? Was it the general category 'dog', or was it the particular dog? The answer is obvious.

The general conclusion, then, is that when one word depends on another, it's typically the dependent's referent that modifies the parent's sense. This is the pattern shown in Figure 8.9, where it's the referent of *Fido* that relates semantically to the sense of *barked*.

This diagram also shows another technicality: the link labelled 'parent sense' which distinguishes the modified 'Fido barking' from the basic sense 'barking'. This link shows that 'Fido barking' is the effect of adding *Fido*, which is helpful when working out the details of modification.

Coreference: a word shares its referent with its dependent

In **COREFERENCE**, the two related words share the same referent.

For example, *a dog* refers to a single entity which isA 'dog', so the sense is supplied solely by *dog*, and neither word modifies the other's sense. On the other hand, the determiner *a* confirms that the referent is a single countable entity, and

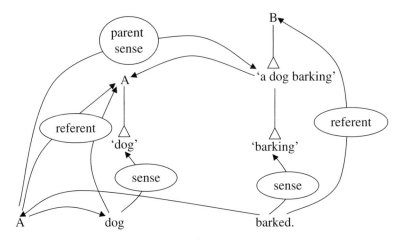

Figure 8.10 *Coreference between a determiner and its complement*

that it isn't definite. The obvious analysis is one in which *a* and *dog* both have the same referent, to which each contributes some information: that it's a single unknown entity (from *a*), and that it's a dog (from *dog*).

This analysis allows us to develop Figure 8.7 into Figure 8.10. We can now see how the words are linked to one another, not only in syntax but also in semantics. As we shall see on page 289, the word *dog* depends syntactically on *a*, but the two words have the same referent, labelled A. The word *a* in turn depends on *barked*, but in this case *a* modifies the sense of *barked*, to produce its own 'parent sense': 'a dog barking'. And lastly, *barked* refers to an event B which is an example of a dog barking.

Coreference is a very common semantic relation between 'grammatical' parent words such as determiners and their 'lexical' complements. It's found in all determiners, and also some auxiliary verbs and prepositions; for example, *will bark* refers to a single event, whose time is set (by *will*) in the future, and in *a book by Dickens*, the preposition *by* shares the referent of *Dickens*, which it links as 'author' to the book. Coreference is also found in the grammatical construction called 'apposition' which I mentioned briefly at the end of Section 7.7, as in *my brother Colin* or *the word DOG*.

Coreference and identity in cleft sentences

Coreference is of course very similar to the effect of the 'identity' relation found in binding (4.6), but the two are structurally different. Take *the dog*, for example. The determiner *the* has two relevant semantic properties. In relation to its complement (*dog*), it requires coreference so that it can mark their shared referent as definite. But because of this definiteness, it has an identity link to its antecedent, such as a dog that's just been mentioned. In one case the referents are simply merged into one node, whereas in the other the nodes are kept separate.

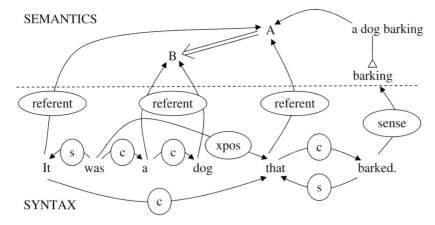

Figure 8.11 *The syntax and semantics of a cleft sentence*

Similarly, one use of the verb BE indicates identity between the subject and the complement, as in (10):

(10)   That building is the post-office.

But the referents of *that building* and *the post-office* must be separate because we can deny the identity, as in (11).

(11)   That building is not the post-office.

The combined effect of coreference and identity is often to reduce a complicated syntactic structure to a much simpler semantic structure, as in the case of cleft sentences (11.6) like (12):

(12)   It was a dog that barked.

This has virtually the same semantic structure as the much simpler example (1), *A dog barked*. Figure 8.11 shows how this effect is achieved, as I explain below.

The syntactic and semantic structures are separated by the dotted line, and the first thing to notice is how much simpler the semantics is. The second is how similar the semantics is to that of *A dog barked* in Figure 8.10. The similarity would have been even greater if I had included a referent for *barked* but I deliberately omitted this because it raises complicated issues about its relation to the referent of *was* which aren't relevant here.

The main point of this diagram is to show the simplifying effects of coreference and binding, which work as follows:

- The referents of *a* and *dog* merge by coreference, as explained above. Their shared referent is node B in the diagram.
- The referent of *it*, labelled A, has an 'identity' link to B thanks to the semantics of *was* in *it was a dog*.
- The relative pronoun *that* has a referent which is merged by coreference with that of *it*, i.e. with A, thanks to the special syntax and

semantics of this particular use of *it* in extraposition, labelled 'xpos' (11.6). The peculiarity of extraposition is a 'dummy' *it* that has an order-irrelevant complement link to a delayed dependent of the verb, in this case the word *that*; and as with the pronouns that we call determiners, this complement link carries semantic coreference. Hence the coreference of *it* and *that*.

This cleft sentence raises important questions about syntactic and semantic analysis. Is it right to give virtually the same semantic analyses to *A dog barked* and *It was a dog that barked*? Surely there are important differences that should be shown in the diagram? The first simply reports the event, whereas the second focuses on the dog (as opposed, say, to a fox).

These differences are indeed important, but is the structure diagram the right place to explain them? Word Grammar, unlike other theories, locates the linguistic structure within a cognitive structure where activation is controlled by attention, and therefore offers a much better explanation for the differences between these two sentences. According to Word Grammar, although their semantic structures are very similar, the syntax of clefting guarantees that more activation centres on 'dog' in one than in the other.

Predicatives: a word's sense is modified by its dependent's sense

We can now consider another alternative to the default pattern in which the dependent's referent modifies the parent's sense. In this alternative, it's the dependent sense, rather than its referent, that modifies the parent's sense. This is what we find in some (but probably not all) predicatives (11.2), the valency pattern where a 'syntactic triangle' lets the verb's dependent share its subject.

For example, (13) illustrates perfectly why the term *isA* is so appropriate for our basic classification relation.

(13)   He is a linguist.

Its syntactic and semantic structure is shown in Figure 8.12. Notice, first, that the predicative *a linguist* doesn't refer to any particular linguist so that we might reply to (13) by asking *Which linguist is he?* (This is a possible interpretation of (13), but not the obvious one.) The crucial thing about *linguist* is its sense, the general category 'linguist'.

The determiner *a* in this case is pure syntax, satisfying the syntactic need for a determiner before a singular count noun; and it's interesting to remember that (13) translates into languages such as French and German without a determiner. The easiest analysis for this use of *a* gives it the same sense as its complement noun.

The verb's meaning is slightly more complicated. Clearly it at least involves the primitive relation 'isA', even though there must also be something extra (which I'm calling 'being') which allows this to be located in time (so that we

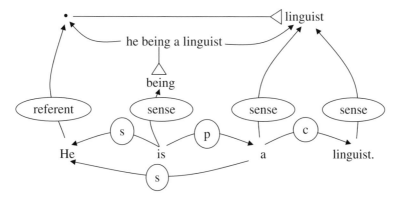

Figure 8.12 *He is a linguist means 'he isA linguist'*

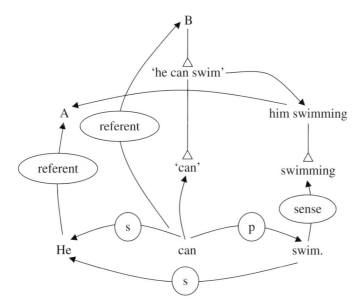

Figure 8.13 *The meaning of* He can swim.

can explain the difference between (13) and *He was a linguist*). But the main point is that 'being' is modified by the sense of *a linguist*, rather than by its referent.

A similar semantic pattern emerges for verbal predicatives such as the infinitive *swim* in (14).

(14)   He can swim.

For this the structure is shown in Figure 8.13.

The structure of *He can swim* is complicated by the fact that *He* is actually the subject of *swim* as well as of *can*, thanks to the triangular 'predicative' relation. This is why the referent of *He* (node A) combines with the sense of *swim*

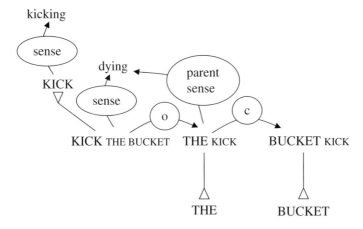

Figure 8.14 *The idiom KICK THE BUCKET*

('swimming') before the latter combines with that of *can* to give 'he can swim'. The result is a structure similar to the one we might give to *Him swimming is possible* or (more syntactically) *It's possible for him to swim*.

But the most relevant characteristic of this diagram is that it is the sense of *swim* that modifies the meaning of *can*, and not its referent. This is what we need because what is possible is not some particular incident of him swimming, but the general and timeless category 'him swimming'. In contrast, the whole sentence does refer to a particular state, labelled B. This is a state in which he can swim, and it is located in time by the present tense (in contrast with the state in *He could swim*, which is located in the past).

Idioms: the effect of the dependent is unpredictable

The last alternative to the default semantic effect of a dependent is irregularity. Such cases are called **IDIOMS**, and the classic example is the idiom KICK THE BUCKET, meaning 'die' (Ayto 2006). Figure 8.14 shows how KICK THE BUCKET is related, as a sublexeme, to the ordinary verb KICK.

As you can see in Figure 8.14, each of the words in this idiom is a special sublexeme of an ordinary lexeme; and what's particularly special about the sublexeme called 'KICK $_{the\ bucket}$' is that it means 'dying'. This is also the 'parent-sense' of its special object.

One consequence of this treatment of idioms is that the same sequence of words, *kick the bucket*, can also be taken literally simply by classifying each word as an ordinary example of its main lexeme.

Semantic phrasing

In each of these patterns, therefore, a word's sense is changed by its dependent from the default sense which it inherits from the lexeme. As I pointed out earlier, this doesn't contradict the lexeme's sense because the new sense belongs to a word-token, and not to the lexeme.

But what about the meaning of the whole sentence? If we attach meanings to individual words, doesn't this prevent us from recognizing that all these word meanings combine into something which is greater than the sum of its parts, the sentence's meaning?

This objection misses the cumulative effect of all these modifications. Take a really simple example, *Fido barked*. If *Fido* modifies the meaning *barked*, then the meaning of *barked* is 'Fido barked' – the meaning of the entire sentence. The meaning of both the words accumulates on *barked* because this is the sentence's root, the word on which all the other words ultimately depend.

The same is true in more complicated examples such as (15).

(15)   A noisy dog in the next house barked all night because he was lonely.

Here too, the entire sentence's meaning is located on its root verb, *barked*. This is modified by its dependents *a*, *all* and *because*, each of which is in turn modified by its dependents and so on; so *barked* actually means 'a noisy dog in the next house barked all night because he was lonely'.

This mechanism of meaning modification also produces intermediate complex meanings, such as 'a noisy dog in the next house', the meaning of *a*. This is a hierarchical semantic structure that I call **SEMANTIC PHRASING** (Hudson 1990: 146–51). This, according to Word Grammar, is where 'phrase structure' belongs, and not in syntax (7.1).

Other issues on the boundary between meaning and syntax

There's a great deal more to be said about how semantic and syntactic structures fit together, but this isn't the place to say it. I'll finish with a short list of important topics that I've discussed elsewhere:

- how semantic phrasing works when a word has two or more dependents, such as a verb with a subject and an object; for example, in *He ate it*, do *he* and *it* each create a separate parent-sense or does *he* have to build on that of *it*, producing an unequal relation between subjects and objects? (Reinhart and Siloni 2006, Hudson 2007c: 122)
- the difference between 'distributed' and 'joint' interpretations of plural (and coordinated) nouns; for example, in *They drank a litre of wine*, was that a litre each (distributed) or a litre between them (joint)? (Hudson 2007c: 229–31)
- the effects of 'quantifiers' such as *each* or *two*, as in *Each of the five students wrote two essays*. How many essays in total? (Hudson 2007c: 228–30)
- the semantic differences between declarative, interrogative and imperative structures; for example, the imperative *Hurry up!* refers to an example of you hurrying up (in the future), which is the purpose of saying these word-tokens. (Hudson 1990: 220–2, 380–3)

None of these published discussions is the last word on the topic, but at least they point the way to a properly researched Word Grammar analysis.

Summary of this subsection:

• Each **dependent** of a word affects its semantics in some way. Typically, the dependent's referent combines with the word's sense, but other possibilities are: **coreference**, the sense–sense relation of **predicatives**, and the irregularity of **idioms**.
• Since a word-token has a separate sense for each dependent, its senses include the meanings of all the dependents (and, recursively, of all their dependents). This produces a **semantic phrasing** which is similar to the syntactic phrase structure of non-dependency theories of syntax.

Where next?

Advanced: Just read on!

8.7.4   Semantic properties

One of the things we all know about meaning is that it's the kind of thing that dictionaries claim to be able to 'define'. However, we also saw in Section 6.6 that dictionary definitions don't really do what they claim, and that what we really need in order to understand a word's meaning is not a definition, but a semantic analysis.

A semantic analysis of a concept is a list of its properties; and in Section 3.5 we saw that properties consist of links to other concepts – what I called the 'network notion'. Consequently, we can be sure that the concepts that we use as word senses are as tightly interdependent as any other concepts we may have.

To take a simple example, the concepts 'bicycle' and 'pedal' define one another, because having pedals is one of the properties of a bicycle and being a moving part of a bicycle is a property of 'pedal'. Likewise for 'bicycle' and 'cycling', and the meaning of the verb CYCLE, since a bicycle is for cycling and cycling is the use of a bicycle.

Recycling and semantic roles

These mutual links don't lead to circularity because the concepts concerned always have other properties, but they do allow concepts to grow in our minds as we find new interconnections. This kind of mental enrichment follows the principle of recycling (3.5): wherever possible, relate concepts to each other.

The main thrust of this principle is to disagree with a very different approach to the study of meaning which assumes that every word should be defined in terms of a fixed set of very general terms called the Natural Semantic Metalanguage (Goddard 2006). In the case of 'bicycle', recycling demands that we should relate it to 'pedal', whereas the Natural Semantic Metalanguage forbids it.

The Recycling Principle also solves one of the most general problems of semantics, namely how to analyse the **SEMANTIC ROLES** that we need in order to distinguish the effects of different dependents.

Take the verb EAT, for example. When I eat a sandwich, the sandwich and I have very different roles in the action. Moreover, when I talk about this event, it's because of these roles that I would be expressed by the subject of EAT, with the sandwich relegated to the object: *I ate the sandwich*, not *The sandwich ate me*. The latter sentence is perfectly grammatical, but requires a considerable imaginative leap because the subject dependency forces the sandwich into the role of eater. The question is how to distinguish these roles.

As I explained in Section 3.2, most linguists assume a small and very general set of role-names such as 'agent' (for me) and 'patient' (for the sandwich). This assumption is problematic because there are several competing sets of roles and it's all too easy to find examples that none can analyse properly because they don't make sufficiently fine distinctions (Pustejovsky 2006).

In contrast, the Recycling Principle means that both language learners and linguists can freely invent new relational concepts as needed, provided only that they can be defined in terms of existing concepts. This is the principle that I applied in syntax, where we had to distinguish different kinds of dependent from one another (7.2, 11.2). The same principle works equally well in semantics and allows us to invent relations that are as general or as specific as we want.

For instance, consider the difference between eating a sandwich and making it. On the one hand, the sandwich has a similar role in both cases. It is deeply changed by the event, and (unlike me) it neither controls the event nor puts any energy into it. To reflect these similarities, we might use the traditional term 'patient' as a name for the sandwich's role. On the other hand, the two events affect the sandwich in very different ways, because one destroys it while the other creates it; so perhaps we should call it the 'effected' when made and 'affected' when eaten. (Again these terms are well established.) But better still, we could combine the two analyses in a taxonomy where 'effected' and 'affected' both isA 'patient'.

Once again, therefore, we find that taxonomies and inheritance are central to the organization of our thinking.

Deixis

One particularly interesting and important kind of semantic property is called **DEIXIS**, from the Greek word for 'pointing' (Green 2006).

Typical examples of **DEICTIC** words are ME, YOU, NOW and HERE, all of which define their referent in relation to the properties of the current word-token – who said it, to whom, when and where. If we take word-tokens as central to language, such words are easy to analyse, and indeed it would be surprising if they didn't exist.

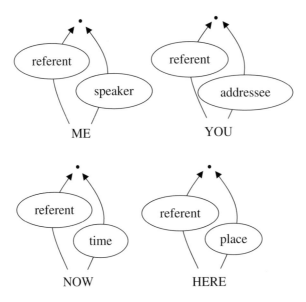

Figure 8.15 *Four deictic words and their meanings*

If John is talking to Mary and wants a word that refers unambiguously to himself, what could be clearer and easier than a word which picks out the current speaker? Whatever else Mary may know, she at least knows that he is talking to her.

Of course, deictic words aren't much use out of context, as in the proverbial message in a bottle washed up on the beach saying 'Help me! I'm here and need help now.' But at least until the invention of modern long-distance communication systems, most word-tokens were produced in face-to-face conversation which is ideally suited for deixis.

The meanings of these four words are defined in Figure 8.15. The relations 'speaker', 'addressee', 'time' and 'place' are crucial for any word-token, but don't reach the lexemes that we derive from most tokens (8.3).

These words are different because the token characteristics allow a simple generalization such as: 'whoever says a token of ME is also the person to whom it refers'. In other words, its speaker and referent are the same.

Tense works in the same way, by locating the time of the event referred to relative to the time when the word is uttered. This is a useful reminder that even the core of grammar cannot be separated either from the general-purpose relations of cognition such as 'before', or from the properties of word-tokens.

Summary of this subsection:

- The senses of different words are typically defined in relation to each other, following the principle of **recycling** whereby concepts build where possible on existing concepts. This principle also allows new **semantic roles** to be defined as needed.

- **Deixis** is a special kind of meaning in which a word's referent is identified in relation to one of the properties of the word-token; typical **deictic** words are ME and NOW, but tense inflections also have deictic meanings.

Where next?

Advanced: Just read on!

8.7.5   Meaning, thought and culture

And finally we come to the Big Question: what does linguistic meaning have to do with thought? Does the language we learn as children have a profound effect on the way we think about the world? And anyway, how much difference is there between one language's semantics and another's?

The last question is easy for anyone who knows anything about more than one language: languages can be very different indeed (Evans and Levinson 2009).

Even languages as similar to one another as English and German show major differences in the concepts they use as word senses. For example, German has no verb which means 'go'. Instead, it has GEHEN for 'going on foot' and FAHREN for 'going in a vehicle'; so *I went home* is translated differently according to whether I went on foot or in a vehicle (in the former case: *Ich bin nach Hause gegangen*, and in the latter: *Ich bin nach Hause gefahren*). Conversely, English has no verb which means the same as FAHREN, which would sometimes be translated as 'go' and sometimes as 'ride'.

The two languages simply divide the world of motion in different ways. As you can imagine, the differences are even more dramatic if we consider more remote languages.

But do these semantic differences affect the way we think about the world? An easy answer is yes, because a sentence's meaning is 'a way of thinking about the world'. If language is part of general cognition, as I have been arguing throughout this book, and if meaning consists of the ordinary concepts of general cognition – concepts like 'dog' and 'barking' – then different semantic structures must, by definition, offer different ways of thinking about the world.

But there's an important qualification that has to be added here. It's possible that these ways of thinking only apply when we're speaking or listening – that they constitute a special kind of thinking called **THINKING FOR SPEAKING** (Slobin 1996). If we know that we're speaking, then we know that we're looking for words to express our thoughts; and that's rarely easy because the words we know often don't match our ideas at all well. Consequently, what we do is to adjust our message to fit into the available words – what we might call cutting our semantic coat to fit our lexical cloth.

For example, an English speaker wanting to say that they had 'gone' home would pick the concept 'going' because this is easy to express, whereas a German speaker would select a more specific concept to match either GEHEN or FAHREN.

But even if this is true, it doesn't necessarily mean that English and German speakers think differently about movement when they're **not** talking – for example, that the German speaker would pay more attention to the mode of transport when planning a journey.

Nor, on the other hand, can we be sure that the linguistic difference **doesn't** affect their non-linguistic thinking. This is a very difficult question which has attracted some very interesting research (Taylor 2006), but the jury is still out.

Part of the difficulty in this research is separating the effects of language and those of general **CULTURE**, the ideas that we learn from others in our community and share with them, and which we learn partly, but only partly, through language.

For example, we all know the concept 'sibling', meaning a brother or a sister, but we must learn it, or work it out for ourselves, without the help of language simply because there's no ordinary word for it. How can we learn it? By learning 'brother' and 'sister', and then inducing a super-concept in the usual way on the basis of their shared similarities (4.4).

This example shows that we can learn cultural concepts without the help of language, and no doubt we learn a high proportion of the properties of most concepts in this way.

Nevertheless, language is undoubtedly the most important guide to the concepts of our culture that we have, and for many concepts it's virtually the only way to find out that the concepts exist, even if we learn properties by more direct experience. I'm thinking here in particular of the abstract values and ideas that have such an important role in a culture and which politicians exploit so effectively – words like FAIR and FREE.

But however reliable a guide language may be to our culture, it may be much less reliable as a guide to reality. For example, can we assume that because we have the word SPIRIT, the concept 'spirit' must have properties which we can find and which will guide us towards some kind of external reality?

In case you think such examples are easy to spot, how about the words DIALECT and LANGUAGE? Can we assume, because we have two words with different meanings, that there must also be a difference in reality that we might find if only we were smart enough?

Summary of this subsection:

- The concepts that we learn as word senses are part of thinking, and since they vary from language to language, we can be sure that language influences the way we think; but it may only influence our **thinking for speaking**.

- On the other hand, language is the main vehicle for a community to transmit its culture to the next generation so it may have more profound affects as well.

Where next?

Advanced: Just read on!

8.8   Social meaning

We end with little more than a nod in the direction of one of the – to me – most interesting areas of language, which we may call its 'social meaning'. This is the territory of **SOCIOLINGUISTICS**, the study of language in relation to society (Hudson 1996, Mesthrie 2006).

Word Grammar is particularly well suited as a theoretical framework for sociolinguistics precisely because it treats language as part of the same cognitive network that also holds what we know about the individuals, social groups and social relations that make up society. This being so, it should be relatively straightforward to relate the two bodies of knowledge to one another, showing how we choose our words so that they fit whatever the social context demands. In this project, 'social meaning' will include any links between words (or other linguistic units such as forms or sounds) and social categories.

8.8.1   Kinship

Taken in this broad sense, social meaning includes a great deal of referential meaning, because our social world is so important to us. Words for talking about social relations are as closely connected as any to our culture, so it's hard to decide, when analysing them, whether one is analysing the language or the culture.

We've already looked at a few examples from a key area of vocabulary, kinship terminology (3.4.1). The network structure of vocabulary is particularly clear in this area because the meanings of two basic terms, MOTHER and FATHER, are 'recycled' in defining slightly less basic words like BROTHER and PARENT, which in turn are recycled in even more peripheral relations such as AUNT and COUSIN.

This is the system that English speakers all apply when speaking, so its effects reach at least as far into our minds as what I called 'thinking for speaking' (8.7.5), and may reach much further if you think of our social behaviour in terms of visiting, sending Christmas cards and so on.

A network analysis is exactly what's needed for teasing out the details, especially since it allows us to consider just the immediate neighbours of each link. This is what you'll see in Figure 8.16, an exploration of the English kinship

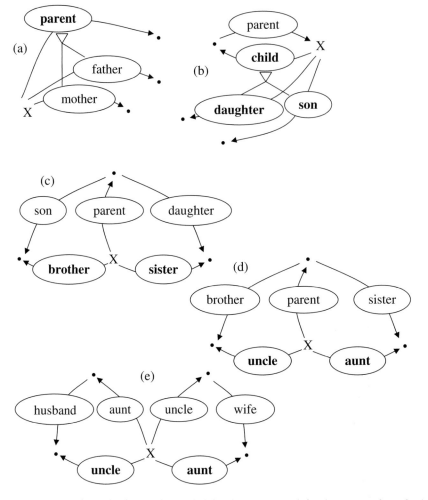

Figure 8.16 *How the English kinship system is defined in terms of 'mother' and 'father'*

system which gradually reaches further into the total network through five mini-networks.

Taking 'mother' and 'father' as the starting point, each network defines one or two new relations (which are in bold) in terms of existing ones as follows:

- Network (a) defines X's parent as either X's mother or father.
- Network (b) defines X's child as anyone whose parent is X, with X's daughter and son as subclasses.
- Network (c) defines X's brother and sister as son or daughter of X's parent.
- Network (d) defines X's uncle and aunt as brother or sister of X's parent.

- Network (e) picks up the peculiar fact that we extend this relation to the spouses of our uncles and aunts.

This is the English system, which meshes reasonably well with the cultures of most English speakers; but there's nothing inevitable about it (Heath 2006). A century of research by anthropologists on kinship terminology has unearthed some wildly different systems, such as the system in which a single term covers not only X's father but also X's uncles (or in some cases, just X's father's brother). Do uncles in such societies have the same rights and responsibilities towards children as fathers do? One would expect so, but it's a matter of fact and research.

The main point is that a language's vocabulary has a network structure which bears some relation to the network structure that its speakers impose on their social relations; and of course it isn't only in kinship that we would expect to find a correspondence between lexical and social structures – think of terms such as FRIEND, COLLEAGUE, FAN and STUDENT.

8.8.2   Social interaction

Another area of social relations in which languages provide guidance is in **SOCIAL INTERACTION**, the relations between us and the people we meet in our social life.

The main interpersonal relations we need to signal are the relations of **power** and **solidarity** that I discussed in 3.4.2. Every language provides ways of signalling these, and in some languages the signals are given in words that lie at the heart of the language. For example, many European languages have two different singular pronouns meaning 'you' according to how intimate the speaker and addressee are. English used to use *thou* and *you* like this, but nowadays the signals are more peripheral: greetings (*hi!* versus *good morning*), politeness terms (*please*, *thanks*) and, above all, the choice of names; so I'm 'Dick' to my wife and friends, 'Dad' to my daughters and 'Professor Hudson' to some colleagues (Hudson 1996: 106–43).

All these words bring social structures into language in a way which is particularly challenging for linguistic theory because it's not just a matter of referential meaning, i.e. properties of the person referred to. Instead, the social relations concern the speaker, who has no place at all in most theories of language.

In contrast, Word Grammar recognizes the speaker as a property of word-tokens, and therefore also as a potential property of some stored word-types or even word-classes. For example, the rule for using English given names such as *Dick* seems to be that they can be used if the speaker and the referent are 'intimately' related (in the sense of 'intimately' that I defined in Section 3.4.2). In network notation, the rule is shown in Figure 8.17. In words, a given name is typically used by someone (the speaker) who is in an 'intimate' relation with the person referred to.

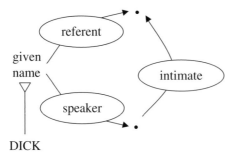

Figure 8.17 *Given names are used only for 'intimates' of the speaker*

Once we recognize that language can 'mean' properties of the speaker which are distinct from the information it gives about ordinary referents, we open up a whole new world of research into language and **SOCIAL IDENTITY** (Joseph 2006). Whenever I talk, I inevitably also give information about my social identity, about how I fit into the larger mental network that I've constructed for society (my I-society); and if you've built a similar network, you'll be able to interpret my 'social meaning' as I intend. Simply by choosing to speak English I give a great deal of information, because I associate talking English with properties such as living in the UK and taking milk in tea; but for a linguist the most interesting choices are those that involve fine details of the language system.

I show my age by saying *Jolly good!* and my education by saying *It's an empirical hypothesis*. I show I'm relaxed and informal by saying *That's nice* (rather than *That is nice*), and I show I'm almost a Londoner by using the occasional glottal stop in words like *hit* (but never in *hitting*, except when I'm jokingly 'putting on an accent'). The methods of quantitative sociolinguistics allow careful and productive research into all these examples of social meaning, and the network notation of Word Grammar offers a theoretical framework for interpreting the results (Hudson 2007c: 246–8, Hudson 2007a, Hudson 2007b).

Summary of this section:

- Word Grammar is a suitable theoretical framework for **sociolinguistics** because it treats language as part of the same general cognitive network as society.
- Vocabulary includes words such as **kinship terminology** whose referential meaning is part of social structure, and which reveals the details of these structures including how some concepts are recycled in other concepts.
- Language also helps us to negotiate **social interaction** by providing linguistic signals, such as the choice of names, for the interpersonal relations of power and solidarity. The social meaning of these signals has to include the 'speaker' relation, which is available in Word Grammar.

- **Social identity** is also closely tied to linguistic choices of many different kinds, ranging from the choice of language to the choice of details of vocabulary or pronunciation.

Where next?

Advanced: You've 'finished'. Congratulations!

PART III

How English works

9   Introduction to English linguistics

English linguistics is the study of English using the ideas and methods of the 'general linguistics' that has pushed forward our understanding of how language works.

In comparison with the study of Latin and Greek, the study of English is fairly young, with the first dictionaries and grammars appearing in the seventeenth and eighteenth centuries (Hanks 2006, Wikipedia: 'History of English grammars'). But serious and systematic grammars of English, as opposed to manuals of 'good usage', are even more recent, dating from the late nineteenth and early twentieth centuries. (Wikipedia: 'Henry Sweet' and 'Otto Jespersen'.)

Even these systematic analyses focused on the history of the modern language rather than on its current organization, and tended to pick out details that were in some way interesting or controversial, and which might be of use to advanced learners of English – the kind of people, in fact, who could read the grammar book. Consequently they ignored elementary information (such as basic word order) and general patterns.

Their historical orientation and their focus on details made them rather dauntingly inaccessible to all but their authors' specialist colleagues, with rather predictable results in education, where a proper understanding of English was most needed. In 1921, an official report on grammar teaching in English lessons concluded as follows: '[it is] impossible at the present juncture to teach English grammar in the schools for the simple reason that no-one knows exactly what it is' (Hudson and Walmsley 2005: 601).

The present boom in English linguistics started in the early 1950s and has been driven by two powerful forces: the position of the United States at the centre of linguistics, and the high profits for publishers in the market for books on English as a foreign language. As far as English grammar is concerned, nobody could now claim that 'no-one knows exactly what it is'.

We know exactly what Standard English is. We know vast amounts of fine detail from large-scale computer-based studies of the usage found in enormous collections of spoken and written English, and these details have been published in a series of mega-grammars covering between 1,000 and 2,000 pages each (Quirk *et al.* 1972, Quirk *et al.* 1985, Biber *et al.* 1999, Huddleston and Pullum 2002, Carter and McCarthy 2006). Moreover, unlike the earlier grammars, these are informed by general theories of language structure, and include generalizations about commonplace patterns as well as the fine details.

No other language has received so much attention in the last few decades, so English has a very special status as the testing ground for theories of language. The dominance of English brings obvious advantages to those of us who know it well, but also carries dangers for linguistic theory that we should at least be aware of.

The main danger is much the same danger that linguistics faced in Europe at the time when Latin was dominant. 'Latinate' grammarians took Latin as a model to be imposed on every other language. When they looked at English they looked for a future tense and a pluperfect (both of which are inflections in Latin) and found them in *will go* and *had gone*, in spite of the rather obvious fact that English morpho-syntax is organized around a two-tense system. Similarly, they found an 'ablative case' in the English preposition FROM, again ignoring the fundamental difference between an inflection and a lexeme.

The danger is that modern grammarians will do the same as the 'Latinate' grammarians did. They may impose the categories and structures of English on other languages, finding determiners, tenses or number inflections in languages that actually have none or distinguishing 'pre-dependents' and 'post-dependents' in languages where no such distinction exists.

Worse still, theoretical grammarians could assume (and indeed have on occasions assumed) that English is a typical language, so a general theory of grammar can safely be built on evidence from this one language. This assumption is simply not true. Given the enormous diversity of the world's 6,000 languages, it's hard to imagine any language being 'typical'; and there's no reason at all to believe that English may be a particularly good candidate for this title.

One issue that arises in English grammar is the contrast between description and prescription discussed in Chapter 5. The grammars listed here, like their historically oriented predecessors, are all 'descriptive' in the sense that their aim is to describe the language rather than to change it. But of course there have been a great many 'prescriptive' grammars too, full of advice about how to improve one's English by avoiding what the grammarians call 'common errors'. One of the main achievements of education seems to be a vast pool of insecurity about such things. (Wikipedia: 'Linguistic prescription'. To get an idea of the depth of this pool, type 'grammatical error' into Google.)

This, then, is the research background to the following very brief introduction to how English works. Within the Word Grammar tradition, it builds on earlier published grammars of English, especially as a heavy monograph and a light teaching textbook (Hudson 1990, Hudson 1998).

Where next?

Advanced: Just read on!

10 English words

10.1 Word-classes

> **Summary of Section 6.3:**
>
> - Like all other concepts, words belong to general categories, variously called **word-classes**, lexical classes or parts of speech.
> - These form a taxonomy in which classes can be divided into subclasses.
> - The broad outline of our modern taxonomy of word-classes was first proposed for Latin and Greek 2,000 years ago.

Section 6.3 included a traditional list of word-classes for English: noun, adjective, pronoun, preposition, verb, adverb, article and conjunction. Not surprisingly, perhaps, the recent attention to English grammar has revealed a number of serious weaknesses in the details of the traditional system which we consider more carefully in Section 10.3, but meanwhile we can review the main changes that are needed when we test the traditional classes against modern theoretical standards.

Most of the traditional classes pass the test with flying colours, which is perhaps part of the reason why they have survived for 2,000 years. Modern grammarians still talk about **NOUNS**, **PRONOUNS**, **VERBS**, **ADJECTIVES**, **ADVERBS**, **PREPOSITIONS** and **CONJUNCTIONS**. These word-classes all play an important part in any modern grammar of English because they each express a bundle of generalizations that couldn't otherwise be expressed. In other words, it would simply be impossible to write a revealing grammar of English without recognizing these classes.

Of course, the actual names we give to the classes are up for negotiation, but there's not much point in looking for modern-sounding alternatives to terms that are as well established as these.

10.1.1 Determiners and pronouns

The only traditional class that really doesn't deserve a place is 'article', which only includes two words: *a/an* and *the*, the so-called indefinite and definite articles. Incidentally, it's helpful to remember that although Greek had (and still has) articles, Latin didn't and Latin grammarians accepted this as a difference between the two languages.

The trouble with the class 'article', as applied to English, is not that its two members are different from each other – they actually have a great deal in common – but rather that they share their similarities with a number of other words. Examples are ANY, THIS, WHICH and HIS, which aren't traditionally called 'articles'. These are the words that modern linguists call **DETERMINERS**, though traditionally they were all called adjectives.

The adjective classification is simply wrong, given the way English grammar works. What it claims is that if we take three lexemes such as ANY, BIG and LINGUISTICS, the first two share more properties with each other than they do with the third. Let's test this.

First, what properties do ANY and BIG share? It's true that they can both combine with a noun, giving *any book* or *big book*, but then so can LINGUISTICS: *linguistics book*. Moreover, when they do combine with a noun in this way, all three stand before it: *any big linguistics book*. As far as I know, there's no property at all that's shared by ANY and BIG but not by LINGUISTICS.

The second question that this discussion prompts is whether there are any properties that distinguish ANY from BIG. There are plenty. To start with, adjectives can be used after BE, but determiners can't:

(1)   The book is big
(2)   *The book is any.

Another important difference is that adjectives are always optional, so they can be dropped without losing grammaticality, but determiners can't:

(3)   Any big book will do.
(4)   Any ~~big~~ book will do.
(5)   *~~Any~~ big book will do.

The rule responsible for this difference says that a noun such as BOOK – what's called a singular **COUNTABLE** common noun – has to combine with a word such as ANY, and a word like BIG simply won't do. In contrast, of course, the determiner isn't essential with the plural *books* or with a **MASS** noun such as COFFEE: *I like books, I like coffee*. What's not allowed is *I like book*.

Another difference between determiners and adjectives is that adjectives can be multiplied, but determiners can't:

(6)   I bought a nice big red book.
(7)   *I bought this his book.

And finally, most determiners can be used without a following noun, but most adjectives can't:

(8)   Any ~~book~~ will do.
(9)   *Big ~~book~~ will do.

These differences explain why all modern linguists separate determiners from adjectives. But once we have the word-class 'determiner', we no longer need 'article' as well because the articles are more or less straightforward determiners. In short, linguists would typically delete 'article' from the list and add 'determiner'. This may look like just a change of name, but this would be wrong because 'determiner' is a different class from 'article', and a much more efficient one because it has more properties and more members.

But Word Grammar actually achieves an even better reorganization of the traditional classes by merging 'determiner' with 'pronoun'. Here's how the argument goes.

The last property of determiners listed above shows a strong link to the class of pronouns. In traditional analysis, when *any* is used on its own, as in (8), it's called a pronoun, and so are the other determiners in our earlier list: *this*, *which* and *his*. Indeed, virtually all the determiners can be used (in traditional terminology) either 'as adjectives' (*I like this book*) or 'as pronouns' (*I like this*).

The obvious exceptions are the articles, THE and A, both of which demand a following noun: **I read the ~~book~~*, **I read a ~~book~~*. But there's another determiner which can't be used without a noun, namely EVERY: **I read every book*. But exceptionality is exactly what we expect, and it would be surprising to find none.

But it's rather odd to say that ANY belongs to two different classes, since this implies two distinct lexemes for ANY: one a determiner, the other a pronoun. And it's even odder to say the same about so many other words: THIS, WHICH, HIS and so on through all the two dozen or so determiners.

Moreover, this dual classification is odder still when you think what it's based on: a mere difference of valency, according to whether there's a following noun. When a verb may be used either with or without an object noun, we don't put it into two fundamentally different classes; for instance, SING is still a verb whether it's used with an object (*sing a song*) or not. So why can't we do the same with determiners?

These objections to the dual classification of determiners have produced wide support for a different analysis with just one word-class and one lexeme per word, and in which the following noun is an optional accompaniment that has no effect on the word-class. In this analysis, ANY belongs to the same word-class whether it is followed by a noun (*Any book will do*) or not (*Any will do*).

The only bone of contention is whether ANY is a determiner which needn't have a following noun, or a pronoun which can have one. Here I disagree with most other grammarians. In my opinion, determiners are simply pronouns that happen to allow (or demand) a following noun.

One of the arguments for this analysis is that the class of pronouns that don't allow a following noun is far larger than the class of determiners that do, so it makes much more sense to treat determiners as a subclass of pronouns. There are other arguments (Hudson 1990: 268–76), but I'll simply take them for granted here.

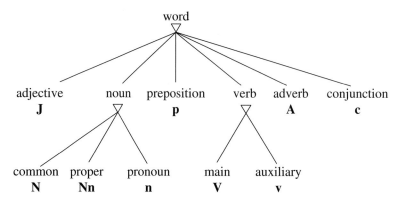

Figure 10.1 *A more efficient taxonomy of word-classes for English*

To summarize, then, the analysis that I present below will treat determiners as pronouns that take a following noun as their complement. But since the difference between them and other pronouns is a matter of valency, not word-class, there's no need to recognize a separate class of determiners. In short, having replaced 'article' by 'determiner', I'm now replacing 'determiner' by 'pronoun'.

But even this isn't the end of the changes needed to the traditional word-classes. What about the relation between pronouns and nouns?

You may have noticed that two of the properties that I listed for verbs mentioned 'noun or pronoun'. This phrase occurs over and over again in traditional grammar books, which suggests that generalizations are being missed and the system of word-classes is less efficient than it might be. If nouns and pronouns can be used in the same way, why not assume that they belong to a single class?

And what better name for this class than 'noun'? In this analysis, then, 'pronoun' isA 'noun', and stands alongside two well established traditional subclasses, 'common noun' and 'proper noun'. In 'pronoun' we find ANY and THE as well as ME, WHO and so on; in 'common noun' we find DOG, IMAGINATION and tens of thousands of others; and in 'proper noun' we find all the names such as DICK and LONDON.

10.1.2   The taxonomy of word-classes and a notation

The outcome of these deliberations is that the taxonomy of word-classes for English looks like Figure 10.1 rather than the one shown in Figure 6.2.

Figure 10.1 rejects the rather flat taxonomy with eight top-level classes and replaces it with a much deeper one that has only six classes at the top. Even this number could probably be reduced by combining adjectives and adverbs into a superclass of 'ad-words' which I still believe could be justified by its efficiency (see Hudson 1990: 168–70); but this idea still needs more work.

This system of word-classes provides a class for almost every word in any English text. The most effective way to build confidence in grammar is to apply your learning, as it grows, to examples, and since we're talking about the real English that you and I have in our minds, we might as well use real examples.

To make this kind of analysis easier, Figure 10.1 also suggests an abbreviation for each of the word-class names. The abbreviations reflect the size of the word-classes: J, N, nN, V and A, with large letters, name large classes, while n, p, v and c name small ones. Example (10) shows how these abbreviations can be applied to an ordinary sentence (which you may recognize).

(10)   This system of word classes provides a class for almost every word
         n   N   p N N   V   n N p A   n   N
         in any English text.
         p   n   J   N

Section 10.3 provides more detailed guidance for novices about how to recognize word-classes. With the help of this guidance and the supporting material on the website you should soon reach the point where you can classify almost all the words in any sample of English, an achievement which many students find rewarding. But even so, it's important to bear in mind that classifying words is only the start, and, in itself, of no particular interest. The interest and real intellectual challenge of grammatical analysis lie in the syntactic relations among the words, which occupy Chapter 11.

Where next?

Advanced: Back to Part I, Chapter 2.3: Generalizations and inheritance
Novice: Explore Part II, Chapter 6.3: Word-classes

10.2   Inflections

Summary of Section 6.5:

- The word-types that are listed in a grammar are of two types: **lexemes** and **inflections**.
- Lexemes (e.g. DOG) are the dictionary words that belong to word-classes and have basic realizations (called **stems**) and basic meanings. Their names are written here in capitals: DOG.
- Inflections (e.g. 'plural') are word-types that have their own properties that play a part in the grammar, independently of the lexemes and word-classes; their realizations are **variants** of a lexeme's stem and their meanings are similarly based on that of this lexeme.
- Lexemes can have any number of **sublexemes** below them in the taxonomy, which allows examples of the same lexeme to be both similar and distinct.

> • The importance of inflections varies enormously from language to language; some languages have extremely rich systems of inflections, while others have none at all.

Like every other language, English has lexemes and sublexemes, but the question here is what inflections it has. The simplest answer is that English does have inflections, but not many.

Most of the familiar European languages have a great many inflections, for the simple reason that most European languages belong to the Indo-European family whose ancestor, spoken about 6,000 years ago, was very highly inflected (Collinge 2006). The Old English of Beowulf and Alfred still had a rich system, comparable with modern German (Wikipedia: 'Old English'), but in the last 1,000 years, English has lost most of these original inflections. The result of these changes is that it's now nearer the uninflected end of the spectrum, approaching languages such as Chinese, Vietnamese and Thai which have no inflections at all.

English nouns have just one inflection, 'plural', but verbs have a few more, which we must now look at in detail.

10.2.1   Basic verb inflections

If we look simply at morphological differences, a regular verb such as COOK has just three distinct forms other than the stem: *cooks, cooked, cooking*. However, that doesn't mean that verbs have just three inflections, because inflections are more abstract than word-forms. Each inflection is a concept, just like 'cat' or the lexeme CAT, justified by a bundle of properties, and not just by one (the morphology).

To see how important other properties are, consider the following examples, both of which contain the form *peeled*:

(1)   He peeled the potatoes.
(2)   The potatoes can be peeled with a knife.

In spite of their shared morphology, these words are very different. One is tied to an event at some time in the past, while the other isn't; the potatoes act syntactically as the 'object' of one verb, but as the other verb's 'subject' (Section 11.1 will explain that a verb's subject precedes it while the object follows it); and one verb can stand on its own, while the other has to be supported by *can be*.

These properties form two bundles, each defining a different concept, so it's important not to be misled by the fact that they happen to share one property. The morphology isn't irrelevant to inflections; but the relationship is a complex one.

Most grammarians accept the need for the verb inflections listed in Table 10.1, which also suggests some abbreviations that can be combined with the word-class abbreviations introduced at the end of Section 10.1.

Table 10.1 *Inflections for English verbs.*

Inflection	Abbreviation	Standard name	Example
Imperative	m	Imperative	Take it!
Tensed	t	Present tense plural	They take it.
Singular	s	Present tense singular	He takes it.
Past	a	Past tense	He took it.
Infinitive	n	Infinitive	He may take it.
Perfect	f	Perfect participle	He has taken it.
Participle	r	Present participle	He is taking it.
Passive	e	Passive participle	It is taken.
Gerund	g	gerund	Taking it is important.

10.2.2   The inflectional taxonomy

Not surprisingly, perhaps, these inflections show similarities among themselves that point to a taxonomy rather than just a flat list. This taxonomy is shown in Figure 10.2.

The superclasses in this taxonomy are important for any understanding of the inflectional system, so I'll now explain why we need them.

TENSED verbs are so called because they have a tense, either past or present.

- A default-tensed verb has no suffix and refers to a state of affairs in the present: *They like syntax. We get up at seven.* Such verbs always have plural subjects (though exceptionally the subject may be *I* or *you*).

- A **singular**-tensed verb is like the default except that it has the suffix {s} and a singular subject: *She likes syntax. He gets up at seven.*

- A **past**-tensed verb refers to a state of affairs in the past: *She liked syntax. They got up at seven.* The subject may be either singular or plural.

The most important distinction among inflections is the one between **FINITE** and **NON-FINITE** verbs. The term 'finite' means 'limited' – the opposite of 'infinite' – as these forms are limited in terms of their subject and their tense. (Wikipedia: 'Finite verb'.) It's easy to see how this applies to tensed verbs, which are all limited to a particular tense or a particular kind of subject. It's less obvious with **imperative** verbs, but even these have an understood *you* as their subject and refer to some event in the future which the person addressed is to carry out: *Hurry up! Take my advice!*

The reason why finite verbs are so important is their unique ability to act as the sentence-root (7.2). They can be used as the only verb in the sentence, whereas all the others have to depend on some other word. Indeed, every word-class except finite verbs needs to depend on some other word, so finite verbs really stand out

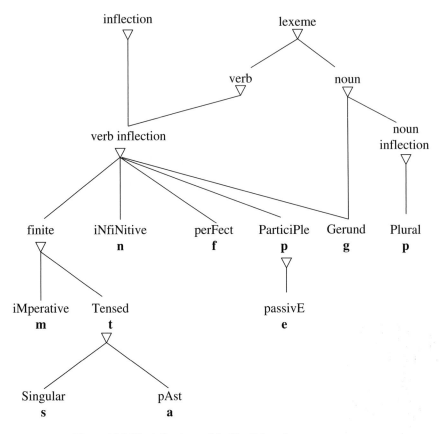

Figure 10.2 *The inflections of the English verb*

syntactically. One of the few useful and almost true rules of traditional grammar was that every sentence needs a finite verb. The truth is actually a little more complicated, but this traditional rule is a step in the right direction.

In contrast with the finite inflections, 'non-finite' inflections are simply the ones that aren't finite, so there's no point in bringing them together. The only general category among non-finites is **PARTICIPLE**, which in my analysis includes just two inflections: present participles (*taking*) and passive participles (*taken*). What these have in common is the possibility of being used to modify a noun, as in *the person taking the photograph* and *the photograph taken by Elizabeth*. The so-called 'past participle' (which I call 'perfect') isn't a participle in this sense because it's only ever used after the auxiliary HAVE (*has taken*).

10.2.3   Gerunds

The one inflection not discussed above is **GERUND**. These are verbs ending in {ing}, but they behave syntactically like both verbs and nouns.

For example, a preposition such as BY can normally only be followed by nouns, so DISCOVERY is permitted but DISCOVER isn't, not even if we provide a subject and object:

(3)   He impressed the world by his discovery.
(4)   *He impressed the world by (he) discovered (new sources of energy).

However, it can be followed by *discovering*, as in (5):

(5)   He impressed the world by discovering new sources of energy.

The possibility of occurring after *by* (along with many other similar observations) shows that *discovering* is a noun.

But now look at what follows it: the noun *sources*. One noun can't be used in this way directly after another noun, as you can see in (6), where I've tried to add *sources* after *discovery*:

(6)   *He impressed the world by his discovery new sources of energy.

If we want to combine these two nouns, we have to use the preposition *of*:

(7)   He impressed the world by his discovery of new sources of energy.

And yet (5) shows that *sources*, without a supporting preposition, can be added to *discovering*, just as it can when DISCOVER is a verb:

(8)   He discovered new sources of energy.

In short, (5) shows that *discovering* has some properties that are only found in nouns (occurring after *by*) and others that are only found in verbs (occurring before *sources* without *of*). The obvious conclusion is that this inflection of DISCOVER is both a noun and a verb (Hudson 2003a, Malouf 2006), which is possible in Word Grammar thanks to multiple inheritance (2.4).

10.2.4   Overview of inflections and abbreviations

The only other possible inflections in English are found in some adjectives and adverbs such as BIG and SOON, which contrast *bigger* and *biggest* and *sooner* and *soonest*. However, it's not at all clear that this is a case of inflection because most adjectives and adverbs use *more* and *most*: *more successful*, *most recently*. If it's not an inflection, then it's an example of the lexical relations discussed in Section 10.4; and for simplicity that's where I assume these patterns belong.

The abbreviations can be combined with those for word-classes to give a complete classification of words. For instance, 'V, a' means 'main verb, past tense' and 'v, n' means 'auxiliary verb, infinitive'. The rather artificial sentence (9) includes one example of each inflection to show how they can be used in analysis.

(9)   Tell them he knows people think he had been helping us by letting
           V,m n,p   n   V,s   N,p V,t   n v,a   v,f V,r n,p p   V,g
           John get beaten.
           Nn   V,n V,e

Inflections make the analysis slightly more challenging than simple word-classes, which in the last resort you can often look up in a dictionary. Inflections require a somewhat more sophisticated analysis that takes more account of the surrounding words. For example, in order to recognize that *think* in (9) is a default-tensed verb, you have to be sensitive to its tense meaning and also to recognize that *people* is its subject.

Where next?

Advanced: Back to Part I, Chapter 2.5: Default inheritance and prototype effects
Novice: Explore Part II, Chapter 6.5: Lexemes and inflections

10.3   Word-class properties

Summary of Section 6.6:

- The only criterion for assessing general cognitive categories such as word-classes is their **efficiency** as tools for expressing generalizations.
- Word-classes have no definition, so there's no point in looking for the 'correct' definition. Instead they have a list of properties that are shared by typical members.
- While novices are learning the more abstract properties of word-classes, **membership tests** may be helpful, provided that the learner can already recognize when two words belong to the same lexeme.

The main idea from Section 6.6 is that categories, including word-classes and inflections, are both justified and recognized by the properties that they combine, rather than by the pseudo-definitions of traditional grammar.

What, then, are the properties that justify the word-classes and inflections summarized in Figure 10.1 and Figure 10.2? A complete answer would consist of nothing less than a complete grammar for English, showing all the intricate ways in which different kinds of words are used. English grammarians are collectively well advanced on the road to such a grammar, but a complete listing of properties isn't at all what novices either need or want.

The most helpful contribution I can make is to offer some elementary 'membership tests'. The list will be highly selective, and the tests won't necessarily be the same as actual properties; but the rather modest aim of this section is to help you to recognize the main word-classes and inflections in ordinary samples of English.

10.3.1   Verbs

Fortunately, the most recognizable class is also the one that provides the best basis for recognizing the others. Verbs are really easy to recognize because of the inflectional possibilities summarized in Figure 10.2 (and expanded in more detail below).

Any lexeme that has a past and present tense is a verb, so if you suspect that some word is a verb, you ask yourself whether it is itself in the past or present tense, and failing that, whether it might have been used (in a different sentence, of course) in either of these tenses.

Take example (1).

(1)   I was writing a book.

Was must be a verb because it's past tense, as you can check by changing it to its present-tense equivalent, *I am writing a book*. This change is relevant because the only difference between the two sentences lies in the change from *was* to *am*. The possibility of replacing *was* in (1) by *am* confirms (in case you were in any doubt) that *was* is past tense; and since it has a tense, it must be a verb.

But what about *writing*? This doesn't have a tense, as you can easily confirm by trying, and failing, to change the tense by substituting some other inflection of WRITE. Nevertheless, it must be a verb because the same lexeme, WRITE, does have the full range of inflections for a verb, including past and present tenses:

(2)   I wrote a book.
(3)   I write a book.

These tense inflections show that the lexeme WRITE is a verb, and if *writing* is an inflection of WRITE, this too must be a verb. QED.

This may sound easy, but it requires quite high-level and complex reasoning. The main challenge is deciding when different word-tokens do belong to the same lexeme and when they don't. This demands attention to a range of different properties, and not just morphology. Particularly important are the accompanying words.

For example, consider *interesting* in (4). Is this a verb?

(4)   It was very interesting.

This looks like the *interests* in (5).

(5)   It interests me.

Since this is clearly a present-tense verb, can we conclude that *interesting* in (4) is also a verb? No, because the two word-tokens actually belong to different lexemes. Here's why.

If they belonged to the same lexeme, they should both share the same abilities for combining syntactically with other words (to be reviewed in 11.2). In the case of *interesting* in (4), it can combine with *very* on the left, and needs nothing at all on the right. If it's an example of the same lexeme as the verb in (5), the same syntactic pattern should be available when we convert it into a present-tense verb. But when we convert *very interesting* in this way, we get (6):

(6)   *It very interests.

Any native speaker of English knows that this is quite impossible.

The conclusion is that *interesting* in (4) does not belong to the same lexeme as *interests* in (5), so there is no evidence that it's a verb. Moreover, we shall see below that the possibility of *very* is typical of adjectives, so all the facts point to the same conclusion: that *interesting* in (4) is an adjective. In other words, the adjective INTERESTING is a different lexeme from the verb INTEREST.

10.3.2   Auxiliary and main verbs

Verbs have two important subclasses, **AUXILIARY** and **MAIN**, for which Section 10.1 provided abbreviations: 'v' for the little class of auxiliaries, and 'V' for the enormous class of main verbs. Typical examples have these two classes combined in the order v V: *will rain, were talking, was seen* and so on.

The terminology is traditional and very well established, but unfortunate because it implies that the principal difference lies in whether the verb 'supports' (in Latin *auxilium* meant 'supporting troops') another verb. This would be a fair description of the relation between the auxiliary *were* and the main verb *talking* in (7).

(7)   They were talking.

The trouble is that although all the auxiliary verbs can be used in this way, so can plenty of other verbs that are not auxiliaries, such as *got* in (8).

(8)   They got talking.

How do we know that *got* isn't an auxiliary? Because it doesn't have a small cluster of properties that distinguish verbs such as *were* (i.e. BE and WILL) from all other verbs. But when we look at these properties, they have nothing to do with 'supporting' another verb.

How, then, can you recognize an auxiliary verb? There are three easy tests, but any one of them will do because they all give the same answer.

- Inversion. Can you make a question by 'inverting' the verb that you're testing and its subject? (I.e. Can you put the subject after the verb instead of in its default position before it?) If you can, the verb is an auxiliary.
- Negation. Can you add *not* after the verb, and then reduce it to *n't*? If you can, the verb is an auxiliary.
- DO. Can you apply inversion or negation by adding DO before the verb? If you can, the verb is **not** an auxiliary.

Let's see how these three tests distinguish *were* and *got* in (7) and (8).

Inversion:

(7)   Were they talking?
(8)   *Got they got talking?

Negation:

(7)   They weren't talking.
(8)   *They gotn't talking.

DO:

(7)   *Did they be talking?
(8)   Did they get talking?
(7)   *They didn't be talking.
(8)   They didn't get talking.

As you can see, the tests work very cleanly and easily.

The conclusion of this little exercise is that BE and GET have different properties, but when we apply the same tests to other verbs, we find that BE lines up with a handful of verbs such as HAVE, WILL, CAN and DO, which are traditionally called 'auxiliary verbs', while GET lines up with all the thousands of other verbs which are traditionally 'main verbs'. This being so, it's obvious what we should call the two classes.

But let's now return to my original point, that the traditional terms are misleading because the distinction has nothing to do with the role of auxiliary verbs as 'supporters' of main verbs. To emphasize this point, I'll test the verb *were* in a sentence where there's no other verb in sight, either explicit or implied.

(9)   They were happy.

When we test this, it comes out as an auxiliary verb:

Inversion: Were they happy?
Negation: They weren't happy.
DO: *Did they be happy? *They didn't be happy.

In short, *were* is just as clearly an auxiliary verb in (9) as it is in (7), in spite of having no other verb to support.

The auxiliary verbs are listed in Table 10.2. If a verb isn't in this list, it's a main verb. As you can see, this is a particularly interesting area of variation and change in Modern English.

10.3.3   Nouns

Nouns are a little more complicated because the obvious inflectional test (having a plural inflection) doesn't apply to a large number of nouns; for example, nouns that name a substance (or 'mass' of stuff) have no plural, so we

Table 10.2 *The English auxiliary verbs.*

Lexeme	Special restrictions	Example
BE	BE is always an auxiliary	I am leaving. I am to go. I am happy.
HAVE$_{pp}$	Only before a perfect participle	I have left.
HAVE$_{poss}$	Only for some speakers	Has he brown eyes?
DO$_{aux}$	Used only when an auxiliary is needed by the syntax but none is needed by the meaning	Did he leave? He didn't leave.
WILL (*would*)		I will leave.
MAY (*might*)		I may leave.
CAN (*could*)		I can leave.
SHALL (*should*)		I shall leave.
MUST		I must leave.
OUGHT (+ TO)	Tending to non-auxiliary	I ought to leave.
USED (+ TO)	Tending to non-auxiliary	I used to leave.
DARE	Always negated or inverted	I daren't leave.
NEED	Always negated or inverted	I needn't leave.

have no obvious plural for STUFF, MONEY or INFORMATION, although they are very clearly nouns.

The easiest test for nouns is that they can be used as the only word to the left of a verb, using a general 'frame' such as '___ *matters*'; so the following sentences prove that STUFF, MONEY and INFORMATION are nouns.

(10)   Stuff matters.
(11)   Money matters.
(12)   Information matters.

To make the test frame more flexible we can ignore the *-s* on *matters*, which allows plurals to qualify as nouns:

(13)   People matter.
(14)   Facts matter.
(15)   Nouns matter.

These sentences show that PERSON (whose plural is the irregular *people*), FACT and NOUN are all nouns. No doubt these examples are obviously nouns to you, because they are typical **COMMON NOUNS**, but many other words pass the test as well:

(16)   Mary matters.
(17)   London matters.
(18)   Africa matters.

These are all **PROPER NOUNS**, or names; but for some proper nouns the frame needs to be more flexible still, with an optional *the*: *The __ matters*. With this change, the frame accommodates all the examples given so far, but also proper nouns such as *the Thames* and *the Sudan*.

Furthermore, the first test frame also accepts most of the traditional **PRONOUNS**:

(19)   It matters.
(20)   We matter.
(21)   Everything matters.

On the other hand, the frame rejects words that are not nouns, such as *sings*, *clever* or *with*, so it makes a very clear distinction between nouns and other words.

The strength of this test is that this one very simple frame picks out exactly the same class of words as many other similar but more complicated frames would give, which indicates a rich bundle of syntactic properties that all converge on the same word-class.

For example, we could also apply the test mentioned earlier (in connection with gerunds – see Section 10.2) after a preposition such as BY, and the results would be exactly the same (provided we could see that pairs like *I* and *me* belonged to the same lexeme).

10.3.4   Common nouns, proper nouns and pronouns

The three subclasses of 'noun' are almost as easy to test for. Here two frames are needed. The first allows only common nouns: immediately after *what* at the start of a question, as in (22) to (24):

(22)   What book do you want?
(23)   What idea came to you?
(24)   What evidence do you have?

Any noun that fails this test must be either a proper noun or a pronoun.

These can be distinguished by the second test frame: occurring straight after *the*. Some proper nouns (such as *the Alps* and *the Nile*) always occur in this frame, but all the others accept it under special circumstances as in (25) and (26):

(25)   He's not the John I knew.
(26)   The London of Charles Dickens was smelly.

In contrast, pronouns can never be used in this way. As with auxiliary and main verbs, this distinction produces very unequal classes in terms of members. Common nouns exist in tens of thousands, proper nouns are a completely open-ended list to which we add every time we hear of a new person or place with an exotic name, but pronouns are a very small class whose members can be listed quite easily under the categories of traditional grammar. Some pronouns have alternative forms which may look rather like inflections, but which are probably better treated in some other way. Table 10.3 is a provisional list of all the pronouns with alternative forms in brackets.

Table 10.3 *The pronouns of English.*

Pronoun class	Members
Personal	ME (*I*), YOU, HIM (*he*), HER (*she*), IT, US (*we*), THEM (*they*)
Reflexive	MYSELF, YOURSELF, HIMSELF, HERSELF, ITSELF, OURSELVES, YOURSELVES, THEMSELVES
Reciprocal	EACH OTHER, ONE ANOTHER
Possessive	MINE (*my*), YOURS (*your*), HIS, HERS (*her*), ITS, OURS (*our*), THEIRS (*their*)
Relative	WHO (*whom*), WHICH, WHOSE, WHEN, WHERE
Interrogative	WHO (*whom*), WHAT, WHICH, WHOSE, WHEN, WHERE, HOW
Demonstrative	THIS (*these*), THAT (*those*)
Indefinite	ONE, SOME, ANY, EACH, EVERY, NONE (*no*)
Compound	EVERYTHING, SOMETHING, ANYTHING, NOTHING; EVERYBODY, etc; EVERYONE, etc; EVERYWHERE, etc.

Section 11.2 will consider the three other pronouns which don't pass the noun test (p. 253): the articles THE and A (*an*), and the word EVERY. It will also argue that the possessive apostrophe, as in *John's wife*, is a pronoun.

10.3.5   Adjectives and adverbs

Once verbs and nouns are in place, the other word-classes are easy to identify. Adjectives can be used before a common noun and also after the verb BE, as illustrated by *big* in (27) and (28):

(27)   A big book stood on the shelf.
(28)   The book was big.

Notice how this test shows that *linguistics* in (29) is **not** an adjective – as indeed we already know because it passes the noun test:

(29)   A linguistics book stood on the shelf.
(30)   *The book was linguistics.

Another useful test for adjectives is that they can typically combine with *very*, as we saw with *interesting* in (4) above.

ADVERBS, on the other hand, can combine with an immediately following verb but can't follow BE. An example is *recently* in (31).

(31)   I recently saw an accident.
(32)   *The accident was recently.

Notice how this test shows that *yesterday* is not an adverb:

(33)   *I yesterday saw an accident.

In case you're wondering what *yesterday* is if it's not an adverb, it's probably a rather unusual proper noun.

Another test for adverbs is use before an adjective:

(34)   It was extremely nice.

But nouns can also be used before adjectives, as in *miles long*, so the test should only be applied to words that aren't already known to be nouns.

10.3.6   Prepositions and conjunctions

Prepositions can be used to join a preceding noun or verb to a following noun. The most common preposition is OF:

(35)   I bought a book of stamps.
(36)   I thought of you.

In these sentences, *of* links the words on either side of it as unequal partners, so a book of stamps is a kind of book, not a kind of stamp, and thinking of you is a kind of thinking (Section 7.1 discusses this inequality in detail).

OF is rather fussy about its syntactic company, and the following noun is absolutely essential; but some prepositions are more flexible. For example, BEFORE can be followed by a noun, by nothing at all, or by a verb:

(37)   Betty had seen Mary before him.
(38)   Betty had seen Mary before.
(39)   Betty had seen Mary before he did.

Examples like these raise a problem for traditional grammar which is forced, by its own definitions, to ignore the similarities among the different uses of BEFORE, distinguishing them as follows:

*   In (37) it's a preposition because it's followed by a noun.
*   In (38) it's an adverb because it's not followed by a noun.
*   In (39) it's a 'subordinating conjunction' because it's followed by a **SUBORDINATE CLAUSE**, a potentially complete sentence which is treated as a subordinate part of a larger sentence. (These syntactic notions are explored more thoroughly in Section 11.1.)

However, the similarities among these three uses of BEFORE are much more striking than their differences; and what's more, BEFORE isn't alone in allowing this particular range of uses (for the most obvious parallels, think of AFTER and SINCE).

Consequently, most modern grammarians treat the old subordinating conjunctions and some apparent adverbs as prepositions (Huddleston and Pullum 2002: 599–600). In this analysis, a preposition is a word which doesn't qualify as a member of any other word-class and which can link a verb and a following noun or verb.

With the traditional 'subordinating conjunctions' removed, only 'coordinating conjunctions' remain – a very small group indeed, whose outstanding members are AND and OR, with BUT, NOR, THEN and (possibly) SO as more exceptional members, each with some restriction that doesn't apply to the core members.

This very small class of words, which I call simply **CONJUNCTIONS**, plays a vital role in grammar (11.5). Their grammatical function is to link words as equals (in contrast with prepositions or 'subordinating conjunctions'), so in (40) the two verbs share equally in their relation to the noun *Fred*:

(40)   Fred sang loudly and talked quietly.

The other conjunctions can also be used in much the same way, so this kind of sentence could be used as a test for conjunctions which excludes various possible candidates such as *whereas*:

(41)   *Fred sang loudly whereas talked quietly.

As with the other word-classes, this membership test builds on just one property among many.

10.3.7   Overview of word-classes and tests

The word-classes and their membership tests are summarized in Table 10.4. It's important not to confuse these tests with a proper grammatical analysis. This will come as I introduce you to more sophisticated theories which allow me to talk, in particular, about the grammatical relations between words.

The tests are presented as very simple frames containing gaps where you can try to insert words, but to use them successfully you actually need a more abstract sense of grammatical structure. Not only do you need to be able to recognize whether word-tokens belong to the same lexeme or not, but you also need to be sensitive to the more abstract ways in which words are related in a sentence.

For instance, to recognize a preposition you really need to know not only whether the word concerned can stand between a verb and a following noun, but also that when it does so, it has the grammatical function of linking them to each other; for example, the fact that *three* can stand between *saw* and *ships* doesn't show that *three* is a preposition.

What we really need in order to talk about such things in a more grown-up way is the idea of 'syntactic dependencies', which we meet officially in Section 7.1; but meanwhile it's important for you to get a toe-hold on word-classes, so we have to make do with what we already know about.

Armed with these tests, as I said on page 255 you should be able to classify virtually every word in any English text. Even though this misses the main point of grammar, which is to express complex meanings by combining words in quite specific ways, you may sometimes find it helpful to talk about word-classes, or even to count them.

Table 10.4 *Tests for the major word-classes of English.*

Word-class	Test	Example
Verb	Past- and present-tense inflections	He walked/walks home.
Auxiliary	Can take negative *n't*	We **weren't**/*gotn't talking.
Noun	(the) ___ matter(s)	**Things** matter. The **Nile** matters. **This** matters.
Common	What ___ ...?	What **things**/*Nile/*this did you see?
Proper	... *the* ___.	I saw the **Nile.**
Pronoun	*... *the* ___.	*I saw the **this**.
Adjective	... ___ [common noun] ...	I bought a **big**/linguistics book.
	... BE ___.	The book was **big**/*linguistics
Adverb	... ___ [verb] ...	I **recently** saw an accident.
	*... BE ___.	*The accident was **recently**.
Preposition	[verb] ___ [noun or verb]	I saw it **before** her. I saw it **before** she did.
Conjunction	[noun] [tensed verb] ___ [tensed verb]	Fred sang loudly **and** talked quietly.

10.3.8   Measuring maturity by counting word-class tokens

For example, it may be interesting to know that the proportion of nouns in a text increases, on average, with the age and linguistic skill of the author (Hudson 2009). How about the words you're reading at the moment?

If you classify all the 302 words in the previous paragraphs (from *The word-classes ...* to *... count them.*) then you'll find the numbers shown in Table 10.5. The first row shows the percentage of word-tokens in this book that belong to each of the word-classes shown in the columns. You can compare these figures with those (in the lower rows) for the two main categories which were distinguished in a million-word collection of written English texts (Hudson 1994).

As you'll see, my writing turns out to be absolutely typical of one particular kind of written English, though not the kind you might expect. Given a major split between 'informational' and 'imaginative' prose, you might expect a textbook on grammar to be firmly in the informational category; but the figures for nouns and verbs show otherwise. I leave it to you, as consumer, to interpret this research finding. I can also boast that although my 19% of nouns is much lower than you might expect in informational writing, at least it's higher than the 17% of the best writers at age 16 (Hudson 2009).

10.3.9   Tests for recognizing verb inflections

As with word-classes, novices shouldn't look for a 'definition', but they do need simple tests as a first step to a more sophisticated understanding.

Table 10.5 *Word-classes as percentages of all the word-tokens in this book compared with a million-word corpus of written English.*

	Nouns	Verbs	Adjectives	Prepositions
	(N or Nn)	(v or V)		
This book	19	21	8	12
Typical imaginative written English	19	22	7	10
Typical informational written English	30	17	8	13

Table 10.6 contains some simple tests for the inflectional categories in Figure 10.2 that students sometimes find helpful.

Where next?

Advanced: Back to Part II, Chapter 6.7: Morphology and lexical relations
Novice: Explore Part II, Chapter 6.6: Definitions and efficiency

10.4   Morphology and lexical relations

Summary of Section 6.7:

- **Grammar** consists of **morphology**, which handles patterns within a word, and **syntax**, which deals with the relations between the words in a sentence.
- Word structure consists of **forms**, which include indivisible **morphs** (which can be further classified as **roots**, **prefixes** and **suffixes**) and more complex **word-forms**.
- In terms of notation, forms are distinguished from words by curly braces: {…}.
- Morphological changes are best handled in terms of '**variant**' relations rather than by realization rules applying directly to morphs.
- Morphological structure is related not only to inflections (variations on a single lexeme) but also to **lexical relations** between distinct lexemes.

We've already seen (10.2) that English has only a few inflections, but that doesn't mean that we don't have much morphology in our words. On the contrary, we have a great deal of it, though most of it is relatively simple compared with some other languages. Most of it has to do with lexical relations rather than with inflections.

Table 10.6 *Tests for verb inflections.*

Inflection	Test for verb V	Example
Finite	V is tensed or imperative and has no preceding auxiliary	*He sleeps/slept.* *Sleep!*
Imperative	V is a bare uninflected verb with either overt or understood *you*, used as a command or invitation	*Sleep!*
Tensed	V has a tense, i.e. you can switch the verb between past and present Default: present tense without {s}	*He sleeps/slept.* *They sleep.*
Singular	V has suffix {s}	*He sleeps.*
Past	V has a clear past-tense form Or V could be replaced by a verb whose past-tense form is clear V doesn't follow the auxiliary HAVE	*He took it.* *I hit it. > I knocked it.*
Infinitive	V is a bare form without suffixes, but (unlike imperative or default tensed) dependent on some other verb such as WILL or SEE, or on TO	*It will be cold.* *I saw him leave.*
Perfect	V is immediately after HAVE, and has either the same form as past, or (in some irregular verbs) a different form	*I have talked.* *I have spoken.*
Participle	V could be used to modify a noun. Default: present participle, with {ing}	*a book written long ago* *It was written long ago.* *the man writing it* *He was sleeping.*
Passive	V is always the same form as perfect, but the lexeme's default subject and object are reorganized, with the object 'promoted' to subject and the subject 'demoted' to follow *by*	*a book written by an expert* *He was interviewed by the committee.*

10.4.1 Lexical morphology and etymology

Take the lexeme MORPHOLOGY and its lexical relations – its similarities to other lexemes. If you think of words that it looks or sounds like, you notice terms such as GEOLOGY, METEOROLOGY, BIOLOGY and THEOLOGY. With the spotlight on them, these words are obviously similar in several respects:

•   they contain a morph {ology};
•   they all mean some area of academic study;
•   they're nouns.

This bundle of properties allows a generalization: words that contain {ology} are nouns that mean an area of academic study.

Is this generalization mentally real for you? The brief and honest answer is that we don't know; or rather, we don't know whether it was mentally real for you before you read this paragraph, but we can at least be sure that it is now. We can also be sure that it's mentally real for anyone who can apply the generalization to new words; so anyone who can work out for themselves that VOLCANOLOGY (or its variant VULCANOLOGY) is the study of volcanoes must know the general pattern, and this is even more certainly true for anyone who can invent a new 'ology' such as LONDONOLOGY, the study of London, or even OLOGYOLOGY, the study of ologies. Any mind that contains this generalization must also contain lexical relations among the various words concerned.

What about the other part of these words? In some cases, this is another morph that has its own generalization, such as the morph {morph} which makes up the rest of {{morph}{ology}}, and which reappears in other lexemes such as METAMORPHOSIS, 'change of shape', and AMORPHOUS, 'without shape'. Clearly {morph} is found in words whose meaning has something to do with shape; but what about MORPHINE, with the chemical morph {ine} that we also find in GLYCERINE and BENZINE? This is an exception, in which {morph} isn't linked to 'shape'. (Apparently, the substance was named after a minor Roman god of dreams who was called Morph because he created shapes in the sleeper's mind; once again this factlet, and many many more, can be found in the online etymological dictionary at www.etymonline.com.)

Exceptions are common in this area of grammar, and often show the effects of changes in our beliefs about the world. To take another example from the ologies, METEOROLOGY nowadays has nothing to do with meteors, but at the time when the word was coined the word *meteor* meant anything high up in the sky, so METEOROLOGY has specialized this meaning in one direction while METEOR has specialized it in a different direction. Exploring word structure is rather like archaeology as the morphology persists long after the original meanings that motivated it vanished into the mists of time.

The main point is that we speakers of English can, and do, analyse words into parts on the basis of their similarities to other words. This is important in English because a lot of our vocabulary is tightly interconnected in this way, but also because the patterns that emerge reflect the rather complicated history of the language.

A great deal of our vocabulary, and especially of our 'academic' vocabulary – the kind of vocabulary you learn at school and university – is borrowed from other languages, and especially from Greek, Latin and French; in fact, one study of the 80,000 words in an English dictionary found that no fewer than 62% were borrowed from one of these languages, and only a quarter were directly descended from the ancestor of Modern English, Old English. (Wikipedia: 'Loanword'.)

In this respect, our discussion of MORPHOLOGY and its relatives was typical, because all the morphs in these words come from Greek or Latin. This explains why some of them can never be used on their own; for example, {geo} and {bio} are only found as word-parts.

Paradoxically, the number of words based on the dead languages Greek and Latin is increasing fast thanks to science and technology. Pharmaceutical companies invent not only new compounds, but also new names for them, and the names are always built out of Latin or Greek morphs such as {mono}, {hydr} and {ster}. On the other hand, these new words are relatively rarely used, and really common words tend to be native to English and its ancestors. In the last sentence, for example, every word comes from Old English except the words *relatively*, *rare*, *really*, *common*, *tend*, *native* and *ancestors*.

10.4.2   Word-formation rules and variants

When a pattern of similarities between words is sufficiently general, we abstract a **lexical relation** involving some combination of word-class, meaning and form. These patterns are often called **WORD-FORMATION RULES** because they allow us to create new words as well as to see relations among existing words.

One example is the 'opposite' relation found between pairs of adjectives like TIDY and UNTIDY. Any English dictionary lists hundreds of words containing the prefix {un} that belong to this pattern: UNABLE, UNACCEPTABLE and so on. This lexical relation generalizes to all adjectives, so a typical adjective is the positive partner of a related negative.

In terms of morphology, the negative adjective has a stem built out of the stem of the positive, with {un} added. However, there are numerous exceptions of different kinds. For one thing, {un} isn't the only prefix for negation, which can also be expressed by {in}, {a} or {non}, as in INACCESSIBLE, AMORAL (or AMORPHOUS, containing {morph}) and NON-COMMITTAL. For another, these prefixes can vary their shape to fit the next sound, as when {in} turns to {im} in IMPATIENT. And finally, the default morphology is overridden in the case of some simple adjectives with negative meanings, such as SMALL and LITTLE (the opposites of LARGE and BIG).

Regardless of these exceptions, though, the general pattern establishes a generalization which applies to all adjectives (Huddleston and Pullum 2002: 1687–91), so we can almost certainly assume that our minds hold something like the informal networks in Figure 10.3.

Network (a) shows the 'opposite' relation itself, while (b) expands the morphological part by giving the default realization for a form's 'un-variant'. This is the regular pattern in UNTIDY, but every generalization allows exceptions, so we find exceptional un-variants (e.g. {{im}{possible}}), opposites that aren't realized by the un-variant of their positive base (e.g. LITTLE) and opposites that

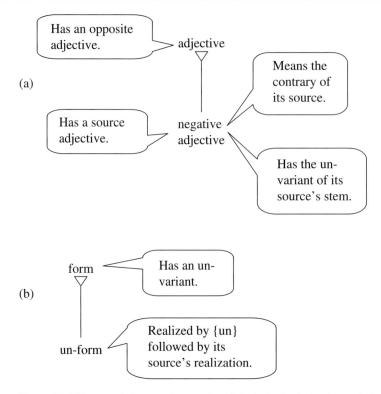

Figure 10.3 *The morphology and semantics of the lexical relation 'opposite'*

don't mean the contrary of their positive base (e.g. UN-AMERICAN, meaning 'anti-American' rather than simply 'not American').

10.4.3   Morphs are meaningless

One of the benefits of treating morphs as meaningless forms is that the same morphological pattern can be used with a range of different meanings. The morph {un} is a good example, because when it's used in a verb it has a very different meaning, namely 'reverse'.

For example, undoing something means reversing whatever you did to it before, rather than simply not doing it; so when you unbutton a coat, you're reversing the previous buttoning, and not simply 'not buttoning' it. In this case the same morphological relation – the un-variant relation – supports a completely different lexical relation.

Such examples are relatively common in English – think of the s-variant which is found in plural nouns and singular verbs (6.7), or the er-variant found not only in agent-nouns such as SPEAKER (6.7) but also in a wide range of other nouns (FIVER, SOUTHERNER) and (probably) also in comparative adjectives like BIGGER – not to mention all the forms that contain {er} without being the er-variant of another stem, such as {{groc}{er}} and {{moth}{er}}.

But the {er} doesn't relate any of these words to another word without {er}, so it doesn't signal a lexical relation; and the {fe} which relates FEMALE to MALE must be mentally real because it's an example of folk etymology (6.7). The perceived link to MALE made our ancestors change *femelle*, from a Latin word *fem-ella*, 'little woman', into *fe-male* (another etymology from the online etymological dictionary).

The conclusion that emerges from such examples is that we can, and do, recognize morphs even when they're shared by only two lexemes. They don't have to show anything as general as a 'rule' or 'variant'.

10.4.4   Recursive structures

The morphology of variants is generally rather simple in English. A form's variant typically consists of that form with some morph added to it, either as a prefix or a suffix as in {{dog}{s}}.

However, many of our words have complicated morphological structures because word-formation rules can apply **recursively**, i.e. one rule can apply to the output of another. The result is a series of increasingly complicated forms such as the following:

- X (= verb) > {{un} X} (= verb, 'reverse effect of X'): ZIP > UNZIP, 'reverse the zipping';
- X (= verb) > {X {able}} (= adjective, 'able to be Xed'): UNZIP > UNZIPPABLE, 'able to be unzipped';
- X (= adjective) > {X {ity}} (= noun, 'property of being X'): UNZIPPABLE > UNZIPPABILITY, 'the ability to be unzipped'.

These patterns are so general that, at least in principle, we can create brand new words. You may be unsure about some of the words in this recursive list – UNZIP is certainly familiar, but what about UNZIPPABLE?

Just to prove that the system allows us to produce genuinely new vocabulary, here's one that you certainly haven't heard before: UNUNZIPPABILITY. Here's how we can prove that it's permitted by the rules:

- X (adjective) > {{un} X} (= adjective, 'not X'): UNZIPPABLE (see above) > UNUNZIPPABLE, 'not unzippable';
- X > X {ity} (above): UNUNZIPPABLE > UNUNZIPPABILITY.

Of course you might have to live quite a long time before you found the need for this monster, but the fact is that it's a possible lexeme of English.

It's sometimes wrongly claimed that the longest word in the English language is ANTIDISESTABLISHMENTARIANISM, with 29 letters. Apart from the existence of technical monsters such as the chemical name of the largest known protein, with 189,819 letters, this is wrong because anyone with enough determination can find some word-formation rule to extend most words; for example, how about the study of antidisestablishmentarianism, ANTIDISESTABLISHMENTARIANISMOLOGY? (Wikipedia: 'Longest word in English'.)

10.4.5   The variety of morphology

Morphology, then, is the study of 'forms', the phonetic and written shapes that realize words, whether these are single morphs or complex forms consisting of multiple morphs.

Morphology reveals similarities and differences that range from the very general, involving a large number of words, to the very specific patterns that are found in only one (such as the {fe} which distinguishes FEMALE from MALE). Where there are generalizations to be made, they can be expressed in terms of 'variants', but generality isn't essential for morphology.

Another contrast which we might expect to be important for morphology is the one between inflections and lexemes. Some morphological patterns belong to an inflection, and others belong to a lexical relation; but a single morphological pattern may be used in both ways (page 135). For example, {ing} is used in some inflections (participles and gerunds), but also in some complex lexemes such as WIRING and PAINTING. What these examples show is that morphology doesn't divide neatly into 'inflectional morphology' and 'lexical morphology', as claimed by some theories.

Where next?

Advanced: Back to Part I, Chapter 2.6: Social categories and stereotypes
Novice: Explore Part II, Chapter 6.7: Morphology and lexical relations

10.5   Social properties

Summary of Section 6.8:

* Since we normally experience language in a social context, we learn how words are used by particular kinds of people; this knowledge relates elements of **I-language** to elements of **I-society**.
* This kind of variation is the subject-matter of **sociolinguistics**.

The point of this section is simply that every English word gives a great deal of social information about its speaker.

The point is obvious if we think of words that are used by particular segments of our society, such as BONNY (used by Scots) and GOSH (used by ex-teenagers of a certain age). But it's important not to lose sight of the fact that simply speaking English links us to a social category, and general accent differences that are audible on most words locate the speaker in one particular English-speaking country. Languages are fundamentally badges of social-group membership, so it's essential to be able to assign social properties not only to individual lexemes but also to the entire language (Hudson 2007c: 239–46).

The fact that English is a world language means that there's a great deal of geographical variation among words, and modern media ensures that most of us can recognize words that are used in other parts of the world. This means that some of the variation which is objectively part of English as an E-language is also part of the I-language of some people, but nobody's I-language includes all of the variation in the E-language.

The same partial knowledge is found in the variation within a single country such as Britain: we're all experts on the E-language in our community but our knowledge of other communities' E-language fades out as our experience of those communities decreases.

Consequently, there can be no question of building a complete model for the I-language of a 'typical English speaker', or even of a 'typical British English speaker'. You and I are bound to have different I-languages, and if we were to meet and look hard for linguistic differences, however tiny, we would certainly find some.

This variation raises serious problems for the methodology of linguistics, but the problem is a lot less serious than it might be precisely because of the feedback mechanism (2.6) which makes us all try to conform like sheep on linguistic matters.

What then are the main links between English words and social information? This breaks down into two different but related questions: How do English words convey social information? and: What kinds of social information do English words convey?

As far as the 'how?' is concerned, the most obvious way is that social meaning is carried by entire lexemes. For example, anyone who uses SIDEWALK sounds to a Brit like an American (whether they are or not).

But lexemes have several different properties, any one of which may carry social information on its own as in the following examples:

- Meaning: If HOOD means the cover over the engine of a car, then the speaker is American (in contrast with Brits, who would use BONNET for this meaning); but Brits also use HOOD for a head-covering.
- Syntax: If ENOUGH is 'completed' by THAT, as in *big enough that it held everything*, then the speaker is American (whereas Brits use TO, as in *big enough to hold everything*).
- Pronunciation: If LUCK is pronounced like LOOK, then the speaker is from the North of England.

The point is that we can't always tie social information in a simple way to the lexeme concerned, but may need to tie it to a particular property of the lexeme.

Turning to the 'what?' question, English lexemes can convey all sorts of different kinds of social information not only about the speaker (as in the above examples) but also about other features of the social contexts in which they're used.

For instance, greetings not only signal the start of social interaction, but give shared information such as the time of day (GOOD MORNING) or the season (HAPPY CHRISTMAS) which confirms a rather minimal level of shared understanding.

What is particularly well developed in English is the linguistic expression of **FORMALITY**, as illustrated in examples like the following:

(1)   John Smith departed this life 1 June 1995. RIP.
(2)   We regret to inform you that John Smith passed away on 1 June 1995.
(3)   Unfortunately, John Smith died on 1 June 1995.
(4)   I'm afraid John Smith died on 1 June 1995.
(5)   John Smith? Oh dear, didn't you know that he died in 1995?

Any English speaker can recognize the social differences that relate to these linguistic differences. A reasonable guess for each would be that (1) is written on a tombstone or in an obituary; that (2) is in a letter from a solicitor; that (3) is in a letter from an acquaintance; that (4) is spoken in conversation between non-intimates; and that (5) is part of a more intimate conversation.

But however obvious such differences are, we don't understand much about how formality works (Wikipedia: 'Register'), so the only guidance Word Grammar can offer is the idea of treating I-language and I-society as separate but related areas of cognition.

Where next?

Advanced: Back to Part I, Chapter 3: Network structure
Novice: Explore Part II, Chapter 6.8: Social properties of words

11 English syntax

11.1 Dependencies

Summary of Section 7.1:

- Traditional **syntactic relations**, like other such relational concepts, are organized in an open-ended taxonomy rather than drawn from a supposedly small and universal set.
- They are **dependencies** because they provide unequal relations between individual words: a **dependent** and its **parent**.
- A dependent is **subordinate** to its parent because it makes the parent's meaning more precise.
- Dependency analysis contrasts with the dominant approach in modern syntax, **phrase structure**, for which the basic relations are **part–whole** relations to phrases rather than traditional syntactic relations. Dependency analysis is preferable because it rests on firmer psychological assumptions and produces simpler analyses.
- One particularly important benefit of dependency analysis is the notion of **dependency distance**, based on the number of words between a word and its parent, which correlates with independent measures of memory load.
- The traditional grammatical relations **subject** and **object** are concepts which are clearly defined by a bundle of properties.
- The logic of inheritance explains why languages distinguish **valents**, inherited from both dependent and parent, from **adjuncts**, inherited only from the dependent.

Since dependencies are the basis of syntax, we now ask which dependencies are needed for English. Novices may prefer to read 11.1.3 (page 283) first.

Our starting point is the set of general dependencies displayed in Figure 7.4 which contrasts valents and adjuncts. Since this contrast is rooted in the logic of inheritance, which applies to all languages, we may expect it to have some relevance in every language, though the details are bound to vary from language to language.

But the taxonomy of dependencies goes well beyond the basic valent/adjunct contrast. The further contrast between subjects and objects shown in Figure 7.4

was introduced just to illustrate some general ideas about dependencies, and wasn't meant to imply that every language must have subjects and objects.

On the contrary, we can expect radical differences between languages if concepts are learned from experience rather than derived from a universal human genetic endowment. The dependency relations that a particular language distinguishes reflect that language's history and the efforts of its speakers to solve the problems that arise in communication.

Consequently, the dependencies we assume for English need not apply to other languages. This is an important difference between Word Grammar and most other theories, which generally assume a small set of grammatical relations suited to the needs of every language (Van Valin 2006).

11.1.1   Pre-dependents and post-dependents

One of the most obvious differences between English and many other languages lies in the rules for word order (7.4). In many languages, word order isn't relevant to distinctions between dependencies, because all dependencies follow (more or less) the same word order. In free-order languages, dependents are all equally free to stand on either side of their parents. In head-final languages, every dependent comes before its parent, and in head-initial languages, every dependent follows its parent. In all these languages – which together constitute the majority of the world's languages – position before or after the head does not distinguish dependents.

But in head-medial languages like English, a dependent's position tends to be fixed according to the dependency. The clearest example of this is the contrast between subject and object which gives *I saw him*, not **Him saw I*. The typical subject precedes the verb whereas the typical object follows it, and that's usually the only way in which we can distinguish them. If we read the sentence *John likes Mary*, we know that it's John, not Mary, who has the feeling because the order of words shows quite unambiguously that the word *John* has to be subject and *Mary* has to be object. As we now expect, there are complications and exceptions such as the possibility of 'inverting' an auxiliary verb and its subject (10.3); and we shall see more exceptions in Section 11.6. But the default rules are both clear and rigid.

But the rules for dependents of other kinds of words are equally clear and rigid. For example, an adjective has to stand before any noun on which it depends, giving *big book* and certainly not **book big*; conversely, a preposition that depends on a noun has to follow it, so *book about linguistics* is possible, in contrast with **about linguistics book*.

Of course you'll notice a major difference between these rules and those for positioning subjects and objects. Word order depends on meaning in the case of subjects and objects, but on word-class for dependents of nouns. We put *John* rather than *Mary* before the verb in *John likes Mary* because we want to show

Table 11.1 *Pre-dependents and post-dependents of four word-classes.*

Word-class of parent	Pre-dependent	Post-dependent
Verb	Mary sang	(Mary) sang it.
Noun	big book	book about (linguistics)
Adjective	very keen	keen on (linguistics)
Preposition	just before (it)	before it

that John is the 'like-er', but when we put *big* before *book* the decision has nothing whatever to do with meaning, and is driven entirely by the fact that *big* is an adjective.

Nevertheless, the fact remains that something, whether meaning or word-class, fixes the word order. And the result is that, once we've decided the meaning and word-class of a dependent, we have very little further control over its position before or after the parent.

In recognition of this fundamental fact about English, Word Grammar (alone among syntactic theories) contrasts two very general dependency types: **PRE-DEPENDENTS**, which precede their parent, and **POST-DEPENDENTS**, which follow it. Table 11.1 shows how this pattern pervades the grammar of English, affecting the dependents of four of the five major word-classes.

For some reason that I don't understand, adverbs aren't affected because they only allow pre-dependents, as in *very quickly*. Even when they're based on an adjective that does allow post-dependents, adverbs don't; for example, even though we can be *indignant at the allegations*, we can't react **indignantly at the allegations*.

Why should English have evolved in this way? No doubt the answer is a complex one involving a convergence of different influences. For subjects and objects the standard explanation is that English increasingly used word order to distinguish them as the old case inflections disappeared.

However, a more general benefit of putting some dependents before the parent and others after it is that this reduces dependency distance (7.1). If a word has two dependents, the only way to guarantee each of them a place immediately next to the parent word is to put one on each side. For example, take *Mary slept soundly*, where both *Mary* and *soundly* depend on *slept*, and are both right next to it, producing the least possible load on memory. In contrast, locating both dependents on the same side, as in **Mary soundly slept* or *Soundly Mary slept*, guarantees that one of them must be separated by the other from their shared parent.

Whatever the explanation, it's clear that the contrast between pre-dependents and post-dependents plays a fundamental role in English syntax. Equally clearly, it's not needed at all in a language where all dependents follow the same word-order rules, even if these rules allow dependents the freedom to occur on either

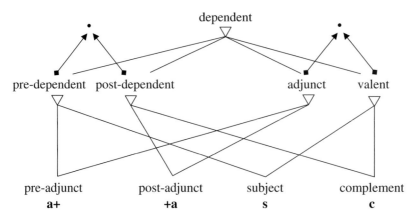

Figure 11.1 *Four basic dependency categories for English*

side of the parent. In a free-order language the position of a dependent isn't inherited from the grammar, so it's not part of the grammar.

It's also important to bear in mind that the pre-/post-dependent contrast is a classification of dependencies, and not a notation for word order. Even if an auxiliary verb's subject is inverted, as in *Are you tired?*, it's still a pre-dependent because subjects are always pre-dependents even when their actual position is exceptional.

11.1.2   Pre- and post-adjuncts, subjects and complements

I've now introduced two fundamental contrasts between dependency types:

- adjunct versus valent, a universal contrast that's dictated by the logic of inheritance;
- pre-dependent versus post-dependent, a contrast peculiar to languages such as English which have head-medial word order.

These categories cut across each other, giving on the one hand pre-adjuncts and post-adjuncts, and on the other subjects and complements, as shown in Figure 11.1.

This diagram shows that the two choices (shown by the choice sets) combine to define four categories. Pre- and post-adjuncts are adjuncts that (typically) precede or follow their parent, abbreviated to 'a+' and '+a' where the '+' is on the same side as the parent. In contrast we have ready-made established terms for valents that typically precede or follow their parents: 'subject' for the first, and **COMPLEMENT** for the second. 'Complement' is a very traditional term (based on the idea of 'completing' the parent) which has been redefined in modern grammar.

Figure 11.2 shows how this kind of analysis applies to a simple example.

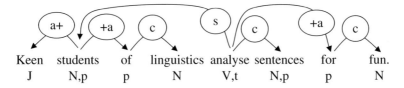

Figure 11.2 *The syntactic structure of a sentence*

This is the first example in this book of a proper Word Grammar analysis of a sentence, so you may want to look at it carefully. Notice in particular how the classification of the words is kept quite separate from the dependency structure that binds them together. The online material includes a great many other examples.

11.1.3   Tests for dependencies

As with word-classes and inflections, novices need simple tests for dependencies. In this case, though, the challenge is more serious, because, unlike words, dependencies aren't laid out for you ready to be classified.

When analysing a sentence's syntax, an expert can take a global approach, but novices generally do best to focus on specifics by considering one word at a time, and asking two questions about each word:

• Which other word, if any, does this word depend on?
• What kind of dependency is there between these words?

I'll explain how you might approach the analysis of example (1) in order to produce the analysis in Figure 11.2.

(1)   Keen students of linguistics analyse sentences for fun.

First classify all the words as well as you can, then start with the **last** word: *fun*. Why start with the last word, not the first? Because most word-tokens in English depend on a word before them – i.e. most words are post-dependents.

Now ask which word *fun* depends on. In this case I recommend always starting with the **nearest** word, in this case *for*, because most words in English depend on a word immediately before or after them. So the question is whether the words *for fun* are bound into a single phrase by a dependency. In this case you can probably trust your instincts and answer yes, because *for fun* is a familiar fixed phrase with a familiar meaning.

But if there's a dependency between *for* and *fun*, in which direction does it go? Does *for* depend on *fun*, with *fun* therefore as the head of the phrase, or the other way round? One way to decide the answer is to ask what kind of question about the rest of the sentence *for fun* answers: a 'why?' question, needing an answer headed by a preposition such as *for*, or a 'what?' question needing an answer headed by a noun such as *fun*. Clearly it tells us why good students analyse sentences, so the head must be *for*.

So far, then, we know that *fun* depends on *for*, so the next question is about the classification of the dependency. Most obviously, *fun* is a post-dependent because it follows *for* (and there's no reason to think this is anything but its default position), but it's also a valent because FOR always has to have a following noun. For instance, we can't say things like **Fun is important, and I always read for*. The outcome of this process, therefore, is that *fun* is the complement – the post-dependent valent – of *for*.

In slightly less painful detail, the remaining words should succumb to the same process of analysis. We continue to work backwards through the words.

- *for* doesn't depend on its neighbour *sentences*, because it tells us why students analyse sentences, not what kind of sentences they analyse; putting together *books for fun* doesn't make sense. Having rejected *sentences*, we move one word to the left, to *analyse*. In this case *analyse for fun* does sound sensible, with *for fun* modifying the meaning of *analyse*. As for the dependency type, *for* must be a post-adjunct because it follows the parent and is completely optional and, indeed, unpredictable.

- *sentences* might depend on either of its neighbours, but we've already rejected any kind of dependency between it and *for*, so *analyse* is the only candidate. The words *analyse sentences* make good sense, and indeed *sentences* must be a complement of *analyse* because something like it is what we expect after this verb.

- *analyse* doesn't depend on any other word because it's a finite verb. (As evidence for this, try changing the tense to *analysed*.)

- *linguistics* might depend on either *of* or *analyse*, but *linguistics analyse* is neither grammatical nor sensible, so *of* is the best bet: *of linguistics*. Since *of* is ungrammatical without a following noun, *linguistics* must be its complement.

- *of* might depend on either *students* or *analyse*, but *students* is by far the better bet, and indeed is right because *students of linguistics* makes perfect sense, with *of* as a post-adjunct (or, possibly, complement – this is a matter of debate and research).

- *students* might depend on either *keen* or *analyse*, but a little thought eliminates *keen* and confirms *analyse*, as *students analyse* makes both excellent sense and good grammar because *analyse* is the form that we expect with a plural subject such as *students* (in contrast with *a student analyses* ...).

- *keen* might in principle depend either on its neighbour *students* or on *analyse*, but as usual the nearest candidate is the winner as *keen students* is the intended meaning.

The point of the example is to show in detail how each dependency brings together a bundle of different properties ranging from word order to word-class and meaning. This is why syntactic analysis is both challenging and worthwhile as a way of developing greater sensitivity to language, not to mention the general mind-training benefits of such mental gymnastics.

The next section will introduce some more dependency types by subdividing 'complement' to recognize dependencies such as the familiar 'object'.

Where next?

Advanced: Back to Part II, Chapter 7.2: Valency
Novice: Explore Part II, Chapter 7.1: Dependencies and phrases

11.2   Valency

Summary of Section 7.2:

- A word's **valency** is the set of dependencies that it needs to satisfy.
- Its **parent-valency** is its need for a parent, and for a parent of a particular kind. A typical word needs a parent.
- Exceptionally, finite verbs may be the **sentence-root** (with a parent that's merely potential, shown in notation by a vertical arrow) because their own semantics includes an **illocutionary force** (e.g. statement, question) that makes them semantically complete.
- A word's **dependent-valency** includes all the dependents that it needs, which (by definition) are all **valents**. In contrast, an **adjunct** merely satisfies its own parent-valency without satisfying any dependent-valency of the parent.
- A word's dependent-valency can allow a number of different valents, but these normally have different constraints which help to distinguish them. These constraints may refer to the valent's word-class, its quantity, its inflection (e.g. its **case**), its word order, its lexeme, or its meaning; and each valent provides one particular element in the word's meaning.
- A word-token's valency may be inherited from different sources in the taxonomy of words, ranging from very general word-classes to specific lexemes.
- A word's valency may include a syntactic **triangle**, in which one word has two parents, one of which depends on the other; in other theories this pattern is called **raising**. The same pattern of relations is found not only in other areas of syntax, but also in other areas of cognition such as kinship.

This section gives a very broad overview of valency in English, starting with parent-valency.

11.2.1   Parent-valency

This is based on the default rule that any word needs one parent, but there are exceptional words which don't need one – *analyse* in example (1) in the previous section, or the verb *are* in the present sentence.

We can define a sentence in terms of dependencies, as a string of words which have dependency links to each other but not to words outside the string. This definition ignores coordination (11.5), but otherwise it's a fair approximation to the principles that we all apply in our writing.

But if all the words in a sentence are linked, either directly or indirectly, by dependency, they must all ultimately depend on one word which doesn't depend on any other word, the sentence root (the 'root' out of which all the other words grow). Although the typical sentence root is a finite verb (see 10.2), there are many other possibilities:

(1)   How about a cup of tea?
(2)   What a good idea!
(3)   If only I could help!
(4)   Oh for the wings of a dove!

Each of these expressions has its own illocutionary force, as a wish, an exclamation or whatever, and is built round a small frame of words which form a lexeme: HOW ABOUT, WHAT A, IF ONLY, OH FOR. Indeed it may be possible in each case to select just one word as the root; for instance, HOW$_{about}$ would be a sublexeme of HOW which has the peculiarities of not requiring a parent, of requiring a token of ABOUT, and of meaning something like 'What do you think of the following suggestion?'

Another aspect of parent-valency is that words are fussy about their parent. One example mentioned earlier is that the adverb VERY accepts only adjectives or adverbs as its parent (e.g. *very quick, very quickly*), but refuses verbs (e.g. **very admire*), which provides a useful test for adjectives.

A more general difference is that adjectives and adverbs depend, as adjuncts, on different word-classes, which is why Standard English distinguishes *quick runner* and *run quickly*, though non-Standard English doesn't. The Standard English contrast gives a useful test for distinguishing gerunds and nouns (see 10.2), showing that *reading* is a noun in *a quick reading of the paper* but a gerund in *quickly reading the paper*.

11.2.2   Dependent-valency

Turning to dependent-valency, we come to the main territory of valency studies that reveals enormous amounts of detail about individual lexemes (Herbst *et al.* 2004).

For example, you might think that at least synonyms would have the same valency, but this isn't so: although TRY and ATTEMPT are synonyms and both allow TO as a complement, this complement is optional after TRY but obligatory after ATTEMPT:

(5)   He told me to try to do it, so I did try, but failed.
(6)   *He told me to attempt to do it, so I did attempt, but failed.

Similarly, LIKELY and PROBABLE have the same meaning but different valencies: although they're interchangeable in (7) they aren't in (8).

(7)   It's likely/probable that it'll rain.
(8)   It's likely/*probable to rain.

The same kind of apparently arbitrary variation appears among determiners, where EACH and EVERY have almost the same meaning but quite different valencies:

(9)   Each/every student wrote an essay.
(10)   Each/*every of the students wrote an essay.

As speakers of English we clearly pick up a great deal of fine detail while listening and reading, and part of the enjoyment of studying English in this way is to discover and explore these details.

The main contribution I can make here is to describe the main dependency-valency patterns, and to comment on a few particularly important cases. The general question is what kinds of valent each word-class allows, and what we shall find is that for some classes the simple contrast between subjects and complements introduced in 11.1 isn't enough.

11.2.3   Dependent-valency for prepositions and 'subordinating conjunctions'

We start with prepositions. Most prepositions just take one complement, which may be either optional (INSIDE, UP, BEFORE) or obligatory (e.g. OF, FOR, TO). In these examples I follow a widely used convention where brackets show optionality, and *(…) shows that omitting the item concerned is impossible – i.e. the item is obligatory.

(11)   I put it inside (the box).
(12)   I was thinking of *(her).

However, a few prepositions allow two valents, which we can call 'subject' and 'complement' because they are, in fact, very similar to subjects and complements of verbs. (Indeed, we can identify this complement with one particular verb complement that we shall recognize below, 'predicative'.) One such preposition is FOR, as in *for … to …*:

(13)   I bought it for you to wear.

Notice that you will be the wearer, so this is a case where we need a dependency triangle (7.2): *you* and *to* both depend on *for*, but *you* also depends on *to*.

The same pattern is found after WITH:

(14)   I saw him with his hat in his hand.

Here *with* has two valents (subject and complement), with the first also acting as subject of the second – which is why the sentence tells us that his hat was in his hand.

Another complication with prepositions is that their complement allows a much wider range of word-classes than was traditionally assumed (10.3). A typical traditional example of a preposition is (15), where the complement of *before* is a noun, *her*. (Remember that according to Section 10.1, 'pronoun' isA 'noun'.)

(15)   He woke before her.

The example of *before* in (16) would traditionally be a subordinating conjunction because its complement is a subordinate clause headed by a verb, *did*.

(16)   He woke before she did.

But the similarities between the two examples point to a unified analysis in which they're both prepositions.

Moreover, if a preposition like BEFORE can have a verb instead of a noun as its complement, why not extend the same analysis to those like IF or ALTHOUGH which allow nothing but verbs? This is how some of the most highly regarded modern grammatical analyses treat most subordinating conjunctions (Huddleston and Pullum 2002: 1012–13), and Word Grammar follows suit.

In a sentence like (16), therefore, *before* is a preposition whose complement is *did*, with *she* as the latter's subject. (The 'subordinating conjunctions' THAT and WHETHER, as in *I know that/whether it's raining*, need a different treatment which is discussed on the supporting website.)

Sentence (17) allows us to summarize the possibilities for prepositions.

(17)   He went *out with* his hat *on because of* the risk *of* sunburn, *although* it rained.

The structure is shown in Figure 11.3.

The example shows that a preposition may have different valency patterns:

- no visible valent at all (*out*, *on*);
- one complement which is a noun (*of*), a finite verb (*although*) or another preposition (*because*);
- a subject and a complement (*with*).

11.2.4   Dependent-valency for nouns

Turning now to nouns, we must recall that nouns include pronouns, which in turn include determiners (10.1). In this analysis, an example like *any*

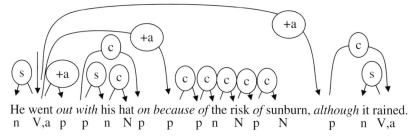

He went *out with* his hat *on because of* the risk *of* sunburn, *although* it rained.
n V,a p p n N p p p n N p N p n V,a

Figure 11.3 *Prepositions can have many different complement patterns*

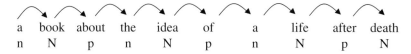

a book about the idea of a life after death
n N p n N p n N p N

Figure 11.4 *A typically simple dependency analysis of a complex noun phrase*

money contains not just one noun, but two, either of which may be used on its own without the other:

(18)   I don't earn (any) (money).

In this example, either of the bracketed nouns may be omitted.

But when a determiner and a common noun combine, which depends on which? The answer is neither obvious nor certain, but on balance I favour the same analysis as one major strand of modern grammar (Payne 2006). In this analysis, the common noun (here, *money*) depends, as complement, on the determiner (*any*; Hudson 2004).

One of the attractions of this analysis is the remarkably simple analysis that it gives to long noun phrases containing prepositions, such as *the bridge over the river at the bottom of the valley* or *a book about the idea of a life after death*; a typical analysis can be seen in Figure 11.4.

Another attraction is the similarity that it reveals to other word-classes. Determiners are often described as 'grammatical' rather than 'lexical' words because of their importance in grammar and lack of ordinary meaning. Given this contrast, the determiner-as-parent analysis makes the lexical word depend on the grammatical word. Just the same is true in preposition–noun or preposition–verb pairs such as *before it* or *before (he) left*, and also (as we shall see below) in auxiliary–main pairs of verbs such as *is working*.

One particularly irritating fact for a grammarian in search of generalizations is that some determiners change shape according to whether they have a complement or not. For example, the one I call NONE is realized as {no} when it has a complement (compare: *I have none* and *I have no money*); and the same is true for most of the possessive determiners: MINE, YOURS, HERS, OURS, THEIRS. This rather trivial morphological fact shouldn't divert us from the underlying unity of these lexemes.

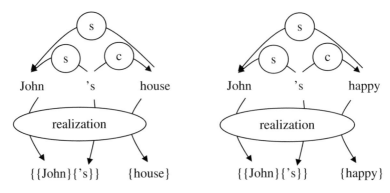

Figure 11.5 *The two 'apostrophe s's as clitics*

11.2.5 The possessive 'S

One particular determiner needs special mention: the possessive 'apostrophe', as in *John's house*. In spite of its lack of substance, there are overwhelming reasons for analysing the suffixed {s} as the realization of a separate word, to which we can give the grand title *the lexeme 'S*.

Although the lexeme 'S is usually attached directly to the possessor noun, as in *John's house*, it turns out that it's actually attaching to the possessor noun's entire phrase. (Wikipedia: 'Saxon genitive'.) This is clear either if the possessor has a post-dependent, as in *someone else* (giving *someone else's hat*), or if there are two coordinated possessors, as in *John and Mary's house*. If the lexeme 'S is a separate word, with the possessor depending on it, this is exactly as we would expect. But if (as some claim) it's a mere inflection, such examples are very hard to explain. The analysis I'm suggesting for the lexeme 'S is the one on the left in Figure 11.5.

But why is the lexeme 'S such a small word? Well, it's no smaller than the verb *is* when this is reduced to *'s* as in *John's happy*. Nobody doubts that this is a separate word, and indeed the root of the whole sentence. So if a single consonant can realize a whole word in this case, why not in the possessive too? The right-hand diagram in Figure 11.5 shows how similar the two cases are. But if we accept this analysis, we're in effect accepting that each of these words is realized, not by a word-form, but by a mere suffix (which actually has just the same form as the suffix found in plural nouns and singular verbs).

There are very good precedents for this analysis, and a technical name: **CLITIC**. (Wikipedia: 'Clitic'.) A clitic is a separate syntactic word which is realized by an affix which has to be glued morphologically to a preceding or following word. Clitics are common in other languages; As in the subject and object pronouns of French are clitics. the French for 'I love you' As in, *Je t'aime*, where both *je* (I) and *t'* (you) are clitics.

But suppose the possessive 'S is a clitic, i.e. a separate grammatical word; what kind of word is it? Clearly, it has all the properties of a typical determiner, a pronoun with a complement (10.1):

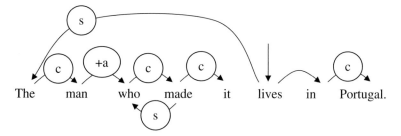

Figure 11.6 *Mutual dependency in a relative clause*

- it allows a following common noun (for the thing possessed);
- no other determiner is possible (e.g. we can't say *the John's house* any more than we can say *the his house*);
- a singular countable noun needs no other determiner (so although we can't say *I like house*, we can say *I like John's house*).

In short, possessive 'S is a determiner, a pronoun that takes an optional common noun as its complement.

But unlike the other pronouns it also has an extra dependent, the preceding noun indicating the 'possessor'. In this analysis, then, *John's house* consists of three words, with both *John* and *house* depending on *'s* – a remarkably similar structure to the one for *John's happy*, containing the clitic verb *'s*. Moreover, both examples seem to need the dependency triangle shown in Figure 11.5 because *John* is directly related both to the adjective *happy* after *is* and to the possessed noun (*house*).

It's only a short step from taking *John's* as two syntactic words to doing the same with the other possessive pronouns; for example, maybe the form {my} realizes two syntactic words, ME and 'S. But we're certainly at the frontiers of research, and enough is probably enough.

11.2.6   Other nouns that have complements

Among nouns, it isn't just determiners that have complements, of course. For instance, a relative pronoun such as WHO has a finite verb as its complement, as in (19), where *who* depends on *man* and *made* depends on *who*:

(19)   The man who made it lives in Portugal.

Examples such as this show the need for **MUTUAL DEPENDENCY** (7.6), because *who* is also a dependent (the subject) of *made*. The structure of (19) is shown in Figure 11.6.

Even common nouns may have complements; for example, in *a student of linguistics*, there are good reasons for analysing *of linguistics* as the complement of *student*. To see why, try replacing the head noun by the 'dummy' noun ONE, as in *a small one* (Huddleston and Pullum 2002: 441). For instance, compare (20) and (21):

(20)   He teaches the students from the English Department but not the ones from French.

(21)   *He teaches the students of English but not the ones of French.

My judgement, indicated by the star, is that (21) is much worse than (20). Why? Because ONE has no complements of its own, so it only allows adjuncts such as the *from* phrases (which could incidentally be expanded into *who are from ...* which again confirms that they are adjuncts). The contrasting badness of (21) shows that *of English* and *of French* are complements.

11.2.7   Dependent-valency for verbs: direct and indirect objects

We've seen so far that most of the main word-classes of English allow valents, but we now come to by far the richest area of valency, that of **verbs**.

Traditionally, dictionaries show verb valencies by classifying them as transitive or intransitive according to whether or not they apply (or 'transit') the action to an object. (Wikipedia: 'Transitivity (grammatical category)'.) However, there's actually much more than this two-way contrast to say about the valency of English verbs.

Take example (22).

(22)   I paid him a pound for the apples.

This sentence shows that the verb PAY allows four valents:

*   the subject – the buyer
*   the first complement – the seller
*   the second complement – the money
*   the third complement – the goods

The three complements aren't interchangeable; for example, the seller and the money can't change positions (unless we add *to* before the seller: ... *paid a pound to him*). This is just one example of a range of differences between these four valents, so we clearly need four distinct dependency types, and not just the basic contrast between subjects and complements.

What we need is a range of further distinctions within 'complement', not only to distinguish co-occurring complements as in (22), but also to distinguish different types of complement when they occur on their own. I can offer a list of categories that I'm fairly confident with, but even this isn't perfect and it certainly doesn't cover all the distinctions that need to be made. This is an area that calls for more research.

The most familiar category is object, which is traditionally divided into 'direct' and 'indirect' object. The direct object is the basic type, so we can recognize this as simply the default object.

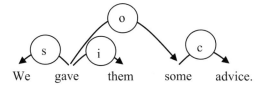

Figure 11.7 *A typical ditransitive verb, with direct and indirect object*

An object is a noun without any preposition, and normally stands immediately after the verb, as in *enjoy linguistics, read books, sing songs*. If the verb describes an action that someone applies to something, then the object normally describes the something, as in *bake a cake* or *eat a cake*. It's hard to separate an object from its verb by, say, an adverb: alongside *enjoy linguistics enormously* we can't say **enjoy enormously linguistics*.

Indirect objects are just the same except that they always occur between a verb and its ordinary object, as in *give Mary flowers, tell me a story, pay the seller a pound*. Consequently, the indirect object is normally the first of two nouns following the verb. It nearly always refers to a person, or at least to an animal or an institution and it's called 'indirect' because it's only indirectly affected by the action. For example, if you give Mary flowers, you pick up the flowers and hand them to Mary, which changes the position and ownership of the flowers, but only indirectly affects Mary.

These two complements are illustrated in Figure 11.7 for a typical 'ditransitive' (having two objects) verb, GIVE. In this diagram, 'i' and 'o' stand for the indirect and direct objects.

11.2.8   Predicatives

A verb's 'predicative' is typically an adjective or a non-finite verb (e.g. *became famous, got moving*), but it may also be a noun (e.g. *are teachers*) or a preposition (e.g. *seemed in a good mood*).

What these examples all have in common is that they describe another valent of the same verb: the object if there is one, otherwise the subject. For example, *angry* describes him in *I got him angry*, but it describes me in *I got angry*. This is quite different from the role of an object, as you can see by contrasting *He met a linguist* and *He became a linguist*. When he met a linguist (object) he met a different person, the linguist; but when he became a linguist (predicative), 'linguist' is simply a description of him after the change.

The term 'predicative' is related to 'predicate', the traditional name for whatever is said about the subject; for instance, *He is a linguist* is said to consist of a predicate 'linguist' applied to the subject 'he'. This kind of analysis often uses the notation 'linguist (he)'. Even for modern grammarians, each predicative has a subject, the person or thing that it describes.

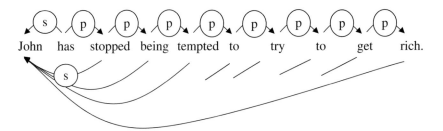

Figure 11.8 *Recursive dependencies in a chain of predicatives*

For instance, in *I got angry*, the word *I* is the subject not only of *got*, but also of *angry*. This is an example of the familiar syntactic triangle (7.2) in which three words are interrelated so that one of them depends on the other two. But the predicative's subject need not be the higher verb's subject: it may also be the latter's object, as in *I got him angry*. In this case, 'angry' is a description of him (after the change), so the subject of *angry* is *him*.

As with other syntactic triangles, predicatives can be applied recursively (7.4) to give sentences like (23).

(23)   John has stopped being tempted to try to get rich.

The analysis of (23) is shown in Figure 11.8, where 'p' stands for 'predicative'.

According to this analysis, no fewer than nine words all share the same subject, *John*. As I explain on the website, the infinitival TO is classified as an auxiliary verb. This analysis is controversial, but explains a number of similarities to auxiliaries such as the possibility of omitting the predicative; for example, just as we can say *I will*, we can also say *I want to*.

11.2.9   Other complements of verbs

Verbs have other types of complement, but their classification is much less certain than objects, indirect objects and predicatives.

For instance, most analyses recognize 'particles', prepositions such as UP or AWAY that are used without a complement and that may stand either before or after the direct object:

(24)   He picked up the book.
(25)   He picked the book up.

But it's not clear how 'particle' fits into the system of dependencies.

On the one hand, we might consider analysing *up* as a predicative; for example, when he had picked the book up, it was 'up', so 'up' is a description of the book. On the other hand, the combination PICK UP is lexically fixed, unlike most predicatives. What other word could you use with PICK when you use this verb to mean 'lift' rather than 'choose'?

In its lexical rigidity, PICK UP is similar to LOOK AFTER, as in (26).

Table 11.2 *The main dependency types for English.*

Dependency	Abbreviation	Example
Pre-adjunct	a+	big book
Post-adjunct	+a	book about linguistics
Subject	s	he slept
Complement	c	about linguistics, the book
(Direct) object	o	wrote it
Indirect object	i	gave her (some)
Predicative	p	is big, make angry

(26)   She looked after the book.

But in this case, *the book* isn't the verb's object as it was in (24). Instead, it's the complement of *after* as you can see by trying to rearrange the words as in (25):

(27)   *She looked the book after.

(27) is impossible because *the book* is the complement of *after*, so it has to follow *after*, in contrast with (25) where *the book* and *up* are fellow complements so they can occur in either order. In other words, *looked* has just one complement, the phrase *after the book*, in contrast with the two complements of *picked*.

How should we classify the complement AFTER of this sublexeme of LOOK? Let's first compare it with the UP of PICK UP. On the one hand, it's like *up* in being lexically fixed; but on the other hand, it has a very different syntactic relation to the accompanying noun, and it certainly doesn't deserve a 'predicative' analysis by virtue of being a 'description' of anything.

We might also compare this AFTER with a direct object. On the one hand, its complement can easily be turned into the subject of a passive verb, as in *The book was looked after by her*. But on the other hand, AFTER is a preposition rather than a noun.

Maybe the best we can do in this state of uncertainty is to classify all the complements other than objects and predicatives simply as default 'complements', with the usual label 'c'.

11.2.10   Summary of dependency types

Table 11.2 summarizes all the dependency types that I've introduced, apart from the supercategories listed in Figure 11.1: 'dependent', 'pre-dependent', 'post-dependent', 'adjunct' and 'valent'.

This completes our brief survey of the valency patterns of English words. Valency is fundamental to syntax because the syntactic structure of a sentence consists of nothing but the valencies of all the individual words, with each valency need satisfied by some other word-token in the sentence.

To take a very simple example, the noun *wine* and the adjective *nice* both need a parent and the verb *tastes* requires a noun as its subject and an adjective as its predicative. Put these three word-tokens together and you have the sentence *Wine tastes nice*, where each word's needs are satisfied by the other words: *wine* and *nice* satisfy the dependency-valency needs of *tastes*, and *tastes* in turn satisfies their parent-valency needs – a perfect case of mutual support. Once we've explained all the dependency pairings of a sentence in this way, the only remaining bit of syntax is coordination (11.5).

Where next?

Advanced: Back to Part I, Chapter 3.3: Choices, features and cross-classification
Novice: Explore Part II, Chapter 7.2: Valency

11.3   Features, agreement and unrealized lexemes

Summary of Section 7.3:

- Some inflections are organized in **morpho-syntactic features**, which are choice sets that list inflections that are alternatives to one another (e.g. the feature 'number' has 'singular' and 'plural' as its competing **values**).
- The only evidence for morpho-syntactic features comes from **agreement rules** (e.g. a determiner agrees in number with its complement) because these cannot be expressed without mentioning features. Inflections that are not involved in agreement are not grouped into features.
- Morpho-syntactic feature-values are properties of the words concerned, so one of the values of a feature may be the '**unmarked**' default with others as '**marked**' exceptions. The basic classification of words is based on the taxonomy, with features as an optional extra.
- In some languages, agreement rules provide conclusive evidence for **unrealized lexemes**, ordinary words which belong to ordinary lexemes and inflections but which have no realization.

English grammar has just two rules of agreement:

- a determiner agrees in number with its complement noun (e.g. *this book* but *these books*);
- a present-tense verb agrees in number with its subject (e.g. *he sings* but *they sing*), with a special rule for the past tense of BE (e.g. *he was* but *they were*).

Both of these rules are actually a little more complicated than they look, but the details are easily available elsewhere (Huddleston and Pullum 2002: 499–511) and this isn't the place for a discussion of how to express them in terms of a Word Grammar network (Hudson 1999).

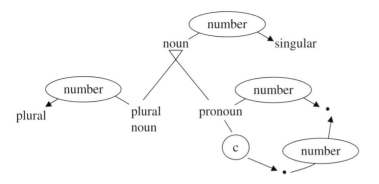

Figure 11.9 *Determiners agree in number with their complement noun*

As far as morpho-syntactic features are concerned, these agreement rules point to just one feature: the number feature which contrasts 'singular' and 'plural' for nouns.

How then do the agreement rules work? The rule for pronouns (i.e. determiners) such as THIS is shown in Figure 11.9. In words, a noun's number is singular by default, but plural if the noun is a plural noun. Moreover, if the noun is a pronoun, its number is the same as that of its complement.

Subject–verb agreement is almost as easy. The only extra assumption needed is that the number feature applies to present-tense verbs, contrasting *think* with *thinks*. (Notice how the morph {s} is associated with plural number for nouns and singular for verbs, a nice illustration of the need to separate morphs from meaning.) The agreement rule is shown in the top network of Figure 11.10, with two simple example sentences shown below. In words, a default tensed verb's number is plural but a singular (present-tense) verb's number is singular and a past-tense verb has no number; if a verb has a number, it's the same as the subject's.

11.3.1   Unrealized subjects

In short, morpho-syntactic features play a rather insignificant role in English grammar. But as we saw in Section 7.3, they're much more important in some other languages, and the agreement rules that involve them provide the best possible evidence for unrealized lexemes – ordinary words that have no realization.

In the absence of such clear evidence, can we assume that English too has unrealized lexemes? Yes, I think we probably can. There are many points where they at least make the grammar easier to write, and in those cases we may also be justified in assuming that language learners take the same short-cuts that tempt a grammarian.

Consider again the case of imperatives that we looked at in Section 7.3. We can probably justify an unrealized YOU as the subject of an imperative by looking at the complications they avoid even in simple examples like (1).

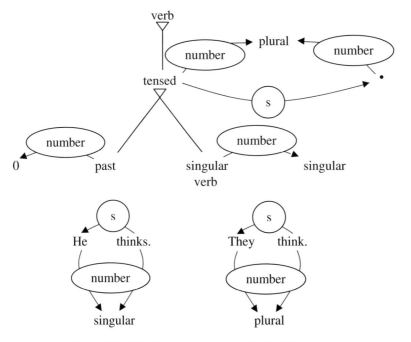

Figure 11.10 *Subject–verb agreement in English*

(1)   Follow me!

How do we know that the request is for 'you', the person addressed, to follow me; i.e. for me to go first, and you second, not the other way round? Rather obviously, we know this because that's how FOLLOW works; and to be more precise, its subject supplies the follower and its object–the 'followed'.

But what if there isn't a subject, as appears to be the case in (1)? In that case, the general rule for FOLLOW doesn't help. Maybe (1) has no follower? No, that's simply wrong because we know it's asking you to follow me. By far the easiest solution is to assume an unrealized YOU as the subject of *follow*, and then everything follows automatically – *follow* has a subject, and the subject's referent, 'you', is the follower.

The benefits of this analysis are even clearer in examples like (2).

(2)   Keep following me!

In this case it's even harder to know how to apply the rule for FOLLOW if there's no subject, because the valency of KEEP normally makes it share its subject with the following verb in a predicative triangle. If *keep* has no subject, then not only is the follower obscured, but it's not clear how the two verbs fit together. But if it does have a subject, business is as usual and the syntactic structure is exactly the same as for (3).

(3)   You keep following me!

The difference between (2) and (3) then lies not in their syntax but in their morphology.

If imperatives can have unrealized subjects, what about other verbs? One of the characteristics of English is that tensed verbs can't have them, so we can't say (4) or (5):

(4)   *Came.
(5)   *Loves you.

In this respect English is different from many other languages such as Spanish, Italian, Russian, Modern Greek, Arabic and Japanese, all of which freely allow tensed verbs to be used without an overt subject. (Wikipedia: 'Null-subject language'.)

But infinitives and participles are often used in English without an overt subject, and in these cases too an unrealized subject can be justified with the same arguments as I used for the imperative subject. For example, consider (6).

(6)   When elderly people are outside in cold weather, it's important to keep moving.

How do we know that it's the elderly people who should move? This is reasonably straightforward if we can assume an unrealized THEM as subject of *to keep*, but without this hidden element it would be really hard.

11.3.2   Other unrealized lexemes

Moreover, there's no reason to think that only subjects can be unrealized. This is a possibility in all cases of ellipsis (8.6.6), i.e. whenever a word that might have been used is omitted.

Take determiners, for example. I argued in Section 10.1 that these are actually pronouns because nearly every determiner that can be used with a following complement noun can also be used without one:

(7)   Those books are his books.
(8)   Those are his.

There's some evidence that at least some pronouns have an unrealized complement noun.

This evidence comes from nouns such as SCALES that have the 'wrong' number for their meaning (often called by grammarians 'pluralia tantum', in honour of their counterparts in Latin; for details see Huddleston and Pullum 2002: 340–4). The problem with SCALES is that it's plural even though it refers to a single object, a machine for weighing oneself in the bathroom which (oddly) we may also call a 'pair' of bathroom 'scales'. Consequently, when we combine SCALES with THIS we use the plural form *these*:

(9)   These scales are broken.

Now the relevant point is that the plural number of *these* doesn't depend on the overt presence of the lexeme SCALES. All we need is an implied reference to scales, as in (10).

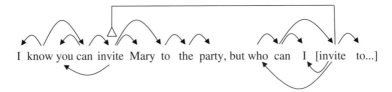

Figure 11.11 *Verb–complement ellipsis as an unrealized lexeme*

(10)   Those scales are ok, but these are broken.

This suggests that the lexeme SCALES has not only been activated but has supplied an unrealized complement for the determiner; and once again, the unrealized complement can be justified by the way it explains the facts when combined with the usual agreement rules.

But if *these* can be complemented by an unrealized SCALES to explain its plurality, what about THEY, which would also be used in these circumstances in preference to IT?

(11)   The scales are broken, so they need to be repaired.

Should we see an unrealized complement after every personal pronoun, or should we reject all unrealized complement nouns on the grounds that examples like (10) can be explained by whatever mechanism explains the plurality of *they* in (11)? I don't know the answer, but unrealized lexemes are certainly among the candidates to consider.

Another kind of unrealized complement may be found in examples like (12):

(12)   I know you can invite Mary to the party, but who can I?

In this case the challenge is to explain the structure of *who can I*. How can so few words mean so much: 'who can I invite to the party?', and how does the pronoun *who* fit in, given that the verb CAN doesn't have a valency which would allow a pronoun other than its subject (in this case, *I*)?

Unrealized lexemes offer a rather satisfying explanation in which *can* has an unrealized *invite* as its complement. This is simply copied, using an isA link, from the earlier overt *invite*, so it inherits almost all the latter's properties, including the sense 'invite to the party'. As usual in default inheritance, the properties are all inherited except those which are overridden: instead of having *you* as its subject, it has *I*, and instead of having *Mary* as its object, it has *who*. This rather tentative analysis is sketched in Figure 11.11, which includes the isA link from the unrealized *invite* to its source, the realized one.

One unsolved problem in this analysis is how to guarantee that the inherited dependents such as *to the party* are also unrealized, but the main point is that the unrealized verb *invite* explains not only why *who can I?* means 'who can I invite to the party', but also how *who* fits in syntactically. This example could take us into the large area of syntax called ellipsis (8.6), and it is possible that unrealized lexemes are the key to understanding the whole of ellipsis, and not just the examples discussed so far.

But that discussion would take us up to the frontiers of research and doesn't belong here.

Where next?

Advanced: Back to Part I, Chapter 3.4: Examples of relational taxonomies
Novice: Explore Part II, Chapter 7.3: Morpho-syntactic features, agreement and unrealized words

11.4   Default word order

Summary of Section 7.4:

- A typical word takes its position from the word it depends on (its **parent**), so the parent is its **landmark**. Landmark relations are properties that words inherit via their dependency relations.
- These inherited landmark relations may simply show which word is the landmark, or they may be more specific, requiring the word to be either '**before**' or '**after**' its landmark.
- Languages with **free word order** impose no specific restrictions on the order of dependents in relation to the 'head' of a phrase, but many languages favour one of three general orderings of a word and its dependents called **head-initial**, **head-final** or **head-medial**.
- The landmark relation is what 'holds phrases together' because the Best Landmark Principle requires a good landmark to be local. This general principle translates, in the case of words, into the **No-tangling principle**: a word's link to its landmark must not cross ('tangle with') any other word's link to its landmark.
- Every non-root word must have one dependency that gives it a landmark, but it may also have other **non-landmark dependencies** which don't carry landmarks. In syntactic triangles, the landmark word is typically the parent on which the other parent depends; this generalization, called the **Raising Principle**, describes the default pattern but allows exceptions where a word is 'lowered' to take the lower parent as its landmark.

These general syntactic ideas apply rather easily to English.

Compared with many other languages, English has rather strict word-order rules because word order carries a great deal of important syntactic information about dependency relations. Its preferred 'head-medial' ordering requires some dependents to stand before their parent, while others have to follow it. This general principle applies to each of the major word-classes, but of course different word-classes have different kinds of dependents so the details vary from class to class, as I explained in Section 11.2.

The grammar shows which of a word's dependents typically stand before it and which after by means of the contrast between pre-dependents and post-dependents introduced in Section 11.1 and summarized in Figure 11.1. From these general dependency types, dependents inherit either 'before' or 'after' as their landmark relation. For example, the subject is before the verb because it isA pre-dependent whereas the object isA post-dependent, and stands after the verb.

Among adjuncts, an adverb such as NEVER isA pre-dependent whereas a more typical adjunct such as *in the morning* isA post-dependent. This explains why (1) is permitted but (2) isn't.

(1)   He never works in the morning.
(2)   *He in the morning works never.

Similarly, some of the adjuncts of a noun have to precede it while others have to follow:

(3)   a short book about linguistics
(4)   *an about linguistics book short

Such rules are clear and rigid, but there are also special arrangements for breaking some of them which we consider in Section 11.6.

11.4.1   The cognitive benefits of the English rules

Are the rules simply arbitrary, or do they reflect more general principles? There are principles, and behind the principles we can see a single general theme: helping the user. Our linguistic ancestors have evolved a system which tries to solve, or at least reduce, two problems:

- multiple dependents: how to hold two or more dependents of the same word in your mind at the same time.
- 'heavy' dependents: how to hold a long chain of dependents in mind.

Every language faces these two problems, and the pressures of everyday communication gradually push a language's users towards some kind of solution, so what follows is simply the English solution.

I've already explained the English solution to the problem of multiple dependencies (11.2). This is the head-medial ordering that reduces dependency distance. For instance, by putting the subject before the verb and the object after, as in *I love her*, we allow both of them to have a dependency distance of 0, in contrast with either *I her love* or *Love I her*, where one of the dependents is always separated by the other from the verb.

'Heavy' words may have just one dependent, but this dependent has a dependent that has a dependent that … For a very clear example of a heavy dependent, think of the children's poem about the house that Jack built, which gradually builds a sentence by adding relative clauses. After a few verses, the sentence is (5):

(5)   This is the cat that caught the rat that ate the malt that lay in the house that Jack built.

(Wikipedia: 'The house that Jack built'.) The word *is* has just one post-dependent, the first *the*, but this is extremely heavy because it stands at the top of a very long chain of dependents (18 in the words quoted here, and the chain is much longer in the full poem).

The metaphor of weight is helpful in thinking about such structures because it translates easily into the metaphor of 'load', in this case the load that a word places on working memory (4.2). A heavy word has to stay in working memory for a long time because its meaning isn't complete until the entire chain of dependents has been processed. For instance, if I tell you to look out for the cat that caught the rat, you don't know which cat I mean until you've finished processing *rat*; and it gets worse as the chain of dependents gets longer.

Now one of the things you'll notice about (5) is that it's actually quite easy to process. This is because you can focus all your mental resources on the cat without having to worry about any other words; and this is because the heavy phrase is at the end of the sentence. To see how important this is, imagine you were processing sentence (6).

(6)   The farmer gave the cat that caught the rat that ate the malt that lay in the house that Jack built some milk.

All the time that you're working on the cat, you're having to remember that *gave* needs a direct object as well. No doubt you agree that (6) is very much harder to understand than (5).

In discussing such examples, grammarians talk about the principle of 'end-weight', which encourages us to put heavy dependents at the end of the sentence. The heavy cat is easier in (5) because it's at the end, i.e. it's the last dependent of *is*. But how can we follow this principle if word order is fixed?

Thanks to the creativity and daring of our ancestors, we have a collection of fixes, the special orders that I discuss in Section 11.6. Other solutions are simply a matter of free choices made by language users. The combined effect is a clear preference for post-dependents to outnumber pre-dependents – typically about two post-dependents to every pre-dependent. If you do a syntactic analysis of ordinary texts, you'll find this trend emerging very clearly; and if you don't, it's probably because your analysis is wrong.

To show the powerful effects of free choice, which is of course almost completely unconscious, it's interesting to look at the choices we make for subjects. These are important because subjects can be heavy; the grammar allows heavy subjects just as it allows heavy words anywhere else, and indeed it's easy to create them on the model of the house that Jack built:

(7)   The cat that caught the rat that ate the malt that lay in the house that Jack built ran away.

But in fact we tend strongly to avoid heavy subjects. One piece of evidence is that we use as subjects two pronouns for every common or proper noun, in contrast with an overall preference which goes in the opposite direction (Biber *et al.* 1999: 236, 1067). Pronouns are inherently much lighter than other nouns because they tend not to have dependents, so we seem to choose our words carefully so that subjects are much lighter than other dependents.

There's more to say about default word order. For instance, a complete grammar of English would certainly say something about the rules for arranging co-dependents that are on the same side of their shared parent such as a verb's subject and pre-adjunct in (8) and (9), and its direct and indirect object in (10) and (11):

(8)   He never slept.
(9)   *Never he slept.
(10)   I gave John a present.
(11)   *I gave a present John.

But the aim of this chapter is to provide a toe-hold on syntax, not a complete grammar; many of these further details can be found on the website.

Where next?

Advanced: Back to Part I, Chapter 3.4.4: Chunking, serial ordering and sets
Novice: Explore Part II, Chapter 7.4: Default word order

11.5   Coordination

Summary of Section 7.5:

- Our memory for complex events allows us to remember **word strings**, ordered lists of words which may or may not have ordinary dependency structure. Word strings are also allowed as the complement of a verb such as SAY.
- Word strings also occur in coordination, where they are the units that are combined by **coordinating conjunctions** (e.g. *and, or*). A coordinating conjunction has two or more word strings as its dependents, but has no parent.
- A coordinating conjunction also signals **dependency sharing**, in which words inside the word string share their dependency relations to words outside the string. Several words share a dependency (either as dependent or as parent) by forming a **set** of words (indicated in notation by a small circle), each of which has the dependency and each of which belongs to a different word string.

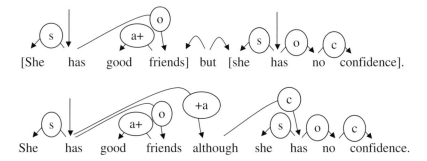

[She   has   good   friends]   but   [she   has   no   confidence].

She   has   good   friends   although   she   has   no   confidence.

Figure 11.12 *Coordination and subordination compared*

- A single word string may contain members of more than one dependency-sharing set, which produces **non-constituent coordination** where word strings do not correspond to phrases.
- In a **layered** coordination, one coordination contains another.

The general discussion of coordination in Section 7.5 was all about English, so novices should read that section first. The following discussion deals with some issues that arise in applying this analysis to ordinary English sentences.

11.5.1   Coordination or subordination?

One question is how to distinguish coordination from 'subordination', i.e. from ordinary dependency. This question arises when two clauses occur together in one sentence, as in (1) and (2).

(1)   She has good friends but she has no confidence.
(2)   She has good friends although she has no confidence.

(1) is a clear example of coordination, but (2) is equally clearly a case of subordination, so the examples need the very different structures shown in Figure 11.12.

(1) has a coordinating conjunction *but* linking two word strings, each of which happens to consist of a complete clause headed by *has*; whereas *although* in (2) subordinates the second *has* to the first.

Why do such apparently similar examples need such different structures? A number of different criteria can be applied to distinguish coordination and subordination (Aarts 2006), but two stand out as the key differences.

One distinguishing characteristic of coordination is the dependency-sharing that allows the coordinated items to share external dependencies. This property of coordination provides a choice between repeating identical words and 'sharing' them – i.e. omitting the 'internal' repetitions. In the example, the word *she* is identical in the first and second clause, so the second one can be omitted; this works fine in (1), but is impossible in (2).

(1a)   She has good friends but ~~she~~ has no confidence.

(2a)   *She has good friends although ~~she~~ has no confidence.

Moreover, the same option exists for the repeated *has*; and once again (1) allows sharing but (2) doesn't:

(1b)   She has good friends but ~~she has~~ no confidence.

(2b)   *She has good friends although ~~she has~~ no confidence.

The second difference between coordination and subordination rests on a property of subordination which coordination lacks: flexibility of position. For reasons that are discussed in Section 7.6, post-dependents such as the subordinate clause *although she has no confidence* can generally be moved to the front of the clause containing them – in other words, turned into pre-dependents. No such movement is possible for coordination, where the conjunction is trapped rigidly between the two word strings. The result is that the parts of (2) can be radically rearranged in a way that's simply impossible for (1):

(1c)   *But she has no confidence, she has good friends.

(2c)   Although she has no confidence, she has good friends.

The differences are dramatically clear, and justify the radically different structures for coordination and subordination.

11.5.2   The coordinating conjunctions

What, then, are the coordinating conjunctions for English? The clearest examples are the lexemes AND and OR, which invariably signal coordination. This is very convenient, since they're also the most common conjunctions. Other coordinating conjunctions are slightly more complicated:

*   BUT as in example (1), but not in *He eats nothing but bananas.*

*   NOR as in (3) but not (4).
     (3)   She neither smokes nor drinks.
     (4)   She doesn't smoke, but nor does she drink.

*   THEN as in (5) but not (6) or (7).
     (5)   She went out, then came back in again.
     (6)   She went out and then came back in again.
     (7)   She went out and she then came back in again.

*   YET as in (8) but not (9).
     (8)   She works hard yet achieves little.
     (9)   She works hard and yet achieves little.

These are the only serious candidates, each with its own special restrictions and peculiarities. What they all share is the possibility of dependency sharing, combined with the rigid word order associated with coordination.

Another detail of coordination in English is that some of the conjunctions can be anticipated by a (so-called) **CORRELATIVE CONJUNCTION**, a word that occurs at or near the start of the first coordinated item. The paired words are:

- BOTH … AND …
- EITHER … OR …
- NEITHER … NOR …
- NOT ONLY … BUT …

However, this pattern isn't confined to coordination, as witness the combination IF … THEN … The correlative conjunctions probably aren't really conjunctions at all, but adverbs with complicated properties of their own.

Coordination is also complicated by a number of patterns of ellipsis which tend to have a more or less 'literary' feel and which are found not only with coordination but more widely in syntactic patterns which contrast or compare items. Perhaps the best known of these ellipsis patterns is called **GAPPING** (Crysmann 2006), and is illustrated in (10) and (11).

(10)   John invited Jean and Bill ~~invited~~ Betty.

(11)   John treats Jean better than Bill ~~treats~~ Betty.

Notice that although (10) combines gapping with coordination, (11) combines it with a very different pattern based on dependency.

The simplest analysis of such examples is to assume that the missing words are present but unrealized (7.3), which gives these examples exactly the same syntax as their full equivalents, with differences only at the level of form. However, the issues are complex (Hudson 1976, Hudson 1988) and a defensible Word Grammar analysis will have to wait for more research.

Where next?

Advanced: Back to Part I, Chapter 3.5: The network notion, properties and default inheritance

Novice: Explore Part II, Chapter 7.5: Coordination

11.6   Special word orders

Summary of Section 7.6:

- Default word order may be overridden by **special word orders** that are allowed by special rules. In the simplest cases, these rules reverse the default orders, but in more complicated cases they require an **extra dependency** which converges on a word defined by an ordinary dependency. The resulting conflict is resolved by default inheritance according to the general principles for complex properties.

- One extra dependency is **extractee**, the relation between a word which has been 'extracted' from its default position and some earlier verb from which it takes its position instead of its usual parent.
- The extractee of one word may also be the extractee of one of its complements, so the extraction relation 'hops' recursively down the dependency chain, producing **long-distance dependencies**; but this hopping is blocked by some kinds of dependency called **extraction islands**.
- The extra complexity of non-default word orders such as those found in extraction benefits us by allowing orders that reduce the demands on our memories, e.g. by reducing dependency distances.

The aim of this section is to survey the options that English offers for overriding default word orders.

11.6.1   Subject–auxiliary inversion

Perhaps the simplest case is subject–auxiliary inversion, which is mainly found in questions but which is also found in other structures:

(1)   **Have you** finished?
(2)   What **have you** finished?
(3)   Not only **has he** finished writing it, but it's actually been published.
(4)   **Had I** known you were coming, I'd have made a cake.

This is only possible with auxiliary verbs (as defined in Section 10.1), so if the sentence's meaning doesn't otherwise require an auxiliary verb, we supply one that has no meaning of its own: the 'dummy auxiliary' DO.

(5)   Did you finish?
(6)   What did you finish?

Since the auxiliary is the sentence root, it must carry the meaning of the entire sentence, including its 'question' meaning. Consequently we can consider 'interrogative auxiliary' as a subclass of 'auxiliary', and associate it not only with a special meaning but also with the special word order. Figure 11.13 shows the relevant part of the grammar, including the forced choice between 'before' and 'after'. In words, a verb's pre-dependent stands before it by default, and this default is normally inherited by its subject. But if the verb is an inverted auxiliary, the subject's position is after it (where 'before' and 'after' are mutually exclusive).

11.6.2   Extraction in topicalization

At the other end of the scale of complexity is **extraction**, which I discussed in Section 7.6. The simplest version of extraction is found in **topicalization**, where a post-dependent is moved to the front of the clause to act as its 'topic' (Sornicola 2006), the element that defines what the clause is about. The

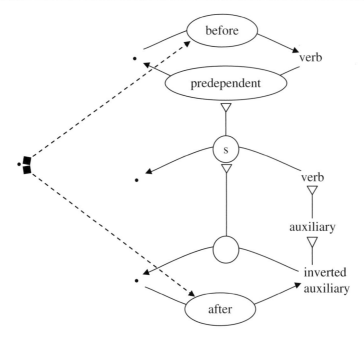

Figure 11.13 *The grammar for subject–auxiliary inversion*

most familiar examples of topicalization involve adjuncts such as expressions of time:

(7)   Yesterday I nearly missed the train.

Yesterday is actually a post-adjunct, in contrast with the pre-adjunct *nearly*, so its default position is after *missed*; but in this example it's been extracted so that it precedes not only *missed* but also the latter's subject and pre-adjunct.

As usual in extraction, repeated 'hopping' down the dependency chain can produce a long-distance dependency in examples like (8), where *yesterday* is still the post-adjunct of *missed*, to which it's attached via a chain consisting of *don't*, *think*, *know* and *that*.

(8)   Yesterday I don't think you know that I nearly missed the train.

In topicalization, the extraction is achieved by adding an extra dependency, an 'extractee', which links the topicalized item to the first verb and then successively to each of the words in the dependency chain down to the word of which it's a post-dependent.

11.6.3   Extracted Wh-pronouns

Most cases of extraction are even more complicated in structure because they involve a Wh-pronoun such as *who* in (9).

(9)   Who did you see?

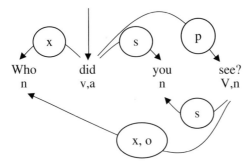

Figure 11.14 *Extraction in a wh-question*

What makes Wh-pronouns complicated is the mutual dependency between them and the following verb (11.2) – a structure, incidentally, which can only be accommodated by the rich dependency structures of Word Grammar (Hudson 2003b).

In short, an apparently simple example like *Who did you see?* requires, in addition to the special order for *did you*, three extra dependencies beyond those in, say, *You saw Mary*:

- *who* is extractee of both *did* and *see*.
- *did* is complement of *who*.

The structure is shown (without the mutual dependency) in Figure 11.14.

Why do we bother to extract words if this requires so much extra structure? Extraction moves words out of their normal position and up to the front of the sentence, but why is that helpful? As usual, it's all about making the sentence user-friendly. If I'm talking to you and start, as in (7) and (8), with a topic such as *yesterday*, this helps you to prepare your mind for the rest of the message. For instance, by activating 'yesterday' you can prepare for a contrast between what happened yesterday and some other event that's just been discussed. Similarly, if I start with *who*, you can prepare for a question about a person.

11.6.4   Extraction in subordinate questions

An even clearer advantage of extraction is to reduce dependency distance when the word concerned depends on another word. Suppose I want to use my question about who you saw as a subordinate clause, and suppose more specifically that I wanted to use it as the object of the verb WONDER. With *who* extracted to the front of its sentence, this gives (10).

(10)   I wonder who you saw.

But without extraction, I would need (11).

(11)   *I wonder you saw who.

Now the relevant fact about WONDER is that its complement must be an interrogative pronoun (or WHETHER or IF, which we can ignore here); in this case,

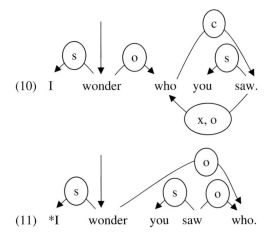

Figure 11.15 *Subordinate questions with and without extraction*

then, its complement is *who*, as shown in the diagrams for (10) and (11) in Figure 11.15.

The main point to notice about the two structures in Figure 11.15 is the dependency distance between *wonder* and *who*, which is 0 in (10) but 2 in (11). It's easy to imagine how the unextracted *who* could have been separated from *wonder* by far more than two other words, thereby posing a serious processing problem for the listener.

Incidentally, you may notice that extraction actually kills two birds with one stone, as explained in 7.6. Not only does it reduce dependency distance, but it also avoids a serious word-order problem in (11), where *saw* has no landmark and *who* has two. Does *who* take its position from *wonder* or from *saw*? And what does *saw* take its position from? In contrast, everything is clear in (10): *who* follows *wonder*, and *saw* follows *who*.

11.6.5   Extraction in relative clauses

The Wh-pronouns in subordinate questions are interrogative pronouns, but a closely related set are the relative pronouns (see Table 10.3 in Section 10.3). These function as post-adjuncts of nouns as in (12).

(12)   I recognized the man who she brought to the party.

In traditional terms we would say that the relative clause *who she brought to the party* modifies *man* (answering the question, 'which man?'); but in dependency terms, *who* is the adjunct of *man* and also extractee, object and parent of *brought*. This structure is shown in Figure 11.16.

In this structure you should particularly notice how the complement link from *who* to *brought* allows a correct landmark structure in which each word has a landmark that links it eventually to the root word *recognized*; if *brought* didn't depend on *who*, it would have no correct landmark.

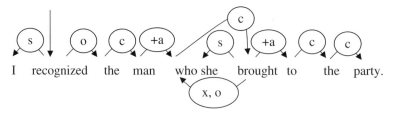

Figure 11.16 *A relative pronoun introducing a relative clause*

11.6.6   Free relative clauses and cleft sentences

Yet another kind of Wh-pronoun is called a free relative pronoun, and in traditional terms it introduces 'free relative clauses' – 'free' in that they don't depend on another noun. (Remember that pronouns are themselves nouns – see Section 10.1.) The clearest example of a free relative pronoun is WHAT, as in (13):

(13)   I couldn't digest what I ate.

Free relatives are quite hard to distinguish from subordinate questions. For instance, *what I ate* could also have been a subordinate question, as in (14):

(14)   He wondered what I ate.

But the two cases are clearly different. For one thing, *what I ate* refers to a concrete object in (13), but to a question in (14), as witness the fact that it can be replaced by *it* in (13) but not in (14). For another, *what* can be replaced in (13), but not in (14), by pronouns such as *everything (which)*. As far as syntactic structure is concerned, however, the structure for *what I ate* is the same in both examples.

Both ordinary and free relative pronouns are important for non-default word orders through their use in **cleft sentences** such as (15) and (16).

(15)   What spoilt the picnic was the weather.
(16)   It was the picnic that the weather spoilt.

Both of these examples provide alternatives to the basic order of words in (17), which express the same meaning:

(17)   The weather spoilt the picnic.

As explained more fully in Section 8.7.3, at least examples like these can be analysed straightforwardly as combinations of a relative clause with the verb BE. (Further details can be found on the website.)

11.6.7   Extraposition

A dummy *it* like the one in (16) is also found in another construction that allows non-default word order: extraposition – positioning something outside (the main body of the sentence). An example can be found in (18):

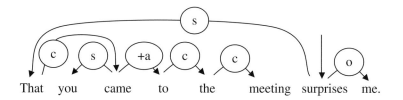

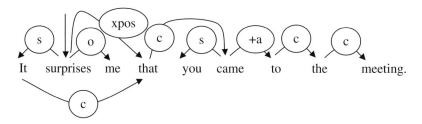

Figure 11.17 *A long subject with and without extraposition*

(18)　　　It surprises me that you came to the meeting.

This has the same meaning as (19):

(19)　　　That you came to the meeting surprises me.

It's easy to see why we prefer (18) to (19) by considering the dependency distances involved: a maximum of one in (18) contrasting with five in (19).

　　The cost of this benefit is a more complex structure, containing two extra dependencies. One is an 'extraposee' (abbreviated to 'xpos') link from *is* to *that*, which essentially turns *that* into a post-dependent in just the same way that extraction turned post-dependents into pre-dependents. The other extra dependency is a complement link from *it* to *that* which allows the pronoun to share all the meaning of the extraposed clause. The structures of the two sentences are shown in Figure 11.17.

11.6.8　　Other ways of delaying heavy dependents

　　　　Extraposition is only one of a number of grammatical devices for displacing the 'heavy' dependents (discussed in Section 11.4) from their favourite position at the end of the sentence. In the following examples of other devices, the displaced phrase is highlighted and the brackets enclose the simpler sentence without displacement.

(20)　　　There arise **a number of serious issues to do with the contract**. (A number of issues … arise.)

(21)　　　In the corner stands **an old oak tree with a heart carved in its trunk**. (An old oak tree … stands in the corner.)

(22)   Books about the psychology of language are more expensive than
         are **those dealing with historical linguistics**. (… than those …
         linguistics are.)

(23)   She put on the table **a basket full of fruit, vegetables and other
         things she'd bought for the feast**. (She put a basket full … feast on
         the table.)

(24)   All the students passed **who took the exam**. (All the students who
         took the exam passed.)

The best analysis for each of these cases probably involves the same mechanism that I introduced for extraction: an extra dependency – in this case, an extra
post-dependency such as 'extraposee'. As in extraction, the dependent isA some
other dependent, and therefore inherits all its properties except its position. Some
cases need an extra word – *it* for extraposition, *there* for patterns like (20) – but
they all change the word order without changing the default dependencies. And
in every case, the effect of the non-default word order is to reduce the dependency distance.

11.6.9   Passives

To conclude this rapid survey of non-default word orders, we must
mention a very different device which is too common to ignore: passive verbs.

For a simple example, consider (25).

(25)   I was impressed by this essay.

This means the same as (26), which is called 'active'.

(26)   This essay impressed me.

The difference lies entirely in the syntactic structure, as shown in Figure 11.18.

What passivization does is to change the verb's default object into its subject,
while at the same time changing the default subject into the complement of a
post-dependent *by*. This *by* is the ordinary preposition BY, whose dependency
I've labelled 'by' for lack of a better label.

A third effect of passivization is to change the verb's inflection from past to
passive (abbreviated to 'e' – see Table 10.1 in Section 10.2); since IMPRESS
is a regular verb the form remains the same, but in some irregulars it changes
(e.g. *John took it > It was taken by John*). This triggers other changes in the
structure because a passive participle can't be the sentence root, so it has to
depend on some other word – in this case, the auxiliary BE. Figure 11.18
shows the extra structure created just to accommodate the inflection as dotted
lines.

One of the benefits of passivization that makes all the extra structure worthwhile is the effect on word order. For example, take the active (27).

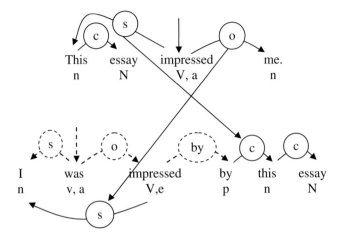

Figure 11.18 *Passivization*

(27)   **All the students who registered for the course** took the exam.

Suppose we want to avoid the long subject and its long dependency. One way to do this is to change the active *took* into the passive *was taken*.

(28)   The exam was taken by **all the students who registered for the course**.

Passives are very common in English because they help us to achieve two completely different ends: either to delay a heavy subject, as in (28), or to avoid mentioning the subject at all, as in (29) – an effect which some people see as the main function of passive verbs (Blevins 2006).

(29)   The exam was taken in the Great Hall.

Once again grammarians have a great deal more to say about passives, but this book isn't the place to say it. They provide me with a convenient opportunity to end the book by enthusing about grammar.

It's possible to see grammar as nothing but rules which prevent us from doing things that we might quite like to do, and this is certainly what prescriptive grammar is all about. But when I try to understand how grammar really works, I'm always impressed to see how enabling and helpful it is. It's a tool for expressing complex meanings, and like any other tool, it has to be designed to fit the circumstances in which it has to be used.

For grammar, the circumstances are the cognitive needs of both the speaker and the listener, and passivization is a good example of how many different and conflicting needs we have. As speakers, we balance inertia (use few words and little structure) against conformity (follow the rules), flexibility (use different patterns for different needs) and limited mental capacity (minimize active word-tokens).

The tool isn't perfect – how could it be? – but it's pretty good; and for that we should thank our linguistic ancestors.

Where next?

Advanced: Back to Part I, Chapter 3.6: Do networks need modularity?
Novice: Explore Part II, Chapter 7.6, or decide you've 'finished' and congratulate yourself!

References

Aarts, Bas 2006. 'Subordination', in Brown (ed.), pp.248–54.

Abbott, Barbara 2006. 'Definite and Indefinite', in Brown (ed.), pp.392–9.

Allan, Keith 2006a. 'Lexicon: structure', in Brown (ed.), pp.148–51.

Allan, Keith 2006b. 'Metalanguage versus Object Language', in Brown (ed.), pp.31–2.

Allerton, David 2006. 'Valency Grammar', in Brown (ed.), pp.301–14.

Altmann, Gerry 2006. 'Psycholinguistics: history', in Brown (ed.), pp.257–65.

Anon. 1987. *Collins Cobuild English Language Dictionary*. London: Collins.

Anon. 2003. *Longman Dictionary of Contemporary English*. Harlow: Pearson Education.

Anward, Jan 2006. 'Word Classes/Parts of Speech: overview', in Brown (ed.), pp.628–32.

Aronoff, Mark and Volpe, Mark 2006. 'Morpheme', in Brown (ed.), pp.274–6.

Asher, Ronald (ed.) 1994. *Encyclopedia of Language and Linguistics*, 1st edn. Oxford: Pergamon.

Atkinson, Martin, Kilby, David and Roca, Iggy 1982. *Foundations of General Linguistics*. London: Allen and Unwin.

Ayto, John 2006. 'Idioms', in Brown (ed.), pp.518–21.

Balota, David and Yap, Melvin 2006. 'Word Recognition, Written', in Brown (ed.), pp.649–54.

Barsalou, Lawrence 1992. *Cognitive Psychology: an overview for cognitive scientists*. Hillsdale, NJ: Erlbaum.

Bauer, Laurie 2006. 'Folk Etymology', in Brown (ed.), pp.520–1.

Beard, Roger, Myhill, Debra, Nystrand, Martin, and Riley, Jeni (eds) 2009. *SAGE Handbook of Writing Development*. London: Sage.

Biber, Douglas, Johansson, Stig, Leech, Geoffrey, Conrad, Susan and Finegan, Edward 1999. *Longman Grammar of Spoken and Written English*. London: Longman.

Blevins, James 2006. 'Passives and Impersonals', in Brown (ed.), pp.236–9.

Bloomfield, Leonard 1933. *Language*. New York: Holt, Rinehart and Winston.

Bock, Kathryn, Konopka, Agnieszka and Middleton, Erica 2006. 'Spoken Language Production: psycholinguistic approach', in Brown (ed.), pp.103–12.

Bouma, Gosse 2006. 'Unification, Classical and Default', in Brown (ed.), pp.231–8.

Brown, Keith (ed.) 2006. *Encyclopedia of Language and Linguistics*, 2nd edn. Amsterdam: Elsevier.

Butler, Christopher 2006. 'Functionalist Theories of Language', in Brown (ed.), pp.696–704.

Carter, Ronald and McCarthy, Michael 2006. *Cambridge Grammar of English: a comprehensive guide. Spoken and written English grammar and usage.* Cambridge University Press.

Coleman, John 2006. 'Design Features of Language', in Brown (ed.), pp.471–5.

Collinge, Neville 2006. 'Indo-European Languages', in Brown (ed.), pp.633–6.

Cornish, Francis 2006. 'Discourse Anaphora', in Brown (ed.), pp.631–8.

Cowie, Anthony 2006. 'Phraseology', in Brown (ed.), pp.579–85.

Creider, Chet and Hudson, Richard 1999. 'Inflectional Morphology in Word Grammar', *Lingua* 107: 163–87.

Creider, Chet and Hudson, Richard 2006. 'Case Agreement in Ancient Greek: implications for a theory of covert elements', in Sugayama and Hudson (eds), pp.35–53.

Crysmann, Berthold 2006. 'Coordination', in Brown (ed.), pp.183–96.

Dabrowska, Ewa 1997. 'The LAD Goes to School: a cautionary tale for nativists', *Linguistics* 35: 735–66.

De Houwer, Annick 2006. 'Bilingual Language Development: early years', in Brown (ed.), pp.780–6.

Dubinsky, Stanley and Davies, William 2006. 'Control and Raising', in Brown (ed.), pp.131–9.

Evans, Nicholas and Levinson, Stephen 2009. 'The Myth of Language Universals: language diversity and its importance for cognitive science', *Behavioral and Brain Sciences* 32: 429–8.

Falk, Yehuda 2006. 'Long-Distance Dependencies', in Brown (ed.), pp.316–23.

Fillmore, Charles, Kempler, Daniel and Wang, William (eds) 1979. *Individual Differences in Language Ability and Language Behavior.* New York: Academic Press.

Fodor, Jerry 1998. 'The Trouble with Psychological Darwinism: review of *How the Mind Works* by Steven Pinker and *Evolution in Mind* by Henry Plotkin', *London Review of Books* 20: 11–13.

Frankish, Keith 2006. 'Nonmonotonic Inference', in Brown (ed.), pp.672–5.

Gleitman, Henry and Gleitman, Lila 1979. 'Language Use and Language Judgement', in Fillmore, Kempler and Wang (eds), pp.103–26.

Goddard, Cliff 2006. 'Natural Semantic Metalanguage', in Brown (ed.), pp.544–51.

Goldberg, Adele 1995. *Constructions: a construction grammar approach to argument structure.* University of Chicago Press.

Gragg, G. 1994. 'Babylonian Grammatical Texts', in Asher (ed.), pp.296–8.

Green, Keith 2006. 'Deixis and Anaphora: pragmatic approaches', in Brown (ed.), pp.415–17.

Gumperz, John and Levinson, Stephen (eds) 1996. *Rethinking Linguistic Relativity.* Cambridge University Press.

Hanks, Patrick 2006. 'English Lexicography', in Brown (ed.), pp.184–94.

Harley, Trevor 1995. *The Psychology of Language.* Hove: Psychology Press.

Harley, Trevor 2006. 'Speech Errors: psycholinguistic approach', in Brown (ed.), pp.739–45.

Hassler, Gerda 2006. 'Meaning: pre-20th century theories', in Brown (ed.), pp.590–6.

Heath, Jeffrey 2006. 'Kinship Expressions and Terms', in Brown (ed.), pp.214–17.

Herbst, Thomas, Heath, David, Roe, Ian and Götz, Dieter 2004. *A Valency Dictionary of English: a corpus-based analysis of the complementation patterns of English verbs, nouns and adjectives.* Berlin: Mouton de Gruyter.

Huang, Yan 2006. 'Anaphora, Cataphora, Exophora, Logophoricity', in Brown (ed.), pp.231–7.

Huddleston, Rodney and Pullum, Geoffrey 2002. *The Cambridge Grammar of the English Language.* Cambridge University Press.

Hudson, Richard 1976. 'Conjunction-Reduction, Gapping and Right-Node Raising', *Language* 52: 535–62.

Hudson, Richard 1984. *Word Grammar.* Oxford: Blackwell.

Hudson, Richard 1988. 'Coordination and Grammatical Relations', *Journal of Linguistics* 24: 303–42.

Hudson, Richard 1990. *English Word Grammar.* Oxford: Blackwell.

Hudson, Richard 1994. 'About 37% of Word-Tokens Are Nouns', *Language* 70: 331–9.

Hudson, Richard 1996. *Sociolinguistics,* 2nd edn. Cambridge University Press.

Hudson, Richard 1998. *English Grammar.* London: Routledge.

Hudson, Richard 1999. 'Subject–Verb Agreement in English', *English Language and Linguistics* 3: 173–207.

Hudson, Richard 2000. '*I Amn't', *Language* 76: 297–323.

Hudson, Richard 2003a. 'Gerunds without Phrase Structure', *Natural Language & Linguistic Theory* 21: 579–615.

Hudson, Richard 2003b. 'Trouble on the Left Periphery', *Lingua* 113: 607–42.

Hudson, Richard 2004. 'Are Determiners Heads?', *Functions of Language* 11: 7–43.

Hudson, Richard 2007a. 'English Dialect Syntax in Word Grammar', *English Language and Linguistics* 11: 383–405.

Hudson, Richard 2007b. 'Inherent Variability and Minimalism: comments on Adger's "Combinatorial variability"', *Journal of Linguistics* 43: 683–94.

Hudson, Richard 2007c. *Language Networks: the new Word Grammar.* Oxford University Press.

Hudson, Richard 2009. 'Measuring Maturity', in Beard, Myhill, Nystrand and Riley (eds), pp.349–62.

Hudson, Richard and Walmsley, John 2005. 'The English Patient: English grammar and teaching in the twentieth century', *Journal of Linguistics* 41: 593–622.

Iacobini, Claudio 2006. 'Morphological Typology', in Brown (ed.), pp.278–82.

Jacobson, Pauline 2006. 'Constituent Structure', in Brown (ed.), pp.58–71.

Joseph, John 2006. 'Identity and Language', in Brown (ed.), pp.486–92.

Julien, Marit 2006. 'Word', in Brown (ed.), pp.617–24.

Jun, Jong 2006. 'Lexical Conceptual Structure', in Brown (ed.), pp.69–77.

Koskela, Anu and Murphy, Lynne 2006. 'Polysemy and Homonymy', in Brown (ed.), pp.742–4.

Kruijff, Geert-Jan 2006. 'Dependency Grammar', in Brown (ed.), pp.444–50.

Kuiper, Koenraad 2006. 'Formulaic Speech', in Brown (ed.), pp.597–602.

Lamb, Sydney 1998. *Pathways of the Brain: the neurocognitive basis of language.* Amsterdam: Benjamins.

Langacker, Ronald 1987. *Foundations of Cognitive Grammar: theoretical prerequisites.* Stanford University Press.

Langacker, Ronald 2006. 'Cognitive Grammar', in Brown (ed.), pp.538–42.

Lasnik, Howard 2006. 'Minimalism', in Brown (ed.), pp.149–56.

Lieven, Elena 2006. 'Language Development: overview', in Brown (ed.), pp.376–91.

McCawley, James (ed.) 1976. *Notes from the Linguistic Underground.* London: Academic Press.

MacLeod, Colin 2006. 'Stroop Effect in Language', in Brown (ed.), pp.161–5.

McNeill, David 2006. 'Gesture and Communication', in Brown (ed.), pp.58–66.

Malouf, Robert 2006. 'Mixed Categories', in Brown (ed.), pp.175–84.

Marslen-Wilson, William 2006. 'Morphology and Language Processing', in Brown (ed.), pp.295–300.

Martin, Robert 2006. 'Meaning: overview of philosophical theories', in Brown (ed.), pp.584–9.

Matthews, Peter 1981. *Syntax.* Cambridge University Press.

Mattys, Sven 2006. 'Speech Recognition: psychology approaches', in Brown (ed.), pp.819–28.

Mesthrie, Rajend 2006. 'Society and Language: overview', in Brown (ed.), pp.472–84.

Nippold, Marilyn 2006. 'Language Development in School-Age Children, Adolescents, and Adults', in Brown (ed.), pp.368–73.

Oakhill, Jane and Cain, Kate 2006. 'Reading Processes in Children', in Brown (ed.), pp.379–86.

Payne, John 2006. 'Noun Phrases', in Brown (ed.), pp.712–20.

Pensalfini, Rob 2006. 'Configurationality', in Brown (ed.), pp.23–7.

Percival, Keith 1976. 'On the Historical Source of Immediate Constituent Analysis', in McCawley (ed.), pp.229–42.

Pinker, Steven 1994. *The Language Instinct.* London: Penguin.

Pinker, Steven 1998a. *How the Mind Works.* London: Allen Lane.

Pinker, Steven 1998b. 'Words and Rules', *Lingua* 106: 219–42.

Pustejovsky, James 2006. 'Lexical Semantics: overview', in Brown (ed.), pp.98–106.

Quirk, Randolph, Greenbaum, Sidney, Leech, Geoffrey and Svartvik, Jan 1972. *A Grammar of Contemporary English.* London: Longman.

Quirk, Randolph, Greenbaum, Sidney, Leech, Geoffrey and Svartvik, Jan 1985. *A Comprehensive Grammar of the English Language.* London: Longman.

Rayner, Keith and Juhasz, Barbara 2006. 'Reading Processes in Adults', in Brown (ed.), pp.373–8.

Reinhart, Tanya and Siloni, Tal 2006. 'Command Relations', in Brown (ed.), pp.635–42.

Reisberg, Daniel 2007. *Cognition: exploring the science of the mind*, 3rd media edn. New York: Norton.

Roelofs, Ardi 2008. 'Attention to Spoken Word Planning: chronometric and neuroimaging evidence', *Language and Linguistics Compass* 2: 389–405.

Rudman, Joseph 2006. 'Authorship Attribution: statistical and computational methods', in Brown (ed.), pp.611–617.

Schütze, Carson 2006. 'Data and Evidence', in Brown (ed.), pp.356–63.

Siewierska, Anna 2006. 'Word Order and Linearization', in Brown (ed.), pp.642–9.

Slobin, Dan 1996. 'From "Thought and Language" to "Thinking for Speaking"', in Gumperz and Levinson (eds), pp.70–96.

Smith, Neil 1999. *Chomsky: ideas and ideals*. Cambridge University Press.

Sornicola, Rosanna 2006. 'Topic and Comment', in Brown (ed.), pp.766–73.

Stemberger, J. P. 1985. *The Lexicon in a Model of Language Production*. New York: Garland Publishing.

Sugayama, Kensei and Hudson, Richard (eds) 2006. *Word Grammar: new perspectives on a theory of language structure*. London: Continuum.

Sullivan, Arthur 2006. 'Sense and Reference: philosophical aspects', in Brown (ed.), pp.238–41.

Taylor, John 2006. 'Cognitive Semantics', in Brown (ed.), pp.569–82.

Theakston, Anna 2006. 'CHILDES Database', in Brown (ed.), pp.310–13.

Touretzky, David 1986. *The Mathematics of Inheritance Systems*. Los Altos, CA: Morgan Kaufmann.

van Gompel, Roger 2006. 'Sentence Processing', in Brown (ed.), pp.251–5.

Van Valin, Robert 2006. 'Functional Relations', in Brown (ed.), pp.683–96.

Wetzel, Linda 2006. 'Type versus Token', in Brown (ed.), pp.199–202.

Winograd, Terry 1976. 'Towards a Procedural Understanding of Semantics', *Revue Internationale De Philosophie* 30: 260–303.

Wray, Alison 2006. 'Formulaic Language', in Brown (ed.), pp.590–7.

Index